Latin America's Struggle for Democracy

A *Journal of Democracy* Book

•

Published under the auspices of
the International Forum for Democratic Studies

Latin America's Struggle for Democracy

Edited by Larry Diamond, Marc F. Plattner, and Diego Abente Brun

The Johns Hopkins University Press
Baltimore

9 8 7 6 5 4 3 2 1

Chapters in this volume appeared in the following issues of the *Journal of Democracy:* chapter 1, October 2004; chapter 19, October 2005; chapter 2, July 2006; chapters 4–5, 7, 10–12, October 2006; chapters 15–17, January 2007; chapter 13, April 2007; chapter 6, July 2007; chapter 3, October 2007; chapters 8–9, 14, April 2008. For all reproduction rights, please contact the Johns Hopkins University Press.

The Johns Hopkins University Press
2715 North Charles Street
Baltimore, Maryland 21218-4363
www.press.jhu.edu

Library of Congress Cataloging-in-Publication Data

Latin America's struggle for democracy / edited by Larry Diamond, Marc F. Plattner, and Diego Abente Brun.

      p. cm. — (Journal of democracy book)
      Includes bibliographical references and index.
      ISBN: 978-0-8018-9058-1 (hardcover : alk. paper)
      ISBN: 978-0-8018-9059-8 (pbk. : alk. paper)
      1. Democracy—Latin America. 2. Democratization—Latin America. 3. Latin America—Politics and government—1980– I. Diamond, Larry Jay. II. Plattner, Marc F., 1945– III. Abente Brun, Diego.

  JL966.L364 2008
  320.98—dc22

                             2008021273

A catalog record for this book is available from the British Library.

CONTENTS

III. Case Studies: Mexico, Central America, the Caribbean

ACKNOWLEDGMENTS

This is the first *Journal of Democracy* book wholly devoted to Latin America. Although we have published a great many essays on the region in the almost two decades since the *Journal* was launched in 1990, we never before felt that we had a "critical mass" of timely essays that would justify their being gathered in a book-length volume. In 2006, however, Latin America had an extraordinary "year of elections," with a dozen countries going to the polls to determine who would hold their highest offices. The majority of these elections were analyzed in individual articles appearing in the *Journal* between October 2006 and April 2008. To these we have added several important thematic essays dealing with the region, as well as a previously unpublished essay by Consuelo Cruz on Central America and an updated version by Daniel Erikson of an earlier *Journal* article on the Caribbean. Though there remain a few gaps in terms of the themes and countries covered here, we believe that this volume presents a very useful introduction to the status of Latin America's continuing struggle for democracy.

We are very pleased that Diego Abente Brun was able to join us in editing this *Journal of Democracy* book. It was fortuitous that Diego, a leading Paraguayan political scientist, came on board as deputy director of the National Endowment for Democracy's International Forum for Democratic Studies, the organization that houses the *Journal,* as we were preparing this volume for publication. Diego was able to share his extensive knowledge of the region during the editing process. He also drafted the book's opening essay, which not only introduces what follows but discusses some key issues not directly addressed by the other contributors.

We are glad to have this opportunity to express our gratitude once more to those we have so often thanked in earlier volumes: the Lynde and Harry Bradley Foundation for its continuing financial assistance to the *Journal*; the National Endowment for Democracy, its Board of Directors, and its president Carl Gershman for their unwavering support of our work; and Henry Tom and his colleagues at the Johns Hopkins University Press for their professionalism in producing this volume, our twentieth *Journal of Democracy* book.

The *Journal*'s executive editor, Phil Costopoulos, deserves special credit for his editing of many of the articles and for the style and clarity of the book as a whole. Our managing editor, Sarah Bloxham, performed her usual magic in organizing and supervising the production process; she made it seem effortless, though that is no doubt an illusion born of her remarkable competence and unflappable demeanor. A number of other current editors (Tracy Brown, Zerxes Spencer, and Marta Kalabinski) and former editors (Sumi Shane and Eric Kramon) also made valuable contributions. And finally, Melissa Aten, our colleague at the International Forum for Democratic Studies, somehow managed to find the time to do an excellent job of compiling the index.

—Marc F. Plattner and Larry Diamond

INTRODUCTION

Diego Abente Brun

The "third wave" of democratization reached Latin America with Ecuador's transition to democracy in 1978. Almost three decades have now passed, and not a single Latin American country that transitioned to democracy has reverted back to military rule. There has never been a comparable period of democratic hegemony embracing almost every country on the continent. Yet this general statement hides a complex reality. First, it obscures the fact that democracy does not mean the same thing everywhere in Latin America, and that the region's democratic regimes often exhibit very different traits. Second, it fails to take account of newly emerging trends that have the potential to alter the political landscape.

These new trends are amply discussed in this volume. One involves the political turmoil and instability (especially in the Andean countries) that have resulted in a striking number of "interrupted presidencies." As Arturo Valenzuela notes, the presidents who have not been able to finish their allotted terms have been toppled not by the military but by "street coups." The vulnerability of Latin American presidents underlines the importance of the constitutional framework. Indeed, strong parliamentary systems would seem much better suited to dealing with the challenges facing Latin America. The resistance to such far-reaching constitutional change, however, is deep and widespread.

Perhaps even more problematic than the presidential system itself is the combination of popular election for the presidency with a European-inspired proportional-representation system for electing the Congress. The use of the plurality system in the one case and proportional representation in the other is bound to bring about a very difficult relationship between the two branches of government, as most presidents are forced to govern without a majority in Congress. In the 1980s, most Latin American countries adopted the "runoff" (or "ballotage") system to elect presidents, but this reform did not quite solve the problem. Even if a president is elected by a majority in the second round, he or she still has only minority support in Congress (whose members are elected in the first round). The problems are likely to worsen when both branches claim the legitimacy derived from popular elections. Witness President Alberto Fujimori's shutting down of Congress in Peru in 1992.

Had copying the French system been the recipe for success, it should have been adopted in its entirety. In other words, the ballotage system should have been employed for Congress as well, replacing the proportional-representation system. This would have accomplished two important goals. First, it would have facilitated the emergence of concurrent majorities in the two branches. Second, it would have provided a strong incentive for presidential frontrunners to negotiate a workable governing coalition *before* the runoff, instead of relying on the hope that they would win the second-round votes of those disliking the other candidate more. Furthermore, this runoff in congressional elections would have mitigated the disproportionality of the first-past-the-post system.

It is widely agreed that there is an emerging "crisis of representation" in much of Latin America. In exploring this problem in the Andean region, Scott Mainwaring notes the paradox of deepening dissatisfaction and disenchantment of the population despite the fact that the representation of previously excluded or marginalized sectors has also increased. Yet rather than pointing to political or electoral institutions as the crucial causal variable, Mainwaring underlines instead what he calls "state deficiencies" or low-quality governance. This explanation may be seen, however, as complementing the one offered by Valenzuela, rather than simply replacing it.

A second recent trend in the region has been described as the emergence, or reemergence, of the left. This issue is addressed here from three different perspectives. Hector Schamis builds on Jorge Castañeda's differentiation between the "two lefts,"[1] but seeks to draw a finer distinction based mainly on policy options and implications. Matthew Cleary, on the other hand, is more concerned with the structural bases of support for the left, and lays out his argument along the lines set forth by Kenneth Roberts's fine work on the subject.[2] Finally, Mitchell Seligson, relying on survey data, argues that Latin Americans are slightly to the right of the world average, a finding that seems to run counter to the argument that Latin America is experiencing a turn to the left (pp. 79–80). Also contradicting conventional wisdom, he presents data indicating that left-leaning individuals in Latin America tend to see the existing democratic systems as less legitimate and are somewhat less likely to favor democracy than right-wing respondents (pp. 83–84).

For the purpose of this discussion, I would make a basic distinction between the *nueva izquierda* (the renewed left) and the *izquierda nueva* (the new left). The former is made up of movements that emerged between the 1930s and the 1960s, developed close ties to the organized working class and to trade unions, and became highly institutionalized.

At one time, many of these parties were deeply anchored in a Marxist-Leninist ideological framework, but they have evolved over the last two or three decades, becoming more akin to the social-democratic parties of Europe. Although they still retain some Marxist tenets, they have shifted from the Bolshevik ideological family into the company of Ferdinand Lasalle, Ferdinand Bebel, Wilhelm Liebknecht, and Karl Kautsky. In this sense, one can argue that the renewed left, present today in Chile, Uruguay, Brazil, and Argentina among other countries, is very similar to today's European left.

On the other hand, there is the *izquierda nueva* (or new left). These are movements of recent appearance, characterized by a lack of organic ties with the working class and by reliance on an amorphous constituency that can only be considered a "multitude."[3] These movements display little institutionalization, no adherence to either Marxist-Leninist or social-democratic ideological tenets, charismatic as opposed to ideological leadership, and no real model of socioeconomic transformation other than utilizing state funds to build a clientelistic apparatus in the framework of an increasingly autocratic political system. *Strictu sensu* this is not the left. These movements may define themselves as such, but they are more properly characterized as authoritarian populists. Venezuela and Ecuador are clear cases of this *izquierda nueva*.

The concept of populism is still useful to characterize an important dimension of politics in Latin America. It is true, as Schamis points out, that today's populism is no longer associated with the import-substitution industrialization of the 1930s through the 1950s. Yet there is still no better term for designating political movements that share the following common traits:

• Appealing to the people (or *populus*) as an undefined, unarticulated whole, rather than to specific constituencies;

• Calling for, but failing to trigger, a political process of constructing new collective identities;[4]

• Eliminating institutionalized channels of communication between leaders and followers, relying instead on the charisma of the leader;

• Resorting to a highly charged nationalistic rhetoric and articulating an "us versus them" dichotomy in terms of the nation versus the anti-nation; and

• Applying economic policies that rely on large transfers of cash and other benefits to selected constituencies without changing significantly the economic structure of production.

A further distinction should be made on the basis of Donna Van Cott's chapter on the emergence of indigenous constituencies. A wholly different setting characterizes countries with large indigenous populations. That is the case in Ecuador, where the indigenous confederation CONAIE has played a central role, and in Bolivia under the presidency of indigenous leader Evo Morales. True, the "left" here does not build its core support around a working-class constituency,[5] but neither does it rely on an amorphous aggregation of clients. Instead, there is an indigenous constituency, with a strong collective identity and a place in the productive system, that "substitutes" for the working class.

It is precisely the massive social transformation that has taken place in Latin America in recent decades and its impact in terms of "informalizing" the labor market that Christopher Sabatini and Eric Farnsworth call attention to in their chapter. The result has been an "increasing wage disparity between skilled and unskilled workers, swelling youth unemployment, declining levels of already-low unionization, incomplete enforcement of existing labor protection, and rapid growth of informal employment caused in part by labor laws that constrain the growth of formal employment" (p. 101). The authors point to the fact that populist leaders have drawn high levels of electoral support from these growing masses of *informales*. This problem may be partially addressed by labor reform, as they argue, but a more comprehensive approach is needed.

Dealing with Poverty and Inequality

All the trends and problems discussed above are closely entwined with Latin America's longstanding poverty and inequality. Indeed, the most strikingly *persistent* characteristic of Latin American societies has been their high levels of poverty.[6] As of 2005, 39.8 percent of Latin Americans—209 million people—lived below the poverty line, with 81 million living in extreme poverty. Equally appalling is the fact that this situation has not significantly improved since 1980, when 41 percent of the population lived in poverty. The preliminary version of *2007 Social Panorama* published by the UN Economic Commission for Latin American and the Caribbean (ECLAC) points to a further reduction for 2006, when the poverty index was estimated at 36.5 percent, and a continuation of this hopeful trend is expected for 2007.[7] Nonetheless, the life of a whole generation has been spent simply trying to catch up with the past—to get back today to where the region was a quarter-century ago.[8]

This dim picture is slightly brightened by real advances in health and education. For example, infant mortality has been reduced significantly, and life expectancy increased from 62 years in 1970–75 to 71 years by 2005.[9] Sadly, however, many of the children who survive and the adults who live longer must still confront a reality of poverty, destitution, and despair.

Progress has also been made in expanding the reach of educational services, especially primary education. Yet lack of progress in secondary, technical, and vocational education leaves those under 25 years of age with an average of only 5.73 years of schooling, compared to more than 6.50 years in East Asia and almost 10 years in most highly developed countries.[10] Even more worrying is the poor quality of education in Latin America. The problem is not so much the level of spending on education as it is the quality of this spending. Although there is a lack of comparative data, the evidence available for a few Latin American countries shows that for *similar* levels of spending, scores in mathematics in countries as different as Thailand, Slovakia, and Poland are between 22 percent and 37 percent higher than they are in Latin America.[11] Furthermore, the structure of educational spending in the region is heavily tilted toward teacher and administrator salaries (which often represent about 90 percent of the total), leaving little resources for investment in school infrastructure, computers, and books.

The problem of inequality is actually worsening in Latin America. While the level of inequality remained high but fairly stable in the 1970s, 1980s, and 1990s, it jumped dramatically in the last decade, making Latin America, already the second most unequal region in the world, even more so.[12]

Moreover, inequality is *not* just a matter of the distribution of income. It also involves the distribution of opportunities for a better life. For example, only 55 percent of Latin Americans with incomes in the lowest quintile of the population have access to secondary education, as compared to 93 percent of those with incomes in the highest fifth. Similarly, only 38 percent of the poorest quintile has access to sewerage, but that percentage rises to 85 percent for the richest quintile.[13] Generally speaking, this reflects a regressive pattern of social spending, vividly illustrated by the fact that only 16 percent of the spending on education, health, and social security benefits the lowest quintile, while almost twice as much, 29 percent, is directed towards the richest quintile.[14]

As survey after survey shows, the social crisis depicted above has generated alienation, anomie, and despair—the breeding grounds for a new brand of populist autocracy. Hence, the sense of despair is not capricious, but well-founded. It must be acknowledged that if Latin American democracies fail to address those challenges effectively, disenchantment will continue to grow, skepticism will widen, and the outmoded criticism of liberal democracy as mere "formal" democracy will be given a patina of credibility.

Latin America's levels of poverty and inequality not only are morally offensive, but also pose a supreme political challenge. Backsliding is unacceptable. Winning the right to live under democracy entailed a long and difficult struggle that cost untold suffering and the lives of many thousands of Latin Americans. They, like those who died combating the scourge of Nazism, lived and died inspired by a simple and powerful conviction, so well summarized by the poet Paul Eluard: "By the power of a word/ I start my life anew/I was born to meet you/to name you/ Freedom."[15] Latin America cannot afford to go backward. In recent decades, leaders in the region successfully met the challenge of producing sound economic policies; now they must confront the contemporary social crisis with courage and vision.

This implies an approach based on three pillars: 1) an all-out but carefully targeted effort to combat poverty; 2) an ambitious initiative to generate adequate domestic resources for this purpose; and 3) carefully designed economic reforms to produce sustainable and equitable growth.

In terms of combating poverty, much has been learned from a variety of recent experiences. For instance, conditional cash-transfer programs such as Bolsa Familia in Brazil, Chile Solidario in Chile, Oportunidades in Mexico, and Juntos in Peru have produced outstanding results in terms of reversing the all-time-high poverty levels of the 1990s and reducing, albeit modestly, income inequality.[16] The cost of these programs, which transfer cash payments to the most impoverished citizens on the condition that their children attend school and receive proper medical attention, has been small, representing on average 0.25 percent of GDP, but their impact has reached as much as 22 percent of the population in Brazil and 28 percent in Honduras.[17]

Much has also been learned from a number of tax reform efforts implemented during the last two decades to deal with the fiscal crisis of the state and to confront the danger of inflationary spending. These reforms have been modestly successful in increasing tax receipts (excluding social security) in the region from 12.6 percent of GDP in 1986–89 to 14.2 percent of GDP in 2000–2003.[18]

Yet when one looks at other dimensions of the tax issue, a darker picture emerges. There is, first, a problem of the overall availability of resources for government expenditures. In 2004, taxes (including social security) as a share of GDP in Latin America reached an average of only 17 percent, compared to 36 percent in OECD countries. Second, there is a question of equity. For example, direct taxes (taxes on income, profits, and capital gains), which are more progressive, represent 5 percent of GDP in Latin American compared to 15 percent in OECD countries.[19] Third and finally, these two factors go a long way toward explaining the failure to reduce high levels of poverty and inequality. In fact, while the average Gini coefficient of .52 before taxes and transfers falls slightly to .50 thereafter, in Europe the Gini coefficient of .46 falls dramatically to .31 after taxes and transfers.[20] This reflects not only the overall tax burden, but also the pattern of spending. In Latin America, spending is highly regressive, with the richest two quintiles benefiting the most, while in Europe it is slightly progressive, with the richest two quintiles benefiting less.[21] The Figure shows the comparative pattern of social spending in Latin America and Europe. This suggests that tax reform must be accompanied by an equally profound improvement in the capac-

FIGURE—PUBLIC TRANSFERS IN LATIN AMERICA AND EUROPE
(INCIDENCE BY INCOME QUINTILE)

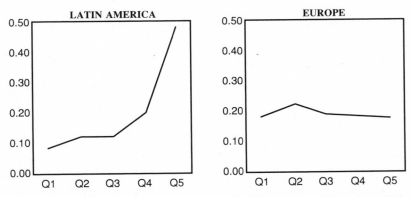

Source: Edwin Goñi, J. Humberto López, and Luis Servén, "Fiscal Redistribution and Income Inequality in Latin America," Policy Research Working Paper 4487 (Washington, D.C.: World Bank, 2008), 19. Graphic corresponds to Figure 10.

ity of the state to deliver quality services, target social spending effectively, drastically reduce corruption, and maintain high and consistent levels of transparency.

The third pillar of this approach is aimed at increasing levels of economic growth in the region. No lasting progress toward combating poverty and reducing inequality can be achieved without sustained economic growth. To be sure, the overall economy has performed quite well in the last five years. According to ECLAC estimates, the region's GDP grew by 5.6 percent in 2007 and, if its projections of a 4.9 percent rate of growth for 2008 are on target, "the region will have marked up a cumulative increase of 23 percent, equivalent to 3.5 percent per year" over the last six years. Such high per-capita GDP growth rates were last experienced during the latter part of the 1960s and lasted until the first oil shock of 1973.[22] Maintaining or increasing this level of sustained growth calls for very pragmatic and wise institutional reform and for continued commitment to certain policies that now enjoy wide consensus. These include a free-market economy (as the most efficient allocator of resources), fiscal responsibility, sound monetary policies, and general macroeconomic stability.

But there also is a new consensus emerging—namely, that strong, efficient, and lean states are just as important as sound policies to ensure properly functioning and free markets.[23] Latin American states, which are generally large but weak, need to be constructed or reconstructed, depending on the case. For they must actively invest in infrastructure, education, health, research and development, the environment, and the quality of life—not only to address social needs but also to foster national competitiveness. Not least, the state will need to encourage entrepreneurship and private investment, rather than erecting bureaucratic obstacles that prevent individuals from becoming productive citizens.

Electoral, Liberal, and Inclusionary Democracy

As this volume shows, the reality of Latin America exhibits not only common challenges but also marked contrasts. Although the process of democratization occurred throughout the region during roughly the same time period, one can see on closer inspection that it did not have the same scope in all countries. In this context, the distinction between electoral and liberal democracies emphasized by Larry Diamond is especially relevant.[24] In all these countries, the basic institutions of *electoral democracy* were installed or restored. In some of them, democratization moved beyond the mode of accessing power to include also the mode of exercising power: These merit the designation *liberal democracy,* which implies limited government, separation of powers, and rule of law *(imperio de la ley).*[25] In a few countries, the process advanced further still, turning these liberal democracies into truly inclusive social systems where the juridical principle of equality before the law translates into reasonably equal opportunities for all in the social realm. These *inclusionary* democracies have managed to reduce poverty and inequality to tolerable levels and to develop a considerable degree of social cohesion. Most observers would agree that, of the seventeen countries of Ibero-America, only Chile, Uruguay, and Costa Rica can be considered inclusionary democracies. In a second tier are countries such as Brazil, Mexico, and Argentina, which have become stable liberal democracies but are still struggling to become inclusionary ones. The remaining eleven countries continue to struggle at earlier stages of the process.

The country studies in the final two sections of this volume are arranged on a geographical basis, with the South American cases preceding Mexico, Central America, and the Caribbean, but here I will treat them in the order of the three categories (or "tiers") to which I have assigned them above. As Arturo Valenzuela and Lucía Dammert show, Chile, the country that is probably closest to being a fully inclusionary democracy, is paying the price of its success. The longstanding rule of the coalition known as the Concertación, composed of the country's leading center-left political parties, came to be seen as lacking sufficient citizen participation. Socialist Michelle Bachelet, the victorious Concertación presidential candidate in 2006, based her campaign on the need to address this shortcoming. But in attempting to implement this promise at the outset of her administration, she quickly found herself in trouble, jeopardizing her backing among party leaders yet unable to gain decisive support from the citizenry. Given that the level of confidence in political parties in Chile is slightly above the Latin American median[26]—and far above the levels found in, say, Ecuador or Paraguay—this was a strategy that involved considerable risk, and she was forced to water it down significantly.

In the second tier of countries stand Brazil, Mexico, and Argentina, Latin America's three largest countries. Brazil has traditionally lagged behind in terms of addressing its social problems, being among the countries with the most unequal distribution of income and the highest levels of poverty. This reality has been changing, however. Lourdes Sola highlights the success of President Lula's administration (2003–present) in reconciling the forces of the market and the social demands of the poor. Indeed, the government of Lula's Partido do Trabalhadores is an excellent example of how to put in practice the old social-democratic saying of "as much market as possible, as much state as necessary." The remarkable success of Lula's social policies (which built on and greatly expanded some of the programs of his predecessor Fernando Henrique Cardoso [1995–2003]) has been sufficient to overcome the severe criticism leveled against officials in his government for acts of corruption, allowing him to win handily his race for reelection in late 2006.

Mexico, by contrast, had a remarkably and uncomfortably close presidential election in 2006, with Felipe Calderón of the center-right National Action Party (PAN) winning a disputed razor-thin plurality over Andres Manuel López Obrador of the Party of the Democratic Revolution (PRD). The contributions to this volume by Luis Estrada and Alejandro Poiré, by Andreas Schedler, and by Jorge Castañeda and Marcos Morales, although centered on the standoff over the 2006 elections, also raise broader questions about the future of Mexican democracy. Fortunately, Schedler's worst-case scenario, according to which Mexico could experience "the extraconstitutional removal of its chief executive through street pressure, much as we have seen in the numerous 'interrupted presidencies' of contemporary Latin America" (p. 244), did not come to pass. Yet the distrust generated by the technical problems of the electoral process, especially against the backdrop of what Estrada and Poiré describe as a deep "north-south" ideological divide, must remain a source of concern. Fully 54 percent of those who voted for López Obrador do not believe that Mexico is a democracy (p. 226). The latest surveys indicate that, from 2006 to 2007, citizen support for democracy declined from 54 to 48 percent and citizen satisfaction with it from 41 to 31 percent.[27] The degree of polarization and the fact that "Mexico is an abysmally unequal society" (p. 243) surely point to more turbulence ahead unless these challenges are effectively addressed.

Argentina seems the most likely candidate to move into the first-tier category of countries. As Steven Levitsky and María Victoria Murillo show, the government of President Néstor Kirchner (2003–2007) was successful in maintaining a 9 percent growth in GDP, lowering unemployment from 20 percent to 9 percent and poverty rates from 50 percent to 27 percent, and increasing private consumption by 52 percent and real wages by 70 percent. Given this record, it is not difficult to understand why President Kirchner's wife, Cristina Fernández de Kirchner, was elected to succeed him in October 2007.

Argentina has always been one of the least unequal countries in the region and has enjoyed relatively low poverty rates. As the recovery from the economic crisis of 2001 proceeds, progress in these areas is likely to advance even further. Problems are more likely to originate in the political realm. In fact, at the national level Argentina has become a de facto "two-Peronist–party" system. The weakness of the non-Peronist opposition creates a severe problem of horizontal accountability and strengthens the concentration of power in the executive.

Levitsky and Murillo show that Néstor Kirchner relied as much as former president Carlos Menem (1989–99) did on ruling by decree *(decretos de necesidad y urgencia)*, thanks to the authority vested in him by Congress in accord with a constitutional provision. At the same time, however, Néstor Kirchner's government failed to address the issue of institution-building, especially in terms of strengthening the enforcement capability of institutions and ensuring the stability of rules. Perhaps these facts help to explain why Fernández de Kirchner ran poorly in the largest urban centers (Buenos Aires, Córdoba, and Rosario), and why socialist Hermes Binner, former mayor of Rosario, was elected governor of Santa Fe, the country's second most important province after Buenos Aires.

The Troubled Andean Countries

Much greater challenges confront the Andean countries, Ecuador, Venezuela, Colombia, and Peru, ordered here from the most to the least troubled. Ecuador has clearly been afflicted by political malaise, suffering three "interrupted presidencies" in less than ten years. The current government of Rafael Correa, who was elected in late 2006, has turned the country into a prime example of illiberal democracy. In her contribution to this volume, Catherine Conaghan describes Correa's presidency as "plebiscitary." This label might suit a president like Argentina's Néstor Kirchner who, with significant popular support, exercised exceedingly broad powers within the framework of the constitution and laws, but there is room for dispute about how well it fits President Correa. The latter did not just close down the Congress, as President Fujimori had done in Peru in 1992; he simply had the majority of congressmen dismissed by an electoral tribunal! It would be difficult to find any conceivable democratic norm to which this kind of behavior would conform.[28]

As a result, as Conaghan points out, Correa may end up remaining in power at least until 2015 and perhaps even until 2019 (p. 211). Furthermore, as she notes, "Correa prefers to forge direct ties with particular constituencies rather than to act through intermediaries such as CONAIE or other organizations of the left" (p. 210). Consequently, all the power has been concentrated in Correa's hands, with political parties and civil society rendered all but superfluous. Conaghan finishes her chapter by cautioning, "Ecuador's political development seemingly hinges solely on Rafael Correa: his personality, his ambitions, and his decisions . . . [that] one man's intentions weigh so heavily in determining the trajectory of change is a worrisome condition" (p. 212).

In short, it would be easy to conclude that Correa has become an autocrat, albeit a popular one. To be sure, the general acceptance and even embrace of his autocratic rule result from the decades-old failure of Ecuador's political parties to address the problems of the population. But despite Correa's strident rhetoric, it does not appear that his policies have much content beyond increasing the state's oil revenues and doubling welfare payments. So there is reason to doubt whether he will be able to bring about lasting social change.

In their chapter on Venezuela, originally published in April 2007, Javier Corrales and Michael Penfold chronicle the relentless and long-successful efforts of Hugo Chávez to transform the country's political system into an authoritarian one. This process appeared to be continuing unabated up to the December 2007 referendum on Chávez's proposed constitutional reform. The surprising defeat of the referendum, however, opened up a whole new phase of the political game. At a general level, it showed that democratic culture still is quite entrenched in the Venezuelan population. At a more specific level, it demonstrated that even many *chavistas* were having second thoughts and that their support for Chávez did not extend to support for the consolidation of an authoritarian political model.

The challenge now facing the democratic opposition is not only to work to dismantle the authoritarian features in Chávez's 1999 Constitution but also to develop a political alternative capable of addressing the needs of the poor not simply through welfare payments, but through a reform of the economic model that can offer them good jobs, decent salaries, and a better life. In fact, despite all the claims made about the benefits brought by Chávez's social policies, Francisco Rodríguez (chief economist of the Venezuelan National Assembly during the first four years of the Chávez government) has demonstrated that they have not, after all, accomplished more than his predecessors' policies.[29]

Colombia has achieved a better record than its neighbors in terms of electoral democracy, but it faces the problem of being the only country in Latin America in which the government does not exercise effective control over all its territory. The thirty-year-old Revolutionary Armed Forces of Colombia (FARC), a one-time political movement that is now deeply involved in drug trafficking and kidnapping for profit, still controls important parts of the country. The equally criminal activities of the paramilitary Auto-Defensas Unidas de Colombia have also contributed to creating a generalized atmosphere of lawlessness and violence.

As Eduardo Posada-Carbó points out in his chapter on Colombia, the success of President Alvaro Uribe in restoring a degree of security goes a long way in explaining his popularity and his landslide reelection in 2006. Yet there is still a long way to go to establish the rule of law in the country, a step that is indispensable even to begin to address other pressing issues, such as enhancing social inclusion. Establishing effective control of Colombian territory is not purely a military challenge, but a political one as well, and it remains to be seen whether that can be accomplished.

Peru is the Andean country that has traveled farthest toward becoming a stable liberal democracy. In the 1980s, it was torn by the violence both of the Sendero Luminoso guerrilla movement (which caused 35,000 deaths) and of a government whose military forces combated it—sometimes within but more often outside the law, systematically violating basic human rights and creating thousands of victims of death squads, torture, and illegal imprisonment.

The following decade was marked by the "successful" authoritarian regime of Alberto Fujimori (1990–2000). Toward the end of that period, however, when Fujimori sought to extend his corrupt regime, Peru's civil society and political forces slowly but surely launched a successful resistance movement leading to Fujimori's ouster. The new century began with democracy restored, and Alejandro Toledo (2001–2006), a Peruvian of indigenous origin, was elected president.

As Cynthia McClintock shows, Toledo's government was highly successful in terms of generating economic growth, but this mainly benefited the wealthiest third of the population. Toledo also had to deal with a hostile press, in many cases linked to the corruption of the Fujimori years. This facilitated the emergence of the populist candidacy of Ollanta Humala in the 2006 presidential election. After winning a plurality in the first round, however, Humala was defeated by former president Alan García in the runoff. García's sound economic policies and the recent approval by the U.S. Congress of a bilateral Free Trade Agreement bode well for Peru's future political stability. Yet the problem of poverty and alienation, especially in the southern highlands, must be effectively addressed.

This volume does not have a separate chapter on Bolivia, but that country is discussed in Donna Van Cott's chapter on indigenous parties and movements, and it deserves a brief mention here. As Van Cott argues, President Evo Morales, after taking office in 2006, manipulated his majority in Congress and in the Constitutional Assembly to push forward an agenda that excluded the concerns of the opposition. Since then, his government has alternated between more authoritarian and more conciliatory stances. The strong resistance mounted by the departments of Tarija, Santa Cruz, Beni, and Pando forced the government in early 2008 to call for the mediation of the OAS. A mission headed by OAS Under Secretary for Political Affairs Dante Caputo is on the way, and one can only hope that a negotiated settlement will be reached that both respects liberal democracy and takes into account the claims of Bolivia's indigenous majority. Only thus can Bolivia avoid becoming a textbook example of what John F. Kennedy warned about more than 45 years ago when he said, "Those who make peaceful revolution impossible will make violent revolution inevitable."

The realities of the countries of Central America, well described by Consuelo Cruz in her chapter, explain why these countries, with the exception of Costa Rica, belong in the third tier. In Guatemala, the political system has become more competitive—just enough to qualify it to be an electoral democracy. El Salvador has yet to produce both order and justice, highlighting the difficulties of moving beyond the basic level of electoral democracy. Nicaragua continues to be the land of patrons, clients, and particularistic pacts. Honduras, like Guatemala, has advanced in terms of consolidating a competitive electoral system but has achieved little more than that. Panama still has a political system dominated by personalism, clientelism, and the overarching influence of a few political families.

Finally, the Caribbean, in spite of having a generally good record in terms of democracy, remains extremely diverse. Among the bigger countries, Jamaica has suffered from a lackluster economic performance and from violence associated with drug trafficking and youth gangs. Trinidad and Tobago exhibits high levels of racial tension between its black and Indian populations, Guyana between its Afro- and Indian-Guyanese populations, and Suriname among its many ethnic constituencies. The smaller islands, although not exempt from the drug and arms smuggling that afflicts the region, seem to be doing rather well in maintaining their democratic systems.

Toward Full-Fledged Democracies

It has been said that the triumph of democracy as a system of government was the most important development of the twentieth century,[30] and nowhere was the impact of that development felt more strongly than in Latin America. The wave of democratization that swept across Latin America during the last decades of the twentieth century did not come about because democrats across the continent chose to import the love of freedom and democracy as exotic merchandise from foreign lands. They drew inspiration from their own history—from the successful but interrupted democratic experiments of the last century, but also from their older and more multifaceted traditions, including the culture of many of their aboriginal peoples; the philosophical works of Francisco de Suárez, Francisco de Vitoria, and Juan de Mariana; and the writings and actions of Latin America's founding fathers.

Nonetheless, there also existed strong countercurrents claiming that democratic regimes would be unable to solve the challenges of the day. Thus when the third wave of democratization began in the 1970s, some doubted that democracy could rise to the challenge of producing sound policies likely to spur the sustained economic growth that could lift people out of poverty. The prevailing view during the bureaucratic-authoritarian era was that only autocratic regimes would be up to the task. But history and emerging new data on comparative economic performance prove otherwise.

Yet the skepticism about democracy persists, although it is now linked to new questions. Today, the central concern is whether democratic systems can find new and creative ways to address the issues of social justice and rule of law discussed above. For this purpose, remaining purely electoral democracies clearly is insufficient. Becoming liberal democracies, based on the effective rule of law, limited government, and checks and balances between the branches of governments, represents a significant advancement, but neither does this go far enough. Only regimes that also uphold the principle of equality under the law in a way that leads to equal opportunities in the social realm can be considered full-fledged democracies. Only when this more ambitious goal is attained will democracy be safe and the future of the people of Latin America be secured. The struggle continues.

NOTES

1. Jorge Castañeda, "Latin America's Left Turn," *Foreign Affairs* 85 (May–June 2006): 28–43.

2. Kenneth Roberts, "Social Inequalities Without Class Cleavages in Latin America's Neoliberal Era," *Studies in Comparative International Development* 36 (Winter 2002): 3–33.

3. Michael Hardt and Toni Negri, *Multitude: War and Democracy in the Age of Empire* (New York: Penguin, 2004). The concept of "multitude" is the functional equivalent of the proletariat in postmodern societies and is therefore entrusted with the power of agency.

4. Unlike what Ernesto Laclau would expect. See his *On Populist Reason* (London: Verso, 2005): 241, *passim*. This debate concerns precisely the nature of politics in systems without strong collective agents such as the proletariat, and puts its faith in the emergence and construction of their sociological and functional equivalent through the concept of the "people."

5. The left in Bolivia played a relevant role for as long as the mining sector remained important. The working-class constituency of Bolivia, made up mainly of miners, has always been a very special working class due to the enclave nature of its process of production.

6. Inter-American Development Bank, *Outsiders? The Changing Patterns of Exclu-*

sion. Latin America and the Caribbean (Cambridge: Harvard University Press, 2008); World Bank, *World Development Report 2006 Equity and Development* (Oxford: Oxford University Press, 2005).

7. *2007 Social Panorama* (Santiago, Chile: ECLAC, 2007), 9.

8. ECLAC, *Panorama Social de América Latina 2006,* 59–60.

9. UNDP, *Human Development Report,* 2006.

10. Robert J. Barro and Jong-Wha Lee, "International Data on Educational Attainment: Updates and Implications," Center for International Development Working Paper No. 42, Harvard University, April 2000, 24–25.

11. OECD, *Latin American Economic Outlook 2008,* 38.

12. World Bank, *World Development Report 2007, 2006, 2003.*

13. OECD, *Latin American Economic Outlook 2008,* 39.

14. OECD, *Latin American Economic Outlook 2008* (for the nine countries for which comparative data are available; it is plausible to presume that the gap would be even greater if countries either not gathering or not providing data were included), 40.

15. Paul Eluard, "Liberté," in *Poésies et vérités* (Paris: Edition de Minuit, 1942). "Et par le pouvoir d'un mot/Je recommence ma vie/Je suis né pour te connaitre /Pour te nommer/Liberté."

16. Sergei Soares et al., "Conditional Cash Transfers in Brazil, Chile and Mexico: Impacts Upon Inequality," International Poverty Centre Working Paper No. 35, UNDP, 2007, 17.

17. Eduardo Lora, "Social Challenges in Latin America," Inter-American Development Bank, March 2007, 29. This was based on data from Handa Sudhanshu and Benjamin Davis, "The Experience of Conditional Cash Transfers in Latin America and the Caribbean," *Development Policy Review* 24 (September 2006): 513–36.

18. Eduardo Lora, "Trends and Outcomes of Tax Reform," in Eduardo Lora, ed., *The State of State Reform in Latin America* (Stanford: Stanford University Press, 2007), 197.

19. OECD, *Latin American Economic Outlook 2008,* 40.

20. OECD, *Latin American Economic Outlook 2008,* 31. The Gini coefficient of inequality ranges from 0 to 1 in ascending order of inequality.

21. Edwin Goñi, J. Humberto López, and Luis Servén, "Fiscal Redistribution and Income Inequality in Latin America," World Bank Policy Research Working Paper 4487, 2008, 19.

22. ECLAC, *Preliminary Overview of the Economies of Latin America and the Caribbean 2007* (Santiago, Chile: ECLAC, 2007), 1–2.

23. Francis Fukuyama, *State-Building: Governance and World Order in the 21st Century* (Ithaca: Cornell University Press, 2004).

24. Larry Diamond, *Developing Democracy* (Baltimore: Johns Hopkins University Press, 1999), 10–15; and Larry Diamond, *The Spirit of Democracy* (New York: Times Books, 2008), 20–26. For a discussion of liberalism and democracy, see Marc F. Plattner, *Democracy Without Borders?* (Lanham, Md.: Rowman and Littlefield, 2007), 40–70.

25. Rule of law could conceivably be translated in Spanish either as *estado de derecho* (a state functioning in accordance to laws) or *imperio de la ley* (the enforcement of laws). Yet whereas the first rendition opens the doors for a distinction between its formal and effective existence (along the lines of the French distinction between *pays légal* and *pays réel*), the second, *imperio de la ley,* has a better and more univocal and unequivocal meaning derived from its Latin etymology: *imperio.*

26. At 20 percent, it stands slightly above the Latin American median. Latinobarómetro, 2007, 94.

27. Latinobarómetro 2007, 80.

28. The dismissal of members of the Electoral Tribunal by the Congress without following the proper procedure cannot be used to justify this measure. Such an act could have been annulled. In no democratic system worthy of the name can elected legislators be sacked unless some kind of mandated revocation procedure is in place and is followed. Doing so makes a mockery of democracy. This selective *fujimorazo* was celebrated by many and ignored by others, as the original one was. Now Alberto Fujimori has stood trial. Time will tell what will be the final outcome in Ecuador.

29. Francisco Rodríguez, "An Empty Revolution: Unfulfilled Promises of Hugo Chávez," *Foreign Affairs* 87 (March–April 2008): 49–62.

30. Amartya Sen, "Democracy as a Universal Value," *Journal of Democracy* 10 (July 1999), 3.

I

Trends in the Region

1

LATIN AMERICAN
PRESIDENCIES INTERRUPTED

Arturo Valenzuela

Arturo Valenzuela *is professor of government and director of the Cen-*
ter for Latin American Studies at Georgetown University. He is the au-
thor of several books and numerous articles on Chilean politics. During
the Clinton administration, he served in the White House as special as-
sistant to the president and senior director for Inter-American Affairs
at the National Security Council. This essay originally appeared in the
October 2004 issue of the Journal of Democracy.

Almost 25 years have passed since Latin America began what has
turned out to be the fullest and most enduring experience it has ever had
with constitutional democracy. While dictatorships were the norm in the
1960s and 1970s—only Colombia, Costa Rica, and Venezuela avoided
authoritarian rule during those decades—today an elected government
rules in every Latin American country except Cuba and Haiti. As David
Scott Palmer notes, between 1930 and 1980, the 37 countries that make
up Latin America underwent 277 changes of government, 104 of which
(or 37.5 percent) took place via military coup. From 1980 to 1990, by
contrast, only 7 of the 37 changes of government in the region took
place through military interventions, just two of which can be fairly described as clearly antidemocratic in intent. The overall number of coups
was the lowest for any single decade in Latin American history since
independence in the early nineteenth century.[1]

The coups of the 1980s were confined to just four countries: Bolivia, Haiti,
Guatemala, and Paraguay. Since 1990, only Haiti and Peru have seen elected
constitutional governments successfully replaced by force. In 1989, Argentines witnessed their country's first transfer of power from one civilian chief
executive to another in more than sixty years. In 2000, Mexico marked its
emergence as a multiparty democracy after more than seven decades of one-
party rule. Most Latin American states have never had so many successive
elected governments come to power without authoritarian reversals.[2]

Nonetheless, the euphoria that accompanied democracy's rise has begun to wane. Opinion polls show that Latin Americans still broadly support democracy and prefer it to dictatorship by a better than four-to-one margin. Yet the same surveys reveal a growing dissatisfaction with democracy and a readiness to question the benefits and the performance of democratic governments.[3]

Particularly troubling is a continuing pattern of instability that affects governance at the highest levels. In country after country, presidents have seen their job-approval ratings plummet while those of legislators and party leaders have tumbled even more steeply. Many a president has left office trailing dashed hopes and enfeebled institutions, but at least has left according to schedule. Fourteen presidents, however, have not. This group has suffered the indignity of early removal through impeachment or forced resignation, sometimes under circumstances of instability that have threatened constitutional democracy itself. A fifteenth chief executive interrupted the constitutional order by closing the legislature.

In the past, militaries were at the heart of the problem. Ambition-driven generals might topple an elected president or bar the implementation of policies that the soldiers and their allies did not like. New figures and forces might gain admission to the military-run "game" of politics if they took care not to advocate anything that sounded too radical or populist. Officers would arbitrate among factions and decide when to call for new elections to restore civilian rule, and coups in turn always enjoyed the complicity of civilian elites.[4] After Fidel Castro seized power in Cuba and set up a revolutionary-communist regime on the island in 1959, polarization intensified throughout the region and military juntas increasingly began to leave behind political refereeing in favor of full-blown "bureaucratic-authoritarian" dictatorship.[5]

Latin American democracy no longer faces threats from U.S.-supported local elites that fear any reform movement as a possible Soviet front. Military governments failed overwhelmingly to cope with the economic and social crises of the 1970s and 1980s. Toward the end of that period, U.S. foreign policy reacted to the winding-down of the Cold War by shifting from support for authoritarian regimes as necessary if distasteful bulwarks against communism to recognition that authoritarianism was thwarting the consolidation of legitimate governments. The United States joined other Western Hemispheric nations in creating mechanisms to stop any forcible disruptions of constitutional democracy.[6] In what has been a sea change since the Cold War, Latin American militaries no longer mix openly in politics.

Failed Presidencies

The ratcheting-down of polarization and the military's withdrawal to the barracks have not, however, ushered in an era of uniformly successful presidential governments. Instability remains a persistent problem and sometimes proceeds along lines that are eerily reminiscent of the unhappy past. For two decades—from Bolivian president Hernán Siles Zuazo's 1985 ouster amid hyperinflation to Haitian president Jean-Bertrand Aristide's 2004 flight before a wave of thugs—a lengthy list of presidents failed to complete their constitutionally prescribed terms (for a complete listing of these "interrupted" chief executives, see pp. 6–7 below).

Three cases differ enough from the others to merit special mention. Aristide has actually been toppled twice. The first coup against him came in August 1991, nine months after he had won a resounding victory in a December 1990 popular election. This was a "classic" military putsch carried out with strong support from a tiny civilian elite fearful of the former radical priest's populism. Restored after a 1994 U.S. military intervention, Aristide hung on through a nonconsecutive second term that began in 2001 while the overwhelming problems of his country (the Western Hemisphere's poorest) festered. They continued to do so even after brigand gangs and disgruntled ex-soldiers descended on Port-au-Prince and forced him—under disputed circumstances—to flee in a U.S.-furnished plane to the Central African Republic on 29 February 2004.

In Peru, President Alberto Fujimori (a political outsider who had won a runoff election after garnering just 25 percent of the vote in the November 1990 first round) executed an *autogolpe* (self-coup). Chafing at the prospect of having to cut deals with a legislature dominated by his foes, he recruited military support and shuttered Congress in April 1992. International condemnation was swift and widespread, but Fujimori's decisive actions (including victories over the Shining Path terrorist movement) helped him to secure both congressional-election victories for his allies and his own reelection to a second term in 1995.

The third unusual case involves the Dominican Republic, where the decision to cut short the final term of longtime president Joaquín Balaguer came before his actual inauguration. In 1994, the aged Balaguer had won a sixth term by a tiny margin, edging an old rival in a bitter race marked by widespread fraud charges and continuing civil unrest. Acting under the strong coaxing of the U.S. State Department (in which I was then serving), Balaguer helped to defuse the situation by letting his term be cut from five years to two and agreeing never to run again.

In the remaining cases, each president left office early amid severe economic, political, and social turmoil that the president's own immediate departure was widely seen as essential to resolving. Some presidents found themselves forced out after they took actions deliberately intended to suspend or undermine democracy. Others found that their position faced erosion not only due to flagging public confidence and surging unrest, but also because military leaders could no longer guarantee order

The Interrupted Presidents, 1985–2004

Raúl Alfonsín (Argentina, 1983–89): Resigned five months before scheduled transfer of power to newly elected president Carlos Menem with economy spiraling out of control, street demonstrations, and inability to implement policies that were being criticized by successor. Minority president, minority in Congress. No military role. Replaced by elected successor.

Jean-Bertrand Aristide 1. (Haiti, 1991): Elected in 1990, deposed in 1991 by military coup. Clashes between presidential supporters and opponents. Majority president, minority in Assembly. Replaced by military junta. **2.** (2001–2004): Elected again in 2000, resigned 2004 amid uprising by former military and deterioration of authority. Authoritarian style of governance, confrontational politics, allegations of corruption. Replaced by Supreme Court chief justice designated by constitution as provisional president. Prime minister appointed.

Joaquín Balaguer (Dominican Republic, 1994–96): Reelected to the presidency in 1994 in highly contested election marred by fraud. Massive protests paralyzed country. Agreed to support constitutional changes shortening his term in office by two years. Majority president. No military role. Replaced by elected successor.

Abdalá Bucaram (Ecuador, 1996–97): Elected 1996, resigned six months later in 1997. Economic crisis, allegations of corruption. Minority president, minority in congress. Military withdrew support after Congress charged him with "mental incapacity." Replaced by congressional appointee, vice-president bypassed.

Fernando Collor de Mello (Brazil, 1990–92): Elected 1989, resigned 1992. Economic crisis, mass demonstrations, allegations of corruption. Minority president, minority in Congress. No military role. Impeached, replaced by vice-president.

Raúl Cubas (Paraguay, 1998–99): Elected in 1998, resigned 1999. Resignation triggered by Cubas's pardon of former army commander, sharp splits in ruling party. Vice-presidential assassination accelerated threat of impeachment amid widespread demonstrations. Congress appointed successor in absence of vice-president.

Alberto Fujimori 1. (Peru, 1990–95): Elected 1990, shut down Congress in 1992 *autogolpe* with strong support of the military. Called for constitutional changes

and support. A final group left under less dramatic circumstances that came down to abysmal performance and nose-diving public support.

On 25 May 1993, Guatemala's President Jorge Serrano tried to break a perceived stalemate with the 116-member legislature (in which his party held only 18 seats) by means of a Fujimori-style self-coup. He arrested congressional leaders, Supreme Court judges, and the national ombudsman, and then announced elections for a constituent assembly to be held within six months. It all soon went sour, however, as the international community, party leaders, business groups, the armed forces, and thousands of student and civic-group demonstrators lined up against him. On June 1, senior officers who had been in touch with the opposition told Serrano that he and his supportive vice-president would have to go. Congress chose the former human rights ombudsman to fill the presidency.

In Ecuador seven years later, it was also high-ranking soldiers who and new election to constitutional assembly. **2.** (1995–2000): Reelected in 1995 and 2000, resigned in 2000 when majority support in Congress crumbled after contested election and widespread accusations of corruption involving his intelligence chief. Chronic demonstrations against illegal elections and corruption. Military played role in president's decision to leave office. Replaced by congressional appointee; first vice-president resigned, second vice-president bypassed.

Jamil Mahuad (Ecuador, 1998–2000): Elected 1998, resigned 2000. Allegations of corruption, mass demonstrations by indigenous groups, splits in ranks of armed forces following protests over IMF-related austerity measures. Minority president, minority in Congress. Military played active role in resignation. Replaced by vice-president.

Carlos Andrés Pérez (Venezuela, 1989–93): Elected 1988, resigned 1993. Serious economic crisis, two military coup attempts, allegations of corruption. Majority president, near-majority in Congress that crumbled. Impeached. Replaced by congressional appointee.

Fernando de la Rúa (Argentina, 1999–2001): Elected 1999, resigned 2001. Economic crisis, demonstrations and street violence, civilian deaths, allegations of corruption. Minority president, minority in Congress. No military role. Vice-president had resigned. Congress appointed series of successors.

Gonzalo Sánchez de Lozada (Bolivia, 2002–2003): Elected 2002, resigned 2003. Mass demonstrations and civilian deaths. Minority president, majority coalition disintegrated. No overt military role. Replaced by vice-president.

Jorge Serrano (Guatemala, 1991–93): Elected 1991, resigned 1993 after attempt to close Congress and arrest members of the Supreme Court. Backdrop of economic crisis led to confrontation with legislature. Minority president, minority in Congress. Military played active role in resignation. Vice-president resigned; replaced by congressional appointee.

Hernán Siles Zuazo (Bolivia, 1982–85): Elected 1982, agreed to resign one year early in 1985 after Church-brokered agreement. Hyperinflation, failing economic policies, mass demonstrations, civilian deaths, allegations of corruption. Minority president, minority in Congress. Military played active role in resignation. Succeeded by elected president.

pressured President Jamil Mahuad out of office after indigenous protestors and rebellious troops occupied Congress to show their anger at the austerity measures that he had proposed to deal with economic stagnation and a ballooning deficit. Mahuad's ouster was part of the deal that the high command had made in order to end the takeover. Mahuad, who had garnered only 35 percent in the first round of the 1998 presidential race and whose party held only 35 out of 121 congressional seats, had lurched from crisis to crisis with scant support.

Ironically, one of the most recent failed presidents turned out to be Fujimori. Riding his early successes in fighting terrorism and boosting Peru's economy, the former agronomics professor leaned heavily on military and secret-police allies and never bothered much with serious party-building or congressional relations. After his 1995 reelection, he began pressing the courts for a constitutional interpretation that would allow him to run for a third term. His public support waned and his hard-line, autocratic style caught up with him when his efforts to rig the April 2000 election sparked mass protests and strong international condemnation. Facing likely impeachment and criminal charges after his spy chief was caught offering bribes, Fujimori went to Japan and sent in his resignation in November 2000. Congress passed over his vice-president and chose its own presiding officer as temporary chief executive pending fresh balloting.

Bolivia's Siles Zuazo had been his country's president from 1956 to 1960. He returned to office in 1982 after years of coups and countercoups, only to face massive economic problems including hyperinflation. With no majority in either house of Congress and a fiercely restive labor movement on his hands, he saw his economic-stabilization policies repeatedly collapse as he strove in vain to bridge the gap between the standards set by the International Monetary Fund (IMF) and the demands of domestic groups.

Nothing seemed to work. Rule by decree, efforts to lobby Congress, and the appointment of a technocratic cabinet proved similarly fruitless as the indecisive Siles Zuazo wavered from one approach to another, finally resorting to a hunger strike as a desperate way to gain public sympathy. With his support crumbling and coup rumors abounding, the president at last agreed to a Catholic Church–brokered agreement under which Congress moved the presidential election forward by a year, cutting his mandate short.

In 1989, observers of Brazilian politics were surprised when an obscure provincial governor named Fernando Collor de Mello managed to parlay charm, good looks, and a media-savvy "antipolitics" message into 28.5 percent of the first-round vote and an eventual presidential-runoff win. Collor, whose ad hoc party held just 5 percent of the seats in Congress, soon alienated the older parties. Congressional moves to limit his powers, plus a faltering, inflation-wracked economy, forced him to move grudgingly toward expanding his legislative coalition. Before he got very far, however, a corruption scandal brought about his impeachment and resignation in 1992.

Venezuela's Carlos Andrés Pérez (1989–93) was exceptional in that both he and his party had won electoral majorities. Pérez had overseen a strong economy during a previous turn as president in the late 1970s, and people reeling from the effects of declining oil prices on the petroleum-dependent Venezuelan economy hoped that he would turn things around. Facing soaring budget deficits and inflationary pressures, Pérez moved swiftly to implement an IMF-approved austerity package that included fuel-price hikes. The result was unrest violent and widespread enough to drive Pérez to declare martial law. His governing style did not help him win support for his policies even among his own partisans. His own party's leaders, many of whom had resisted his candidacy, resented him for not adequately informing them of his initiatives and for ignoring their reform proposals. In October 1991, Pérez lost ground in internal party elections. The year following, two unprecedented military uprisings (army colonel and future president Hugo Chávez led the first) left 120 people dead. As Pérez's own party abandoned him amid charges that he had misused secret presidential funds, his efforts to recruit support from a dissident wing of the main opposition party fell short, and he found himself impeached and removed from office in December 1993.

A Flawed System?

How to account for this list of failures? Scholars point out that establishing democracy is one thing, while consolidating it is something else entirely. As Dankwart A. Rustow put it, democracy needs time to "habituate" itself.[7] Reformers have stressed the need for time to strengthen state institutions, develop rules and procedures for greater transparency and the rule of law, create and improve political parties and civil society organizations, and build effective working relations between the executive and legislative branches of government. Democratic governments must cope with daunting economic and social challenges, and need improved state capacity, accountability, and representativeness in order to meet the stern tests of governance. Donor agencies and international financial institutions have generated long lists of goals, from strengthening local governments to creating more transparent methods for handling legal matters.

Peter Hakim recently described the multiple hurdles now facing Latin America's nascent democracies.[8] While he stressed his belief that there is "no single cause or common set of causes that can explain Latin American malaise," he also singled out stronger political parties and better leadership as necessary preconditions for successful governance. From a methodological point of view, it is unclear why the strengthening of particular institutions or sets of institutions should improve the overall rate at which democracies succeed in establishing themselves and remaining functional. Much more work will be needed to enable us to distinguish the truly essential factors from those that are helpful but not crucial.

Studying the failed presidencies described in this essay may help us make that distinction. Two dynamics are particularly noteworthy. The first flows from the heat that the president and other officials can feel from protest movements seeking concrete solutions to real problems. This is hardly something new in Latin America, where the state—and at its head the president—tends to be seen as the source of all power and the final bearer of responsibility. In many cases, the political costs that came attached to IMF-compliant policies form a prominent theme. Indeed, not only presidents Mahuad and Pérez, but also Argentina's Fernando de la Rúa (driven from office in December 2001) and Bolivia's

Gonzalo Sánchez de Lozada (forced out by violent demonstrators in October 2003) felt the sting of protests against austerity measures that each had adopted in order to stabilize a troubled national economy. And yet it is also true that presidents who avoided strong steps for fear of public outcry—this group includes Collor de Mello, Siles Zuazo, and Serrano as well as Argentina's Raúl Alfonsín and Ecuador's Abdalá Bucaram— have paid a price for their relative inaction as national currencies have collapsed and inflation has spiraled out of control.

Protests can face a president with a quandary. Unchecked demonstrations may rage beyond bounds, but the use of force against them can backfire. The personalization of authority in the figure of the president adds a particularly vexing dimension. Failures of government are viewed not as failures of a party or movement, but as failures of the chief executive himself. The heavy symbolic trappings carried by the head of state, combined with often-overblown folk memories concerning powerful and nondemocratic past presidents, lead citizens to expect that a leader must fix the country's problems or face bitter charges of incompetence and corruption.

In presidential systems, a crisis will often cease to be primarily about specific grievances and their redress, and become instead a question of whether the chief executive himself should go. The police and military, fearing association with an unpopular or discredited leader, may underreact to threats against public order. If unrest mounts, the fixed-term president may find his position growing untenable, with no ready-made exit strategy available to match the dissolution of parliament and call for new elections that would be the solution in a prime-ministerial regime. Pressure from the street (including the worrisome possibility of violence) and congressional actions that push the limits of constitutional propriety may be what it takes to make a failing president face his fate. In the meantime, the political confrontations and turbulence caused by the issue of his removal can threaten to transform a government crisis into a full-blown crisis of the constitutional order itself.

The second dynamic dovetails with the first and helps to explain it. Although the citizenry expects a head of state to resolve deep-seated problems, Latin American democratic presidents are for the most part extraordinarily weak—they "reign" rather than "rule." The weakness of state institutions is usually less at fault than the sheer difficulty of building and maintaining support in a political environment of fragmented parties with little or no internal discipline. Compounding this problem is a lack of institutional incentives to prevent unchecked party splits, floor crossings, and the like. In the absence of congressional majorities, presidents struggle to generate legislative support, only to find that legislators—often including members of the president's own party—have no interest in either collaborating with a weak chief executive or aiding the success of a strong one. Rather than generating a logic of cooperation, presidential regimes seem to give rise to a logic of confrontation precisely because the president's foes see a successful chief executive as bad for their own interests and a failed president as someone to avoid.

The need for a solid capacity to practice the "politics of addition" and build governing coalitions becomes especially apparent when one realizes how many failed Latin American presidents have been bereft of *prima facie* majority support. Among the 14 interrupted mandates that this essay discusses, only Haiti's Aristide, Venezuela's Pérez, and Paraguay's Raúl Cubas came into office on the strength of absolute majorities won in a single round of voting. Alfonsín and de la Rúa of Argentina each topped 48 percent, while the remaining nine presidents were runoff winners who came in well short of that in the first round. Bucaram, Fujimori, and Sánchez de Lozada each initially won less than 25 percent of the vote.

At the same time, only Pérez and Cubas (who was Paraguay's chief executive for less than a year in 1998–99) commanded legislative majorities. One study covering all presidential elections in 18 Latin American countries from 1978 to 2000 found that presidents averaged more than 50 percent of the vote in only half the countries. Majority legislative support for the president was even rarer, occurring in only about one of every four presidential terms covered by the study.[9]

The more fragmented the opposition and the smaller the president's own party, the greater becomes the challenge of cobbling together a majority ruling coalition. Legislators may ignore programmatic considerations entirely and seek instead to gain as many advantages as possible for specific constituency interests. Coalitions will then be short-lived and ad hoc, aimed at grabbing the main chance or weathering the crisis of the moment rather than representing a stable majority of legislators. Even majority coalitions may have little to do with adopting a common program across a range of policy matters. Opposition parties will often stand to get no credit for successful policies but risk blame for failures, giving such parties scant reason to rally to the president, even if promised cabinet posts. Should opposition forces come to think that they will get more out of causing a president to fail than helping him to succeed, the presidency in question may go into a death spiral. With no prospect of fresh elections to resolve impasses and generate working majorities, executive-legislative relations will wind up bitterly deadlocked in what Juan J. Linz has called the "zero-sum game" of presidentialism.[10]

On the president's side, the travails of coalition-building may result from a simple unwillingness to surrender cabinet authority and executive freedom of action to often-amorphous and potentially antagonistic partners. Thus for presidents, too, the costs of power-sharing may exceed its perceived benefits, leading to the perverse situation of a president who lets his administration remain weak and politically isolated rather than bend his prerogatives to the demands of allies.

Although "minority presidents" are more likely to face difficulties than those backed by clear legislative majorities, strong party representation in congress is no guarantee of presidential success. Both Pérez and Cubas disdained dealing with their own parties and faced political revolts (the former's attempt to make up for this by recruiting opposition legislators into a new coalition fell flat, as we have seen). A president may find defeated rivals (perhaps including figures within his own party whom he bested for the nomination) becoming his harshest congressional critics. Making the problem worse may be former presidents eager to return to office and unafraid to pull their old parties apart in the process.[11] When the going gets rough, allies will desert to save their viability in future elections. In contrast to the situation that obtains in a parliamentary system, legislators can defect without either risking their own seats or affecting the president's ability to remain in office.

To make all this worse, chief executives often find it tempting to attack congress while trying to bypass it with decrees. The precipitous drop in the credibility of legislatures, parties, and politicians—often quite rightly cited as a serious problem in Latin democracies—is due not merely to sensationalist journalism and critical NGOs, but also to the deliberate rhetoric of presidents who seek to boost their own standing at the legislature's expense. Typically, the more decree powers a president possesses, the worse will be his relations with congress. The increasing exertion of such executive prerogatives risks turning the legislature from an arena of compromise and "getting to yes" into a forum for saying no to executive plans. By resorting to decree powers presidents may become stronger, but the presidential system becomes weaker and more brittle, encouraging confrontation rather than accommodation.

The paradox of Latin American politics is that democratically elected chief executives are undermining democratic institutions in the very act of trying to shore up their own weaknesses as presidents. Even those who do not fail outright all too often leave behind a legacy of missed opportunities. The plebiscitarian temptations that come with presidentialism, combined with the popularity of rhetorical assaults on "politics as usual," can occasionally lead to the concentration and even abuse of power in the leader's hands. The cautionary tales of Fujimori, Aristide, and most recently Chávez in Venezuela, show how presidentialism can be perverted into quasi-authoritarianism or even dictatorship.

Is Parliamentarism the Answer?

These observations suggest that the problem of governance in Latin America may be due to more than just the episodic weaknesses of particular parties, leaders, or institutions. Can it be that presidentialism by its very nature makes confrontations sharper, cooperation more elusive, party discipline harder to achieve, and party fragmentation easier and more reasonable-seeming? Is it time for reformers in the region to think once again about the wisdom of shifting from presidentialism to parliamentary government?[12]

Although "presidentialism" and "parliamentarism" are types that admit of considerable internal variation, and although there are mixed forms of government that combine elements of both, for expository purposes the two systems can be sharply differentiated on several key dimensions.[13] Presidential regimes feature "competing legitimacies." The executive and the legislature can each claim its own electoral mandate to exercise its distinct, though occasionally overlapping, powers. Presidents or congresses may choose cooperation or confrontation; the rules of the system (whether formal or informal) fail to require either. Under parliamentary government, by contrast, the legislature generates the executive, which then serves at the pleasure of the legislative majority, whether as a majority or a minority government. Cabinet government means that members of parliament hold responsible executive posts. This not only requires that senior party leaders and would-be ministers must run for legislative office, but also provides a means by which legislators can gain serious executive-branch experience and a more strongly felt stake in how the country's affairs are run, thereby encouraging more skilled and sober leadership.

Under presidentialism, moreover, the chief executive is both head of state and head of government. In the former capacity, the president receives ambassadors and potentates, travels to official funerals, and embodies the nation in times of triumph and tragedy. As head of government, the president enjoys wide latitude in naming cabinet and sub-cabinet officials, although some of these may need legislative consent or be subject to congressional oversight. In parliamentary regimes, the "ceremonial" and "effective" roles are divided, with the head of state (whether a constitutional monarch or a president) filling a symbolic function and perhaps acting as a moderating force at times of crisis. Prime ministers as executive chiefs run collegial governments that reflect party and coalition imperatives. Although in the media age prime ministers have become more visible as chiefs of government and enjoy considerable authority and prominence in their own right, their post by its very nature still demands that they lead by maintaining the trust of their parties and ultimately a majority of parliament.

Third, the direct election of presidents means that someone may reach the highest office in the land without strong party or governmental experience or support, propelled by direct media appeals in races crowded with candidates. To be successful, a president must work with congress—despite the sometimes-overwhelming temptation to bash it—and must achieve this cooperation mostly by using political rather than statutory or constitutional powers. The leadership of the president's own party will be split among congress, the higher levels of the executive branch, and those attached to the party organization. Each of these three groups will often have its own goals and incentives as its members make their various calculations about how best to position themselves for future political success. Prime ministers in cabinet governments are typically not media-driven political amateurs, but rather veteran party leaders with substantial ministerial experience and every incentive to stay close to rather than "run against" their own parties and coalition partners in the legislature.

Fourth and finally, presidents and congresses are elected for fixed, often staggered terms, which can lead to a situation where the legislative majority changes hands even while the president has years left in office. In parliamentary regimes, the government can change either when the prime minister's party loses a majority (whether through general-election defeat or a coalition breakup) or when the prime minister's party rebels and calls for new leadership. Any crisis of leadership or government, in other words, trips automatic institutional "safety valves" such as ministerial resignations, parliamentary dissolution, or fresh elections. Crises of government, therefore, rarely become crises of regime. This suppleness of parliamentarism stands in sharp contrast with the intrinsic rigidity of presidentialism, under which a defect in leadership or failure of policy can quickly tailspin into institutional and even mass confrontations with a frightening potential for violent instability and all the human and political costs it portends.

In sum, parliamentary regimes are based on a political logic that urges cooperation and consensus within the context of coherent policies. The unification of legislative and executive power places a high premium on working together to maximize success and avoid new elections. The underlying logic of presidentialism is far more conflict-prone, meaning that miscalculations or other personal failures of leadership can more easily set loose the perverse logic that leads legislators to hope for the president's failure, particularly late in a term or at a time of special difficulty when citizens become peculiarly eager for a savior—or failing that, a scapegoat.

What's Stopping Parliamentarism?

While the case for adopting parliamentarism might seem compelling to political scientists, the idea of such a shift is plainly anathema to most Latin American citizens. The overwhelming symbolic authority attributed to presidentialism leaps out from the pages of the region's history and bestrides its politics like a colossus. Even if successful democratic presidents have been few and far between, there have been enough legends such as Mexico's Benito Juárez (1861–63, 1867–72) to keep Latin America the region of presidentialism *par excellence*. Brazil, which is unique in Latin America for having remained officially a monarchy from the time of its independence in 1822 until 1889, decisively defeated a 1993 referendum on shifting to parliamentarism. The compelling reason seems to have been a fear that doing away with presidentialism would strip citizens of vital representation.

Aside from the potent appeal to tradition, the argument against ditching presidentialism most heard in the region is that parliamentary government would fail precisely because of weak leaders, parties, and legislatures, thereby provoking greater instability. This argument ignores how the political-incentive structure based on separation of powers aggravates party fragmentation and indiscipline and encourages weak leadership. It also ignores the substantial evolution in parliamentary governments that has taken place since the wobbliest days of the French Third and Fourth Republics (1870–1940, 1946–58) or the "musical-chairs" cabinets of Italy in the years following World War II.

It is noteworthy that the post-Soviet democracies of Eastern Europe have overwhelmingly evolved into either parliamentary systems or semipresidential systems (based on the French Fifth Republic) where popularly elected presidents with specific powers, including authority in foreign and security matters, coexist with prime ministers whose governments must enjoy the support of parliament to survive.[14] Given Latin Americans' reluctance to abandon the presidential system, semipresidential formulas might be considered a more realistic alternative. The problem is that semipresidentialism may not solve some of the inherent problems of presidentialism, and indeed could make them worse by reifying the conflict between the two state powers and personalizing them in the figures of the president and the prime minister.[15]

Preferable to semipresidentialism would be a parliamentary system with a popularly elected but somewhat less powerful president—something closer to the Portuguese rather than the French system. The president would be limited to a crisis-intervention role when governments need to be formed or parliaments dissolved. The president would not be able to compete with the prime minister in designing or implementing policy. But a parliamentary government in Latin America should adopt two measures that Portuguese voters have yet to approve: 1) the constructive vote of no confidence, whereby any vote to bring down a government requires proposing a new one; and 2) the option under which the prime minister can declare any legislative proposals a matter of confidence, to be approved automatically unless parliament votes to dismiss the government.[16]

If presidentialism cannot be replaced, can we list elements that might at least promote stability while providing safety valves for failed presidents? Such measures could include concurrent elections for all elective legislative and executive posts; closed or even straight party-list electoral systems; and a presidential prerogative to dismiss one congress and schedule the election of a new one. An additional step might require the president to resign upon failure to command a majority in any new congress, which would then be charged with naming a new president to finish out the existing term. These measures, however, would not change the basic confrontational logic that prevails in presidential regimes, nor would they encourage the creation of collegial forms of government based on strong parties and a different form of governmental leadership.

The record compiled by Latin American presidentialism is grave and deeply worrying. It is no exaggeration to say that this sad arc of failure is among the reasons why democracy's future now hangs in the balance across a huge swath of the Western Hemisphere. What better moment could there be for citizens across Latin America to ask themselves whether their presidentialist traditions are so dear that they must be conserved even at the expense of hopes for democracy's consolidation? The visionary framers who laid down the U.S. Constitution—the model for all pure presidential regimes ever since—had a supreme sense of the peculiarities and even the idiosyncrasies of the particular case for which they were writing a prescription. In their own varying circumstances more than two centuries later, perhaps Latin Americans would do better to imitate the spirit of prudence that actuated the U.S. framers rather than cling to the letter of the system that those framers created. If Latin Americans were to choose such a course, they might also reflect that Europe, in 1787 a haven of autocracy, today can boast models of democratic and predominantly parliamentary governance that deserve at least a fair hearing without *a priori* dismissal merely on the grounds of custom.

NOTES

1. David Scott Palmer, "Peru: Collectively Defending Democracy in the Western Hemisphere," in Tom Farer, ed., *Beyond Sovereignty: Collectively Defending Democracy in the Americas* (Baltimore: Johns Hopkins University Press, 1996), 258.

2. For background, see Jonathan Hartlyn and Arturo Valenzuela, "Democracy in Latin America Since 1930," in Leslie Bethel, ed., *Latin America Since 1930: Economy, Society, and Politics* (Cambridge: Cambridge University Press, 1994).

3. Marta Lagos, "A Road With No Return? Latin America's Lost Illusions," *Journal of Democracy* 14 (April 2003): 161–73.

4. A classic study is Charles W. Anderson, *Politics and Economic Change in Latin America* (Princeton: Princeton University Press, 1967). See also John J. Johnson, *The Military and Society in Latin America* (Stanford: Stanford University Press, 1964) and Edwin Lieuwen, *Generals vs. Presidents: Neomilitarism in Latin America* (New York: Praeger, 1964).

5. Guillermo O'Donnell, *Modernization and Bureaucratic-Authoritarianism: Studies in South American Politics* (Berkeley: University of California Press, 1973).

6. See Tom Farer, ed., *Beyond Sovereignty*.

7. Dankwart A. Rustow, "Transitions to Democracy: Towards a Dynamic Model," *Comparative Politics* 2 (April 1970): 337–63. See also Juan J. Linz and Alfred C. Stepan, *Problems of Democratic Transition and Consolidation* (Baltimore: Johns Hopkins University Press, 1996).

8. Peter Hakim, "Latin America's Lost Illusions: Dispirited Politics," *Journal of Democracy* 14 (April 2003): 121.

9. J. Mark Payne et al., *Democracies in Development: Politics and Reform in Latin America* (Washington, D.C.: Inter-American Development Bank, 2002), 74, 211.

10. Juan J. Linz, "Presidential or Parliamentary Democracy: Does It Make a Difference?" in Juan J. Linz and Arturo Valenzuela, eds., *The Failure of Presidential Democracy* (Baltimore: Johns Hopkins University Press, 1994), 18–19.

11. Rafael Caldera, a former president of Venezuela (1969–73) and an architect of the elite agreements that ended authoritarian rule, had an even more negative effect on his party when he succeeded Pérez after the latter's impeachment. Having failed to win the nomination of the party that he had founded, Caldera insisted on running as an independent. Repeat candidacies of former presidents are the stuff of legend in Latin American history. The pattern has continued into recent decades, featuring not only Caldera and Fujimori but also figures as dissimilar as Balaguer, Fernandez of the Dominican Republic, Eduardo Frei of Chile, Alan García of Peru, Hipólito Mejía of the Dominican Republic, Carlos Saúl Menem of Argentina, and Julio María Sanguinetti of Uruguay.

12. In addition to Juan J. Linz and Arturo Valenzuela, *Failure of Presidential Democracy,* see Juan J. Linz, "The Perils of Presidentialism," *Journal of Democracy* 1 (Winter 1990): 51–69 and Arturo Valenzuela, "Latin America: Presidentialism in Crisis," *Journal of Democracy* 4 (October 1993): 3–16. Critics of these views, while acknowledging the problems with presidentialism, tended to overstate the success of presidential regimes in the early years of democratic transition. See the essays in Scott Mainwaring et al., eds., *Presidentialism and Democracy in Latin America* (New York: Cambridge University Press, 1997).

13. An essential work in the field is Matthew Soberg Shugart and John Carey, *Presidents and Assemblies: Constitutional Design and Electoral Dynamics* (New York: Cambridge University Press, 1992).

14. Juan J. Linz and Alfred C. Stepan, *Problems of Democratic Transition and Consolidation,* 276–82.

15. Arend Lijphart makes this argument in signaling a preference for parliamentary government. See his "Constitutional Design for Divided Societies," *Journal of Democracy* 15 (April 2004): 102. Linz also has expressed skepticism regarding semipresidential formulas.

16. I am indebted to former Portuguese prime minister António Guterres for relaying these insights to me in personal conversation. Arend Lijphart notes that this combination of rules from the German and French parliamentary systems would protect cabinet effectiveness, while ensuring the parliament's prerogatives to replace the government with another or force elections. See Lijphart, "Constitutional Design for Divided Societies," 104.

2

THE CRISIS OF REPRESENTATION IN THE ANDES

Scott Mainwaring

Scott Mainwaring *is Eugene Conley Professor of Political Science and director of the Kellogg Institute for International Studies at the University of Notre Dame. He is coeditor of* The Third Wave of Democratization in Latin America: Advances and Setbacks *(with Frances Hagopian, 2005) and the author of* Rethinking Party Systems in the Third Wave of Democratization: The Case of Brazil *(1999). This essay, which originally appeared in the July 2006 issue of the* Journal of Democracy, *is based on his book,* The Crisis of Democratic Representation in the Andes *(2006), and draws upon work coauthored with Ana María Bejarano and Eduardo Pizarro.*

Over the past decade and a half, disaffection with democracy, political parties, and legislatures has spread to an alarming degree in the five countries of the Andean region—Venezuela, Colombia, Ecuador, Peru, and Bolivia. Between 1992 and 2005, popular and elite discontent cut short the terms of democratically elected presidents in all but Colombia. In Peru, a 1992 palace coup led to the collapse of the country's democracy, and in 2000 President Alberto Fujimori was forced to flee the country. In Ecuador three successive democratically elected presidents were forced out of office in 1997, 2000, and 2005. In Venezuela, President Carlos Andrés Pérez resigned under pressure in 1992, and a 2002 failed coup attempt briefly unseated President Hugo Chávez. In Bolivia, both the president who was democratically elected in 2002 and his constitutionally installed successor resigned under pressure. In the 1990s, massive discontent with existing parties caused wholesale collapses of the party systems in Peru and Venezuela. Traditionally strong parties have eroded or even disappeared throughout the Andean region, allowing for the rise of political outsiders and a surge of popular mobilization against the political establishment. In Bolivia in 2005, Evo Morales, a former leader of the country's coca farmers, won a landslide electoral victory running on a ticket (MAS, the Movement to Socialism) that did not even exist in the 1990s. He, too, railed against the established parties and promised a different, supposedly more participatory kind of democracy.

The widespread dissatisfaction with the quality and vehicles of democratic representation is a core ingredient in the political crisis that afflicts the Andean region today and threatens to spread throughout Latin America and beyond. A careful examination of this crisis challenges many assumptions that are common in studies of political representation. Scholars have mostly analyzed how representation works in the advanced industrial democracies, and they have generally assumed that patterns of representation remain fairly stable over time. Analyzing the Andean cases allows us to examine why in many countries representation sometimes *fails* to work and why patterns of representation are sometimes beset by instability. In the Andes, the failures of democratic representation are profound and widespread. Moreover, whereas most of the established literature assumes that democratic representation is based on programmatic linkages between voters and parties,[1] in the Andes representation is often based on clientelistic and personalistic bonds.

The five Andean countries have very divergent histories. During the 1960s and 1970s, Venezuela and Colombia were among the most democratic countries in Latin America. They enjoyed relatively stable and legitimate democratic representation, while Bolivia, Peru, and Ecuador remained largely mired in dictatorship. But Venezuela's once-solid democracy began to face serious challenges as early as 1989, with the outbreak of massive popular protests against President Pérez. In 1992, future president Chávez attempted a military coup, which despite its failure signaled the growing disenchantment with the existing political system. A deepening repudiation of the establishment parties then led to Chávez's election as president in 1998. Similarly, Colombia's democracy began to erode in the early 1990s, the victim of an armed conflict between drug lords, paramilitary forces, and left-wing guerrillas, and of deteriorating government control in the rural areas.

The political convergence among the Andean countries has not been entirely in a negative direction. As the Third Wave of democratization reached Latin America in the late 1970s and early 1980s, Peru, Ecuador, and Bolivia emerged from authoritarian rule. Discounting Peru's brief foray into dictatorship in 1992, all five Andean countries have been ruled by democratic or semidemocratic regimes since the Bolivian transition to democracy in 1982. For the first time in history, all five countries have simultaneously enjoyed an extended period of representative democracy.

While coming from very different starting points, today the Andean countries all face severe challenges to the legitimacy, stability, and efficacy of democratic representation. In all five countries, party outsiders or political independents burst onto the scene and vied for the presidency—winning that office in Bolivia (2005), Colombia (2002), Ecuador (2002), Peru (1990, 1995, 2000, 2001), and Venezuela (1993, 1998). Since the 1990s, electoral volatility has escalated, reflecting citizen discontent with existing party options. In all these countries except for Venezuela, public-opinion surveys indicate poor evaluations of parties and Congress, the two main pillars of democratic representation, and support for democracy itself is fairly low. Thus today the Andean countries have come to share a crisis of democratic representation that sets them apart as a distinctive subregion within Latin America.

Signs of Crisis

Democratic representation denotes a specific type of principal-agent relationship, one in which voters (the principals) choose politicians or parties (the agents) to represent their interests in a democratic regime. The core of democratic representation lies in the relationship between citizens, on the one hand, and elected politicians, parties, and assemblies, on the other. While in a democracy there exist other vehicles through which citizens pursue their interests—such as nongovernmental organizations, interest groups, and social movements—democratic representation in the strict sense refers only to the relationship between voters and their elected agents.

Among the agents of representation, political parties have long held a privileged place in democratic theory and practice. Parties establish an institutional linkage between voters and their representatives. They help to aggregate and to synthesize bundles of issues and to provide information shortcuts for voters. For these reasons, parties are central both to the study of democratic representation and to democracy itself.

The legitimacy and stability of a country's democratic representation are continuous variables. A crisis of democratic representation refers to one end of this continuum, where patterns of representation are unstable and citizens believe that they are not well represented. Such a crisis can be gauged by both attitudinal and behavioral indicators. The attitudinal indicators involve citizen perceptions: Large numbers of citizens are dissatisfied with the way in which they are represented, or they do not feel represented at all. The behavioral indicators are actions by citizens rejecting existing mechanisms of democratic representation—for example, withdrawing from electoral participation, voting for new parties (especially antiestablishment ones), voting for political outsiders, turning to antisystem popular mobilization efforts, or joining revolutionary struggles. In the Andes, both the attitudinal and behavioral indicators today show widespread disenchantment with and rejection of parties and legislatures.

Survey data consistently show a profound lack of trust in representative institutions in the Andean countries, except for Venezuela. Trust in parties and legislative bodies has increased in Venezuela since Hugo Chávez's election in 1998, but in the other four countries it has remained chronically low. In the 2003 Latinobarómetro survey, very few respondents expressed "some or a lot of confidence" in political parties: 5 percent in Ecuador (down from 18 percent in 1996), 6 percent in Bolivia (16 percent in 1996), 8 percent in Peru (18 percent in 1996), and 9 percent in Colombia (11 percent in 1996). The percentage was only slightly higher, 14 percent, in Venezuela (up from 11 percent in 1996).[2] These figures are low not only compared to other countries but also compared to the confidence expressed in other institutions in the Andean countries.

A crisis of democratic representation also manifests itself in measurable kinds of behavior. One indicator of voter dissatisfaction with parties is electoral volatility—the net share of votes that shifts from one party to any other party from one election to the next. High electoral volatility persisting over two or more consecutive electoral periods suggests that many voters are seeking alternative representative vehicles because they are dissatisfied with the way in which they are represented. Hence it is a likely sign of a crisis of democratic representation.

Electoral volatility has been high in Bolivia, Ecuador, and Peru since the restoration of democracy in the late 1970s and 1980s, and in the 1990s it rose sharply in Colombia and Venezuela. Since 1978, mean volatility in lower-chamber elections has been 22.1 percent in Colombia, 31.3 percent in Venezuela, 36.4 percent in Ecuador, 39.8 percent in Bolivia, and 51.9 percent in Peru—one of the highest levels of electoral volatility in the world. (This compares to an average volatility of 3.2 percent in the United States for 1978–2002.)

High electoral volatility in the Andes reflects not just shifts in electoral preferences for established parties, but the rapid rise of new parties and the decline of longstanding ones. In Peruvian elections since 1985, on average 60 percent of the lower-chamber vote went to parties less than a decade old. Over the past 15 years, all five Andean countries have elected at least one president from a party that had existed for no longer than one previous election. These new parties typically differ from the traditional ones; they have weak organizations and rely more on personalistic connections to voters, established primarily through the media. Political outsiders have also displaced established political parties at the subnational level. In Peru in 2004, independent regional movements controlled 13 of the 25 regional governments and 1,634 of the 2,281 jurisdictions.[3] Independents have also flourished at the local level in Colombia.

The dramatic rise of new parties has resulted in the withering or disappearance of some traditionally important parties. Today, Venezuela's Democratic Action (AD) is a shadow of the party that won five out of seven presidential elections between 1958 and 1988, and the Social Christian Party (COPEI), which won the remaining two, no longer exists. These two parties were the main pillars of Venezuelan democracy between 1958 and 1993. Of the four parties that occupied Peru's political center stage during the 1980s, the American Popular Revolutionary Alliance (APRA) surprisingly resurrected itself in the 2001 election, but the other three—the United Left, Popular Action, and the Popular Christian Party—are gone for good. In Bolivia, Nationalist Democratic Action (ADN), one of the three main electoral contenders from 1982 until 2002, has been reduced to irrelevance. The other two—the Nationalist Revolutionary Movement (MNR) and the Movement of the Revolutionary Left (MIR)—suffered withering electoral setbacks in 2005, and their survival prospects are unclear.

The traditional parties that have managed to survive bear faint resemblance to what they once were. During their heydays, Venezuela's AD, Bolivia's MNR, and Peru's APRA integrated the masses politically and forged strong party loyalties and identities; today, little if any of that fervor remains. Similarly, Colombia's Conservative Party, one of two parties dominating electoral competition from 1886 until the mid-1990s, experienced serious electoral erosion in the 1990s and did not field a presidential candidate in the 2002 election. In the 2006 congressional and presidential elections, the Liberals suffered their worst setback since the restoration of democracy in 1958.

The inability of parties to adequately represent their voters has been most profound in the two cases of party-system collapse, Peru and Venezuela. In both countries, the party systems of the 1980s disintegrated in the 1990s. The collapse of a party system is a dramatic and unusual expression of a crisis of democratic representation; it is the result of the electorate's repudiation not only of individual parties but of *most* existing parties. Citizens prefer to risk the unknown rather than to stick with the existing options.

The Rise of Outsiders

As the traditional parties have crumbled, antiestablishment political outsiders have flourished especially in Venezuela, Peru, and Bolivia, where they now thoroughly dominate politics.[4] Some observers might initially be inclined to applaud the demise of old parties and the rise of new competitors and of outsiders. If these newcomers rise to power because of voter dissatisfaction with traditional parties, is that not simply the result of a fair democratic process? The answer requires a closer look at the political outsiders and new parties that have taken over Andean politics in the past decade and a half.

By the time of their demise, Venezuela's AD and COPEI were widely viewed as the pillars of an old, failed order. Similarly in Bolivia, Evo Morales won a landslide victory in 2005 by presenting himself as an alternative to the old elite-dominated system. Peruvian presidents Alberto

Fujimori (1990–2000) and Alejandro Toledo (2001–2006) presented themselves in much the same way. Ollanta Humala, the populist leftist who won the first round of the 2006 presidential election in Peru, appears to be of the same ilk as Chávez and Morales. So, why not allow for "new blood" to reinvigorate these countries' political systems?

My purpose here is not to exalt the party systems of the 1980s. Among the five Andean countries, only Venezuela had a relatively vibrant democracy for any length of time—and even there, democratic success coexisted with poor economic performance from the late 1970s on. The traditional Colombian party system, which provided democratic stability from 1958 to 1991, rested on a conservative, relatively exclusionary pact. Yet for all their flaws, these party systems provided structure to democratic politics in all five countries.

The decline of traditional parties and the rise of political outsiders occur in a weakened institutional landscape. Newcomers present themselves as champions of fresh ideas and efficient and ethical government (and in most cases, of popular causes). They claim to be more democratic than the old system. But as they delegitimize party systems and discredit legislative assemblies, these self-proclaimed "democrats" pave the way for plebiscitarian forms of representation in which populist presidents displace parties as the primary vehicles for expressing the popular will.[5] Plebiscitarian representation chips away at democratic institutions, and sometimes paves the way to authoritarian or semiauthoritarian regimes, as occurred with Peruvian president Alberto Fujimori in the 1990s and Venezuelan president Hugo Chávez after 1998.

Fujimori was elected as an outsider in 1990, capitalizing on the public's profound disenchantment with outgoing president Alan García and the traditional parties. Fujimori portrayed Congress as ineffective and out of touch with Peruvian realities, and in April 1992 he mounted a coup, shutting down the Congress altogether. Initially, he won tremendous popular approval for this *autogolpe* (self-coup), but it soon became clear that Fujimori was far from a democratic reformer. The remainder of his tenure revealed the ugly side of populist political outsiders, as he attacked institutional checks and balances and tolerated widespread corruption. His ignominious downfall in 2000 left Peru with greatly weakened political institutions. In a similar vein, Chávez has railed against the old establishment and won considerable popular support but has persistently undermined democratic checks and balances. Notwithstanding his claims to the contrary, Venezuela is less democratic today than before 1998.

These two examples suggest a broader point. Leaders who are elected on the basis of direct populist appeals, sometimes aided by demagogic claims and often with the express intention of weakening parties, usually end up undermining democratic institutions. What starts out as plebiscitary representation easily slides into nondemocratic or even antidemocratic representation. Thus, far from compensating for a crisis of democratic representation, the rise of plebiscitarianism usually exacerbates it.

What Lies Behind the Crisis?

What lies behind the crisis of representation that is endangering Andean democracy? A common view is that the crisis arises from the exclusion of many citizens from the political process, the lack of popular or direct democracy, or the inadequacy of existing mechanisms of representation. Believing that such deficiencies were largely to blame for citizen disaffection with parties and representation, political reformers in the Andean countries in the 1980s and 1990s carried out major constitutional reforms intended to open up their political systems and promote greater participation (Venezuela in the 1980s, Colombia in 1991, Bolivia in 1993, and Ecuador in 1996). This diagnosis may have been accurate at the time of these reforms, but it is doubtful today.

In fact, there has been a dramatic expansion of democratic representation since 1978 in all five countries, especially in Bolivia, Ecuador, and Peru. In the past few decades, all five countries have seen democratic representation enhanced in four different respects: the massive incorporation of new citizens, qualitative changes in citizenship, political reforms such as the introduction of direct elections for governors and mayors, and new political openings for indigenous peoples.

Between the 1950s and the 1990s, regimes across the region broadened citizenship to include larger parts of their countries' populations. The numerical expansion of the electorate was particularly remarkable in Ecuador and Peru, primarily due to the enfranchisement of the illiterate in 1978–79. In Ecuador, election participation jumped from 12.1 percent of the population in the 1958 legislative election to 41.7 percent in 2002. In Peru, 45.3 percent of the population voted in the 2001 presidential election, compared to 14.9 percent in 1956. In Bolivia, the increase was also significant, from 27.4 percent of the population in the 1960 presidential election to 35.4 percent in 2002.

Accompanying this numerical expansion in the ranks of the represented were profound qualitative changes in citizenship. The percentage of those living in urban areas increased sharply in all five countries, with a significant impact on the makeup of the electorate. In the 1950s, poor rural residents—constituting majorities in Bolivia, Colombia, Ecuador, and Peru—faced limited choices in the "electoral market," which in rural regions was dominated by clientelist exchanges. Because local patrons controlled the peasant vote, there was limited real competition. By the 1990s, urbanization and expanded enfranchisement meant that the share of voters subjected to direct personalistic manipulation had fallen sharply.[6]

Levels of education have also risen dramatically in all five countries since the 1950s, further improving the odds for high-quality representation. Secondary-school enrollment has increased at a stunning rate in Colombia, Peru, and Ecuador. In Colombia, secondary-school enrollment went up from 12 percent in 1960 to 67 percent in 1996; in Peru, it increased from 18 to 73 percent in the same time period; and in Ecuador, it grew from 12 to 50 percent between 1960 and 1994.[7] In Bolivia and Venezuela, the percentage of secondary-school age students who were enrolled tripled and doubled, respectively. Better-educated voters have more knowledge and information about the electoral market, which in principle should serve to improve the quality of representation.

Another enhancement of democratic representation occurred as a result of political decentralization. Prior to the 1980s, all five countries were centrally governed, and mechanisms of representation were concentrated at the national level. Governors and most mayors were appointed rather than elected. In Bolivia, Colombia, and Venezuela, decentralization created local arenas of democratic representation during the 1980s and 1990s.[8] During the same time period, the Andean region's indigenous peoples—historically marginalized both socially and politically—were formally incorporated into the political system and won special recognition and rights, especially in Bolivia.[9]

These sweeping changes in the nature of citizenship and democratic representation do not imply that citizenship has been extended evenly to all individuals. The exercise of rights in the Andes is still far from equal across different classes, races, and genders. Despite persistent inequalities in the exercise of citizenship, however, the expansion of citizenship in the Andean region is impressive.

If limited access to representation—what we might call truncated representation—were primarily responsible for the present crisis, then the individuals with the least access would express the least confidence in representative institutions. This proves false, however. The poor and the less educated are most subjected to truncated representation; yet education and socioeconomic status have a weak impact on confidence in parties and legislatures in the Andean region. Dissatisfaction with the agents of representation is widespread across all levels of income and education.

State Deficiencies

If the Andean crisis is not due to "truncated representation," where can its source be found? In my view, the primary cause of the crisis is what might be called "state deficiencies." The concept of state deficiencies implies something more than merely poor government performance—it means that the state fails to fulfill some of its basic governance, legal, and security functions. The state includes a vast and complex array of institutions; most important for the present analysis are the national executive branch, the judiciary, the police, and the armed forces. These four state institutions have long been deficient in the five Andean countries, though with differences from one country to the next and from one administration to the next.

The economic and social performance of the Andean countries has been poor since the early 1980s. Venezuela's per-capita income has declined over a long period, beginning in the late 1970s. High unemployment (ranging in 2005 from 9 percent in Bolivia to 14 percent in Colombia in urban areas) and underemployment afflict the economies of all five countries. States by themselves cannot resolve these economic problems, but state policies have a large impact on economic performance.

Hand in hand with poor economic performance goes rampant corruption. Elites and citizens perceive corruption to be very extensive in Bolivia, Ecuador, and Venezuela, and fairly extensive in Colombia and Peru. On Transparency International's 2005 Corruption Perceptions Index—where 10 designates the lowest-possible level of perceived corruption and 1 the highest—Colombia's score was 4.0, Peru's 3.5, Bolivia's and Ecuador's 2.5, and Venezuela's 2.3.[10]

These numbers are not surprising. Since the early 1990s, all five Andean countries have experienced corruption scandals involving public officials. Venezuelan president Pérez's 1992 impeachment was triggered by a corruption scandal. Colombian president Ernesto Samper (1994–98) was blemished by the widely known fact that he had accepted millions of dollars in campaign funds from a drug cartel. Ecuadorian president Jamil Mahuad (1998–2000) was forced to resign after widespread demonstrations against his allegedly corrupt government. In Peru, ex-president Alan García (1985–90) was widely believed to have been involved in corruption and was forced into exile for much of the 1990s. His successor, Alberto Fujimori, became implicated in massive corruption scandals after resigning in 2000. In public-opinion surveys, a large majority of citizens in all five countries agrees that corruption has increased greatly in recent years.

A widespread perception of official corruption erodes voters' confidence in representative institutions. Simply put, citizens do not trust politicians who plunder the public coffers. While citizens might understand that politicians sometimes fail to deliver economic goods as a result of difficult circumstances, citizens cannot accept corruption among public officials, especially in times of economic hardship.

All five Andean states have also fallen short in two other key areas that are direct state responsibilities: ensuring personal security and protecting the legal rights of citizens. The police forces and judiciaries of the region have failed with respect to these tasks. High crime rates adversely affect the quality of life. In Peru, an estimated 69,000 people died as a result of political violence during the armed conflict of 1980–93. In Colombia, guerrillas and paramilitary forces hold sway over large swaths of the countryside. Throughout the region, judiciaries have been deficient in carrying out their responsibility for upholding citizen rights.

The Andean states have made little or no progress in addressing such issues as poverty, corruption, crime, and education. Poor state performance has negatively affected citizens' trust in their representative institutions. Citizens need and expect the state to devise policies that address their key concerns—jobs, income, housing, education, and personal security—and that enforce their rights. When states fail to perform these tasks adequately, citizens understandably become disenchanted with representative institutions.

Poor state performance can affect citizen confidence in representative institutions in two ways. First, there is evidence that *objective* macro-level performance directly affects confidence in institutions. According to the 1995–97 World Values Surveys, in 23 countries worldwide that had a certain level of democracy (a combined Freedom House score of 8 or less), confidence in parties and legislatures was higher where 1) per-capita income was higher, 2) economic growth was higher over the preceding decade, 3) inflation was lower, 4) more students of secondary-school age were enrolled, 5) unemployment was lower, 6) the Transparency International score was higher, and 7) the homicide rate was lower.

Second, citizens' *subjective* perceptions of poor state performance can erode their confidence in representative institutions. If disgruntlement with democratic representation stems from state deficiencies, this should be reflected in survey data. Individuals with the most negative perception of the state's performance should also express the least confidence in the institutions of democratic representation. Statistical results based on the 1998 Latinobarómetro survey confirm that in the Andean region, those respondents who regarded state performance as substandard also expressed low confidence in parties and legislatures. In all five countries, individuals who held the poorest opinion of national economic performance had the least confidence in parties and congress. Individuals with a more favorable assessment of the national economic situation were much more likely to express confidence in parties and legislatures.

According to these surveys, citizen assessments of crime and corruption also powerfully influence their confidence in parties and legislatures. In Bolivia and Ecuador, individuals who believed that corruption had worsened in recent years expressed a low level of trust in parties. In Colombia, citizens who believed that both crime and corruption had worsened expressed little confidence in parties and legislatures. And in Peru and Venezuela, respondents who believed that crime rates had increased also voiced a notable distrust in parties and legislatures.

Confidence in parties and legislatures was hardly affected by gender, level of education, or socioeconomic status in all five countries. In societies marked by egregious inequalities, the less privileged had reason to be more skeptical about democratic institutions, yet the effect of education, gender, and socioeconomic status on confidence in parties and assemblies was weak. In fact, in Bolivia and Venezuela, better-educated citizens expressed lower confidence in parties than did the less educated. Whereas the social marginalization of respondents had little impact on their trust in parties, their subjective assessments of state performance had a profound effect.[11]

These survey data suggest that state deficiencies are at the core of the Andean crisis of democratic representation. If states were more effective, citizens would have more favorable evaluations of the situation in their country, and their confidence in the core institutions of democratic representation would improve. If this analysis is correct, political reforms should focus first and foremost on making states more effective and only secondarily on making systems of representation more open. The formal systems of representation in these countries are already open. The truly grave deficiency is in state capacity.

Other survey evidence further corroborates the hypothesis that the main cause of the Andean crisis is poor state performance rather than the extent of democratic representation. Many survey respondents state that they would welcome abolishing legislatures and would accept a "strong" leader if state capacity improved. Many were even ambivalent about the value of democratic government itself. Both in the Andean countries and elsewhere in Latin America, large numbers of respondents agree that "in certain situations, an authoritarian government can be preferable to a democratic one," or that "it doesn't matter whether we have a democratic or nondemocratic government." In the 2005 Latinobarómetro survey, Venezuela was the only Andean country where a majority agreed that "democracy is always the best form of government." A lot of people in the Andean countries are unsure of the benefits of representative democracy, and might under some circumstances even be willing to forgo it.

In the Andean countries, state deficiencies extend well beyond presidential administrations—the state's "high command"—to include other important state agencies, most notably the justice system and the police. In Colombia, the armed forces have failed for an extended period in defeating nonstate armed combatants. Even during good democratic administrations, such as that of Bolivian president Gonzalo Sánchez de Lozada's first term (1993–97), other parts of the state continued to have serious deficiencies. A good administration can achieve significant change in some policy areas during its tenure, but it is unlikely to manage far-reaching reform of other state institutions in the same time frame.

Just as the concept of state deficiencies differs from the notion of poor governmental performance, it also differs from the concept of state collapse (or a failed state).[12] State deficiencies involve problems that, while of greater scope and longer duration than those merely reflecting poor performance of a particular government, are still less profound than a state collapse. A failed state is one that loses its ability to govern, to provide physical security for its citizens, and to control its territory. A polity that suffers state deficiencies fails to provide citizens with an important array of public goods, but nonetheless it still functions.

Nowhere in the Andes in recent decades has there been a state collapse. State failure in the Andean region has been partial and limited to specific subregions: the areas in Colombia controlled by guerilla groups and, to a lesser degree, those controlled by paramilitary forces (because they are less destructive of the state and cooperate with it more); and the areas of Peru where Sendero Luminoso had a pervasive presence between 1980 and 1993. Otherwise, problems of "stateness" in the Andes have been far less acute than those that have plagued such countries as Sierra Leone, Rwanda, the Democratic Republic of the Congo, Liberia, Bosnia, Sudan, and Afghanistan over the past two decades.

The Paradox of Democratic Representation

According to many indicators, the last few decades saw a boom in democratic representation in the Andes. The policies that excluded people from formal citizenship and the practices that produced truncated representation became less pervasive. More people became citizens in a formal sense, and fewer were subjected to traditional forms of personalistic domination. A greater number and diversity of parties emerged. Yet along with greater democratic representation came a growing disenchantment with the institutions of representation. How do we explain this apparent paradox?

In principle, the expansion of representation might have satisfied citizens, creating a perception that the political system was open and legitimate even if other aspects of the polity were not working well. In practice, however, it has probably had the opposite effect, reinforcing among citizens the subjective sense of a crisis of representation.

The incorporation and empowerment of new citizens, even in countries with staggering social inequalities, has bred heightened political expectations and an awareness of the right to demand from government certain collective and particularistic goods. More people have more opportunities to express disappointment with the political system and to place demands upon it. Citizens understandably direct their frustration against the suppliers of representation—that is, parties and politicians—when their policies fail to produce results. Although the police, the judiciary, bureaucrats, and other public-sector agencies share responsibility for poor state performance, elected officials are the most visible representatives of the state and are ultimately supposed to control it.

Elections provide an easy way in which citizens can register their displeasure with state performance—by voting against parties and politicians who seem to fail them. They cannot easily take action against other state actors that contribute to state deficiencies, except through such unusual means as legal action or filing a complaint with the ombudsman. From this perspective, a crisis of representation may occur not despite an increase in representation, but rather partly because of it.

In the past few decades, the region has seen an increase in poverty, income inequalities, and crime; job generation has been poor; economic growth has been sluggish; and there is a widespread perception that governmental corruption is rampant. States have failed to adequately address the needs of their populations, causing citizens to lose trust in parties and legislatures. The real problem is the failure to achieve effective results, not deficiencies in the formal mechanisms of representation.

This distinction has important consequences not only for understanding the crisis of representation, but also for responding to it. If the core problem were truncated representation, a lack of diversity in the competing parties, or a lack of accountability of elected politicians to voters, electoral reforms might have remedied the situation. Since the root of the crisis is state deficiencies, however, efforts to enhance democratic representation are unlikely to solve the problem. Indeed, some institutional reforms intended to enhance representation might exacerbate state deficiencies, thereby deepening the crisis. In particular, reforms that foster participation at the expense of state capacity threaten to do more harm than good.

These remarks raise the difficult question of *why* state performance has generally been so poor in the Andean countries. Unfortunately, there is little empirical research on state deficiencies, whether in or beyond contemporary Latin America. One can nonetheless consider various potential explanations. To some degree, the answer is a long-term historical one. Compared to Argentina, Chile, and Uruguay, the Andean countries have suffered from a history of patrimonialism, social and political exclusion, and dependence on extractive industries—a legacy that has not fostered successful state-building.

But if long-term historical factors were all-determining, analysts and policy makers might throw up their hands and proclaim the task of state-building hopeless. Besides, such factors cannot explain why state performance has worsened over the last quarter-century in many important arenas—job creation, economic growth, citizen security, and, in Colombia and Peru, control of the national territory. Some more historically proximate causes also merit attention. One important contemporary factor is the debt crisis of the 1980s, which bankrupted most Latin American states and spurred inflation throughout the region. In the face of spiraling inflation and stagnant economies, most countries undertook far-reaching economic reforms, many of which were necessary to restore stability. While some neoliberal reforms were needed to stave off state bankruptcy, others weakened the state. In the 1990s, state-bashing was fashionable in some circles, and some reformers disregarded the essential role of the state in regulating certain aspects of the economy, formulating policies, correcting market deficiencies, providing and enforcing a legal framework, protecting property rights, combating crime, providing education, and ensuring individual rights. The state cannot resolve all problems, but without an effective state, society and the market do not function well. Some policy makers were so eager to shrink the state that they failed to appreciate how important its proper working is for democracy and economic performance. Dismantling the state, rather than striving to make it more efficient, sometimes became the goal.

Andean states have a weak tax base, which leaves them with limited resources to perform their functions and meet citizen demands. Some states have been further weakened by patrimonial practices on the part of parties and politicians. Other important factors that have hampered state performance in the Andean region are idiosyncratic. In Bolivia, Peru, and Colombia, the growth of the cocaine industry fueled criminality and weakened the justice system. In Peru and Colombia, revolutionary guerrilla movements (and in Colombia, paramilitary forces as well) sowed widespread destruction that debilitated the state.

Improving state performance is the key to promoting greater citizen confidence in the institutions of representative democracy—and satisfaction with democracy in general. The Andean states today are unable to generate enough jobs, to provide adequate opportunities for education and advancement, and to ensure the personal security of their citizens. When democratic governments fail to meet the basic needs of their people for an extended period, citizens will become dissatisfied with the institutions of representative democracy. Therefore, building a state that can satisfy reasonable citizen demands is essential.

Effective state-building must be at the core of the contemporary policy agenda. This is easier said than done, but posing the issue in this way suggests some broad alternatives and rejects other paths. Reducing the size of the state without thinking about how to build a more effective state is misguided. Neither resorting to the state-led development of the past nor to a market with a feeble state is viable. Trying to expand participation or to decentralize without building state capacity is equally problematic. The critical need is to build a state that protects its citizens and guarantees their rights, that is efficient, and that interacts effectively with markets and with civil society to meet the challenges facing democracy in the twenty-first century.[13]

NOTES

1. For a classic example, see Philip Converse and Roy Pierce, *Political Representation in France* (Cambridge: Harvard University Press, 1986).

2. See *www.latinobarometro.org* for Latinobarómetro surveys cited here and later in this article.

3. Data from Carlos Meléndez, personal communication.

4. On the dominance of political outsiders in Peru, see Catherine M. Conaghan, "The

Irrelevant Right: Alberto Fujimori and the New Politics of Pragmatic Politics," in Kevin J. Middlebrook, ed., *Conservative Parties, the Right, and Democracy in Latin America* (Baltimore: Johns Hopkins University Press, 2000).

5. On the rise of political outsiders and the potential danger they represent for democracy, see René Antonio Mayorga, "Outsiders and Neopopulism: The Road to Plebiscitary Democracy," in Scott Mainwaring, Ana María Bejarano, and Eduardo Pizarro, eds., *The Crisis of Democratic Representation in the Andes* (Stanford: Stanford University Press, 2006); Guillermo O'Donnell, "Delegative Democracy?" *The Journal of Democracy* 5 (January 1994): 55–69; Martín Tanaka, "From Crisis to Collapse of the Party Systems and Dilemmas of Democratic Representation: Peru and Venezuela," in Scott Mainwaring, Ana María Bejarano, and Eduardo Pizarro, eds., *The Crisis of Democratic Representation in the Andes.*

6. On the expansion of citizenship in Peru and its ongoing limitations, see Sinesio López Jiménez, *Ciudanos Reales e Imaginarios: Concepciones, desarrollo y mapas de la ciudadanía en el Perú* (Lima: Instituto de Diálogo y Propuestas, 1997).

7. World Bank, *World Development Indicators,* 1998. *www.worldbank.org/wdr/wdr98/ contents.htm.*

8. On decentralization, see Kent Eaton, *Politics Beyond the Capital: The Design of Subnational Institutions in South America* (Stanford: Stanford University Press, 2004); and Kathleen O'Neill, *Decentralizing the State: Elections, Parties, and Local Power in the Andes* (Cambridge: Cambridge University Press, 2005).

9. On the development of indigenous people's movements and political parties, see Donna Lee Van Cott, *From Movement to Parties in Latin America: The Evolution of Ethnic Politics* (Cambridge: Cambridge University Press, 2005), and Deborah J. Yashar, *Contesting Citizenship: The Rise of Indigenous Movements and the Postliberal Challenge* (Cambridge: Cambridge University Press, 2005).

10. Transparency International Corruption Perceptions Index 2005, available at *www. transparency.org/cpi/2005/cpi2005_infocus.htm.*

11. For theoretical analysis of the state's importance for democracy, see Guillermo O'Donnell, "On the State, Democratization and Some Conceptual Problems: A Latin American View with Glances at Some Post-Communist Countries," *World Development* 21 (August 1993): 1345–69; Guillermo O'Donnell, "Democracia, desarrollo humano y derechos humanos," in Guillermo O'Donnell, Osvaldo Iazzeta, and Jorge Vargas Cullell, eds., *Democracia, desarrollo humano y ciudadanía* (Rosario, Argentina: Homo Sapiens, 2003), 25–147; and Juan J. Linz and Alfred C. Stepan, *Problems of Democratic Transition and Consolidation: Southern Europe, South America, and Post-Communist Europe* (Baltimore: Johns Hopkins University Press, 1996), 16–37.

12. On state collapse or failed states, see Robert I. Rotberg, ed., *When States Fail: Causes and Consequences* (Princeton: Princeton University Press, 2004).

13. On the importance of building a state that interacts effectively with markets to promote development, see Alejandro Foxley, "Más Mercado o más estado para América Latina?" paper for the Inter-American Development Bank seminar, Lima, Peru, March 2004.

3

LATIN AMERICA'S
INDIGENOUS PEOPLES

Donna Lee Van Cott

Donna Lee Van Cott *is associate professor of political science at the University of Connecticut and author of* From Movements to Parties in Latin America: The Evolution of Ethnic Politics *(2005). Her forthcoming book,* Radical Democracy in the Andes, *assesses the implications for democracy of indigenous peoples' experiences in local government. This essay originally appeared in the October 2007 issue of the* Journal of Democracy.

Among the key influences shaping the quality of democracy in Latin America today are the recent political mobilization and formal incorporation of indigenous peoples. In countries where such peoples make up a large share or even a majority of the populace, their legal and political incorporation into the state signifies a major power shift and the weakening of institutions that had been built to exclude them. Where indigenous peoples constitute a smaller share of the electorate, their recent inclusion denotes a more generalized opening of the political system to excluded and vulnerable sectors of society.

The political incorporation of indigenous movements and parties helps in diverse ways to improve democratic quality. Yet this incorporation also challenges fragile and stressed liberal-democratic regimes and generates social and institutional conflicts whose full implications remain uncertain. Anthropological and journalistic accounts of indigenous peoples' rising political power often present rosy visions of a multicultural utopia, whereas conservatives (of the global North and South) often sketch a dire scenario of racial confrontation, political apartheid, and state dismemberment. The actual and potential impact of this phenomenon most likely lies somewhere between these two accounts.

Indigenous peoples today form about 11 percent of Latin America's total population of 540 million.[1] High concentrations of indigenous cultures are located in the centers of the great pre-Columbian civiliza-

TABLE—ESTIMATED INDIGENOUS POPULATIONS
IN LATIN AMERICAN COUNTRIES

COUNTRY	INDIGENOUS POPULATION	PERCENTAGE OF TOTAL
Bolivia	5,914,000	71
Guatemala	8,342,000	66
Peru	12,696,000	47
Ecuador	5,556,000	43
Belize	47,000	19
Honduras	938,000	15
Mexico	14,049,000	14
Chile	1,217,000	8
Guyana	56,000	8
El Salvador	429,000	7
Panama	168,000	6
Suriname	26,000	6
Nicaragua	241,000	5
Paraguay	168,000	3
Colombia	794,000	2
Venezuela	471,000	2
Costa Rica	36,000	1
Argentina	370,000	1
Brazil	332,000	0
Uruguay	1,000	0

Source: "Operational Policy on Indigenous Peoples and Strategy for Indigenous Development," Inter-American Development Bank, 22 February 2006, 47, *http://idbdocs.iadb.org/wsdocs/getdocument.aspx?docnum=691261*.

tions—the Aztec and Mayan empires in southern Mexico and Central America, and the Incan empire, which extended at its height from what is today northern Colombia south into Chile along the Andes Mountains. Although precise figures can be difficult to determine with certainty,[2] it is generally agreed that indigenous peoples form statistical majorities in Bolivia and Guatemala, and amount to significant minorities in Peru, Ecuador, Belize, Honduras, and Mexico (see Table).

The majority of indigenous peoples today are bilingual, speaking at least one indigenous language as well as Spanish or another European language. For example, Mexico's 2000 census defines indigenous individuals as those speaking an indigenous language, but 60 percent of these individuals also speak Spanish.[3] Rates of European-language acquisition are higher among men, who tend to have more years of schooling than women and are likely to have more interaction with the nonindigenous through military service and employment. The rise of indigenous social movements in the last few decades has generated greater interest among the indigenous population in preserving and even learning once-lost languages. This is particularly the case regarding the various Mayan languages in Guatemala, and it is also a trend visible far to the south in the Andes, where millions speak Quechua. Nevertheless, there are dozens of indigenous groups, such as the Coconuco in Colombia, whose members retain a strong sense of collective identity and follow distinct cultural traditions but no longer speak an indigenous language.

Most indigenous people live in rural communities, farming small plots while engaging in artisanal production or a variety of forms of paid labor, since most family holdings are insufficient for subsistence. Many men today must spend at least part of the year away from their home communities in order to earn income. The majority of contemporary indigenous organizations have roots in the struggle to gain back land from *haciendas* (plantations) or to protect traditional community lands from settlers and other intruders. Nevertheless, the proportion of indigenous peoples living in cities is increasing rapidly. Migrants have created predominantly indigenous neighborhoods in or on the outskirts of Buenos Aires, La Paz, Lima, and Mexico City, though most maintain ties to rural communities that they visit regularly to participate in community life.

The history of Latin America's indigenous peoples has been difficult. The European invasion and conquest in the fifteenth and sixteenth centuries was catastrophic for the estimated 50 to 100 million indigenes who lived in what has since become Latin America. In the century after Christopher Columbus's first landing in 1492, violent attacks by Europeans, disruption of productive activities, and diseases of domestic and foreign origin wiped out an estimated 90 to 95 percent of the native populations. Spanish policies had the effect of atomizing large-scale political organization, as they forced Indians to settle in small Spanish-style towns, tied them as serfs to *haciendas,* or made them work in mines.

Colonial rule did provide indigenous cultures with a degree of internal autonomy and collective land rights. But these were destroyed after the Latin American colonies won their wars of independence from Spain, as the classical-liberal politicians of the late nineteenth and early twentieth centuries seized what remained of collectively held arable land and nullified colonial and church-based corporate rights. Influenced by the progressive European social thinking of the day, many Latin American states in the 1930s adopted the ideology of *indigenismo,* which promoted the preservation of indigenous cultural history while mainstreaming indigenous children into Spanish-language schools and forcibly "modernizing" indigenous social and economic systems.

The conservative military regimes of the 1960s and 1970s quashed independent indigenous political activity. Fledgling groups of intellectuals in Argentina and Chile were among those who saw their efforts crushed. Even states that held elections all too often raised various legal bars against voting by indigenous peoples. Ecuador and Peru, for example, imposed literacy tests for voting until each country made the transition to civilian rule. But even after literacy requirements were dropped and indigenous voters were legally enfranchised, fraud, barriers to registering new parties or gaining identity documents, plus the scarcity of nearby polling places, restricted indigenous political participation.

Until the 1990s, when barriers to party registration were lowered and constitutional reforms in many countries allowed civil associations to compete for some public offices, indigenous citizens wishing to become involved in politics had no choice but to join clientelist, corporatist, and leftist parties. Such parties trapped indigenous communities in relations of dependence. Top-down corporatist relationships—often an extension of dominant, elite-driven parties such as the Peronist party of Argentina and the Democratic Action and Social Christian parties of Venezuela—restricted indigenous political activity. Leftist parties embraced the socioeconomic demands made by the indigenous as peasants, while ignoring the oppression of their cultures, restricting indigenous politicians to subordinate candidacies, and perpetuating the same racist practices as conservative parties.

Organizing and Reform

Things began to change in the 1970s as indigenous social-movement organizations sprang up from Mexico to Argentina. These organizations typically began as local movements seeking to defend land rights. As their geographic scope increased so did the tendency to embrace distinctly cultural issues such as bilingual education and respect for customary systems of law and self-government. Many contemporary indigenous organizations broke away from groups that the Catholic Church, evangelicals, or political parties had established in the 1970s to coopt the indigenous. Others split off from peasant organizations sponsored by labor unions or leftist political parties, as these too persistently failed to acknowledge the racial and cultural roots of indigenous oppression.

By the 1980s, with help from international actors and donors—including human rights organizations, scholars, churches, and environmentalists—national-level indigenous organizations had formed in Argentina, Bolivia, Brazil, Colombia, Ecuador, and Venezuela, while organizations covering significant regions, departments, or states within a national space were active in Chile, Mexico, Nicaragua, Panama, and Peru. Some of these national organizations had little money and only tenuous connections to more cohesive local organizations, but they provided a platform for interaction with national and international actors regarding economic development and human rights policies.[4]

Bringing diverse indigenous groups into unified organizations has not been easy. In Ecuador, the largest indigenous-language group, the Quichua, contains seventeen distinct subgroupings, while the Amazonian region contains twelve more indigenous nationalities ranging in size from 600 (the Achuar) to around 40,000 (the Shuar) people. Colombia's minuscule indigenous population is divided into 81 groups speaking 64 languages. These linguistic and cultural differences are in constant tension with the need of indigenous movements to construct and project an aggregate indigenous identity.

Indigenous organizations that span geographic regions also must contend with strong regional identities. Indigenous peoples initially organized separately in distinct ecological zones, with densely settled indigenous communities in mountainous regions acting in concert, while more dispersed lowland groups formed regional confederations. Indigenous communities also are divided by religion, with Catholic and evangelical Protestant groups sometimes in open conflict, as in Chiapas, Mexico, and highland Ecuador. And like nonindigenous movements, they are divided by ideology and personal rivalries.

During the 1980s, the most effective regional and national indigenous organizations made impressive gains in areas such as greater access to bilingual education and collective land titling. But most substantive gains were not achieved until the 1990s, after indigenous social movements had devised networks and strategies capable of mounting widespread protests and marches lasting weeks or even months. In the early 1990s, indigenous activists and their allies formed transnational movements and organizations that spanned the global North and South and coordinated subregional activism. The increasing maturity of organizational networks enabled indigenous movements to act both informally (as interest-group lobbies and protestors) and formally (as participants in constituent assemblies and government officeholders).

The efforts of elite politicians to shore up failing democratic regimes by reforming political constitutions inspired indigenous organizations and their supporters in the academic and human rights community to mobilize in order to secure their rights. The skillful, peaceful, and dignified manner in which three indigenous delegates to the 1990–91 Colombian National Constituent Assembly gained a stunning array of indigenous rights inspired indigenous movements elsewhere to study the Colombian model and develop their own strategies. As they were feeling pressure from well-organized indigenous groups and their supporters, constitutional reformers were responding to broader societal demands to legitimize ailing democratic regimes by improving mechanisms for representation and participation, extending the rule of law and public authority into rural areas, and strengthening protections for a modern, internationally promoted set of individual and collective human rights.

Constitutional reform was not successful everywhere. The indigenous rights promised in Guatemala's 1996 peace accords failed to pass in a 1999 constitutional-reform referendum. Mexican Indians' efforts to secure comparable reforms failed in 2001, when Congress passed a watered-down version of the 1996 San Andrés Accords between the government and Zapatista rebels. States such as Chiapas and Oaxaca, however, have passed constitutional changes recognizing stronger collective rights.[5]

By 2000, a "multicultural regional model" of constitutionalism had emerged. Its five key features are: 1) rhetorical recognition of the existence of indigenous peoples as collective entities preceding the establishment of national states; 2) recognition of customary indigenous law as binding public law, typically limited by international human rights or higher-order constitutional rights, such as the right to life; 3) protection of collective property rights from sale, dismemberment, or confiscation; 4) official status for indigenous languages; and 5) access to bilingual education.

Various sources have ranked Latin American countries on the extent of their commitment to these rights. I place Colombia, Ecuador, Panama, and Venezuela in the "strongly multicultural" category. All countries in this category recognize most or all of the above-listed rights, while providing a high degree of legal and political autonomy in specified indigenous territories. Argentina, Bolivia, Brazil, Costa Rica, Guatemala, Honduras, Mexico, Nicaragua, Paraguay, and Peru provide "modest" recognition of some indigenous rights. Countries that recognize few or no rights include Belize, Chile, El Salvador, Guyana, and Suriname.[6]

The Rise of Indigenous Parties

The process of participating effectively in constitutional reforms proved crucial to the next breakthrough in the formal inclusion of indigenous peoples: the formation of viable political parties. Indigenous organizations overcame huge financial and logistical barriers to elect their own delegates in constituent-assembly elections in Colombia (1990), Ecuador (1997), and Venezuela (1999). Indigenous delegates, notwithstanding their small numbers, skillfully constructed alliances in favor of far-reaching reforms, while indigenous organizations lobbied constitutional reformers or protested in the streets. These successful, national-level political experiences gave indigenous movements—which previously had confined their activities mainly to the informal sphere—the confidence, experience, and political allies to move into formal politics by spawning their own political parties or, where permitted, competing in elections as civil society organizations.

Indigenous leaders understood that the implementation of their newly minted constitutional rights hinged upon votes in congress. Recent constitutional reforms themselves had fostered indigenous-party formation by instituting local and regional elections. Decentralization created political spaces in which geographically concentrated indigenous parties could successfully compete—even where special constitutional rights had not been secured. And so it was that Bolivia's coca growers swept municipal elections in their base in the Chapare of Cochabamba in 1995, a base that they soon used to construct a formidable national party. Moreover, some new constitutions (such as those of Colombia and Ecuador) lowered barriers for party registration in order to open restrictive party systems to new entrants.

The electoral gains scored by indigenous political parties have been dramatic. In 1991, Colombia's indigenous peoples elected three dozen municipal councilors and sent four representatives to Congress, including two indigenous senators guaranteed seats by the 1991 Constitution. They achieved this notwithstanding their geographical dispersion, low rates of voter registration, scant financial resources, and constant acts of intimidation and violence against their candidates. By 1997 they had elected one governor, eleven mayors, and about two hundred municipal councilors. Colombia's indigenous parties continue to be among the most durable of the numerous popular electoral vehicles created in the country since 1991.

The Colombians' success inspired indigenous organizations elsewhere. The most impressive results have been achieved in Ecuador and Bolivia. In Ecuador, the Pachakutik Movement of Plurinational Unity, which first competed in the legislative election of 1996, was part of the coalition that elected President Lucio Gutiérrez in 2002. Pachakutik was badly battered by its participation in the disastrous Gutiérrez administration, which crumbled in April 2005, but the movement retains a significant presence in Congress and controls dozens of local governments, often in alliance with leftist parties. In Bolivia, coca growers and other peasant and indigenous organizations founded the Assembly for the Sovereignty of the Peoples to compete in the 1995 municipal elections. After an internal split in 1999, the stronger faction, running under the registration of the Movement to Socialism (MAS), won the presidency in 2005 with 53.7 percent of the vote—the most decisive victory since the country returned to democracy in 1982. The MAS also holds absolute majorities in the Chamber of Deputies (the lower house of Congress) and in the Constituent Assembly for constitutional reform, which was elected in 2006.

The astounding and rapid success of indigenous parties in Colombia, Ecuador, and Bolivia inspired indigenous organizations with smaller bases amid less auspicious political and constitutional environments to form electoral vehicles for the first time. In Venezuela, an indigenous organization in the state of Amazonas formed the United Multiethnic People of Amazonas (PUAMA) to fight (successfully) for state-level constitutional rights. PUAMA won state-level office in 1998 and elected a representative to the 1999 Constituent Assembly. In 2000, allied with the leftist party Fatherland for Everybody, PUAMA elected the first indigenous governor of Amazonas and three of the state's seven mayors, and sent a representative to the National Assembly. Even in Guyana, where political conditions are manifestly unfavorable to aspiring parties, the Amerindian Guyana Action Party finished third in the March 2001 national elections, captured two seats in parliament representing the two indigenous-majority districts, and swept local elections in the Rupununi region.[7]

The meteoric rise of indigenous movements and parties should be understood in the context of the collapse of the political left in the late 1980s and its steady recomposition and resurgence in the last decade. In Colombia and Argentina, indigenous parties entered politics in the absence of a viable leftist option, attracting votes from nonindigenous voters searching for an outsider alternative to elite parties and neoliberalism. In Bolivia, Ecuador, Mexico, and Peru, indigenes emerged as important actors after a once-dynamic left had declined or moved toward the center. In the 1990s, indigenous movements and parties in these countries were the most dynamic voices critiquing unchecked neoliberalism; their protests helped to galvanize diffuse opposition to free trade. In the central Andes, Guatemala, and Mexico, surging indigenous movements absorbed the flotsam of a defeated and divided left, creating cross-ethnic coalitions that promoted the expansion of democratic participation and curbs on neoliberalism. Indigenous peoples' dense organizational networks provided the "mass-mobilizing capacity" to advance socialist critiques of capitalism in the absence of effective class-based movements.[8] Indigenous movements revitalized a moribund left by injecting more content and legitimacy into a sterile socialist discourse, and by manipulating nationalist images to make the left more appealing to a wider segment of society.

Yet one must ask what contributions indigenous movements and parties have made to democratic quality, and what challenges they pose. They have had a cumulative impact that has affected Latin American democracy—for better and for worse.

Impact on Democratic Quality

The political inclusion of indigenous peoples improves the representational dimension of democracy by giving once-excluded citizens more say in how decisions are made. Equally important, it demonstrates that poor and excluded peoples can mobilize human and social capital—such as cultural identity, dense organizational networks, and an ethic of reciprocal support and solidarity—to defeat powerful and well-funded elites. Indigenous political parties spend little on media advertising, yet they attract media attention by offering compelling images and appeals that resonate with a broader population.

The old view that the poor cannot effectively compete in Latin American politics is no longer valid. Perhaps the greatest indicator of their success is that political parties which had subordinated indigenous candidates to low-ranking or "alternate" places on electoral lists now recruit indigenous leaders for top positions. In Bolivia in 2002, for example, not only did the MAS finish second in the national election, but seventeen indigenous legislators entered office representing nonindigenous parties. The same year, the Indigenous Movement of the Peruvian Amazon had trouble finding candidates for Peru's regional elections because so many prospects were running instead with better-financed nonindigenous vehicles. In addition to inspiring other excluded groups, indigenous political parties provide a healthy model of collective political action for civil society associations because they are organically linked to deeply rooted social movements. The presentation of a successful alternative model for empowerment is crucial in Latin America, where political parties are failing at the task of linking political institutions to voters.[9]

Indigenous movements expand definitions of democracy by emphasizing economic equality and social justice. They offer an attractive, culture-based alternative to neoliberalism that is woven into a traditional socialist critique. Perhaps the indigenous have been more effective advocates for the impoverished because they are more visible and photogenic than the millions of urban and rural poor, who lack distinct, newly valued cultural identities. Indigenous peoples' oppression and exclusion points to more fundamental problems with Latin American democracy: a disconnect between the state and civil society; a marked imbalance in access to wealth and resources and the political power derived therefrom; and the challenge that powerful international economic actors present to national sovereignty and the autonomy of national and subnational cultures. Cohesive, autonomous voluntary associations and the political parties that they sponsor are the most important and effective counterweight to the concentration of economic and political power. In Dietrich Rueschmeyer's words, indigenous movements increase the "cultural influence" of subordinate groups, destabilizing the political balance of power—a necessary step toward reducing inequality and thereby improving democracy.[10]

Indigenous movements question the legitimacy of the traditional Latin American state model and its norms of personalism and populism, clientelism and corporatism. They challenge exclusively representative models of democracy in favor of more participatory models that can engage citizens in public-policy decision making and hold leaders accountable. Their critique is based on traditional indigenous self-governing practices that emphasize consensus-seeking, community participation, leadership rotation, and reciprocity—norms and institutions that constitute valuable social capital. Such values and practices are becoming institutionalized in many municipalities where indigenous political parties

now govern.[11] This is most notable in Ecuador, where the Pachakutik
Movement has introduced innovative institutions into local government,
including participatory budgeting processes (based on the successful
model of Porto Alegre, Brazil) and *sui generis* deliberative institutions
that link civil society and local-government actors and mobilize unpaid
labor on community projects. Development professionals are trying to
disseminate Pachakutik's models to other municipalities.

Even where indigenous movements have gained only a modest political foothold, they may improve democratic quality by offering real
programmatic alternatives and accessing legislative and media fora to
alert the public to issues that might not otherwise receive attention. Like
the European environmental parties, even when they do not gain power,
they may force other parties to address their issues, and with their strong
presence they challenge the status quo in ways that can be good for
democratic governance.

Challenges for Democracy

Yet indigenous movements can also hinder democracy. As Rueschmeyer cautions, highly mobilized and angry newcomers can overload
weak states, leading to protracted instability that delays democratic progress. Indigenous movements toppled or destabilized weak governments
in Ecuador in 1997, 2001, and 2005, and in Bolivia in 2003 and 2005.
The despised administrations usually are replaced by politicians and parties that are equally flawed, perpetuating a cycle of unrest and cathartic
victory that increases electoral volatility and party-system disintegration
without strengthening existing representative institutions or constructing
new ones. Indigenous movements and parties ably articulate widespread
public dissatisfaction with contemporary politics, but have yet to define
viable national strategies for governing across the ethnic divide.

The destruction of party systems and the rise of indigenous "outsider"
personalist candidates and populist electoral vehicles in some countries
have failed to offer voters real solutions. In the name of justice and
constituency loyalty, some triumphant indigenous parties have refused
to share newly gained power and state resources with the groups that
they replaced. Some are explicitly "antisystem" and may seize power
and destroy a failing system of representation before a new one can be
put into place. The absence of party systems to organize and moderate
political life makes legislative negotiation difficult, encourages executives to rule without restraint, and leads civil society organizations to
seek redress in the streets.[12] This syndrome occurred after party-system
collapses in Peru and Venezuela, and also emerged in Bolivia in 2006.

Since taking office as the MAS standard-bearer in January 2006, Bolivian president Evo Morales has manipulated his absolute majority in the
lower house of Congress and in the Constituent Assembly to avoid negoti-

ating with the remnants of traditional parties. He has encouraged supporters to take to the streets to pressure democratically elected opponents.

After a conciliatory first year, Morales took a decidedly authoritarian turn at the end of 2006, placing himself in the populist and power-grabbing current of the contemporary left. The economic windfall to the treasury from increased hydrocarbon revenues has fueled these authoritarian moves. In the populist-authoritarian tradition of Mexico's Lázaro Cárdenas (1934–40), Argentina's Juan Perón (1946–55; 1973–74), and Venezuela's Hugo Chávez (1999–), Morales is using the hydrocarbon windfall and strident nationalist and anti-imperialist slogans to maintain his popular base, placate the middle class, and destroy the traditional elite. He has appointed political cronies with questionable credentials to important policy positions and packed a rebellious Supreme Court with four new political appointees. In the process he is not only tarnishing his own democratic credentials, but, as the region's most prominent indigenous politician, he is also tarnishing by association the credentials of other indigenous candidates and movements. Bolivia is at risk of becoming an authoritarian "petro-left" regime in the mold of Chávez's Venezuela rather than the multicultural democracy for which many had hoped.[13]

Indigenous movements that are rooted in socialist unions and parties often maintain authoritarian and confrontational styles of politics that are more appropriate for earlier eras of armed struggle. Many such organizations—in order to survive the threat of violence from the military, state agents, and armed landowners—have been governed by norms that impose conformity and forbid internal criticism as a threat to survival.[14] Accustomed to feeling besieged by an external threat, some indigenous organizations are finding it hard to make the switch to the openness and tolerance for give-and-take that properly characterize representative democracy. Local affiliates of indigenous movements and parties may use violence against adversaries and be unwilling to negotiate, fearing that this may be viewed as a sign of weakness.

Although they have come a long way since the 1980s, contemporary indigenous organizations, communities, and political parties exhibit sexist norms. Few poor, rural women hold authoritative positions in movements or parties because women often lack basic education, are kept in the role of children's caretakers (in contrast to middle-class women), and must face their husbands' objections. For these reasons, Bolivia's indigenous political parties—the MAS and the smaller, now struggling Pachakuti Indigenous Movement—have had a harder time than *mestizo* parties finding enough qualified and willing female candidates to meet the demands of female-quota laws, failure to comply with which will result in a party's being banned from competition. When indigenous women do gain office, they may suffer physical abuse and intimidation from male colleagues, while their lower educational levels preclude effective autonomous action.

Elsewhere in the world, it is common wisdom that identity-based politics generates more intractable conflicts than class-based politics. The scholarly literature on ethnic political parties, which is derived mainly from cases outside Latin America, demonstrates the danger to democracy of allowing ethnicity to order political life, particularly in systems where culture aligns with economic exclusion.[15] This danger exists to a lesser degree in Latin America, owing to the mutability of ethnic and racial identity in the region. Latin America's most successful ethnic parties—Colombia's Indigenous Social Alliance, Ecuador's Pachakutik, and Bolivia's MAS—have built alliances that cross class and cultural lines on the basis of shared dissatisfaction with representative democracy, the failure of neoliberalism to improve welfare, and rampant corruption. Yet deep-seated internal conflicts generated by endemic interethnic confrontation have at times bedeviled all three parties. The rise of predominantly indigenous parties has raised awareness of ethnic inequality, while also emphasizing difference and generating a more extreme and racist discourse on both sides of the ethnic divide.

Distinct visions of indigenous-communitarian and liberal-individualist democracy may also generate ideological conflicts. Indigenous cultures tend to privilege collective identities and interests above those of individual community members. Thus indigenous movements and parties may fail to give sufficient importance to individual liberties or to foster citizenship on an individual level. Indigenous individuals accustomed to participating in politics through community organizations may feel unable to question group norms, to use their rights as citizens, or to act without the group.

For centuries, indigenous communities have used their own systems of internal dispute regulation and justice in the absence of accessible, culturally sensitive state systems. In the 1990s, Bolivia, Colombia, Ecuador, Nicaragua, Panama, Paraguay, Peru, and Venezuela explicitly recognized some jurisdiction for customary law in their constitutions. Most of these, as well as an additional set of countries—Argentina, Brazil, Costa Rica, Guatemala, Honduras, Mexico, and Nicaragua—ratified the International Labor Organization's Convention 169 on the rights of indigenous and tribal peoples, which requires states to adjust national legislation to permit the exercise of indigenous customary law. This recognition substantially expanded the coverage of legitimate public law in rural areas. Indigenous community justice is typically quick, inexpensive or free, and supplied in the local language. Such systems enjoy high legitimacy in indigenous communities, rarely result in serious conflicts, and should not be confused with recent episodes of vigilantism against criminal suspects or corrupt officials in the face of police inaction or collusion.

Yet most indigenous justice systems lack features that democratic theorists commonly associate with the rule of law. Rather than basing decisions and sanctions on written, preexisting universal norms, authorities typically fit each decision to the case in an attempt to restore community harmony and reconcile opposing parties. Indigenous law is authoritative because it is exercised by legitimate authorities, who administer it using traditional processes. Typically, there is less emphasis on the actual content of the law, which changes over time to accommodate circumstances. Defendants are usually not allowed a formal defense, and must rely instead on their own testimony and social prestige. There seldom are higher bodies to whom defendants can make appeals. Sanctions may include corporal punishment, expulsion, and even execution—although such drastic measures are reserved for the most serious cases. These breaches of liberal-democratic norms of justice are troubling. In most cases, indigenous peoples are incorporating features of Western systems to deflect opposition to the implementation of constitutional reforms that recognize customary law.[16]

A difficult process of adjustment to the formal incorporation of indigenous peoples is underway. Where indigenous parties have been in power for some time, in some cases disillusionment and frustration have set in already and public support is declining. Some indigenous leaders have succumbed to the temptations of corruption, while many organizations are riven by partisan politics. As resource constraints prevent indigenous politicians from improving indigenous constituents' economic well-being in the short or medium term, some once-energized indigenous organizations are disengaging from democratic life.

In sum, Latin America's indigenous social movements and political parties have invigorated local and national politics and bestowed legitimacy on democratic institutions by their inclusion in them. These movements and parties offer unique perspectives for addressing democratic deficiencies, as well as the capacity to mobilize social capital for democratic ends and to forge consensus on common political projects. They are expanding public expectations of democracy by insisting on greater participation, the reduction of inequality, and the protection of collective rights.

Yet fundamental and durable improvements in the region's quality of democracy require that contradictory visions of democracy be reconciled. Traditional elites must accept that indigenous peoples are now permanent players in politics; their needs must be addressed and their cultures respected. Elites must allow political institutions to facilitate greater participation for individuals and groups and make reducing inequality and injustice their highest priority. By the same token, indigenous politicians and groups must shift their perspective from that of excluded outsiders to protectors of democratic institutions, laws, and values. The minority of indigenous politicians who have not demonstrated their commitment to democracy should seek reconciliation, not retribution, and incorporate the best features of Western liberal democracy into their multicultural visions.

What the future holds for indigenous peoples and democracy in Latin

America is likely to depend upon the balance of power and incentives for cooperation among indigenous peoples, the nonindigenous left, and neoliberal elites. In countries such as Bolivia and Ecuador, where the center-right opposition is internally divided and has nothing new to offer middle-class voters, we may see a form of "populist multiculturalism" continue, featuring a single hegemonic populist leader or party with ties to indigenous organizations amid fragmented politics and persistent social unrest. Should these regimes generate levels of corruption, economic mismanagement, or human rights violations markedly higher than their predecessors, we are likely to see a backlash against indigenous movements, as urban and middle-class voters choose security over social justice. In countries such as Mexico and Chile, where the Marxist left is fragmented and market-oriented elites maintain relative unity, we are likely to see continued "neoliberal multiculturalism."[17] This will mean modest cultural and political-rights gains for ethnic minorities and indigenous peoples, within a context of neoliberal economic policy and political continuity. Only where all three forces are relatively balanced and equally committed to the rule of law, accountable governance, and the protection of universal individual human rights and collective rights for distinct cultural groups, will we see the most desirable outcome: the multicultural democratic state.

NOTES

I wish to thank Shannan Mattiace for useful critical comments on a previous draft.

1. Richard S. Hillman, ed., introduction to *Understanding Contemporary Latin America,* 3rd ed. (Boulder, Colo.: Lynne Rienner, 2005), 5.

2. National censuses and surveys taken by anthropologists and development professionals struggle with and differ over issues of methodology, classification, and distrust between census takers and subjects, all of which make the task of measurement more difficult.

3. Shannan Mattiace, *To See with Two Eyes: Peasant Activism and Indian Autonomy in Chiapas, Mexico* (Albuquerque: University of New Mexico Press, 2003), xi.

4. For useful overviews of this process, see Alison Brysk, *From Tribal Village to Global Village: Indian Rights and International Relations in Latin America* (Stanford: Stanford University Press, 2000); and David Maybury-Lewis, ed., *The Politics of Ethnicity: Indigenous Peoples in Latin American States* (Cambridge: Harvard University Press, 2002).

5. On Guatemala, see Kay Warren, "Voting Against Indigenous Rights in Guatemala: Lessons from the 1999 Referendum," in Kay B. Warren and Jean E. Jackson, eds., *Indigenous Movements, Self-Representation, and the State in Latin America* (Austin: University of Texas Press, 2002), 149–80.

6. For other rankings of Latin American countries with respect to indigenous rights, see Cletus Gregor Barié, *Pueblos indígenas y derechos constitucionales en América Latina: un panorama,* 2nd ed. (Distrito Federal, Mexico: Inter-American Indigenous Institute, 2004). For analyses of indigenous constitutional rights, see Willem Assies et al., eds., *The Challenge of Diversity: Indigenous Peoples and Reform of the State in Latin America* (Amsterdam: Thela Thesis, 2001); and Donna Lee Van Cott, *The Friendly Liquidation of*

the Past: The Politics of Diversity in Latin America (Pittsburgh: University of Pittsburgh Press, 2000).

7. For electoral data on indigenous parties up to 2005, see Donna Lee Van Cott, *From Movements to Parties in Latin America: The Evolution of Ethnic Politics* (New York: Cambridge University Press, 2005).

8. See Matthew R. Cleary, "Explaining the Left's Resurgence," pp. 62–76 of this volume; and Kenneth M. Roberts, "Social Inequalities Without Class Cleavages in Latin America's Neoliberal Era," *Studies in Comparative International Development* 36 (Winter 2002): 15–16.

9. Kenneth M. Roberts, "Party-Society Linkages and Democratic Representation in Latin America," *Canadian Journal of Latin American and Caribbean Studies* 27 (Spring 2002): 9–34.

10. On democratic quality and inequality, see Dietrich Rueschmeyer, "Addressing Inequality," *Journal of Democracy* 15 (October 2004): 80–86.

11. See Anthony Bebbington, Gonzalo Delamaza, and Rodrigo Villar, "El desarrollo de base y los espacios públicos de concertación local en América Latina," 2005, *www.innovacionciudadana.cl/latinoamerica/espacios.asp*; and Ana María Larrea and Juan Pablo Muñoz, eds., *Organizaciones Campesinas e Indígenas y Poderes Locales: Propuestas para la Gestión Participativa del Desarrollo Local* (Quito: Red Interamericana Agricultura y Democracia, 1998).

12. See Scott Mainwaring, "The Crisis of Representation in the Andes," pp. 18–32 of this volume; and Hector E. Schamis, "Populism, Socialism, and Democratic Institutions," pp. 48–61 of this volume.

13. Schamis, "Populism, Socialism, and Democratic Institutions," 29–32. Robust earnings from hydrocarbon taxes and royalties raised 2006 tax receipts by 46 percent over 2005 levels, to US$1.71 billion. Earnings from additional revenues are expected to bring the government approximately $1 billion annually after 2007. See "Gas Boost for Morales," *Latin American Regional Report: Andean Group* (Latin American Newsletters), November 2006, 15.

14. George Simmel, *Conflict and the Web of Group Affiliations* (New York: Free Press, 1955).

15. The classic source on ethnic parties is Donald L. Horowitz, *Ethnic Groups in Conflict* (Berkeley: University of California Press, 1985).

16. On the importance of the rule of law in democracies, see Guillermo O'Donnell, "Why the Rule of Law Matters," *Journal of Democracy* 15 (October 2004): 32–46. On indigenous peoples' customary-justice systems, see Rachel Sieder, "Recognizing Indigenous Law and the Politics of State Formation in Mesoamerica," in Rachel Sieder, ed., *Multiculturalism in Latin America: Indigenous Rights, Diversity and Democracy* (London: Palgrave Macmillan, 2002), 184–207; and Raquel Yrigoyen Fajardo, "The Constitutional Recognition of Indigenous Law in Andean Countries," in Assies et al., *The Challenge of Diversity*, 197–222.

17. Charles Hale coined this term in "Does Multiculturalism Menace? Governments, Cultural Rights and the Politics of Identity in Guatemala," *Journal of Latin American Studies* 34 (August 2002): 485–524.

4

POPULISM, SOCIALISM, AND DEMOCRATIC INSTITUTIONS

Hector E. Schamis

Hector E. Schamis *is associate professor in the School of International Service at American University in Washington, D.C. He has written on democratization and market reform in Latin America and ex-communist countries. His current research is on transitions from subnational authoritarianism, and on the effects of democratic institutions on economic cycles in new democracies. This essay originally appeared in the October 2006 issue of the* Journal of Democracy.

Just as in the 1990s, when specialists on Latin America acknowledged the emergence of a "new right," today they are coming to terms with the rise of reinvigorated left-wing politics. Influential publications such as *Foreign Affairs* and the *Economist,* as well as a host of academic venues, have focused on Latin America's current swing of the pendulum. Understanding the meaning of this change and assessing its implications for the future of democracy have become priorities for observers and practitioners alike.

Yet while all left-wing parties in Latin America invoke the aspiration for a more egalitarian capitalism and a more inclusive political system—among other issues that define the left—the political landscape is far more diverse than their similar discourse may suggest and analysts have so far been able to capture. In fact, current debates on governments that generally qualify as left of center have for the most part not gone beyond broad references to at most two brands of leftist politics, reiterating familiar discussions regarding the factors that have historically shaped progressive agendas in the region.

For example, a recent, widely read essay by the Mexican academic and diplomat Jorge Castañeda categorizes one type of left as having first sprung from communism and the Bolshevik Revolution, later identifying itself with Fidel Castro's Cuban Revolution. Leninist in its ideological and organizational roots, this left has somewhat unexpectedly turned toward pragmatism and moderation in recent years, adhering firmly to democratic institutions. The other type of left, meanwhile, draws freely on nationalist and populist symbols from the past. This left appeals to the poor, but through inflammatory rhetoric and redistributionist programs financed by fiscal expansion. Government spending booms during periods of largesse, only to contract dramatically when relative prices worsen and impose new macroeconomic constraints. Democracy suffers in these contexts, for the political process is reduced to a mere by-product of economic cycles, while broad discretionary powers in the hands of a personalistic leader erode the polity's institutions.[1]

Although Castañeda's distinction between two types of left is a step in the right direction, further differentiation is needed to account for the various lefts that have emerged in Latin America's recent past. We need more fine-grained characterizations and more precise classifications of the cases, not just for the sake of taxonomical consistency but also to map out complexities that a typology of two is unable to capture. This can also help us to avoid the mistake of classifying our observations on the basis of concepts that have far less meaning today than they did fifty years ago, when socialism and populism each put forward a vision of the future—of a classless society in the former case, and of autarkic industrialization in the latter—that could capture the imaginations of vast sectors of society. To be sure, progressive politics in Latin America will inevitably draw from the historical legacies of socialism and populism. The tenuous, inorganic, and amorphous manner in which these legacies now find expression, however, suggests that they can hardly inform useful analytical categories today.

If anything, the left in this part of the world often looks like a mishmash of *post*socialism and *post*populism. For example, how do we classify the Workers' Party of Brazil (PT)? Although hardly Bolshevik (yet officially a socialist formation), it is a party that emerged from the ashes of labor-based traditions associated with President Getúlio Vargas (1930–45; 1950–54). Yet the PT's fiscal discipline since taking office in 2003 means that it cannot be considered populist. What is the significance of the word populism—in Venezuela and elsewhere, and with or without Hugo Chávez's "Bolivarian socialism"—in the absence of that mainstay of Latin American populist political economy, import-substituting industrialization? How do we make sense of "left-wing populist" Néstor Kirchner of Argentina, a president elected by the same Peronist party that had earlier catapulted "right-wing populist" Carlos Menem to power?

The study of today's lefts opens a useful window on the polities of Latin America and their uneven democratic systems, but the challenge is to identify stable and consistent criteria that will allow us to tell one type of left from another. This entails using conceptual instruments within their proper historical contexts, since concepts removed from their original place and time of birth tend to lose their explanatory power. Notions such as a Leninist and a populist left (or populist right, for that matter) in Latin America perform more of a metaphorical function today, much like categorizations that speak of a "fascist" right (typically applied to the far right regardless of location) or a "Maoist" left (often applied to peasant mobilization across the developing world).

Accordingly, we should examine the left's record by means of more proximate factors. I thus identify a variety of lefts by using as my analytical basis of division the character of the party system, which can range from institutionalized and well-functioning to disjointed or even collapsed. Looking at the operation of party systems offers a deeper insight into the left and the quality of democracy more generally, for what is often predicated about the different lefts is also valid for parties of the right and the center. That is, in countries where the left is moderate, prone to parliamentary compromise, and respectful of institutions, so tend to be the other parties. Conversely, wherever the left disregards the rule of law, curtails the independence of the media, and ignores the other branches of government, so does the right.

A related question, then, is why the region's party systems have developed so erratically since the democratic transitions of the 1980s. I tackle this question by examining the path-dependency of the democratization process, the behavior of political elites, and the economic policies that have either ameliorated or magnified the effects of economic cycles. While accounting for the multiple types of left, these three factors also illuminate important differences in the operation of party systems and the uneven performance of democratic polities in Latin America.

Institutionalized Party Politics

Regardless of whether the left or the right is in power, institutionalized party politics promotes moderation and mutual accommodation, and with them democratic stability. Some Latin American countries have reached that neighborhood, while others have not. The factors that have allowed some countries to arrive at a democratic polity based on a stable party system also explain the behavior of the parties of the left.

Chile's redemocratization since the late 1980s is a case in point. From the outset, that process has had a strong institutional basis owing to the constitution that General Augusto Pinochet's military regime enacted via a plebiscite in 1980. This document included a formula and a schedule to guide the termination of military rule, calling for a 1988 plebiscite that would either keep Pinochet as president for another eight years or lead to 1989 national elections and the beginning of a democratic transition. This confronted the opposition parties with a choice: perpetuate the stalemate that dated back to the overthrow of President Salvador Allende in September 1973, or be part of the political process under the military regime's rules, which entailed the possibility that voters might legitimize the very dictatorship that the opposition had been contesting for more than fifteen years. Initially, only a handful of leaders from the Christian Democratic Party favored the latter option, but they managed to persuade their own rank-and-file as well as their counterparts in the Socialist Party.

In the end, participation paid off. The parties of the center-left, clustered together as the Concertación, prevailed in both the October 1988 plebiscite and the December 1989 general election. Chile returned to democratic rule with the start of Patricio Aylwin's presidency in March 1990. Despite doubts and mistrust, the Pinochet government transferred power to the new democratic government, as mandated by the constitution that the military regime itself had written. That transfer process was itself an exception, for rarely do autocratic regimes establish norms that specify, well in advance and with great detail, when and how the regime will abandon power.

Seen in retrospect, therefore, the military regime was constrained by the very constitutional framework that had granted it power. The 1980 constitution turned out to be a blessing in disguise. It not only reduced the uncertainty of the transition, but also—by remedying the longstanding problem of presidents elected with a popular-vote minority and by requiring larger congressional majorities to pass legislation—removed instabilities that had troubled the previous institutional order. Chile's experience reinforced centripetal tendencies, deepening and enriching a learning process that had already been under way.

In a country with a history of growing ideological polarization that had exploded into violence in the 1970s, the survival of democracy also depended on the resocialization of the political elite. The new institutional incentives facilitated this process. It was telling that somebody like Alejandro Foxley, minister of finance from 1990 to 1995 and foreign minister today, recognized early in the first democratic government that the constitutional rules left by Pinochet had "somewhat ironically fostered a more democratic system," for they forced major actors into compromise rather than confrontation and, by "avoiding populism," increased "economic governability."[2]

Consequently, since 1990 Chile has embraced the goal of poverty alleviation along with those of macroeconomic discipline and export orientation, avoiding the exogenous shocks that have hit the region over the last decade and a half. The typical portrayal of Chile as Latin America's "champion of neoliberalism" misses how pragmatic, if not counter to the mainstream and heterodox, the country's economic policies have actually been—from the emphasis on a competitive exchange rate to a free-trade agreement with the United States, from the tight regulation of the banking sector to the fine-tuning of interest rates, and from restrictions on capital flows to the creation of a fund to cushion the economy against fluctuations in the world price of copper (Chile's key export and always a state-owned resource). Such policies have flowed from a setting in which congressional bargaining has prevailed over street politics and compromise over executive discretion. Progressive politics in Chile is a matter not of sweeping transformations but of piecemeal reforms. The center-left Concertación, built around the Christian Democrats and the Socialists, has governed since 1990 and turned the country into a model of democratic capitalism and stable party politics in the region.

Although owing more to the behavioral dispositions of the political elite than to institutional incentives, strong centripetal tendencies have also developed lately in Brazil. Since the PT took office in 2002 under President Luiz Inácio "Lula" da Silva, these tendencies have become all the more noticeable and indeed remarkable, if one takes into account how fragmented Brazil's party system is and how strongly the country's constitution exacerbates political competition at the local level. The fractured party system is the legacy of two decades of authoritarian rule that ended in a top-down, protracted fashion and left behind slow-evolving parties created by the military regime itself. The excessively decentralized, hyperfederal constitution is a product of the primacy of territorial politics and the unwavering capacity of subnational interest groups to impose constraints upon the center.

The fragmented party system, the constitutional framework, and the weight of a populist past that tended to deepen labor-capital and urban-rural cleavages made for fragile parliamentary coalitions and overly strong incentives for pork. Brazilian politics became a zero-sum game that often paralyzed the policy-making process and left the country open to prolonged macroeconomic distress, made worse by unfriendly external conditions going back to the 1980s. Indebtedness, inflation, and volatile cycles of boom and bust—the archetypal features of Latin American macroeconomics—beset Brazil during its period of democratic transition. It was as late as 1994 that then–finance minister Fernando Henrique Cardoso implemented a successful stabilization program, laying the basis for his election and then reelection to the presidency in 1994 and 1998. Initially, the "Plano Real" paid off, but after five years of real exchange-rate appreciation the policy had become unsustainable. A sharp devaluation and deep recession kicked in just as Cardoso's second term began in January 1999.

Yet the lessons of earlier mistakes had sunk in, and Brazil would not return to the troubled legislative processes of the past. As president, Cardoso had managed to organize coherent and consistent legislative support. He successfully changed the terms of the relationship between the central government and the states, particularly in such crucial areas as fiscal policy and domestic-debt management. The currency-devaluation crisis of early 1999 was the litmus test of this new relationship, a test that the government certainly passed. As of that moment, a more flexible exchange-rate regime came into being (Brazil's Central Bank stopped pegging the value of the real to the U.S. dollar) and the banking sector was reorganized. Stability returned relatively soon, and the economy recovered its competitiveness.

It was in this context that Lula won a close October 2002 election over Cardoso's handpicked successor, José Serra of the Brazilian Social Democratic Party. Twenty-two years after its creation, and after compiling a record of successful municipal and state administrations across the country, the PT had finally made it to national office. Coming as it did in the wake of the Argentine collapse and debt default of 2001–2002, the rise of a leftist union leader to the presidency of Latin America's largest country made economic and financial elites nervous. The challenge was serious, but Brazil's top political leaders rose to it. Appearing together with their respective economic policy-making teams, sitting president Cardoso and president-elect Lula allayed fears by agreeing clearly and publicly on such crucial terms of the transition as the need to maintain macroeconomic discipline, to deploy a consensual strategy in negotiations with the country's creditors and the IMF, and to strengthen democratic practices and institutions.

It is no exaggeration, therefore, to say that Lula's PT government marks a watershed in Brazilian democracy. Originally socialist, the PT embodies a novel and pioneering form of leftist politics. Though it has roots in the populist traditions of working-class politics in São Paulo, the PT embraces true bottom-up decision-making methods that are also a far cry from the traditional leftist practice of democratic centralism. As in the much-discussed experiment with participatory budgeting in the city of Porto Alegre, the party leadership relies on the input of local-level councils whose deliberations and votes, funneled up to state and national leadership, shape the party's agenda. This consultation process also includes a variety of social movements, most notably the often-radical Landless Rural Workers' Movement (MST)—the world's largest movement of the rural poor—which since its founding in 1984 has pushed for a deepening of agrarian reform.[3] While generally responsive to the MST, the PT leadership has nonetheless remained firmly within its role of governing party, playing an evenhanded game of parliamentary give-and-take. Under Lula's balanced leadership, Brazilian democracy appears to have finally entered the era of institutionalized party politics.

The same can be said of Uruguayan democracy, but with significant additions. With the November 2004 victory of Tabaré Vázquez of the left-of-center Frente Amplio coalition, the century-old two-party system of the Blancos and Colorados gave way to multipartism. The outstanding characteristic of this sea change is that it took place within a context of peace and stability. There was nothing like the sort of political crisis that frequently accompanies (if it does not trigger) such a party-system transformation. Furthermore, the main group within the governing coalition and largest congressional bloc happens to be "Espacio 609," created and led by former Tupamaro guerrillas of the 1970s. The presence of José Mujica—a Tupamaro cadre who spent fourteen years in jail—as president of the Senate and third in the line of presidential succession closes the most traumatic period of Uruguayan history. A stable democratic system based on robust and effective party politics is now firmly in place.

Disjointed Party Politics

In disjointed party systems, incentives for parliamentary negotiation tend to be weak. Taking political disputes to the streets is routine, and the executive branch enjoys ample room for autonomous action. The economic cycle typically drives the political process. When prices are favorable and the economy is growing, the incumbent chief executive rides high, often circumventing established institutional routines and concentrating power in the office of the president. The basic traits of the typically strong Latin American presidential system gain extra force, leading to a "superpresidency" whether a leftist or a rightist is in office. When the wheel turns, with prices falling and growth waning while an angry opposition nurses its accumulated grievances, instability frequently follows and the superpresident becomes an embattled (and sometimes a former) president.

Argentina is a case in point, made so by the deterioration of its party system since the democratic transition of 1983. In 1989, reeling under the effects of the debt crisis and hyperinflation, the incumbent Radical Party lost office to Peronist Carlos Menem. Fighting inflation was a priority for the new government, which tackled the task by fixing the Argentine peso to the U.S. dollar under a currency board. By 1992, the stabilization measures were yielding results. As the terms of trade were improving and foreign investment was beginning to return, Menem that year embarked on a comprehensive privatization program. As he had done with the stabilization package, he carried out privatization by using his executive-decree authority and granting broad policy-making powers to his economy minister. The distribution of state-owned assets among private actors was also a political tool, an effective rent-seeking mechanism to garner support among the country's most powerful economic elites.

With economic recovery under way and broad discretionary powers in his hands, Menem next packed the Supreme Court and engineered a constitutional change that permitted him to run for a second term. Part of his strategy was to shift the balance of power within the state to favor the executive branch over the judiciary and the legislature. Menem's maneuvering generated resentment, not only among opposition groups but also among members of his own party, who grew bitter at his antics and his preference for political appointees recruited from conservative groups outside the Peronist party structure. In the end he was reelected, but it was a pyrrhic victory given the damage that it inflicted upon the party system and such fundamental principles as separation of powers and checks and balances.

By the second half of the 1990s, external conditions were again changing—this time for the worse. The Mexican currency devaluation of 1995, the continual appreciation of the U.S. dollar, and the devaluation of the Brazilian real in 1999 could only add up to bad news. It was time for a change, but the peg of the peso to the dollar was a straightjacket against countercyclical monetary policy, and Menem had become wholly identified with price and exchange-rate stability. Moreover, with growing public expectations of zero inflation, voter preferences regarding the trade-off between full employment and low inflation had begun to shift decidedly in favor of the latter, evincing a higher tolerance for recession. That is how Fernando de la Rúa of the center-left Alianza coalition saw things while running for president in 1999. He promised to keep the currency board and to continue servicing the swelling debt, much of which was subject to skyrocketing interest rates.

Problems were compounded by the way de la Rúa exercised power. First he pushed his coalition partner aside, which led to the resignations of his vice-president and a prominent cabinet member. Then he turned his back on his own party, gathering around himself a "friends and family" inner circle of unelected, nonpartisan advisors, several of whom had no previous political experience. Lastly, he appointed none other than Domingo Cavallo, once Menem's economic czar and the architect of peso-to-dollar currency stabilization, to a ministerial post with extraordinary powers over economic policy, further ignoring the political parties and marginalizing Congress. In December 2001, after four years of recession and with unemployment around 20 percent, a government freeze on bank accounts sent people into the streets. Rallies, food riots, and looting spread across the country. With democratic institutions lying seriously wounded, the economic emergency turned into a grave political crisis and the president resigned. De la Rúa fell in the same way that he had governed, cut off from the average citizen, severed from political society, and estranged from his own party.[4] In January 2002, after devaluing the currency and defaulting on its debt, Argentina plunged into its worst economic crisis ever.

The story comes full circle with Néstor Kirchner, a left-of-center Peronist governor from a small province who won election to the presidency in April 2003, succeeding a transitional administration led by Eduardo Duhalde. Thanks to the stability that Duhalde had managed to recover, Kirchner found more auspicious domestic and international economic conditions. Argentina restructured its debt, obtaining an unprecedented reduction of 70 percent, and improved its fiscal condition. At the same time, prices for its major exports began to rise again. With a competitive exchange rate, it acquired a large trade surplus that has spurred three consecutive years of rapid growth and mounting foreign exchange. Riding the boom, Kirchner has also found opportunities to accumulate power, especially since he did well in the October 2005 midterm elections. He has since sacked all independent-minded members of his cabinet (most notably Roberto Lavagna, the architect of the economic recovery), exploited his weakened opposition by coopting leaders from other parties, played on regional and factional divisions, and blatantly employed fiscal resources to grease the wheels of Peronist party politics. Moreover, he has flirted with unconstitutionality by extracting from Congress extraordinary powers to make unilateral decisions regarding such critical matters as foreign-debt negotiations and the budgetary process.

Kirchner's politics could be seen as reflected in "Menem's mirror"—the image is transposed from left to right, but otherwise the picture is identical. Whether democratic procedures are circumvented, twisted, and violated "to quickly achieve market efficiency and enter the First World," as in Menem's narrative, or in pursuit of "social justice and independence from the U.S. and the IMF," as Kirchner puts it, makes little difference. Disjointed party systems tend to weaken the legislature, tilting the balance of power in favor of the executive whether the left or the right is in office.

In Peru as well, democratization has failed to go together with the development of robust and stable party politics. The events leading to the June 2006 comeback win of former president Alan García and his left-wing American Popular Revolutionary Alliance (APRA) form no exception. To understand the multiple challenges posed by a party system unable to reproduce basic democratic routines, one must start with García's first presidency. It lasted from 1985 to 1990 and was by all accounts—including his own—a colossal failure.[5] Fiscal expansion generated an initial boom, but it was soon followed by raging inflation, massive disinvestment, and deep recession. In response, García repudiated Peru's foreign debt and nationalized the banks, thus ending up internationally isolated and in conflict with domestic business interests. As all this was occurring, the poverty rate was soaring and the violence of the Shining Path guerrillas was on the rise in the cities and the countryside alike.

As a result, by 1990 democracy was in shambles. The traditional political parties were so discredited that the two main electoral contenders were outsiders Mario Vargas Llosa, the country's most prominent writer, and Alberto Fujimori, a little-known agronomist. Fujimori and his newly created Cambio 90 won the contest and governed with the goal of eradicating the Shining Path—an end accomplished through state-terrorist methods—and recovering stability, investment, and growth, which the new president achieved through a corruption-ridden privatization and reform program. In 1992, Fujimori staged a self-coup, closed Congress, and rewrote the constitution. He had managed to start a third term when his autocratic rule began to come under challenge in the late 1990s. Alejandro Toledo, another relative outsider (this time with an indigenous ethnic background and a Stanford doctorate) lost to Fujimori at the polls in April 2000 and later led protests against him. In November 2000, with his administration unraveling amid corruption scandals, Fujimori fled into Japanese exile. Toledo and his own new party, Perú Posible, won the next election in June 2001.

Marred by scandals and internal disputes, the Toledo presidency came to an end with the election of June 2006. The runoff pitted García against former army officer and coup plotter Ollanta Humala, a political newcomer running under the banner of the Union for Peru (UPP). From the outset, the contest was influenced by the explicit intervention of Venezuela's Hugo Chávez, who sided with, and according to some observers even financed, Humala's campaign. Casting himself as a moderate social democrat in the mold of Chile's Ricardo Lagos and Michelle Bachelet, García eked out a narrow win. The problems that he faces are monumental—poverty, ethnic divisions, and regional inequalities. What will make his task all the more challenging is the dysfunctional institutional setting within which he will have to work. With Congress fragmented, García will have a hard time reaching much-needed parliamentary accords—a daunting prospect in light of the ephemeral character of Peru's political parties and the volatility of the party system as a whole.

The Petro-Left

Democracy does not fare well in oil-producing countries, at least not in the long term. Oil-export revenues spur an appreciation of the exchange rate that hurts the competitiveness of the manufacturing sector and crowds out investment. Because of this, not only do countries rich in oil grow slowly but they do so in unbalanced ways, which create intense regional and sectoral cleavages, and through sharp cycles associated with price and exchange-rate fluctuations, which foster instability. More often than not, the political economy of oil engenders a patrimonial system of domination—a polity in which extensive clientelistic networks seek control of the resource in order to distribute its proceeds among insiders. This tends to produce a "sparse" state that is unable to define and enforce rights, centralize the means of administration, or collect revenue efficiently. In such a setting the left side of the political spectrum can all too easily become a peculiar "petro-left," just as the right becomes a "petro-right." Oil distorts the entire political and economic picture, whether in a collapsed party system such as Venezuela's or a disjointed and fragmented one such as Bolivia's.

Oil was the cornerstone of the Venezuelan political arrangement after 1958. The so-called Pact of Punto Fijo, signed by the relevant political and economic actors after years of military rule, institutionalized a power-sharing democracy under which the center-left Democratic Action (AD) party and the center-right Social Christian Party (known as COPEI) built the dominant political machine. Through the 1960s and 1970s, while most of Latin America was under authoritarian rule, in Venezuela oil paid democracy's bills.[6] The problem, however, was that oil could do so only as long as prices remained high. When they began to dip around 1983, unprecedented fiscal constraints exposed the nature of the arrangement—a system of collusion among politicians of both parties who doled out the oil windfall to their cronies while largely ignoring the demands of the urban poor. In February 1989, long-simmering discontent burst into violence during the so-called Caracazo, a series of riots against the structural-adjustment program of then-president Carlos Andrés Pérez that left a death toll estimated at between one and three thousand.

While the Caracazo signaled the demise of *puntofijismo*,[7] the system's death certificate was signed by a pair of 1992 coup attempts, followed by Pérez's impeachment and removal from office the next year. Lieutenant-Colonel Hugo Chávez, a coup leader who had risen to prominence by condemning AD and COPEI as arrogant and corrupt, capitalized on the crisis. His ardent rhetoric resonated with the shantytown dwellers who turned out in unprecedented numbers for the 1998 election. With both parties virtually disbanded, Chávez ran and won with 56 percent of the vote. *Chavismo* had begun.

Once in power, Chávez opened a tumultuous chapter in Venezuelan history, one that is still being written and whose long-term implications remain unclear. What started as a genuine electoral victory gradually deteriorated into a simulacrum of democratic rule. In 1999, Chávez convened elections to choose a national constituent assembly. This body revised the 1961 Constitution, mandating a switch from a bicameral to a unicameral national legislature, the removal of control over the army from the legislature's hands, an extension of presidential tenure from five to six years, and authorization for the incumbent president to seek a consecutive second term. In a country that had become deeply divided while political parties had become irrelevant, conflict intensified. After being reelected under the newly amended constitution in July 2000, a weakened Chávez barely survived a two-day attempted coup in April 2002. But survive he did, and then went on comfortably to defeat a recall referendum in August 2004. Subsequently, he packed the Supreme Court with seventeen loyal justices, replacing five and adding a dozen new ones.

Oil is the factor that explains how Chávez transformed himself so quickly from the damaged, almost-ousted president of 2002 to the assertive figure of 2004 and after. As the price of crude oil has soared, Chávez's ambitions have become easier to finance. These include not only his comprehensive fiscal stimuli and far-reaching social programs, but also his new international persona—projecting himself as a regional leader, meddling in the domestic politics of Peru and Mexico, destabilizing the Andean Pact, entering Mercosur while challenging Brazil, and ratcheting up his rhetoric against the United States and the Bush administration (even as most of Venezuela's offshore exploration remains contracted out to

U.S. firms and all the country's oil continues to be refined in Louisiana). Chávez's rule represents an oil-funded, twenty-first century version of patrimonial domination. Along with the vague populist oratory and nebulous socialist goals come clearly undemocratic methods. The question is whether, with a shift in the price cycle, his "Bolivarian Revolution" will collapse just as the Punto Fijo arrangement did in the late 1980s and, if that happens, how much farther from stable and democratic party politics Venezuela will then be.

Although perhaps less prominently than in Venezuela, the traits of a petro-left are also visible in Bolivia. While party politics, however fragmented and disjointed, still plays more of a role there than in Venezuela, Bolivian democracy has deteriorated rapidly since President Gonzalo Sánchez de Lozada's term came to a premature end with his resignation in October 2003. With a mobilized labor movement and a divided party system, the Sánchez de Lozada administration suffered from defective circumstances at its very outset. When the June 2002 election had produced no candidate with the required majority, an agreement between the two traditional parties in Congress (known by their acronyms as MIR and MNR) had made Sánchez de Lozada president. The close runner-up, coca-growers' leader and Movement Toward Socialism (MAS) candidate Evo Morales, viewed the agreement as a behind-the-scenes conspiracy and usurpation. The fierce mass mobilizations that he and his allies sparked undermined the new president's legitimacy and doomed his administration from the outset.

After two interim presidents failed to restore stability, a December 2005 election gave Morales a solid 53.7 percent first-round victory and made him Bolivia's first president elected by a majority in more than two decades. Morales had rallied his base with such classic leftist issues as the rights of indigenous peoples, the end of restrictions on coca growing, and full state control over the hydrocarbon sector. It was not too surprising, then, that with the enthusiastic support of Fidel Castro and the ever-growing influence of Hugo Chávez, Morales nationalized Bolivia's oil and gas sector on May Day, 2006. With great fanfare and nationalistic fervor, Morales even ordered troops to occupy foreign-run oil and gas fields. Upon reviewing the event and its images, one cannot help remembering Lenin's great concern with "leftism," that "infantile disorder," especially given that one of the main casualties of the nationalization turned out to be Brazil's Petrobras, the state-owned oil company of a Latin American country governed by a socialist labor leader.

The leftward tide has divided Latin America more sharply than it has been at any time since the return of democracy two decades ago. Under Chávez's petro-financed foreign policy, the Andean Pact has been seriously damaged by Venezuela's departure, Mercosur's purpose has become uncertain with Venezuela's challenge to Brazil's leadership, and the worsening of relations between Bolivia and Brazil has made a chimera of the old hopes for regionwide energy integration. This suggests the need to come to terms with the multiple types of left that are in office today in Latin America, and to examine their differences in terms of stark contrasts among their respective countries' party systems as well as the uneven performance of their democratic institutions.

The Left and the Future of Democracy

Populism as a political actor is history—we should perhaps drop the concept altogether. Once classic import-substituting industrialization ceased to be a feasible strategy—a result of the increasing market integration and financial openness that has come about since the mid-1970s—the economic incentives of the multiclass, urban coalitions that had sustained populism disappeared. Without material bases of support, populism's structural foundations vanished. Such strains of "populism" as have come to power since the transitions of the 1980s have been crude imitations of the original, capable of recreating its rhetoric and rituals but unable to reproduce its substance. Similarly, socialism is a thing of the past. Once state socialism disclosed its ugly face and its irrational economics, the system and its ideology collapsed together. Notions such as a classless society, central planning, and state ownership of the means of production lost meaning and traction, in Latin America and elsewhere.

Yet the essential progressive concerns of populism and socialism are as alive as ever. Decades after the end of military rule, longstanding goals such as a welfare state, social justice and political inclusion, substantive equality and dignity for working people, and rights for disadvantaged groups remain unfulfilled and continue to spark mobilization. Political vehicles from the past, however, are no longer viable in their original form. The issues remain the same, but new strategies are needed to address and resolve them. Socialists have generally found a new script with relative ease, for they have had somewhere to look. Felipe González had already turned Spain into a model of social democracy by the mid-1980s. By the mid-1990s, even the Hungarian and Polish ex-communists were being elected to take their countries "back to Europe."

Populist politicians, however, have been less successful in turning their mass movements into viable political parties. For the most part, these leaders have had difficulty finding a narrative that can contribute to democratic stability in a consistent manner. The specter of old-fashioned populism keeps coming back, perhaps as a witness to how incomplete the political incorporation of Latin America's poor remains, and as a painful reminder that the region is still the world's most unequal. The populist conundrum confronts Latin America with the familiar yet complex challenge of promoting substantive democratization while reinforcing the procedures that make up democracy itself. The need to accomplish both tasks continues to present thorny issues in a region where the very word "institution" has long been taken to mean little more than a bag of tricks that ruling elites use to deceive, exclude, and impoverish the people. Frequently, leaders who have pursued socially just ends have not felt compelled to do so through consensual means. In a sad irony, such leaders have ended up weakening the very rights and institutions that the poor and destitute so desperately need, further worsening the inequalities that the leaders were supposed to correct.

Righteousness, however, does not make a good recipe for a democratic society. If right-wing Carlos Menem deserves criticism for packing his country's highest court, so does left-wing Hugo Chávez, regardless of their quite dissimilar goals. In a democracy, means are substantive and not merely formal, because rules are the only thing upon which contenders can always agree. Procedures are thus the glue that holds the polity together. This is the ultimate challenge for the left in Latin America today, to reconcile the substantive goals of inclusion and equality with the goals—the equally substantive goals, I emphasize—of robust procedures and institutions. There are countries in the region where this twin challenge has been addressed and even met. The common denominator in those success stories is the existence of a stable system of party politics and a decision-making process run not by executive discretion, but by legislative bargaining. Across the rest of Latin America, much remains to be done in this regard, but good examples stand near at hand. They must be emulated.

NOTES

I thank the Interdisciplinary Council on Latin America at American University for its support and Patrick Quirk for his research assistance. I also thank Michael Shifter for comments.

1. Jorge Castañeda, "Latin America's Left Turn," *Foreign Affairs* 85 (May–June 2006): 28–43.

2. Alejandro Foxley, "Surprises and Challenges for a Democratic Chile," in *Global Peace and Development: Prospects for the Future* (Notre Dame: Helen Kellogg Institute for International Studies,1991), 5–8.

3. Patrick Quirk, "The Power of Dignity: Emotions and the Struggle of Brazil's Landless Movement (MST)" (M.A. thesis, American University, Washington D.C., 2006).

4. Hector E. Schamis, "Argentina: Crisis and Democratic Consolidation," *Journal of Democracy* 13 (April 2002): 81–94.

5. Michael Shifter, "A Conversation with Alan Garcia," *Washington Post,* 4 June 2006, B2.

6. Terry Lynn Karl, "Petroleum and Political Pacts: The Transition to Democracy in Venezuela," in Guillermo O'Donnell, Philippe C. Schmitter, and Laurence Whitehead, eds., *Transitions from Authoritarian Rule: Latin America* (Baltimore: Johns Hopkins University Press, 1986).

7. For a comprehensive overview of *puntofijismo* and its aftermath, see Jennifer L. McCoy and David J. Myers, eds., *The Unraveling of Democracy in Venezuela* (Baltimore: Johns Hopkins University Press, 2004).

5

EXPLAINING THE LEFT'S RESURGENCE

Matthew R. Cleary

Matthew R. Cleary *is assistant professor of political science in the Maxwell School of Citizenship and Public Affairs at Syracuse University. He studies Latin American politics and has recently published* Democracy and the Culture of Skepticism: Political Trust in Argentina and Mexico *(with Susan C. Stokes, 2006). This essay originally appeared in the October 2006 issue of the* Journal of Democracy.

The left is back in Latin America. Over the past decade, leftist candidates have won presidential elections in Venezuela (1998), Chile (2000 and 2006), Brazil (2002), Argentina (2003), Uruguay (2005), Bolivia (2006), and Peru (2006).[1] Mexico's leftist candidate finished just shy of victory in July 2006, but the leftward trend may still spread later this year: The left will either win or place a strong second in the November 2006 presidential election in Nicaragua, and leftist incumbents are heavy favorites for reelection in Brazil and Venezuela.[2] This is a stunning turn of events for a region in which previous leftist victories (such as Salvador Allende's in Chile in 1970, or Alan García's in Peru in 1985) occurred so rarely and ended so disastrously. And it comes as a surprise to most observers, who had interpreted the dearth of leftist victories in the 1980s and 1990s as evidence that the left was permanently hamstrung by "pacted" transitions, which tilted the electoral playing field to the right, and by the hegemony of neoliberal economics, which constrained the possibilities for redistributive policy making and decimated labor and other mass organizations. Leftist electoral victories in such a context seemed impossible.[3]

As a result, when leftist victories have occurred, scholars have framed them as isolated and singular events—as exceptions to the rule. For example, we can explain the Brazilian case in terms of President Luiz Inácio ("Lula") da Silva's personality, charisma, and persistence; we portray the Venezuelan case as a unique reaction against the failures of the mainstream parties in the early 1990s; we view the Chilean case in the singular context of its authoritarian past, which even today looms over the country's gradual and cautious democratization.[4] The heterogeneity of the left has also contributed to the common view that each case is unique. Much has been made, for example, of the stark differences in substance and style between the populist left, purportedly dangerous and radical, and the "social-democratic" left, which is more moderate.[5] Distinctions like these make it difficult to see the rise of the left as a regional wave. How, for example, can a single regional process account for the ascendancy of a bombastic populist like Venezuela's President Hugo Chávez, on the one hand, and a moderate fiscal conservative like Chile's President Michelle Bachelet on the other?

These differences within the left, while real, are often overemphasized. In contrast to how it is sometimes portrayed in the press, the left in power is predominantly moderate. Chávez is the only sitting president who is unambiguously "populist," in the sense that he actively undermines independent sources of institutional authority and draws his political power primarily from a charismatic and paternalistic connection with the masses. Others, including Argentina's President Néstor Kirchner and even Bolivia's President Evo Morales, are more moderate, in that they show greater respect for the rule of law and a limited willingness to personalize and concentrate political power.[6] Most electorates seem to favor moderation as well—comparisons to Chávez clearly hurt presidential candidates in Peru (Ollanta Humala) and Mexico (Andrés Manuel López Obrador). In sum, the contemporary Latin American left is more homogenous, and more moderate, than many would argue.

As leftist victories accumulate, it becomes increasingly clear that they represent a regional trend rather than a series of isolated events. In this essay I offer a general explanation for this trend, without focusing on cross-country differences within the left. Thus, I define the left in broad terms: as a political movement with historical antecedents in communist and socialist political parties, grassroots social movements, populist social organizations, or other political forces that traditionally have had antisystemic, revolutionary, or transformative objectives.[7] The mobilizational form and the degree of radicalism may vary across countries. But in all cases the left shares (at least rhetorically, and usually substantively) a concern with redistribution and social justice, and it finds mass support among segments of the population that are severely disadvantaged under the current socioeconomic order.

The rise of the left in Latin America cannot be adequately understood without considering the regional and international factors that have helped to shape this wave of electoral victories. Domestic economic and structural factors have generated support for the left, while international political and economic factors have sustained the left in power by producing incentives for moderation on the part of both leftist governments and their traditional antagonists. This leftward shift in electoral competition will endure. The left will not always win, but its newfound competitiveness will be a permanent feature of electoral politics in most Latin American countries.

Structural Bases of Support for the Left

The underlying reason for the left's success in Latin American elections is obvious, and yet it is helpful to state it: Severe economic inequality is endemic throughout Latin America, and this inequality gives the left a natural support base that typically encompasses a majority of the population.

Latin Americanists often refer to the region as the most unequal in the world. In fact, inequality is more pronounced in sub-Saharan Africa, but what makes Latin American inequality so remarkable is that it exists in the context of relatively high levels of wealth and development. For example, inequality in Argentina, Chile, and Mexico (as measured by Gini coefficients) is roughly comparable to that in Nigeria, Zimbabwe, and Malawi. But the GDP per capita of the former three countries exceeds that of the latter three by an order of magnitude.[8] Globally, inequality tends to fall as countries become richer, but Latin America does not follow the pattern. All Latin American countries except Jamaica are significantly more unequal than we would predict based on their levels of wealth. Furthermore, the available evidence indicates that Latin America's relatively good macroeconomic performance in recent years has done little to equalize the distribution of wealth.[9]

Given this state of affairs, most Latin American countries are ripe for a socioeconomic cleavage in which the median voter supports the radical redistribution of wealth. According to some recent work in political economy, this is precisely the reason that wealthy elites worked so hard, and so successfully, to undermine the combination of democratic institutions and mass political participation that arose across Latin America in the mid-twentieth century.[10] For the moment, let us leave aside the theoretical difficulty involved in reconciling extreme inequality with democratization (I will return to this problem below). Taking democratic institutions and free participation as given, the electoral dominance of the left has an obvious explanation: The left succeeds because most Latin Americans are poor and a small minority is quite wealthy.

Yet inequality alone cannot account for variation in the left's resurgence across countries, since inequality is ubiquitous. For every country in which the left has been flexing its electoral muscles in recent years (for example Brazil or Chile), we can point to another in which the left remains weak and ineffectual (for example Colombia or El Salvador). The additional factor that explains why the left has found success in some countries but not others is the nature of mass political mobilization. Inequality has translated into electoral success for the left almost exclusively in countries that historically have had an organizational basis for mass mobilization. For example, Brazilian president Lula da Silva has benefited from the close ties between organized labor, leftist social movements, and the Brazilian Workers' Party (PT). Mexico's Party of the Democratic Revolution (PRD) draws mass support from leaders who gained their popular base while serving within the long-ruling Institutional Revolutionary Party (PRI), from social movements, and from an array of preexisting leftist groups. In Ecuador and Bolivia, the left draws support from indigenous political parties that grew out of unusually strong social movements in the 1990s. In some cases the organizational structure of the left has deep historical roots; in others, it was cobbled together only after redemocratization. What all of these cases have in common is that the development of mass-mobilizing structures preceded leftist electoral victories by at least a decade.

These organizational bases of support for the left do not exist in all Latin American countries. One useful way to identify the countries that have them comes from a study by Kenneth Roberts, who divides Latin American party systems into "elitist" and "labor-mobilizing" varieties. Elitist party systems have segmented (or vertical) cleavages, in which parties organize *across* lines of socioeconomic class. Labor-mobilizing party systems have stratified (or horizontal) cleavages, in which parties tend to organize *along* class lines. Roberts offers evidence to indicate that labor-mobilizing party systems arise in countries with higher union density, larger manufacturing sectors, and greater public investment in economic development.[11]

Like many scholars, Roberts doubted the ability of leftist groups to succeed in new Latin American democracies, primarily because the elitist party systems in many countries inhibited the ability of leftist groups to mobilize voters around a socioeconomic cleavage, even in conditions of extreme inequality. A fresh look at his typology shows his prediction to be quite accurate with respect to countries with elitist party systems. But his classification also reveals a striking correspondence between countries with labor-mobilizing party systems and leftist electoral success (see Table on p. 67). Among the eight countries with labor-mobilizing party systems, six (Argentina, Bolivia, Brazil, Chile, Peru, and Venezuela) currently have leftist presidents. In Mexico, the leftist presidential candidate López Obrador fell less than a percentage-point short of winning in July 2006; in Nicaragua, former president Daniel Ortega of the leftist Sandinista Front is a leading candidate for the November 2006 elections. Thus, the left either is in power or is a credible contender for power in *all* countries with labor-mobilizing party systems.

In the countries that Roberts classifies as having elitist party systems, the left has fared much more poorly. The only such country with a true leftist in power is Uruguay, where socialist Tabaré Vázquez won the presidential election in 2005. Ecuador may also be an interesting case in this respect. Although Roberts (correctly) classifies Ecuador as having an elitist party system, the rapid growth of indigenous social movements and their incorporation into the party system give Ecuador the type of mass-mobilizing capacity that is necessary for leftist victories. Unsurprisingly, the left has found a certain level of success in Ecuador, for instance in Lucio Gutiérrez's election in 2003. But Gutiérrez was forced from office after he lost the support of the leftist groups that had brought him to power, and as of this writing (September 2006), the outlook for the October election remains cloudy.

This evidence suggests that the left needs a mass-mobilizing capacity to translate latent and diffuse support into electoral success. In most cases, this capacity has come from a historically mobilized labor sector. Interestingly, voters from the lower and working classes often remain politically active even in countries where the organizations that originally mobilized them have deteriorated, as many have under neoliberalism. In a few cases, leftist parties have also relied on social movements, indigenous organizations, and other popular groups for mass support. While the exact form of mobilization differs from one country to the next, the common theme is that leftist victories in the current wave have been built on preexisting organizational structures that facilitate class-based mobilization.

The Timing of the Resurgence

The left has succeeded in Latin America where it has had the capacity to mobilize large groups of voters along an economic cleavage, yet both the inequality that generates support for the left and the organizational structures that help leftist parties to channel that support existed well before the current wave of leftist victories. This raises the question of timing: Why are we witnessing leftist victories only now, some 20 to 25 years after redemocratization in most countries? Two factors combine to explain the timing of the leftist wave: a gradual tactical shift in the left's approach to electoral politics, and the constraints imposed by the pacted nature of many Latin American transitions.

In contrast to earlier eras, the left in many Latin American countries has freely and consciously entered the electoral game, abandoning revolutionary and violent ideologies while reorganizing partisan, labor, and civic organizations with a view to electoral success. In most countries, this strategic shift happened only gradually in the decade or so after redemocratization. As Francisco Panizza notes, "Historically, the Latin American left has had an uneasy relationship with liberal-democratic institutions," and the embrace of the electoral process "has been a significant ideological change."[12] In the 1960s and 1970s, most Latin American countries were home to leftist political parties or social groups that advocated

TABLE—ELITIST AND LABOR-MOBILIZING PARTY SYSTEMS
IN LATIN AMERICA

ELITIST PARTY SYSTEMS			LABOR-MOBILIZING PARTY SYSTEMS		
COUNTRY	PEAK TRADE UNION DENSITY (%) 1970–95	MANUFACTURING SHARE OF GDP (PEAK SCORE 1970–80)	COUNTRY	PEAK TRADE UNION DENSITY (%) 1970–95	MANUFACTURING SHARE OF GDP (PEAK SCORE 1970–80)
Colombia	9.2	19.0	Argentina	50.1	28.0
Costa Rica	15.4	22.2	Bolivia	24.8	15.9
Dominican Republic	17.0	18.5	Brazil	24.3	28.7
Ecuador	13.5	20.2	Chile	35.0	25.0
Honduras	8.5	17.0	Mexico	32.1	29.9
Panama	17.0	17.2	Nicaragua	37.3	24.3
Paraguay	9.9	17.5	Peru	25.0	25.6
Uruguay	20.9	24.0	Venezuela	26.4	17.7

Source: Kenneth Roberts, "Social Inequalities Without Class Cleavages in Latin America's Neoliberal Era," Studies in *Comparative International Development* 36 (Winter 2002): 15–16, especially Tables 1 and 2.

Marxism, socialism, or other ideologies of revolutionary social change, including economic nationalization and radical forms of redistribution. These groups commanded majority support only rarely, if at all. But they were important political forces with significant mass support, as indicated by Salvador Allende's electoral performance in 1964 and 1970, and by popular support for insurgent groups such as the Nicaraguan Sandinistas. With few exceptions, adherence to democratic practices like free and fair elections was simply not a priority for these groups; for the most part, the left deliberately avoided electoral competition altogether.

In contrast, the contemporary left has embraced the electoral process, and its leading figures (such as Chávez and Lula) have won national elections on multiple occasions, often with majority support. In this sense, the modern Latin American left appears as a genuinely new political force. Yet it would be a mistake to miss the organizational links between the contemporary left and its historical precursors: in fact, there is a high degree of continuity in most cases. As noted above, union organizations and social movements were critical to the formation of Brazil's PT (Lula himself first entered political life as a labor leader in the late 1970s). Mexico's PRD began as a coalition between dissident members from the ruling PRI and several smaller leftist groups. In Chile, the Socialists who have been in power since 2000 are the direct political descendants of the Socialist Party that functioned before the 1973 coup.

Where the left has truly broken with its past is in terms of strategy. Most significant leftist groups, including communist and socialist political parties, no longer advocate violence, revolution, or other antisystemic approaches to resolving issues of social justice. Instead, they have made a conscious decision to compete for elected office, and have either reorganized themselves as electorally viable political parties or allied themselves with established left-of-center parties.[13] To be sure, many social movements across the region remain committed to contentious forms of protest politics, including strikes, demonstrations, and roadblocks. But increasingly, these methods of protest are seen as a legitimate form of civil disobedience within a democratic system, rather than a direct challenge to the system itself. Furthermore, these strategies are increasingly used *in conjunction with* electoral contestation rather than as an alternative. Regionwide, the left is now more committed to the electoral process than at any time in the past.

The second reason that the left has emerged as an electoral force only gradually is that the return to democracy in many Latin American countries took the form of pacted transitions, which have worked against the left in several ways. In some cases, the political marginalization of leftist groups was an explicit requirement of the outgoing authoritarian regimes. For example, Chile's post-authoritarian electoral system was clearly and intentionally constructed to be biased against the left. In other cases, the left was disadvantaged more implicitly, as the old regimes negotiated peaceful transitions only when they had reasonable certainty about the identity of their civilian successors, who were invariably from centrist or center-right parties. In most cases, the danger of "going too far to the left" was internalized by voters and even by leftist groups, which seem to have recognized that electoral support for centrist candidates would help to ensure a smooth transition and the reestablishment of democratic institutions. Everyone perceived that authoritarian "backsliding" was a real possibility and that moderation was the order of the day.

In Brazil, for example, the transition in the early 1980s required prodemocracy forces to proceed with caution. The electoral college that was to elect a new president in 1985 originally seemed to favor the Brazilian Social Democratic Party (PSDB), which had close ties to the military. But a faction of PSDB delegates defected and voted for Tancredo Neves, the candidate of the Party of the Brazilian Democratic Movement. This was a surprising turn of events, but Neves had long been a member of the political establishment and had assiduously advertised his moderation to the military and other conservative political forces. As it happened, Neves fell ill and died after winning the election, and was replaced by José Sarney, the vice-president elect. Sarney was also a member of Brazil's political elite, and in fact had previously been a leader in the PSDB. Brazil's return to democracy in the 1980s was thus characterized by moderation and continuity, as the leading political figures, including elected presidents, were members of the political establishment who had been active in politics during the period of military rule.

A similar dynamic played out in Chile. Although General Augusto Pinochet (who ruled from 1973 to 1990) was obliged to allow a free election after losing the 1988 plebiscite, he still exercised enormous influence over the process of redemocratization. All sides recognized this fact, which is why the center-left coalition (the Concertación) nominated Patricio Aylwin of the Christian Democratic Party. Aylwin is usually portrayed as an antagonist to Pinochet and a hero of the transition period. To a large extent this is true, but Aylwin was also an establishment politician who had a long history of moderation with respect to the dictatorship. In fact, as a senator in 1973, Aylwin openly agitated for the military to intervene against Allende's government, and he publicly supported the coup after it succeeded.[14] After Pinochet's defeat in the 1988 plebiscite, Aylwin was a central figure in negotiations with the military that resulted in constitutional changes which limited the impact of redemocratization and preserved many of the military's prerogatives. Given his posture toward the military regime both in the early 1970s and the late 1980s, Aylwin was clearly a moderate candidate whom the outgoing regime viewed as acceptable. The Chilean Socialist and Communist parties recognized this, and made a strategic decision to support Aylwin's candidacy within the Concertación. They would later also support the Christian Democrat Eduardo Frei, who led Chile from 1994 to 2000.

Thus the process of Latin America's democratization in the late twentieth century led to a generation of centrist or conservative leaders, invariably from the political establishment and representing the economic and social elites of their countries. This pattern often lasted for two or three presidential terms, and in several ways it set the stage for the current wave of leftist victories. One reason for this is that elections in presidential systems tend to produce opposition victories sooner or later. In Latin America this dynamic was augmented by the fact that the first generation of center-right administrations generally failed to perform well in office. In some cases they performed quite poorly, not only in terms of economic stewardship, but even to the point of destroying their own party organizations. Additionally, political parties and citizens grew increasingly comfortable with the stability of democratic institutions, and thus were more likely to express support for the left as memories of authoritarian rule began to fade.[15] This dynamic process helps to explain the decidedly gradual nature of the left's electoral resurgence, even amid longstanding and relatively constant conditions of severe socioeconomic inequality.

International Incentives for Moderation

It would be naïve to assume that military coups are a thing of the past, given Latin America's long history of military interventions in politics. Indeed, we do not need to hearken back to an earlier era to find examples.

Hugo Chávez was deposed in a short-lived military coup in April 2002. The military in Ecuador is heavily involved in politics, and has either directly intervened or tacitly supported the removal of three democratically elected presidents in just the past decade (1997, 2000, and 2005). Nevertheless, there is a clear difference between the way in which traditional power structures (including the military) reacted to leftist victories in the past, and the way in which they have reacted to the current wave. There are two reasons for this: The first is that international norms of respect for democracy (or at least for elections) are increasingly powerful in the region, making coups more costly. The second reason is that international economic integration and the dominance of neoliberalism have constrained leftists, once in power, from pursuing the types of radically redistributive or socialist policies that instigated military coups or right-wing destabilization efforts in the past.

At least since the end of World War II, the United States, international organizations, and most Latin American governments have consistently voiced respect for democracy within the region, though their actions have not always matched their words. The United States in particular repeatedly saw fit to subvert democratically elected governments in Latin America when it judged those governments to be pro-Soviet, Marxist, or in some other way antagonistic to U.S. economic and security interests. For their part, Latin American governments often acquiesced to U.S. intervention in neighboring countries, and in some cases actively favored it. Thus, concern for democracy often took a backseat to concerns about security and stability in general, and about Soviet expansionism in particular.

Since the end of the Cold War, Latin American governments (acting both unilaterally and as members of international organizations) have become increasingly assertive in encouraging respect for the democratic process. In 1991, the Organization of American States (OAS) issued Resolution 1080, which requires the secretary-general to convene a strategy meeting within ten days of any "irregular interruption of the democratic political institutional process or of the legitimate exercise of power by the democratically elected government" of any member state. The Inter-American Democratic Charter, signed in 2001 by the United States and all Latin American countries except Cuba, contains even stronger language, and allows the OAS to suspend any state in which an interruption of the democratic order has occurred.[16] Over the past 15 to 20 years, the OAS has become more active in election monitoring and more assertive in dealing with threats to democratic institutions, such as Alberto Fujimori's irregular reelection in Peru in 2000.

Freed from the constraints of its Cold War security imperatives, the United States has also placed increased importance on respect for democratic institutions, and has actively discouraged coups or other threats to democratic institutions on several occasions. The United States formally protested Fujimori's *autogolpe* (self-coup) in 1992, as a result of which

"Fujimori reluctantly and grudgingly backed away from his effort to install an openly authoritarian regime and started a process of redemocratization."[17] In 1993, the United States condemned a military-backed self-coup by President Jorge Serrano in Guatemala, cutting off almost US$70 million in aid and threatening Guatemala's trade status. Serrano was forced to resign, and constitutional order was soon restored. According to Wendy Hunter, U.S. actions not only contributed to Serrano's failure, but also discouraged President Itamar Franco from attempting a similar move in Brazil later that year.[18]

The U.S. response to the short-lived coup against Hugo Chávez in 2002 shows that U.S. commitment to democratic institutions is still not absolute. But while U.S. actions were less than admirable, the incident also shows just how powerful international democratic norms have become in Latin America. With the possible exception of Cuba's Fidel Castro, no leader is more antagonistic to the United States than Chávez. The George W. Bush administration has not looked kindly on Chávez's anti-U.S. rhetoric, his courtship of Cuba and Bolivia, or his oil politics. Furthermore, by dissolving Congress and packing a new constitutional assembly with his own supporters shortly after taking office, the former *golpista* Chávez revealed his own ambivalence toward democratic principles. It is hard to imagine a case better suited to test U.S. commitment to democratic norms. Yet even in these circumstances, the United States did not actively support the coup, and was quickly forced to renounce it after being embarrassed by its own silence and by accusations (later substantiated) that it had known of the coup plans ahead of time. For its part, the OAS issued a strong statement against the coup. Domestic support within Venezuela waned, the coup-plotters lost their resolve, and Chávez was restored to power within days. One must wonder whether in earlier eras such a coup attempt would have been successful, or even actively supported by the United States and other Latin American governments.

It will be a long time before scholars of Latin American politics lower their guard against the possibility of military coups, and with good reason. But clearly, the increased salience of democratic norms, institutionalized in organizations such as the OAS, makes coups less likely today than they were 20 or 30 years ago. Even where traditional power structures might favor the removal of a leftist president, as they clearly did in Venezuela in 2002, military coups are increasingly costly in the modern era of respect for democratic institutions.

Neoliberal Economics and the Left

One of the most notable, and in some circles disheartening, characteristics of the current wave of leftist administrations is the high degree of continuity with their predecessors' neoliberal economic policies. Historically, of course, the Latin American left had promoted policies for poverty alleviation and redistribution that included high levels of social spending and state involvement in the economy. Today, with few exceptions, the left's commitment to such policies is tepid. The main reason for this moderation is that leftist administrations (and in fact, all administrations) are constrained by the regionwide commitment to economic neoliberalism and by increased levels of international economic integration. Constraints are most obvious in the areas of monetary and fiscal policy. Governments can no longer easily subsidize social spending by printing money or assuming large amounts of debt. In other policy areas, leftist governments have more room to maneuver and experiment with policy, but they have still exercised great caution in departing from neoliberal orthodoxy. In all cases, governments are more constrained where capital is mobile.

Almost by definition, neoliberal economic policies are anathema to leftist governments. The left is surely correct to argue that Latin America's existing neoliberal systems do not sufficiently prioritize poverty alleviation, redistribution, and human development. Important segments of most Latin American countries do, however, credit neoliberal policies with ending the specter of hyperinflation, and with achieving what moderate economic growth the region has experienced in the past decade. Thus, leftist governments that might be inclined to challenge neoliberal policies more aggressively must consider whether such a course would either curtail their ability to construct broad political coalitions, or worse, provoke serious macroeconomic problems like a new bout of inflation. Similarly, international economic integration has constrained governments that are dependent on liberalized trade and international capital from pursuing policies that might threaten capital inflows. In addition, neoliberal policies have often been institutionalized and insulated, making change difficult even for leftists who are willing to accept the risks involved.[19]

Economic elites and other traditional power structures in Latin America recognize the constraints that these regional economic factors place on leftist administrations, and this makes the rise of the left seem less threatening. These elites also tend to have a vested interest in stability, and so they have reason to support democracy even when the left is in power. Neoliberalism and economic integration have thus produced incentives for moderation on the right as well. Put another way, the same factors that prevent the left from pursuing more radical economic policies are also responsible for the ability of the left to remain in power without provoking antisystemic behavior on the part of opposing political forces.

The Venezuelan case is instructive on this point, because it illustrates how difficult it is for Latin America's leftist governments to escape the dictates of the international economic order. Venezuela's oil reserves (and current high prices) make it the only country in the region with a truly independent source of wealth, and this gives Chávez increased maneuverability. Other leftist leaders lack the freedom that resource wealth can bring, which makes it much more difficult for them to mount a fundamental challenge to the regional economic system. For example, even with the limited bargaining power provided by Bolivia's natural-gas reserves, Evo Morales has been forced to moderate his anti-neoliberal aspirations, and so it is difficult to see how a truly radical break with the region's neoliberal system could succeed there.

This dynamic helps to explain why Latin America's socioeconomic inequality has not been more damaging to democratic stability. A recent study by Carles Boix suggests that highly unequal and asset-specific societies are infertile grounds for democracy because the wealthy fear the severe redistribution that majority rule would entail.[20] But in Latin America, democracy does coexist with inequality, at least partly because the constraints placed on democratic governments by capital mobility and regional economic integration discourage the type of radical redistribution that would otherwise lead the wealthy to undermine the democratic process.

What Future for the Left?

The underlying structural conditions (inequality and mass mobilization) that have facilitated the recent wave of leftist victories are longstanding, if not permanent, features of Latin America's political and economic reality. The international factors (democratic norms and economic integration) that have contributed to this process also seem to be with us for the long term. Thus the current leftward shift in electoral politics most likely represents a fundamental and enduring transformation in the nature of political competition in Latin America. The left will not always win—but in a region where it was largely absent from the electoral arena for some thirty years, the left is back, and it will remain competitive in much of Latin America well into the future.

Still, the left faces some challenges, and its success will be contingent both on its own chosen strategies and on future structural conditions in Latin America. On a short-term basis, the success of the left might depend on any number of local or idiosyncratic conditions. For example, leftist candidates have clearly benefited from being perceived as outsiders in countries where political insiders are widely assumed to be corrupt. If the left becomes tainted by corruption scandals, it could easily lose this advantage. The basic socioeconomic cleavage that motivates most political competition in Latin America might also be trumped on occasion by other considerations, such as security. This may help to explain the strong electoral performance of right-of-center parties (widely perceived to be "law and order" parties) in Mexico, Colombia, and some Central American countries where crimes related to drugs and gangs are serious problems and looming political issues.

Thinking longer-term, one remaining question is how broadly the current wave might spread in Latin America. To this point, the left's resurgence has largely been confined to countries with a history of mass-mobilizing party systems. It remains to be seen whether the left will also become more competitive in countries lacking such structures. The Ecuadorian case may prove to be a bellwether in this respect. Ecuador does not have a strong history of labor mobilization, but the recent incorporation of indigenous groups into the electoral system shows that other forms of mobilization are possible. And after some near misses, the left may finally succeed in winning the presidency and establishing a stable administration when elections are held in October 2006. This suggests that the leftist wave may expand into other countries, but only if the left can identify and exploit methods of mass mobilization.

One final threat to the left's future in Latin America, and in some cases even to the future of democratic institutions, would be a break with the current commitment to policy moderation. It would be a mistake to assume that traditional power structures will remain conciliatory if the left pursues more radical policies of poverty alleviation and redistribution. Again, the Venezuelan case illustrates the point. Even if we accept that Chávez's extreme rhetoric is not always matched by his actions and by government policies, the attempted coup in 2002, the general strike in 2002 and 2003, and recurring violent protests clearly demonstrate that a lack of moderation can threaten the stability of democratic institutions.

Bolivia may yet head down a similar path. To this point, Morales's rhetorical extremism has been accompanied by moderation on the ground. But any truly radical move, such as confiscation of privately (and legally) held lands, could precipitate political violence and destabilize his regime. Paradoxically, the increasing international salience of democratic norms might have a destabilizing effect in such cases, by making democratically elected leftist governments bolder than they would otherwise be. The threat of an authoritarian reaction should never be discounted in such cases.

It is also important to note that antidemocratic interventions, including interventions by the military, are not the exclusive domain of the right. In fact, the classic right-wing military coup is increasingly rare in Latin America. Of fifteen Latin American presidencies identified by Arturo Valenzuela as ending prematurely in the past two decades, only one (Haitian president Jean-Bertrand Aristide's ouster in 1991) could plausibly be described as a military coup against a leftist president. It has been far more common for the military to intervene against (or support the removal of) centrist or center-right presidents, as in Ecuador on several occasions, in Bolivia in 1985, or even in Peru in 2000.[21] Both the credibility of the left and the stability of democracy itself will be seriously endangered if the left politicizes the military, as it seems tempted to do in Venezuela, Bolivia, and perhaps Ecuador.

These are serious concerns. Yet the potential pitfalls identified here seem either improbable or unlikely to precipitate a durable shift away from the left in the region's electoral politics. Thus the most likely course of events for the foreseeable future in Latin America is the continuation, and possible expansion, of an active electoral left. Proponents of traditional leftist politics may lament the relative moderation of current Latin American leftist administrations, and may prefer to place their hopes in such nonelectoral forms of politics as protests, social movements, and nongovernmental organizations. Yet it remains true that problems of inequality and social justice are probably better served by a moderate left in power than by a more radical left that intentionally camps on the fringe of politics and stands in opposition to liberal-democratic institutions. The future of the left in Latin America will in large part depend on its ability to strike a balance between the pragmatic need for moderation and the moral imperative to pursue strategies for poverty reduction, redistribution, and development.

NOTES

I would like to thank Pablo Beramendi, Carles Boix, Mark Hibben, Marcelo Nazareno, Kenneth Roberts, and Susan Stokes for useful comments and suggestions.

1. Some observers would add Ecuador under Lucio Gutiérrez to this list, since he was elected on a leftist platform. Gutiérrez's actions in office did not match his campaign rhetoric, however, and leftist groups withdrew support from his administration within a year, contributing to his ouster. I discuss this case further throughout the essay. See Ronald Chilcote, "The Left in Latin America: Theory and Practice," *Latin American Perspectives* 30 (July 2003): 10–15.

2. Left-of-center, if not truly "leftist" presidents are also in power in the Dominican Republic, Haiti, Honduras, and Ecuador.

3. See for example Kenneth Roberts, "Social Inequalities Without Class Cleavages in Latin America's Neoliberal Era," *Studies in Comparative International Development* 36 (Winter 2002): 3–33; and Kurt Weyland, "Neoliberalism and Democracy in Latin America: A Mixed Record," *Latin American Politics and Society* 46 (Spring 2004): 135–57.

4. See Wendy Hunter, "Brazil's New Direction," *Journal of Democracy* 14 (April 2003): 151–62 (especially p. 153); or Steve Ellner, "Introduction: The Search for Explanations," in Steve Ellner and Daniel Hellinger, eds., *Venezuelan Politics in the Chávez Era: Class, Polarization, and Conflict* (Boulder, Colo.: Lynne Rienner, 2003), 7–26.

5. See Jorge Castañeda, "Latin America's Left Turn," *Foreign Affairs* 85 (May–June 2006): 28–43.

6. Evo Morales has certainly been provocative, but his actions to this point have not been as radical as his rhetoric. His "seizure" of natural-gas fields, for example, was actually a ploy to renegotiate contracts with foreign companies, and he later moderated his position.

7. For a similar definition and discussion, see Francisco Panizza, "Unarmed Utopia Revisited: The Resurgence of Left-of-Centre Politics in Latin America," *Political Studies* 53 (December 2005): 716–34.

8. According to a recent UNDP report, GDP per capita in Brazil, Mexico, and Chile is US$12,000, $10,000, and $9,000, respectively. The figures for Nigeria, Zimbabwe, and

Malawi are $1,050, $2,400, and $600. All six countries have similar Gini coefficients, ranging from 50.3 to 57.1. See Kevin Watkins, *Human Development Report 2005* (New York: United Nations Development Programme, 2005).

9. See Kenneth Roberts, "Social Inequalities Without Class Cleavages," 7.

10. For the general argument see Carles Boix, *Democracy and Redistribution* (Cambridge: Cambridge University Press, 2003).

11. Kenneth Roberts, "Social Inequalities Without Class Cleavages."

12. Francisco Panizza, "Unarmed Utopia Revisited," 720–21.

13. Ronald Chilcote, "The Left in Latin America: Theory and Practice"; and Jeffrey W. Rubin, "From Che to Marcos: the Changing Grassroots Left in Latin America," *Dissent* 49 (Summer 2002): 39–47.

14. Arturo Valenzuela, *The Breakdown of Democratic Regimes: Chile* (Baltimore: Johns Hopkins University Press, 1978).

15. For example, Susan Stokes finds that "security-oriented" candidates, as opposed to "efficiency-oriented" candidates, are significantly more likely to win elections as the number of years since the democratic transition increases. See Susan Stokes, *Mandates and Democracy: Neoliberalism by Surprise in Latin America* (Cambridge: Cambridge University Press, 2001), 94–95.

16. Peter Hakim, "Dispirited Politics," *Journal of Democracy* 14 (April 2003): 108.

17. Kurt Weyland, "Neoliberalism and Democracy in Latin America: A Mixed Record," *Latin American Politics and Society* 46 (Spring 2004): 139.

18. Wendy Hunter, "Brazil's New Direction," 157.

19. In a recent interview, Evo Morales complained that he was unable to take measures to help the poor because the presidential palace is "full of padlocks. . . . I feel like a prisoner of the neo-liberal laws." See Paul Mason, "Evo Morales 'Padlocked' in Palace," *BBC News,* 5 April 2006.

20. Carles Boix, *Democracy and Redistribution.*

21. Arturo Valenzuela, "Latin American Presidencies Interrupted," on pp. 3–17 of this volume.

6

THE RISE OF
POPULISM AND THE LEFT

Mitchell A. Seligson

Mitchell A. Seligson *is Centennial Professor of Political Science at Vanderbilt University and directs the Latin American Public Opinion Project (LAPOP), which conducts the AmericasBarometer surveys. He serves on the Advisory Board of the Inter-American Program on Education for Democratic Values and Practices of the Organization of American States. This essay originally appeared in the July 2007 issue of the* Journal of Democracy.

Latin America's "left turn" was the focus of a cluster of thoughtful articles in the October 2006 issue of the *Journal of Democracy*. Since then, the trend toward the left and toward populist governments has deepened. In South America, the rise of the left is unmistakable, with Argentina, Bolivia, Brazil, Chile, Ecuador, Guyana, Peru, Uruguay, and Venezuela led by presidents with varying degrees and shapes of leftist ideology, while further north, in Mexico, a leftist presidential candidate was defeated by the narrowest of margins in the 2006 election. And of course, one must not forget about Cuba, the remaining dictatorship in the region, still firmly in the hands of the socialist left in spite of the protracted and serious illness of Fidel Castro. The most recent additions to the populist left are Bolivia's Evo Morales, who took office in 2006, and Ecuador's Rafael Correa, who began his presidency in early 2007. In Paraguay, the decades-old hegemony of the Colorado Party is being challenged by suspended Roman Catholic bishop Fernando Lugo, who espouses a mixture of leftist and populist rhetoric.

These are remarkable changes for the region. While leftists have held power in the past, never before in Latin America have so many countries been governed by presidents of the left. It should be added that the ideological variations among them are great, however. Presidents Luiz Inácio "Lula" da Silva of Brazil and Michelle Bachelet of Chile support free trade and close ties with the United States, while Hugo Chávez of

Venezuela employs a rhetoric replete with praise of socialism and attacks on capitalism and the United States.

Populist governments are also on the rise. Latin American populism comes in right-wing as well as left-wing forms, and has a history that reaches back to the 1930s. The term "populism" is sometimes confused merely with charismatic, personalistic leaders who appeal to a broad voter base that crosses class lines. Populism properly defined, however, must include a core belief that the institutions of classical liberal democracy, especially legislatures and courts, are anachronistic, inefficient, and inconsistent with the true expression of "the people's will" (or at least the populist officials' interpretation of it).[1] Populist leaders typically propose instead to "listen to the people" with the aim of personally carrying out their will while isolating "rejectionists" who would deny it. In practice, populism often can mean running roughshod over fundamental democratic guarantees of civil liberties, especially free expression and the right to due process.[2]

What are we to make of the rise of the left and the resurrection of populism? The first of the two phenomena almost certainly betokens the maturation of democracy in the region, as the polities of the region adapt to the coming to power of the opposition via the ballot box without serious threat of military intervention. As such, these trends may add up to little more than one of those pendular swings of the voters' "mood" such as periodically occur in many established democracies. Alternatively and more ominously, the rise of populism and some varieties of leftist rule could represent a threat to democratic stability.

In order to take the full measure of the situation, investigating several key questions will be helpful. The first asks whether leftist political sympathies predominate in the region, and whether there is evidence of a shift to the left among the populace. A second would inquire as to whether Latin Americans support populism, meaning a style of governance that would do away with representative and judicial institutions in favor of concentrating power in the hands of the chief executive. Finally, it is worth investigating whether those who favor a leftist or a left-populist orientation are less supportive of democracy and more likely to favor some alternative system.

Answering these questions requires studying the beliefs and attitudes of Latin American[3] citizens across the region, as well as examining how these beliefs have changed over time. Our ability to tap into the opinions of citizens worldwide has been greatly enhanced by the recent widespread expansion of crossnational surveys. The World Values Survey (WVS) is foremost among them, with the broadest coverage.[4] Unfortunately, outside the advanced industrial nations, coverage by region is spottier and in Latin America very limited. This gap can be filled, however, by regional surveys—a growing enterprise in the developing world. Many of these surveys use as their monikers variations on the name of the Eurobarometer, the grandfather of the genre, though problems of sample design and execution mean that the data are not necessarily of uniformly high quality.[5]

The fullest coverage of the Western Hemisphere comes from the AmericasBarometer, a survey periodically carried out by the Latin American Public Opinion Project (LAPOP) of Vanderbilt University and its consortium of more than twenty academic partner institutions, anchored at the Universidad de Costa Rica. The AmericasBarometer provides a rich—and indeed, the sole—source of data covering Latin America, the Caribbean, and North America.[6] The AmericasBarometer's questionnaires and studies provide detailed coverage of democratic values and behaviors, and are publicly available at *www.lapopsurveys.org*. The data itself is available for free public online analysis at that same site; the raw data rests in selected university repositories, and can be acquired directly from LAPOP.

In 2006, the AmericasBarometer interviewed more than thirty-thousand people in nineteen countries, including all the countries in Central America, much of South America, key cases in the Caribbean, and North America.[7] The inclusion of the United States and Canada, the hemisphere's quintessential democracies, provides a unique baseline of comparison missing from most other efforts.

A Threatening Trend?

How far "left" are Latin American citizens, and are they trending in that direction overall? Surprisingly, it turns out that ideologically, Latin Americans are actually slightly to the *right* of most respondents worldwide. We are able to say this because for many years, beginning with the Eurobarometer and the early iterations of the WVS, public-opinion questionnaires around the world have included a 10-point left-right ideology scale, with a score of 1 selected by those who place themselves on the far left of the political spectrum, and a score of 10 by those who place themselves on the far right. The arithmetic midpoint on this scale would be 5.5, but since whole numbers are accepted as the only possible choices, focus-group studies show that respondents almost universally tend to view 5 as the neutral (neither left nor right) point on the scale.[8]

Respondents in most countries cluster heavily near the center of the scale, although there are exceptions: The mean figure for Belarus in 1990 was 3.88, while that for Bangladesh in 2000 was 7.56. The average score for the world, however, was 5.56. This comes from pooled WVS data encompassing more than 267,000 interviews across 84 countries and spanning the years from 1981 to 2004. This indicates a slight leaning to the right worldwide.[9] Unfortunately, the WVS's coverage of Latin America and the Caribbean has been limited, but the four countries included in the most recent (2000–2001) round yield the following average values:

Chile, 5.22; Mexico, 6.55; Peru, 5.69; and Venezuela 6.32. In sum, both worldwide and in the limited set of Latin American countries studied via the WVS, opinion skews just slightly to the right of center.

The AmericasBarometer data for 2006 reveal a regional average of 5.77, which places Latin America slightly to the right of the 5.56 world average.[10] The 2004 figure for the Latin American countries that were included in both the 2004 and 2006 rounds was 6.17, however, so it appears that there has been a recent shift to the left. Averages can, of course, be deceiving, but in this case they are not. Looking at countries that can be compared directly in the 2004 and 2006 AmericasBarometer rounds, all but two of them moved to the left, and of the ones that did not, only one experienced a statistically significant shift to the right. Thus the slight "shift to the left" has indeed occurred, and the trend is regionwide, but the magnitude of the shift is small and the center of gravity remains somewhat to the right. Moreover, longer-term trend data would need to be examined before we could be confident about the existence of any secular long-term trend.

For ideology to matter, it must translate into behavior—such as voting for candidates who espouse leftist or rightist positions—which is consistent with this or that ideological orientation. Since the AmericasBarometer includes questions not only on ideology but on party preference as well, we can analyze the relationship between those two and then go farther by examining election results as they relate to social class, employment, and other factors that might form the substance of various "cleavages" within a given society. What emerges is that ideological dispositions along the classic left-right continuum do indeed have a meaningful impact on partisan orientations for many Latin Americans, but national contexts matter a great deal.

In some countries, for instance, parties (and voters) split sharply into leftist and rightist camps, while in other places parties are hard to tell apart as far as ideological preferences go. Finding left-versus-right differences among the major Costa Rican parties is nearly impossible, while Nicaragua's and especially El Salvador's respective party scenes display sharp ideological splits. In Figures 1 and 2, the mean ideology score of those who supported particular presidential candidates is indicated by a small circle, and the 95 percent confidence interval around that mean is shown by a horizontally placed "I," such that the larger the number of respondents who selected that candidate in the survey, the narrower the confidence interval.

In Costa Rica, the average ideology score on the left-right scale in 2006 was 5.9, and as can be seen in Figure 1, all the candidates who received significant numbers of votes in the election that year fell very close to that mean. The greatest deviation was only 0.6 of a point, and that was for voters supporting the Libertarian Party, which is at the very fringe of the Costa Rican political spectrum. The traditional right-of-center Social

FIGURE 1—IDEOLOGICAL DISPOSITION AND PRESIDENTIAL VOTE CHOICE: COSTA RICA

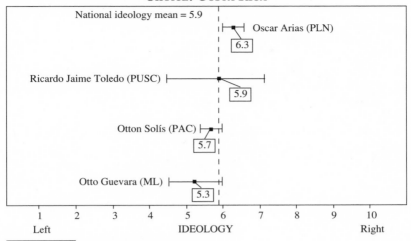

Horizontal lines indicate 95 percent confidence intervals.
Source: AmericasBarometer by LAPOP.

Christian Unity Party (PUSC), which saw its electoral support collapse in 2006 amid scandals involving two former presidents, coincides directly with the national ideological mean. Interestingly, supporters of the traditionally left-of-center National Liberation Party (PLN) averaged 6.3, slightly to the *right* of the national mean. These findings dramatically illustrate the electoral realignment taking place in that country but speak even more directly to the very narrow range of ideological difference in Latin America's oldest and most stable democracy. Even though the electoral scene has been marked by declining voter participation and evidence of declining support for the system,[11] Costa Rica remains at the top of all the countries in the region in terms of political legitimacy, and, as these results show, the ideological disagreements are very limited.

As noted above, Costa Rica's Central American neighbors Nicaragua and El Salvador present considerably more polarized pictures (see Figure 2). In the former country, those who supported Sandinista leader Daniel Ortega—who in late 2006 won back the presidential office from which the voters had ejected him in 1990—are predictably a fair distance to the left of their fellow citizens who supported President Enrique Bolaños (r. 2002–2007) of the Constitutionalist Liberal Party (PLC). More importantly, the left-right ideological gap is far wider in Nicaragua than it is in Costa Rica—which one would expect to be the case if one holds, as we do, that ideology still matters. In El Salvador, the ideological chasm is much broader still. There, supporters of the 2004 presidential candidacy of Schafik Hándal (d. 2006) of the Farabundo Martí National Liberation Front (FMLN)—the leftist party that emerged from the guerrilla forces

FIGURE 2—IDEOLOGICAL DISPOSITION AND PRESIDENTIAL VOTE
CHOICE: NICARAGUA AND EL SALVADOR

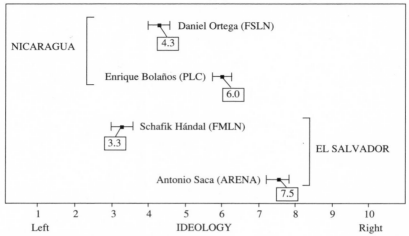

Horizontal lines indicate 95 percent confidence intervals.
Source: AmericasBarometer by LAPOP.

of the 1980–92 civil war—averaged a 3.3 as compared to the 7.5 ideology score registered by backers of Antonio Saca, the candidate of the
rightist ARENA party that has won the presidency in every election since
democracy was restored to that country.

Ideological cleavages also stand out in Chile, where Socialist Party
candidate Michelle Bachelet won the presidency in a January 2006 runoff
by attracting voters who were closest to the national ideological mean
(see Figure 3). Far to her left was Tomás Hirsch, who espoused a more
radical program during the campaign but won only a small vote share
(which explains the wide confidence interval around the mean of the survey respondents who say that they voted for Hirsch's party). The rightist
candidate, Joaquín Lavin, attracted voters who were ideologically furthest
to the right, while the center-right Sebastián Piñera, whom Bachelet beat
in the runoff, had the backing of voters whom the AmericasBarometer
data show as closer to the center than Lavin's. In short, Chile's voters in
2005–2006 held ideological preferences that mapped perfectly onto the
spectrum of candidates from which the electorate had to choose.

Three key conclusions emerge from this review of ideology in Latin
America. First, even as the region puts more "leftists" into presidential
palaces, the median voter remains slightly to the right of world opinion
(which itself is slightly right of center). Second, within the "slightly rightist" orientation that predominates among Latin Americans, voters have
clearly moved somewhat toward the left even during the brief span from
2004 to 2006. Third, the role of ideology in defining the electorate varies
sharply from one country to another. In some cases, voters (and thus viable

FIGURE 3—IDEOLOGICAL DISPOSITION AND PRESIDENTIAL VOTE
CHOICE: CHILE

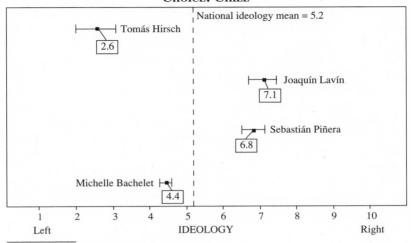

Horizontal lines indicate 95 percent confidence intervals.
Source: AmericasBarometer by LAPOP.

candidates) cluster heavily in the center, while in other countries, vast
ideological chasms separate voters, who in turn align behind candidates
spanning the left-right spectrum. In short, the end of the Cold War has
not meant any "end of ideology" (to borrow Daniel Bell's famous phrase)
for Latin America.

The Shift to the Left and Democratic Values

Beyond the ballot box, the AmericasBarometer data show that ideology
is relevant to the far deeper question of support for democracy. According to the survey, it is generally the case that people who self-define as
more leftist also tend to view their political systems as less legitimate,
and are less likely to favor democracy as a political system. A frequently
used approach to measure democratic support in many contemporary
democracy surveys is drawn from the work in postcommunist Europe
of William Mishler and Richard Rose. The item has become known as
the "Winston Churchill question," after that statesman's famous remark
about democracy being the worst system of government except for all the
other forms that have been tried from time to time. The survey measures
agreement or disagreement with this statement: "Even though democracy
has many problems, it is better than any other form of government."[12]

Another key dimension in democratic support is legitimacy, as defined in the classic works of Seymour Martin Lipset and David Easton.[13]
The AmericasBarometer uses a 10-point scale to measure the Churchill
item, and a five-variable composite index (each of the five variables is

measured on a 7-point scale) to measure legitimacy, thus avoiding the way that other research uses yes-or-no or 4- or 5-point scales—crude gauges ill-suited to capturing subtle but significant variations of opinion among citizens. As shown in Figure 4, the further ideology trends to the left in Latin America as a whole, the lower will tend to be both belief in the Churchillian view of democracy as the best system possible *and* belief in the legitimacy of the actually existing political system. This is a disturbing finding, especially in light of the findings reported above that a leftward trend is running and that ideology makes a difference in how voters view candidates. For the region as a whole, the finding that citizens of the Americas who line up on the left are less likely to prefer democracy than those on the right suggest that the movement to the left adds up to a move away from democracy, while the measurements taken using the legitimacy scale suggest that the left questions the authority of the regime to govern. Important exceptions are Chile and Bolivia, where it is the left that expresses higher support for democracy on the Churchill item.

With these worrying trends in mind, a search of the AmericasBarometer data for additional evidence points to a less democratic left in many, but not all countries of the Western Hemisphere. For example, respondents were asked: "There are people who say that what we need is a strong leader who does not have to be elected via the ballot. Others say that even though things don't work, electoral democracy, that is, the popular vote, is always the best." Only in Chile and Guatemala did respondents whose answers qualified them as left-of-center predominantly support electoral democracy and reject a strong leader. Everywhere else, it was rightists who were more likely than not to favor electoral democracy (it should be added that in several countries the difference between leftist and rightist respondents was not statistically significant).

Similarly, probes of political tolerance reveal that in most countries— Chile, Guatemala, and Mexico are exceptions—left-wing respondents are no more tolerant than their rightist fellow citizens. Interestingly, in prior studies of Latin America that LAPOP has conducted, leftists have often been found to be more tolerant than rightists. The questions used to measure tolerance have centered on the willingness of respondents to grant to opposition minorities basic civil liberties, such as the rights to vote, run for office, protest, and speak freely. It may well be that with the left now in power across much of region, left-wingers have become *less* tolerant of the now mostly out-of-office right. Testing such a hypothesis, however, would be a task well beyond the scope of this brief essay.

Is there evidence that citizens of Latin America would prefer populist-style governments rather than liberal democracies? As already noted, populism has many and varied meanings, but the current interest in it is directly linked to the growing South American trend to make constitutional changes, often through constitutional conventions or constituent

Figure 4—Impact of Ideology on Legitimacy and Belief that Democracy Is the "Best System"

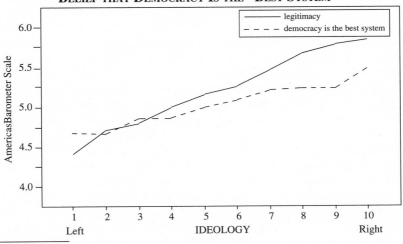

Sig.<.001
Source: AmericasBarometer by LAPOP

assemblies, that focus power in executive hands while weakening judges and legislators. The most dramatic example is Venezuela under Hugo Chávez, but similar patterns are observable in Bolivia, Ecuador, and elsewhere. Do the surveys provide hard evidence that a preference for populism over liberal democracy is afoot?

Nearly all surveys of Latin America have found that citizens hold their national legislatures and judiciaries in low regard. The AmericasBarometer data confirm that picture. Respondents are read a long list of institutions and asked how much they trust each one. When we convert the numbers arrayed along the AmericasBarometer's 1-to-7 scale to a more intuitively comprehensible 0-to-100 scale, the church scores at the top, with a mean trust score of 69 out of a possible 100 across the region as a whole. At the very nadir of public trust sit political parties, whose collective score of 35 is half what the church averages. The justice system averages 43, the legislature and supreme court score a 44, and law-enforcement agencies notch a 46. Of all the state institutions about which the surveys ask, only the armed forces—which garner a score of 60—manage to climb above 50 on the 0-to-100 trust scale. All the key representative institutions of liberal democracy languish in the negative (below-50) zone—a clear token of the public's lack of confidence in them.

How low are these scores? The WVS uses a different metric, scoring trust in these institutions along a mere 1-to-4 scale. Yet an examination of the WVS rank-ordering shows that the lowest average trust score across all countries worldwide belongs to political parties, with the legislature and then the justice system the next least-trusted institutions. Across the globe, as in Latin America, the military is the most trusted state institution of all, and no state institution enjoys the level of trust that religious institutions do. In this sense, Latin America conforms precisely to the international pattern.

To obtain a more nuanced look, it is instructive to compare the Latin American results with identically worded and scaled questions and answers drawn from AmericasBarometer research done in the United States and Canada. Although confidence in parties is low in both Canada (49.1) and the United States (42.9), the Canadian score is the Hemisphere's highest, while the U.S. score ranks fourth from the top. In only one other country do parties average a trust score that exceeds 40, while in Paraguay and Ecuador the figures are below 30. When it comes to the supreme court, the gap with Latin America is greater. The highest courts of Canada and the United States score a 71.3 and a 67.1, respectively, while throughout Latin America and the Caribbean no court scores above 60, and half of them score below 50. The least trusted high courts are found in Ecuador (24.7), Paraguay (30.2), and Haiti (31.4). When it comes to public trust in the justice system as a whole, the pattern is the same: The United States and Canada are the only countries where the score is above 60. The Hemisphere's least-trusted justice systems belong to Ecuador (28.0), Paraguay (31.0), and Peru (32.6). Costa Rica, Latin America's oldest established democracy, comes closest to the United States and Canada with a score of 52.9.

With citizens placing so little trust in the traditional institutions of liberal democracy, one might expect to find the urge to jettison them running high along with a spring tide of populist sentiment. Yet this is not entirely what the survey evidence shows. Support for parties may be low, but when the 2006 AmericasBarometer asked: "In your opinion, can there be democracy without political parties?" only 44 percent regionwide agreed. (Outliers included Ecuador and Haiti, where 50.5 and 62.2 percent, respectively, agreed that there can be democracy without parties.) In most countries, a majority rejects the notion that there can be democracy without parties, yet a strong minority accepts the idea. It is hard to say whether this is good news or bad unless we dig deeper in search of a better way to interpret what these findings say about Latin Americans' willingness to accept populist rule.

To gain further insight into the appeal of populism, LAPOP developed a new set of items for the 2006 AmericasBarometer. These questions were designed specifically to gauge citizens' willingness to push aside parties, legislatures, and courts in order to hand power to the executive. The LAPOP consortium built five items that formed a single dimension (using factor analysis) when the data were analyzed. One item, for example, read: "With which of these two opinions do you agree more: 1) For the progress of the country, it is necessary that our presidents limit the voice and vote of the opposition parties; 2) There is no reason that

FIGURE 5—IMPACT OF EDUCATION ON SUPPORT FOR POPULISM

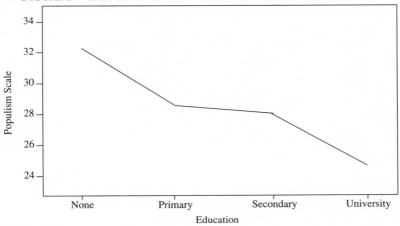

Sig.<.001
Source: AmericasBarometer by LAPOP

would justify that our presidents limit the voice and vote of the opposition parties, even if they hold back the progress of the country."

The experts from LAPOP also created an overall scale to measure "support for populism." According to this gauge, more than a third (36.3 percent) of all respondents refused to accept any populist measure, and only 15.2 percent of the respondents would support more than two of the five populist measures. Yet nearly half (48.4 percent) of the respondents in the pooled data set were willing to accept two of the five measures, and almost two-thirds (63.7 percent) were willing to accept at least one such measure. By this reckoning, then, while only a small minority of citizens in Latin America and the Caribbean favor a wide variety of measures to strengthen the presidency at the expense of representative, liberal-democratic institutions, a substantial majority would accept at least one sharp cutback in the separation of powers.

What of the minority that rejects liberal democracy? In democracies, minorities can be important, especially if they assert their preferences with great intensity or are concentrated in a homogeneous sector of the population. Under certain sets of election rules, for example, mobilized minorities with a unified position can achieve victory when the opposition is divided. Minorities also can carry great weight in the street, should they decide to embark upon demonstrations, civil disobedience, or terrorism. It is important to know, therefore, where minority support for populist rule is strongest in Latin America. Seymour Martin Lipset's classic work on "working-class authoritarianism" finds support in the contemporary data from the region. A regression analysis on the pooled data finds that populist sentiment is significantly higher among the poorer and less educated (see Figures 5 and 6).[14]

FIGURE 6—IMPACT OF WEALTH ON SUPPORT FOR POPULISM

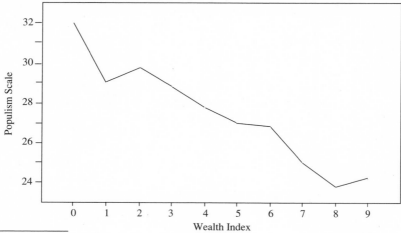

Sig.<.001
Source: AmericasBarometer by LAPOP

A surprising finding, however, is that even when we control for wealth and education, the *younger* the age of the respondent, the more likely he or she will be to support populist measures at the expense of liberal democracy and its guarantees of rights and freedoms. The surprise flows from the old and widespread assumption that older people are "set in their ways" and therefore more likely to support a government that puts limits on dissent. Fully explaining what draws today's Latin American youth to populism will require more analysis, but one plausible hypothesis posits that many older citizens of the region, having lived through the military dictatorships of the 1970s, are "immunized" against populist-authoritarian appeals in ways that younger citizens simply are not. The young know only the disappointments of the current democratic period, when economic growth across much of Latin America has been less robust than expected, and worse, has largely failed to reach the poor. Moreover, it may well be that older citizens are more jaded in general, having seen politicians of all stripes come and go, and therefore less willing to rally behind the latest political "flavor of the month." Perhaps it is not surprising, therefore, that Chile and Haiti—which have seen such political extremes in the last several decades—are the two countries where the older one is, the more likely one is to reject populism. Across the region as a whole, however, the results regarding age and populism should be seen as sobering. For they suggest that as the young people of today become tomorrow's electoral majorities, populism's appeal against the many checks, balances, rules, and frustrations of liberal democracy will only grow.[15]

The AmericasBarometer data point to some overall trends that merit careful attention. The ideological center of gravity in Latin America is, by world standards, slightly to the right, yet attitudes are moving to the left. Ideological cleavages in Latin America, long after the Cold War's end, still line up along a distinct left-right dimension, and voters support parties consistent with their ideological orientations. The gap between left and right is very narrow, however, in some countries (Costa Rica) but strikingly wide in other countries (Chile, El Salvador, and Nicaragua).

Being on the left in Latin America has implications beyond the ballot box. For the region as a whole, those on the left are less likely to believe that their country's political system is legitimate, and are less likely to believe that despite all its flaws, democracy is still the best available form of government. Moreover, in most countries, the left is more likely to support strong leaders who offer weak support or even hostility to the checks, balances, and procedures that mark liberal democracy. A second and related trend is the rise of populist figures and governments, especially in South America. This trend emerges, no doubt, in part from the very low level of trust that many citizens place in key institutions of liberal democracy—especially parties, the courts, and the legislature. In some countries, such as Ecuador, trust in these institutions is abysmally low. This should come as no surprise given the events in Ecuador over the past decade, in which a succession of democratically elected presidents were forced by the legislature to leave office early even as the executive branch eviscerated the independence of the country's judiciary.

While demand for across-the-board measures that would add up to dictatorial rule is still very much a minority sentiment across the region as a whole, close to two-thirds of respondents would even now accept at least some sharp reduction in the institutional autonomy of the courts, the legislature, and opposition parties. Support for measures that would result in what Larry Diamond calls a "hollowing-out" of democracy[16] is moreover closely associated across the region with the poverty, lack of schooling, and youth of respondents. On the other hand, it is hard to underestimate the importance of the fact that Latin Americans now have genuine choices of party and ideology that can be expressed in free and fair elections, so not all trends are negative. But the negative trends are real enough, and their potential effect on democratic stability in the region remains to be seen.

NOTES

I thank Kirk and Darren Hawkins, José Miguel Cruz, María Fernand Boidi, and John Booth for their suggestions and comments on an earlier draft of this essay.

1. Kurt Weyland defines populism as: "a political strategy through which a personalistic leader seeks or exercises government power based on direct, unmediated uninstitutionalized support from large numbers of mostly unorganized followers. This direct, quasi-personal relationship bypasses established intermediary organizations or deinstitutionalizes and subordinates them to the leader's personal will." Kurt Weyland, "Clarifying a Contested Concept: Populism in the Study of Latin American Politics," *Comparative Politics* 34 (October 2001): 14.

2. Among the classic works exploring the elements of the populist tradition are Michael L. Conniff, ed., *Populism in Latin America* (Tuscaloosa: University of Alabama Press, 1999); and J.M. Malloy, *Authoritarianism and Corporatism in Latin America* (Pittsburgh: University of Pittsburgh Press, 1977). For a more recent view, see Kenneth M. Roberts, *Changing Course: Parties, Populism, and Political Representation in Latin America's Neoliberal Era* (Cambridge: Cambridge University Press, forthcoming).

3. The AmericasBarometer covers Latin America plus four Caribbean countries and the United States and Canada. In this article, when the term "Latin America" is used, it includes the Caribbean as well.

4. Ronald Inglehart et al., *Human Beliefs and Values: A Cross-Cultural Sourcebook Based on the 1999–2002 Values Surveys* (Mexico City: Siglo XXI, 2003), 200.

5. Some regional surveys present a mix of national samples and urban samples, while others limit themselves to the official national language, excluding significant linguistic minorities; since intranational variation on many opinion and behavior variables is often wider than international variation, direct comparisons of samples with sharply varying coverage can be seriously misleading. See Mitchell A. Seligson, "Improving the Quality of Survey Research in Democratizing Countries," *PS: Political Science and Politics* 38 (January 2005): 51–56.

6. The countries were stratified into a small number of geographical regions (usually numbering four to six). Within each region, moreover, the samples were substratified into urban or rural zones. Questionnaires translated into widely spoken indigenous languages, such as Quechua and Aymara in Bolivia, and three Mayan languages in Guatemala were used where appropriate in each country.

7. As in the case of the AfroBarometer and the World Values Survey, careful survey work covering a wide array of countries is often practically impossible to accomplish within a single year. Additional countries are being added to the AmericasBarometer in 2007, but the data for those countries will become available only after this essay goes to press. Experts from participating countries met in Costa Rica in May 2006 to agree on a standardized core questionnaire, after which each country's delegation was free to add items related to specific issues relevant to their home country or to specific interests of the researchers. For the training manual and questionnaires, visit *www.lapopsurveys.org.*

8. A 0-to-100 scale would have provided a true neutral point, but the AmericasBarometer conforms to the World Values Survey standard of a 1-to-10 scale.

9. The WVS has expanded its range of countries over the years, moving from a concentration on advanced industrial democracies to one that now includes many countries from the developing world. Looking exclusively at the seventy countries surveyed since 1999, the mean ideology score is 5.58, nearly identical to the entire series since 1981, indicating no worldwide shift in the post–Cold War epoch. Worldwide, nonresponse on this question is typically higher than on other survey items. The WVS mean is based upon 193,531 individuals who responded to the ideology question on at least one wave of the WVS. The AmericasBarometer encountered a nonresponse rate of about 20 percent, which is typical for many surveys.

10. This comparison includes a subset of ten countries from 2004 that were also surveyed with the identical survey item in 2006.

11. See Fabrice Lehoucq, "Costa Rica: Paradise in Doubt," *Journal of Democracy* 16 (July 2005): 140–54, as well as the subsequent exchange between Lehoucq and former Costa Rican president Miguel Angel Rodríguez in the April 2006 issue of the *Journal of Democracy.*

12. William Mishler and Richard Rose, "Five Years After the Fall: Trajectories of Support

for Democracy in Post-Communist Europe," in Pippa Norris, ed., *Critical Citizens: Global Support for Democatic Governance* (Oxford: Oxford University Press, 1999), 78–99.

13. See, for instance, Seymour Martin Lipset, *Political Man: The Social Bases of Politics* (Garden City, N.Y.: Doubleday, 1960); and David Easton, *The Political System: An Inquiry into the State of Political Science* (New York: Knopf, 1953). We measure legitimacy by a 5-item series, each item in which is scored on a 1-to-7 scale and then transformed into a 1-to-10 index. Details can be found in John A. Booth and Mitchell A. Seligson, "Political Legitimacy and Participation in Costa Rica: Evidence of Arena Shopping," *Political Research Quarterly* 59 (December 2005): 537–50; Mitchell A. Seligson, "The Impact of Corruption on Regime Legitimacy: A Comparative Study of Four Latin American Countries," *Journal of Politics* 64 (May 2002): 408–33; and Mitchell A. Seligson, "The Measurement and Impact of Corruption Victimization: Survey Evidence from Latin America," *World Development* 34 (February 2006): 381–404.

14. Analysis of individual country data, not reported here, finds variation in these regression patterns. Extensive studies regarding each of the AmericasBarometer countries are available at *www.lapopsurveys.org*.

15. An obvious alternative explanation is that as today's young people age, they will come to resemble their elders and therefore will be equally resistant to populist appeals. Unfortunately, the panel data that would help us to distinguish between those effects related to age in general and those related to membership in a specific generational cohort do not exist. See Glenn Firebaugh, *Analyzing Repeated Surveys* (Thousand Oaks, Calif.: Sage, 1997).

16. Larry Diamond, *Developing Democracy: Toward Consolidation* (Baltimore: Johns Hopkins University Press, 1999).

7

THE TRANSFORMATION OF THE LABOR ARENA

Christopher Sabatini and Eric Farnsworth

Christopher Sabatini *is senior director of policy at the Americas Society and Council of the Americas and the editor-in-chief of* Americas Quarterly. *From 1997 to 2005 he served as director for Latin America and the Caribbean at the National Endowment for Democracy.* **Eric Farnsworth** *is vice-president of the Council of the Americas. He served in the State Department and Clinton White House as an advisor on Western Hemisphere affairs. This essay originally appeared in the October 2006 issue of the* Journal of Democracy.

Among the defining but often overlooked characteristics of modern Latin American electorates is their "informality."[1] The economic reforms of the 1990s and the subsequent failure of labor markets to absorb unemployment have left more than half the region's urban working (and voting) population on the economic margins and without attachments to organized channels of political participation. Behind the much-noted resurgence of populism[2] in Latin America lies this fluid and heterogeneous popular sector. Incorporating it into formal political and economic life is the region's greatest challenge.

According to regionwide surveys, unemployment and job security remain Latin Americans' greatest concerns, and with good reason. Unemployment has risen since the 1990s even as such measures of job quality as employment security, labor-rights guarantees, and access to benefits have declined dramatically. The dilemma of what to do with a growing pool of jobless or underemployed and disaffected people is not unique to Latin America or even the developing parts of the globe. As antiglobalization riots were enveloping the 4–5 November 2005 Mar del Plata Summit of the Americas in Argentina, across the Atlantic unemployed youths from poor, immigrant neighborhoods in France were in the midst of a weeks-long series of car burnings and riots in and around Paris and other large cities. In early 2006, the French government moved tepidly to relax labor-market rigidities (such as severe limits on employers' freedom to dismiss workers) that were widely blamed for exacerbating immigrant unemployment. Those who felt their own interests threatened by such changes reacted with disruptive and sometimes-violent protests of their own that rose to a crescendo in March. The twin outbreaks of unrest in late 2005 and early 2006 left French premier Dominique de Villepin's government badly shaken. They also suggest that Latin America's governments, like their counterpart in France, face a choice: They can enact labor-market reform and risk political instability now, or else allow a demographic time bomb to keep ticking away as more and more young people come of age whom the rigid job market cannot absorb.

Despite the hopes of technocrats, multilateral organizations, and some politicians, the economic and fiscal reforms of the 1990s (measures now known disparagingly as the Washington Consensus) failed to generate employment at the anticipated rates. The privatization of state enterprises and the restructuring of private firms resulted in huge formal-sector layoffs. Reformers had assumed that in a new macroeconomic environment purged of fundamental inefficiencies and energized by liberalized trade, displaced workers would find new jobs relatively quickly in sectors fueled by foreign direct investment and the region's enticingly low labor costs.

Growth did follow the reforms, but it was not enough to offset the effect of the layoffs plus the entrance of new workers into the labor market. Across Latin America, urban unemployment nearly doubled, going from 5 percent in 1989 to 9 percent in 2003.[3] In stark contrast to expectations, those hardest hit by the jobs downturn were unskilled and semiskilled workers and youth. But more important was the *quality* of the jobs that were generated during the period. Throughout the region, the 1990s continued the trends of the 1980s: Manufacturing and public-sector jobs became rarer, employment in services climbed, and informal-sector jobs grew dramatically. By 2001, estimates placed the percentage of workers employed in the informal economy at more than half the region's urban workforce.

These patterns deepened the split between skilled workers (who benefited from the growth of export-oriented jobs) and unskilled and semi-skilled workers, many of whom lost jobs in the restructuring and with them the social-welfare benefits that the state and labor unions had typically provided.

In the post–Washington Consensus environment, in which the public sector no longer provided the primary source of employment and the state no longer protected certain industries, firms had to boost productivity in order to compete internationally. Doing so meant cutting labor costs. But existing and mostly unreformed labor laws have kept nonwage labor costs artificially high and hence have pushed growing businesses toward extralegal hiring. While unemployment (temporary or otherwise) has been a consequence of market reforms, the explosion of informal employment has sprung from the failure to push reforms to completion.

Every country in Latin America has a welter of laws governing relations between employers and employees. Many of these laws date from the 1930s and 1940s, and have remained largely unchanged since then. Anachronistic laws make Latin American labor markets among the most restrictive, rigid, and cumbersome in the world. Legal "job-security provisions" typically saddle employers with lengthy notice requirements, mandate compensation for dismissal without adequate cause (which in many cases cannot include the employer's economic difficulties), and award "seniority premiums" to long-serving employees.[4] For employers calculating the costs of hiring or firing, the costs of complying with these laws can be staggering.

To cite a few specifics, Argentina's labor laws mandate two months' notice or two months' wages before dismissal, at which point the fired worker becomes entitled to a twelfth of his or her salary and bonuses from the last year, plus vacation, all multiplied by the total number of years worked. Moreover, to avert massive layoffs during Argentina's 2001 financial crisis, dismissal payments were temporarily doubled. In Peru, labor legislation guarantees each dismissed employee one and a half times the worker's monthly salary (in contrast to the one month's annualized salary in Argentina) times the number of years worked, capped at twelve years total. Chilean labor laws provide for a month's salary, plus vacation multiplied by the number of years worked, up to ten years.

Reforms introduced in the 1990s did little to improve the overall labor market. Most aimed at allowing firms formally to contract temporary workers. Peru introduced a parallel and more flexible system that allowed for temporary hiring and probationary periods by small and medium-sized enterprises and several key industries. Chile permitted the use of temporary and less binding labor contracts and established a government subsidy for the first four months of a contract with a private company. Later reforms also changed the requirements for registering and recognizing the authority of new unions. Argentina approved a three-month probationary period for new employees. In response to these legal loopholes for hiring, the percentage of workers employed under temporary contracts shot up.[5]

But these were only half-measures, introduced by governments afraid to face the heat that any broader reform of labor laws would generate. The root problem, which concerns long-term rather than temporary employees, remained untouched. Moreover, the backdoor created for temporary hiring also limited workers' ability to gain access to the benefits of full employment and union organization. Finally, even after the opening of these temporary-employment loopholes, the average costs associated with dismissing a formally hired, full-time worker in Latin America were still the highest in the entire industrialized world.[6]

Businesses must of course take carefully into account the long-term legal and financial costs and commitments associated with hiring new regular employees. The high incidence of job-security provisions serves as a disincentive to thinning the numbers of unproductive laborers or shifting them to other areas. At the same time, the risk of being saddled with expensive, hard-to-fire workers discourages firms from making new hires. The result, most of the time, is that expanding businesses seek extralegal means of adding employees. Predictably, higher dismissal costs correlate with higher rates of self-employment and informality. Job-security provisions that "lock in" the employment of existing workers tend to bar new workforce entrants, who are disproportionately young and female. According to one study, the effect of job-security provisions is twice as great on youth as it is on other sectors.[7]

Informal employment is a two-way street, with both firms and workers calculating costs and making choices. Firms hire informally or extralegally in order to avoid the costs (financial and administrative) associated with formal, full-time employees. Among these costs, broadly construed, is the risk that regular employees will be more likely to organize or join unions that can later press for higher pay and benefits. Hiring informally promises not only a cheaper but also a more quiescent labor force. Yet the very precariousness of informally contracted labor may arguably dampen productivity in the long run, making it less obviously a good bargain for employers or societies as a whole.

Research suggests that the border between formal and informal employment is fairly porous and more voluntary than previously thought.[8] Workers sometimes opt for the informal sector to avoid having to direct some of their salary to benefit plans. The decision is often based on both the low level of formal wages and a lack of confidence that benefits such as pensions and unemployment insurance will ever materialize in countries where employers can refuse to pay while governments refuse to make them. Rather than pay portions of their salaries into a system which offers few guarantees that they can collect their contribution and the expected match, many workers prefer to be paid directly in cash.

Whether because workers choose it or simply lack options, the informal sector has swelled over the last two decades. According to a 2005 International Labor Organization (ILO) report, during the 1990s the rate of job growth in Latin America's informal sector was almost twice what it was in the formal economy.[9] While estimates vary depending on how "informal" employment is defined, most current studies calculate that close to half of Latin America's nonagricultural workforce is now informal.[10] In countries such as Ecuador, Honduras, and Peru, that number is probably closer to 60 percent, while in Chile—whose rate of informality is the region's lowest—just under 40 percent of nonagricultural workers are not formally employed.

Life on the Edges

While informal employment may have helped to cushion the blow of economic reforms in the absence of a more efficient labor market, it is hardly a desirable employment outcome. There is a fair amount of variation concerning how people enter the informal sector and their degree of choice in doing so. Yet there can be little doubt that informal-sector employment is generally a suboptimal situation for a worker. Those who toil on the fringes of the formal economy all too often have limited access even to minimal job security or basic benefits and safety protections.

Frequently it is women and youth who suffer most. According to a number of studies, women and younger workers make up the majority of those employed informally.[11] That women and youth should be over-represented in the informal sector is to be expected given the proven discriminatory effect that existing labor law has on aspiring entrants to the labor market. This effect looms particularly large in a region where more than a third of the populace is under 16.[12] This "youth bulge" will mean that Latin American labor markets will have to absorb a flood of new workers when already, according to the ILO, unemployment among youth (18.8 percent) is more than double the overall unemployment rate of 9 percent.[13]

Falling employment in public and manufacturing jobs plus dramatic increases in informal and temporary hiring have meant plummeting rates of unionization throughout Latin America. Unions find their traditional structures and orientations under pressure as never before. The large public sectors and protected industries on which union organizers and leaders once focused gave way during the decade of the Washington Consensus to privatization programs and a reduced role for state intervention. In the past, the heavy role of the state in the economy meant that unions' advocacy efforts and relationships were oriented primarily toward the government and elected officials. Economic reforms involving the passage of public enterprises into private hands have cut public payrolls, reduced state intervention, deprived the unions of a central site for negotiations, and heightened the need for new strategies of organization and bargaining.

At a time when unionization has declined across the world, it has dropped especially sharply in Latin America. While comparable data are difficult to find, levels of unionization have decreased by almost 50 percent in Argentina, Colombia, Peru, and Venezuela since 1980. In Colombia and Peru, the unionized share of the workforce is just 5 to 8 percent.[14]

Union membership has grown in just two countries: Brazil and Chile. Brazil's President Luiz Inácio ("Lula") da Silva has launched a campaign to grant informal-sector workers semiofficial recognition as laborers by giving them workers' identity cards, thus providing access to state-provided health and pension benefits. While the loose incorporation of informally employed workers into union ranks has sparked tensions within the formal union movement, the plan has increased membership (albeit via an ill-defined category) in formal labor unions. The policy points to a future path for reform for the region.

In Chile, the rise in union membership has been the result of a labor-law reform that has left few limits on the ability of small workers' groups to gain recognition as unions and bargain collectively. Membership in these groups went up after the reform, but what was in effect a diffusion of the right to organize has also left worker representation in a dramatically fragmented state.

The movement of so much of the working class beyond the reach of traditional union-organizing efforts has had implications for both economic and political representation. Established unions have become increasingly marginal, and along with their waning influence has shrunk that of the old-line labor-based parties which these unions have long supported. Argentina's General Confederation of Workers (CGT) and Peronist party, Mexico's Confederation of Mexican Workers (CTM) and Institutional Revolutionary Party (PRI), and Venezuela's Confederation of Venezuelan Workers (CTV) and Democratic Action (AD) party are classic examples of mass unions and the parties that depended on them. With the organized segment of the working class in eclipse, such parties have either declined or, as in the case of the Peronists, have begun to seek new constituents amid the growing ranks of informal workers.

For unions, the task of organizing the informal sector presents a dilemma. Heterogeneous and dispersed, this sector has few easily identifiable or unified interests and little sense of common identity. The informal sector is a world of small producers, casual laborers, street vendors, illegally contracted workers, and domestic employees. In this world, it is hard to apply the usual union model of banding large numbers of workers together in order to negotiate with employers by leveraging the collective power of the workers' labor. Such workers' organizations as are found in the informal sector typically take the form of sector-specific groups or neighborhood associations. While such small groups may have coherent interests, they do not add up to meaningful nationwide movements able to facilitate large-scale inclusion.[15] Despite these challenges to collective action, the traditional orientation of Latin American unions toward the state rather than employers may mean that unions will be well-equipped to act as political advocates for informal workers in the future.

For now, absent an existing structure or logic for mass mobilization and representation, the informal sector remains a fluid or at best loosely attached electoral base. In several countries, political entrepreneurs and outsider candidates have effectively leveraged informal workers' votes by means of populist movements and rhetoric. But as with the typical populist project, these efforts have so far failed to create and consolidate stabler and more institutionalized channels for sustaining informal workers' participation and representation in political life. Over the past decade, in countries such as Venezuela, Peru, Guatemala, Ecuador, Bolivia, and even Argentina, the presence of this unattached base has spelled high levels of electoral volatility as well as erosion in the coherence of party systems. More recently, the swelling pool of informal workers has helped to feed a populist backlash against the organized political system. In all this, ideology has mattered little.

Populist Leaders, Informal Followers

The list of political leaders who have tapped the power of the informals ranges from Peru's former president Alberto Fujimori (1990–2000) to Venezuela's current president Hugo Chávez. The means and ends to which these leaders have sought to mobilize these sectors have varied, as has the extent to which they have sought to build more institutionalized links to these sectors.

In his first campaign in 1990, one-time agronomy professor Fujimori was at best a long shot against the world-famous and erudite Peruvian novelist Mario Vargas Llosa. Nevertheless, the social and economic destruction wrought by the first administration of once-and-future-president Alan García (1985–90, 2006–) had exploded traditional partisan and social alliances. When García left office after his first term, Peru's economy was in tatters, inflation was raging at 7,000 percent, the international community had turned its back, and the Peruvian people were suffering from the violent assaults of the Maoist Sendero Luminoso (Shining Path) terror group. Running as an outsider with no organized structure except a loose electoral machine called Cambio 90, Fujimori appealed to Peru's marginalized and in particular its many informals. He railed against political elites and promised a host of programs oriented toward the informal sector—the legalization of street vendors, the creation of lending projects for microbusinesses, and a program to grant land titles to squatters—and even included leaders from the informal community on the Cambio 90 ticket.

Fujimori's programmatic and rhetorical appeal to Peru's dispossessed worked. During his early years in power, the urban informal sector formed an important part of his popular constituency. After his election, Fujimori directed many of the proceeds from the unexpected wave of privatization toward projects targeting the needs of the poor. Yet the president's lack of interest in institutionalizing a broader movement quickly became clear. He built personalistic relations with the business class, forged an alliance with sectors of the military, and then set out to create a new political movement with each election. After his April 1992 dissolution of Congress and *autogolpe* (self-coup), he called elections for a constituent assembly to draft a new basic law and then dissolved Cambio 90 in favor of a new political machine, Nueva Mayoria (New Majority). A few years later, in 1998, he formed Vamos Vecino (Let's Go Neighbor) for that year's municipal elections, and soon created a party called Perú 2000 to promote his bid for a controversial third term amid major corruption scandals and calls for his ouster.

In all these instances, the focus was on mobilizing voters behind Fujimorismo rather than crafting a coherent structure for representation. Even the programs aimed at serving the needs of the underclass quickly became personalized. Fujimori had these programs organized and run out of his office, and personally announced and delivered them, especially at election time. Changes to the labor law that granted businesses greater leeway for temporary hiring also served to augment the president's base of informal-sector workers while weakening the labor unions lined up against him. As with other changes in Latin American labor law that made temporary hiring easier, the Fujimori-era reforms did little to help informal workers in the long term.

After Fujimori fled into exile in 2000, his poorly institutionalized electoral machine collapsed. Six years later, in the May 2006 presidential election, many of the popular sectors to which Fujimori had appealed swung behind another outsider candidate. Ollanta Humala used populist appeals to the dispossessed, denunciations of the political class, and the promise of radical change to woo voters. The strategy worked in the shantytowns that ring Lima and the poor, rural regions of southern Peru and the Andean highlands. While this was not enough to win the presidency, Humala secured a plurality for his party in Congress and came within 5 percentage points of the repentant Alan García. The question now is if the one-time traditional populist García can organize a new political base to head off the latest breed of populists who succeeded him and now nip at his heels.

Even before Hugo Chávez arrived on the political scene, Venezuela's growing informal sector had been eating away at the base of the country's once-dominant national labor union, the CTV. One CTV leader estimated in 2002 that the proportion of workers who lay beyond the organizational framework of the union—and hence also that of its ally, the AD party—had over the years approached 53 percent.[16] These nonunionized, informal workers became a base ripe for political mobilization against the two-party dominance that had corroded democratic accountability and led to massive corruption. Many informals resented the CTV leadership as part of this old, corrupt system.

Following his failed 1992 coup attempt and a resulting jail term, former army lieutenant-colonel Chávez won the presidency in a 1998 landslide. Shunning the traditional power structures as vestiges of the bankrupt old order and emphasizing his dark skin and indigenous features, Chávez sought direct contact with the unorganized base of his poor followers. Like Fujimori in Peru, Chávez claimed to represent the improverished masses whom decades of cozy upper-class power-sharing had ignored and brushed aside. To those on the margins of the economy looking in, the old-line parties and unions seemed tokens of the exclusiveness and clubby self-dealing that Chávez was promising to sweep away.

Once elected, he quickly set out to dismantle or wear down many of the old order's pillars, including the CTV. Rallying his base among the working poor and his own circle of labor leaders, Chávez attempted first to remake the CTV into a Chavista labor organization by allowing unaffiliated workers to vote in union elections. Stiff resistance from the CTV and international labor groups led to elections that produced a president from the union's traditional base, though pro-Chavista union leaders won seats on the CTV board. With the "inside" strategy of taking over the CTV via internal elections having produced such mixed results, in 2003 Chavista labor leaders turned to the "outside" approach of creating a parallel, pro-Chavista union known as the National Union of Workers (UNT). Their hope was that the UNT would offer a means of both splitting the traditional labor movement and mobilizing informal-sector workers.[17] Nevertheless, recent labor-related clashes that have pitted the UNT against the government and various publicly owned enterprises have cast doubt on the regime's commitment to creating a vehicle for worker representation which can effectively defend workers' rights before the state.

The Chávez regime has paired its efforts at labor organizing with a less centralized grassroots campaign to set up local committees of the working poor. Through organizations such as the Bolivarian circles (similar in structure and function to block committees), social-development missions, and cooperatives, the government has sought to reach into poor neighborhoods and the networks of the informal sector. More than a structured source for representation, however, many of these regime constructs are conduits for state patronage. Their connection to President Chávez's party, the Fifth Republic Movement (MVR), is tenuous; they remain primarily a set of decentralized and diffuse channels for clientelism tied to the president's personal influence.

In Bolivia, the political trajectory of President Evo Morales has followed much the same pattern. An Aymara elected in December 2005 as his country's first indigenous president, Morales draws his largest support from a coalition of indigenous rural voters and working-poor informals from places such as El Alto, the rapidly growing and heavily indigenous slum that looms above the capital of La Paz. While his opposition to the U.S.-backed coca-leaf eradication program as leader of the coca growers' union consolidated his base among indigenous rural voters, as Morales's stature grew he and his party (the Movement Toward Socialism, or MAS) tapped into the growing urban working class. In recent years, the cities in Bolivia's highlands and even in its flatter and more Europeanized east have seen a wave of rural migrants, mostly indigenous people, who often wind up working informally as vendors or in small businesses.

During his run for the presidency, Morales held his heterogeneous, loosely structured popular base and party together by directing anger and protest against the ruling class and the international economic order. This was an easy tactic to master: Strikes and protests (including highway blockages around La Paz) made life hard for an elected government headed by politicians tied to the economic and business classes of Bolivia's east. Now that he has secured power, however, Morales must face the more difficult task of governing. Early actions such as the 1 May 2006 armed seizure and nationalization of internationally owned natural-gas fields and the calling of an assembly to draft a new constitution have kept the base united with a fresh dose of defiance and a new common project. Yet signs of strain are evident as well. A series of compromises have sparked protests from within Morales's own movement by more radical groups which charge that the president is not sticking to the revolutionary pledges that he made on the campaign trail. Morales's attempts to take a more moderate line in recent land conflicts with Bolivian settlers on the Brazilian border, to resist demands that he quickly nationalize mines as well as a host of sectors in addition to gas, and to moderate his stated opposition to U.S. policies aimed at discouraging coca growing have provoked dissent on the part of leaders and organizations with ties to his popular base.

The New Environment

It is difficult to imagine a more dysfunctional situation than the conditions that workers face in Latin America today: increasing wage disparity between skilled and unskilled workers, swelling youth unemployment, declining levels of already-low unionization, incomplete enforcement of existing labor protections, and rapid growth of informal employment caused in part by labor laws that constrain the growth of formal employment.

Among the principal political challenges facing Latin America as a whole are those of incorporating groups left behind by formal economic growth in recent decades and stemming the flow of new workers into the growing pools of informality. Given the region's demographics, labor markets already stretched to their limits are going to have to absorb an even greater flood of workers. At the same time, democracy has provided, for the first time, a means to give voice to the disenfranchised, displaced, and traditionally ignored. In prior decades, protest based on unmet economic expectations might merely have been suppressed, by force if necessary. Now, democratic governments take such actions at their peril.

Populism, with its potential for irresponsibility and plebiscitarianism, is just one upshot of the new demographics of labor in Latin America. Another and still more risk-laden prospect is suggested by what has unfolded since the November 2005 campaign of car burnings and assaults in France. The French system is good at protecting workers who already have jobs, yet these very protections make it much less effective at creating jobs for new entrants. Those who bear the brunt of the French rigidities are newcomers and those outside the traditional channels for education and recruitment of new employees—which in France means primarily minority and immigrant youth, the cognates of Latin America's recently urbanized indigenous peoples.

The reforms that the Villepin government attempted to adopt in order to help prevent more disturbances like those of November 2005 would have established a short probationary period for new employees in place of the old arrangement that put new hires on a fast track to guaranteed lifetime employment. Among the protestors who demonstrated so vehemently against this tepid proposal were university students and trade-union members who made it clear that they would accept nothing less than the coveted job-for-life guarantees of the existing labor system. In a country that prides itself on revolution and progress, the protests demonstrated a deep desire by French youth to preserve the past, at the risk of excluding the poor. Although reforms (albeit of an even more minimal nature) eventually passed, the price in turmoil and disorder that France had to pay highlights the difficult realities faced by Latin American leaders who would attempt to reform labor codes in any way that might reduce the benefits of the privileged. From highway shutdowns in Argentina to wildcat strikes and protests in Bolivia, Ecuador, and Venezuela, recent outbursts of opposition to Latin American governments have raised the possibility that the real threat may be less from the election of this or that irresponsible leader or government than from a long-term undermining of any government's capacity to govern democratically.

Democracy cannot be sustained if a majority of a country's populace stands outside its formal economy and political system. As the case of Peru shows, arguably the least that one can expect under such circumstances is extreme electoral volatility as a fluid mass of unattached, uncommitted voters swings wildly from one movement and one election to the next. The stable system of interest representation that helps democracy to become firmly established will have a hard time forming in such a fluctuating political climate.

Addressing this problem will stretch the bounds of traditional organizations and established political constituencies. The heterogeneity and diffuseness of the informal sector does not lend itself to easy organization or interest aggregation. There are few clear economic incentives that bind the various producers, retailers, and service providers who make up the informal sector. Indeed, as Ruth Berins Collier and Samuel Handlin have argued, the "particularistic nature" of the popular associations that represent the informal sector is more "conducive to clientelism and cooptation" than the formation of broader movements for mass political representation.[18]

A Route to Reform

Despite these organizational obstacles, there may be a path for reform. A solution could lie in changes to law and policy that will grant workers, including those in the informal sector, better protection for core labor rights and access to social services in exchange for reductions in the burdens that employers must shoulder when making hiring and firing decisions. The former set of changes promises the possibility of improving the conditions for informal laborers at the same time that it would help them to integrate themselves politically as formal citizens. The latter set holds the prospect of longer-term change that will give Latin America's labor markets the flexibility that they will need to cope with the influx of new workers and those currently shunted to the margins.

In order to navigate such a course, governments will first need consistently to defend the basic rights of labor. Securing full citizenship rights for organized and unorganized workers will require as an initial step that governments enforce the core rights of labor that are already on the books: freedom of association and bargaining, freedom from forced labor and invidious discrimination, and eradication of child labor. Throughout the region, these rights have received imperfect protection at best. Labor courts remain notoriously slow, corrupt, and politicized.

Second, governments should develop effective means of ensuring basic benefits (meaning among other things pension programs and health-care access) to workers—informal and formal alike—via a creative mix of private and public initiatives. As mentioned earlier, some employees opt for informality because they expect that the benefits promised by formal employment will never materialize. Along these lines, Lula's administration in Brazil has launched an innovative program to grant limited benefits to employees in the informal sector. The effort has spawned some concern among labor leaders that the policy may lead to an attenuation of worker representation and collective power. Nevertheless, it represents one of the first serious efforts to incorporate the unorganized informals into the labor movement around the demand for public benefits. In Chile, the government of recently elected President Michelle Bachelet has outlined its own plan to extend benefits to informals.

While the idea of incorporation in Brazil is to bring informals under the umbrella of state protections—more than to bring them within the ambit of formal political representation per se—in many ways unions in Brazil and in the region are particularly well suited to undertake this form of representation and negotiation. The main job of Latin America's unions has historically been that of persuading governments to give greater benefits and wages to employees of the state and state-owned enterprises. Since economic reforms began thinning the ranks of such employees in the 1990s, many unions have found themselves struggling to craft strategies for dealing with private employers. The informal-sector dilemma plays in many ways to unions' traditional strength.

Third, the keystone of reform has to be the updating of outmoded labor codes, especially insofar as these make the cost of dismissing workers unreasonably and destructively high. Unreformed, these laws will continue to act as a deadly drag on new hiring, investment, economic expansion, and prosperity. Important change could be achieved by lowering or eliminating the sums that firms are required to pay in order to shed unnecessary workers and in several cases (where such provisions do not exist) allowing for economically motivated dismissals. Ultimately, the long-term path to creating more formal jobs for Latin American workers lies in this area. Without more freedom to make economically rational personnel decisions, firms will continue to be shackled by high labor costs, and more workers will continue to be forced into the marginal world of informal labor. Labor-law reform is by no means a panacea, but labor markets need the flexibility to be able to respond to the inevitable expansion and contraction of the market.

Fourth, new job-training programs must accompany any scaling back of job-security provisions. Studies show that when companies no longer face high costs for shedding workers, layoffs go up. The same studies indicate that time to reemployment is shorter when these costs are lowered (easier firing also means easier hiring).[19] Training programs can provide a speedier route to new jobs and a buffer against the painful, even if relatively short-term, dislocations that labor-market fluctuations can cause.

What will unions get out of all this? For one, as established union leaders in countries such as Peru and Venezuela have discovered, politicians who base their popularity on the masses of unorganized, informal laborers will often find that traditional unions and their officials present tempting targets for populist attacks. In contrast, a broad reform of labor law promises to augment the ranks of formal-economy workers, and with them the recruiting and organizing prospects of old-line unions. They and their leaders could find themselves newly relevant—precisely at a time when the pressures and demands associated with globalization make stronger voices for workers' rights so urgently needed. But getting to such a point will require unions to sharpen their vision and rethink their traditional strategies and political positioning.

In Latin America, the politics surrounding labor issues have always been explosive. But the growing threats of populism and even graver political disorders should citizens' hunger for jobs not be met offer a real opportunity for governments to strike a politically innovative balance. The tradeoff would provide governments with the political capital to rewrite outdated labor laws and, by incorporating a new generation of workers, profoundly recast politics and labor relations in ways that would help the whole region steer away from the pitfalls of populist promises and protest.

Latin America may be approaching a historic turning point in the areas of political incorporation and labor relations. The levels of economic and social dislocation and political flux in the region are opening up an opportunity for creative, entrepreneurial leaders to change the direction of employment, labor rights, and politics for a new generation. Doing nothing will ensure only that the promising shores of opportunity become the menacing shoals of crisis as the unbending realities of demographics, globalization, and populist opportunism threaten the political and economic fortunes of the region.

NOTES

The authors wish to thank Stan Gacek for commenting on an earlier draft; Matias Zaldua and Juan Cruz Dias for conducting some of the basic research on labor laws; and Talisa Anderson for finding statistical and other data on the informal sector and youth. Any errors or omissions remain the authors' responsibility.

1. While disagreements among experts about the precise meaning of economic "informality" make defining (not to say measuring) the phenomenon a tricky business, we use the term "informal" here to refer to firms and the self-employed that conduct their hiring operations (and perhaps all their operations generally) outside labor codes and other formal legal requirements.

2. At its most basic, the term "populist" generally denotes a movement that mobilizes those who feel themselves to be disadvantaged by socioeconomic and political dislocation, as well as a leadership style that draws on a sense of disaffection from the established political system and elites. For the evolving debate on the nature and definition of modern-day populism in Latin America, see Kenneth Roberts, "Populism, Political Conflict, and Grass-Roots Organization in Latin America: A Comparison of Fujimori and Chávez," *Comparative Politics* 38 (January 2006): 1–39; Steve Ellner, "The Contrasting Variants of Populism of Hugo Chávez and Alberto Fujimori," *Journal of Latin America Studies* 35 (February 2003): 139–62; and Kurt Weyland, "Neopopulism and Neoliberalism in Latin America: Unexpected Affinities," *Studies in Comparative International Development* 31 (Fall 1996): 3–31.

3. World Bank Development Indicators database, Latin America and the Caribbean, Unemployment, total (percent of total labor force), 1989–2003. See *http://devdata.worldbank.org/data-query*.

4. In Colombia, Ecuador, Panama, Peru, and Venezuela, veteran workers receive a seniority premium not only if they are laid off, but even if they quit.

5. Víctor Tokman, "Integrating the Informal Sector in the Modernization Process," *SAIS Review* 21 (Winter–Spring 2001): 45–60.

6. James Heckman and Carmen Pages, "The Cost of Job Security Regulation: Evidence from Latin American Labor Markets," *NBER Working Paper No. W7773,* June 2000.

7. Heckman and Pages, "The Cost of Job Security Regulation," 29.

8. See for example, William Maloney, "Does Informality Imply Segmentation in Urban Labor Markets? Evidence from Sectoral Transitions in Mexico," *World Bank Economic Review* 13 (May 1999): 275–302; and Jaime Saavedra, "Labor Markets During the 1990s," in Pedro-Pablo Kuczynski and John Williamson, eds., *After the Washington Consensus: Restarting Growth and Reform in Latin America* (Washington, D.C.: Institute for International Economics, 2003), 213–64.

9. The growth rate in the informal sector was 3.9 percent, while in the formal sector it was 2.1 percent. See International Labor Organisation, *Global Employment Trends Brief,* February 2005, 6.

10. Most research on the informal sector in Latin America places the total size of the sector regionwide at around or just over 50 percent of the urban workforce. The International

Labor Organisation's 2002 Labor Overview calculated the rate at 46.3 percent. Nicolai Kristensen and Wendy Cunningham estimate the range throughout the region as 30 to 70 percent, and Tokman, citing International Labor Organisation numbers, says that the sector provides about 57 percent of total urban employment in Latin America. Nicolai Kristensen and Wendy Cunningham, "Do Minimum Wages in Latin America and the Caribbean Matter? Evidence from 19 Countries," World Bank Policy Research Working Paper 3870, March 2006; and Tokman, "Integrating the Informal Sector in the Modernization Process."

11. International Labor Organisation, *Global Employment Trends Brief,* February 2005, 6.

12. Economic Commission for Latin America, *Boletín demográfico: América Latina y Caribe—Estmaciones y proyecciones de población, 1950* (Santiago, Chile: United Nations, 2002), 38, Table 11a, "América Latina: Estimaciones y Proyecciones de la Población Total."

13. International Labor Organisation, *Global Employment Trends Brief,* February 2005, 7.

14. Jaime Saavedra, "Labor Markets During the 1990s," 246.

15. Ruth Berins Collier and Samuel Handlin, "Shifting Interest Regimes of the Working Classes in Latin America," *Institute of Industrial Relations Working Paper Series* (Berkeley: University of California, 2005), 7.

16. Anonymous interview conducted by Christopher Sabatini, Caracas, Venezuela, 25 June 2002.

17. Steve Ellner, "Organized Labor and the Challenge of *Chavismo,*" in Steve Ellner and Daniel Hellinger, eds., *Venezuelan Politics in the Chávez Era: Class, Polarization and Conflict* (Boulder, Colo.: Lynne Rienner, 2003).

18. Ruth Berins Collier and Samuel Handlin, "Shifting Interest Regimes of the Working Classes in Latin America," 14.

19. Studies done for the Research Network of the Inter-American Development Bank have found a negative relationship between high barriers to firing and employment demand in Argentina, Colombia, and Peru, as well as Barbados. See Research Network Working Papers R-388, R-391, R-393, and R-394 at *www.iadb.org/RES/pub_List.cfm?pub_type_id=RNP.* The most rigorous cross-country analysis of the effects of firing costs on employment concludes that a reduction in the costs associated with shedding workers reduces worker tenure but is also associated with a decline in the duration of unemployment. See Heckman and Pages, "The Cost of Job Security Regulation."

II

Case Studies: South America

8

ARGENTINA:
FROM KIRCHNER TO KIRCHNER

Steven Levitsky and María Victoria Murillo

Steven Levitsky *is professor of government at Harvard University.* ***María Victoria Murillo*** *is associate professor of political science and international affairs at Columbia University. Together they edited* Argentine Democracy: the Politics of Institutional Weakness *(2005). This essay originally appeared in the April 2008 issue of the* Journal of Democracy.

Argentina's 28 October 2007 presidential election contrasted sharply with the one that preceded it. The 2003 race took place in the aftermath of an unprecedented economic collapse and the massive December 2001 protests that toppled two presidents in a span of ten days. That election—which was won by little-known (Peronist) Justicialist Party governor Néstor Kirchner—was held in a climate of political fragmentation and uncertainty. Little uncertainty surrounded the 2007 campaign. After four years of strong economic growth, and with the opposition in shambles, a victory by the incumbent Peronists was a foregone conclusion. The only surprise was that Kirchner, who remained popular, chose not to seek reelection. Instead, his wife, Senator Cristina Fernández de Kirchner, ran in his place.

Cristina Kirchner captured 45 percent of the vote, easily defeating Elisa Carrió of the left-of-center Civic Coalition (23 percent) and Kirchner's former economics minister, Roberto Lavagna (17 percent), who was backed by the Radical Civic Union (UCR). In addition to winning more than three-quarters of Argentina's 23 governorships, the Justicialist Party (PJ) and other pro-Kirchner allies won large majorities in both legislative chambers. In the Chamber of Deputies, the lower house of Argentina's bicameral National Congress, progovernment Peronists and other Kirchner allies (including pro-Kirchner Radicals) won 160 of 257 seats, while dissident Peronists won another 10 seats. The loosely organized Civic Coalition won 31 seats, while the UCR won 30 seats. In the

Senate, the Kirchnerista forces controlled 47 of 74 seats after the election, while another 5 seats were held by dissident Peronists. The PJ thus emerged from the election in a dominant position. Opposition forces were split into at least three blocs (the UCR, the Civic Coalition, and the center-right Republican Proposal [PRO]), and thus posed no serious challenge. Indeed, future challenges seemed more likely to come from within the PJ.

Cristina Kirchner is the first woman ever to be elected president of Argentina. (Isabel Perón, who had been elected vice-president as her husband Juan Perón's running mate in 1973, succeeded to the presidency upon his death the following year.) Kirchner's success, however, was rooted not in her gender—she performed better among men than among women—but in her status as the candidate of a successful incumbent government.

Néstor Kirchner left office as the most popular outgoing president in modern Argentine history. After taking office in the aftermath of Argentina's worst-ever recession, Kirchner presided over four years of export-led growth, rooted in a competitive exchange rate and soaring commodity prices. The economy grew 9 percent a year between 2003 and 2007, and consequently, living standards improved immensely. Private consumption increased by 52 percent between 2002 and 2007. Unemployment and poverty rates were halved: Unemployment fell from 20 percent in 2002 to 9 percent in 2007, and the poverty rate fell from nearly 50 percent to 27 percent.

Support for Kirchner was also rooted in public policies. Within the parameters of an export-led model and conservative fiscal policy, the Kirchner government pursued several heterodox policies that generated broad support. For one, Kirchner's hard-line position in debt renegotiations following Argentina's 2001 default resulted in the largest debt "haircut" in history (a debt swap worth about 30 percent of the defaulted debt)—an outcome that both won public support and eased the fiscal situation. Second, Kirchner reversed a decade-long pattern of wage-depressing policies by encouraging unions' collective bargaining and pushing through a series of minimum-wage increases.[1] These policies—along with tight labor markets—brought a 70 percent increase in real wages. Kirchner also pushed through a social-security reform that extended access to unemployed and informal-sector workers, thereby bringing more than a million new people into the system. Investment in public works increased more than fivefold under Kirchner, producing a major expansion in housing and infrastructure, while funding for public education and scientific research rose considerably. Overall, public expenditure expanded by more than 30 percent in 2007—a massive election-year increase.

Several noneconomic policies also enhanced public support for Kirchner, particularly among middle-class voters. For example, Kirchner led an overhaul of the Supreme Court, which had been packed by President Carlos Saúl Menem in 1990 and was widely viewed as politicized and corrupt. Encouraged by Kirchner, Congress impeached or forced the resignation of six of the nine Supreme Court members and replaced them with respected jurists. On the human rights front, Kirchner pushed successfully for the annulment of laws limiting prosecution for human rights violations during the 1976–83 dictatorship—namely, the 1986 Final Point Law establishing a deadline after which new human rights cases could not be launched, the 1987 Due Obedience laws protecting junior officers from prosecution, and the 1990 pardon of top generals responsible for the Dirty War.

Cristina Kirchner's victory was also rooted in the continued strength of the Peronist party machine. Argentina's only mass party, the PJ possessed a stable electoral base as well as a grassroots organization and activist base that dwarfed those of its rivals. PJ networks operated throughout the country, mobilizing voters through a mix of clientelism and other appeals. In many interior provinces, where clientelism is most extensive and Peronist machines are most dominant, Cristina Kirchner's victory was overwhelming. In some northern provinces (for example, Formosa, Salta, and Santiago del Estero), she won more than 70 percent of the vote, more than quadrupling her nearest rival.

Although the PJ was highly fragmented, with two and even three rival Peronist lists competing in many provinces, the electoral cost of this fragmentation was limited by the phenomenon of *listas colectoras* (fusion candidacies), in which multiple mayoral and gubernatorial candidates supported—and shared a ballot with—the same presidential candidate. Effectively a substitute for party primaries, the *listas colectoras* allowed Cristina Kirchner to accumulate the votes of diverse and competing tickets that might otherwise have backed her rivals.

Finally, Kirchner's victory was a product of opposition weakness. The middle class–based UCR—the only non-Peronist party ever to win a clean election in Argentina—weakened considerably during the 1990s, and after the disastrous Radical presidency of Fernando de la Rúa (1999–2001), it began to disintegrate. After suffering important defections on its right (Ricardo López Murphy) and left (Elisa Carrió), the UCR finished sixth in the 2003 election, with barely 2 percent of the vote. Under Néstor Kirchner, five of the UCR's six governors and more than a third of its 476 mayors rejected the Radical leadership and instead backed the government, earning the label "K Radicals." In the 2007 election, the K Radicals supported Cristina Kirchner, not UCR-backed candidate Roberto Lavagna, and one of them, Julio Cobos, became Ms. Kirchner's running mate.

None of the opposition parties that emerged in the wake of the UCR's collapse—most notably, Carrió's Alternative for a Republic of Equals (ARI), López Murphy's Federal Recreate Movement (MFR), and Mauricio Macri's PRO, possessed a national organization or a significant activist base. According to a survey carried out by Ernesto Calvo and María Victoria Murillo, the PJ has nearly 300,000 activists (almost 1 percent of the population) across the country. This is nearly ten times as many activists as ARI and PRO combined.[2] Indeed, the opposition's activities were confined largely to urban centers. Consequently, although elections in the major metropolitan areas remained highly competitive (Cristina Kirchner lost in Buenos Aires, Córdoba, and Rosario—the three largest cities in the country), the PJ was virtually unchallenged in many peripheral provinces.

Why Argentina Is Not Venezuela

Néstor Kirchner's presidency was characterized by a significant concentration of executive power. Like Carlos Menem during his first presidential term (1989–95), Kirchner governed at the margins of Congress and other institutions of horizontal accountability. Through November 2007, Kirchner issued 232 executive decrees, a rate (4.3 decrees per month) which matched that of Menem (4.4 per month). Kirchner retained the emergency powers delegated to the executive by Congress during the 2001 crisis, and in 2006 Congress granted him vast discretionary power to modify the budget after its legislative approval. Although Kirchner's reform of the Supreme Court was widely applauded, other executive actions encroached on judicial independence, most notably his successful promotion of a law that enhanced executive control over the Magistrates' Council, the body responsible for overseeing the appointment and removal of federal judges.

Finally, Kirchner concentrated executive power vis-à-vis the provinces. He did this by opening up new sources of revenue (particularly export duties and fees on public services) that unlike existing taxes were not shared between the federal and provincial governments. As a result, the provinces' share of overall revenue fell to barely half of what it had been a decade earlier, which increased provincial governments' dependence on fiscal transfers from the federal government.[3]

The combination of Kirchner's concentration of power and the PJ's growing electoral dominance generated concern that Argentine politics was taking an authoritarian turn. Such characterizations are misleading. The core institutions of democracy remain strong in Argentina: Elections are clean, civil liberties are broadly protected, and the military—author of six coups between 1930 and 1976—has withdrawn from politics. Indeed, despite a Weimar-like hyperinflationary crisis in 1989 and a collapse into depression in 2001 to 2002, the constitutional order has never been interrupted since Argentina's return to democracy. The lopsided PJ victories in the 2005 midterm elections and in 2007 were products of opposition weakness, not abuses by incumbents. The Kirchner government's record on civil liberties was good, and in some areas (such as police handling of public protest), it was clearly superior to the performance of its predecessors.

Argentina's relatively strong democratic record is not a result of its presidents' leadership or good will; rather, this record is rooted in the constraints that society and the polity impose upon the executive. Argentine democracy is buttressed by a broad societal commitment to civil liberties and an extensive infrastructure of civil society organizations committed to their defense.[4] Argentine governments confront a "permanent associative network for the supervision of state authorities."[5] Civic and media organizations serve as agents of "societal accountability," exposing and denouncing (and thus raising the political cost of) state abuse.[6] During the 1990s, for example, large-scale civic campaigns compelled judicial action in response to the 1990 murder of teenager María Soledad Morales (in which members of the governing clan in the province of Catamarca were implicated) and the 1997 killing of news photographer José Luis Cabezas (arranged by a mafia boss with ties to the government). In December 2001, when President de la Rúa declared a state of siege and violently repressed protesters, public repudiation was so overwhelming that he was forced to resign, and when police killed two street protesters *(piqueteros)* in 2002, the intensity of the public outcry led interim president Eduardo Duhalde to shorten his mandate.

Under the first President Kirchner, societal "antibodies" manifested themselves around the reelection issue. After the PJ's landslide victory in the 2005 legislative elections, some critics worried that Kirchner would seek to change the constitution—as he had done while governor of Santa Cruz—to permit unlimited reelection.[7] Thus when Kirchner backed an initiative by Misiones governor Carlos Rovira to rewrite his province's constitution to permit unlimited reelection, the issue quickly gained national attention. Although Peronists dominated Misiones politics (winning six consecutive gubernatorial elections between 1987 and 2007), local civic and opposition forces, led by the Catholic Church, organized a broad opposition campaign and defeated the PJ in the constituent-assembly election. The defeat had an immediate and powerful impact at the national level: Governors in Buenos Aires and Jujuy abandoned reelection projects, and any sort of national initiative became unthinkable.

Argentine presidents are also constrained by other democratically elected actors, particularly governors. Governors and other provincial bosses are powerful players in Argentine politics, not least because they often dominate the nomination process for national legislators. Because most legislators owe their nomination to a provincial boss rather than the national party leadership, discipline within the PJ's legislative bloc hinges to a considerable degree on the president's ability to maintain the support of the governors.[8] Thus, even powerful Peronist presidents such as Menem and Kirchner have never been able to govern unilaterally, as Chávez has done in Venezuela. Rather, they have governed in coalition with—and with the negotiated consent of—party bosses.[9] Kirchnerista efforts to build a "transversal" movement—composed of progressive Peronists and non-Peronist leftists—at the margins of the PJ machine never gained traction. Although Kirchner initially alienated some party bosses, he ultimately needed them to deliver the vote. Prior to the 2005 election, he made his peace with the party machine, and the transversal project was abandoned.

In sum, Néstor Kirchner's ability to concentrate power was limited by robust democratic institutions, a strong civil society, and the nature of his own Peronist coalition. Consequently, he never approached Chávez's centralized and autocratic rule—even at the peak of his popularity and political strength.

It is also important to note that several of the Kirchner government's initiatives enhanced the quality of Argentine democracy. For one, Kirchner improved the quality of the Supreme Court by nominating qualified and independent justices, establishing new procedures—such as public hearings—to ensure greater transparency and accountability in the judicial-nomination process, and reducing the size of the Court from nine justices (a product of the 1990 Court packing) to seven and eventually five. In reducing the Court to its original size (a move that had been demanded by numerous legal, human rights, and civil liberties groups), the government deprived itself of the opportunity to appoint two additional justices. The independence of the remade Supreme Court became manifest in the 2006 *Badaro* case, in which the Court forced the government to index pension payments, and the 2007 *Rosza* case, in which the Court limited the government's use of interim appointments (which are not subject to legislative approval) to fill judgeships. At the time of the ruling, about a fifth of all Argentina's federal jurists held interim appointments.

Néstor Kirchner also made important strides in the area of human rights. As noted above, his government pushed successfully for the nullification of the Alfonsín-era Final Point and Due Obedience laws, which had limited the scope of human rights trials. By 2006, more than five-hundred former military and police officers had been brought up on charges.[10] Kirchner also pushed the courts to annul Menem's 1990 pardon of the top generals responsible for the Dirty War. In July 2007, the Supreme Court declared one of the pardons unconstitutional, which may pave the way for the annulment of all of the pardons.[11]

Finally, Kirchner restored a minimum of public trust in government. The 2001–2002 crisis of governance and the economy triggered a massive withdrawal of public trust from the political elite. According to the Latinobarómetro survey, the percentage of Argentines expressing confidence in their country's political parties fell from 29 percent in 1997 to a stunningly abysmal 4 percent—the lowest in Latin America—in 2002.[12] This crisis of representation was seen in the 2001 midterm election when, in a striking protest against the entire political elite, 22 percent of voters cast blank or spoiled ballots. In two of the country's largest districts, the city of Buenos Aires and the province of Santa Fe, the number of blank and spoiled ballots exceeded that for *all* parties combined. The crisis of representation was also seen in December 2001 protests, when middle-class protesters surrounded each branch of government and chanted *Que se vayan todos!* ("Throw them all out!"). Citizen anger reached such heights that politicians were often physically attacked when they ventured out in public—on downtown streets, in restaurants, and even in their own neighborhoods.

This extraordinary erosion in public trust was rooted in several factors, but one was a widespread perception that the government had grown almost entirely unresponsive to voters' demands. The gap between public opinion and public policy grew particularly acute under de la Rúa, whose Alianza coalition had campaigned on a platform of clean government and social justice but failed to deliver either.[13] The Alianza government was implicated in a Senate bribery scandal in 2000, and its repeated austerity measures convinced many Argentines that de la Rúa was more responsive to international creditors and bond markets than to voters.

Kirchner reversed this pattern. Whereas de la Rúa appeared constrained to the point of paralysis, Kirchner sought to expand the government's (real or perceived) room for maneuver by launching high-profile battles against the very entities that were seen to constrain his predecessors: the military, the IMF, bondholders, and foreign and domestic capitalists. Although the economic merits of some of these initiatives (such as price controls or paying off the IMF debt in full) were open to question, the *political* consequences were clear and important: Argentines perceived their government as having responded to public demands, and consequently their support for Kirchner, optimism about the future, and support for democracy all rose considerably.

Challenges for Argentine Democracy

Although Argentine democracy is robust, it nevertheless remains more crisis-prone than those of comparable middle-income countries in Latin America. Two problems continue to undermine the quality of Argentine democracy. The first is the weakness of the non-Peronist opposition. The Argentine party system has suffered a partial collapse.

Although the PJ survived the 1989 and 2001–2002 crises, the UCR—the only other significant national party since the 1940s—has ceased to be a national force. The Radicals' share of the presidential vote fell from more than 50 percent in 1983 to just 2 percent in 2003, and in

2007 their representation in Congress (30 of 257 seats) reached a historic low. The party's decomposition—which began with the defection of leaders such as Carrió and López Murphy after 2001—continued under Kirchner with the emergence of the "K Radicals." The UCR is not necessarily dead. It retains a national infrastructure of local leaders and activist networks, which creates the potential for a future recovery (as occurred with APRA in Peru). However, the Radicals have not seriously contended for the presidency since 1999, leaving the party's status as a national-level electoral force very much in doubt.

The UCR's collapse has not been accompanied by the emergence of stable new parties. The spread of mass-media technologies has reduced politicians' incentives to invest in party organization, and the volatility of the urban middle-class electorate that became "available" after the UCR's collapse has made it difficult to consolidate new partisan alternatives. With numerous forces—including, beginning in 2003, the Kirchner government—competing for ex-Radical votes, no significant non-Peronist alternative has taken root. All the major new parties that emerged during the 1980s and 1990s were weakly organized and failed to extend beyond the major metropolitan centers. None survived for much more than a decade. The two new parties that emerged in 2003, ARI and the MFR, have fared little better. The MFR received just 1 percent of the vote in 2007 and has been effectively displaced by the center-right PRO (another Buenos Aires–centered party). The ARI, meanwhile, suffered a serious schism following the 2007 election.

Since the 1940s, only the Peronists and the UCR have built national organizations, mobilized large memberships, and established stable identities in the electorate. With the collapse of the UCR, the non-Peronist half of the party system has become a fragmented collection of personalistic vehicles, local patronage-based machines, and short-lived programmatic parties. The result has been increasing fragmentation and fluidity.

The weakness of the non-Peronist opposition has several important consequences. Most obviously, it leaves the opposition increasingly incapable of challenging the PJ in the electoral arena. In both 2003 and 2007, non-Peronist forces were divided into two or three camps, none of which posed a credible electoral (much less governing) alternative. As a result, the PJ emerged as the de facto dominant party. In the 2003 presidential election, the top two finishers were *both* Peronists, and in the 2005 legislative elections, no non-Peronist party won even 10 percent of the national vote. In presidential elections, opposition-party weakness might be overcome with relative ease. Because much of Argentina's large middle-class electorate leans anti-Peronist, a coalition of non-Peronist forces (as in 1999), or even a candidate who emerges as a focal point for non-Peronist voters, might be sufficient to defeat PJ presidential candidates.

At the provincial and legislative levels, however, the implications of opposition weakness are more serious. Because the smaller interior provinces—where PJ dominance is greatest—are overrepresented in Congress, non-Peronist representation in that body is eroding. After the 2007 election, the pro-Kirchner bloc in the Chamber of Deputies was more than twice the size of the three largest opposition blocs combined. In the Senate, PJ dominance was reinforced by malapportionment and an electoral rule, established in 1994, that grants two Senate seats to the first-place finisher in each province and a third seat to the party that finishes second. Due to a combination of opposition weakness and provincial-level Peronist schisms, which led to the emergence of two and even three pro-Kirchner tickets, pro-Kirchner slates finished first *and* second (thus collecting all three Senate seats) in provinces such as Salta, Santiago del Estero, and Rio Negro (where the minority seat was won by a K Radical). Pro-Kirchner forces captured 42 of 72 Senate seats, which—together with allied provincial parties—gave them nearly two-thirds of the upper house.

Danger Signs Ahead

Although the PJ's electoral dominance is unlikely to lead to the emergence of a hegemonic regime, it is likely to have several negative consequences for democracy. First, although opposition forces remain capable of winning the presidency, they are increasingly incapable of governing. As Calvo and Murillo have argued, opposition parties' weakness in the legislature, in the provinces, and in society make governing extremely difficult,[14] since non-Peronist presidents are almost certain to confront Peronist-controlled legislatures and mostly Peronist governors. And given opposition parties' limited grassroots presence and weak ties to unions, business associations, and other social actors, non-Peronist presidents would be vulnerable to the kind of governability crises that destroyed the Alfonsín and de la Rúa presidencies.

Opposition-party collapse may also exacerbate Argentina's crisis of political representation. The failure of the Alianza government in 1999 to 2001 left much of the non-Peronist electorate without effective partisan representation. It was largely these "orphaned" voters who cast blank and spoiled ballots in the 2001 election and swelled the ranks of the *Que se vayan todos!* protests in 2001 and 2002.[15]

Finally, even if Néstor and Cristina Kirchner are unlikely to violate seriously the democratic rules of the game, the absence of a credible opposition or serious electoral competition threatens to diminish executive accountability even further. At the very least, the lack of oversight and accountability increases the risk of major policy mistakes. As Argentine history has shown repeatedly, moreover, low executive accountability also increases the likelihood of corruption and other serious abuses.

A second challenge facing Argentine democracy is the persistent problem of institutional weakness.[16] Institutional strength may be defined along two dimensions: 1) *enforcement,* or the degree to which the rules that exist on paper are complied with in practice; and 2) *stability,* or the degree to which formal rules survive minor fluctuations in the distribution of power and preferences.[17] Many Argentine political and economic institutions are weak on one or both of these dimensions.

Between 1930 and 1983, Argentina suffered a long era of regime instability—marked by six military coups—during which the Constitution, the electoral system, Congress, the Supreme Court and other institutions were repeatedly suspended, circumvented, or modified. This established a pattern of institutional fluidity that persisted for decades. To take one example, from 1928 to 2003, not a single presidential term prescribed by the constitution was ever complied with in full. In 1930, 1962, 1966, 1976, 1989, and 2001, elected presidents were removed before the end of their respective mandates. Two presidents—Perón and Menem—completed their terms, but both of them modified the constitution to permit a second term. Similarly, although the constitution guarantees Supreme Court justices lifetime tenure, this constitutional guarantee has been routinely violated since the 1940s, as incoming governments—both civilian and military—have routinely removed unfriendly justices and replaced them with allies.[18]

Argentina's core democratic institutions—elections, civil liberties, and civilian control of the military—strengthened considerably after 1983. Nevertheless, many areas of political and economic life remain plagued by institutional weakness. During the 1990s, the rules of the game governing executive-legislative relations, the judiciary, federalism, candidate selection, taxation, and central-bank independence were repeatedly challenged, violated, manipulated, or changed. Some patterns of institutional manipulation continued under Kirchner. Examples include the reform of the Magistrates' Council, the 2006 "superpowers" law that granted the president vast discretionary authority over the budget, the elimination of open primaries to nominate presidential candidates (a law established in 2002), and the government's assault on the once-independent state statistical agency, INDEC, by firing INDEC technocrats and creating dubious new procedures for calculating inflation.

In other areas, the Kirchner government respected the letter of the law while violating its spirit. Thus, although Congress's impeachment or threatened impeachment of six of nine Supreme Court justices—which was encouraged by Kirchner—was legal, it reinforced the pattern of executive encroachment that has existed since the 1940s. More ambiguous, perhaps, was Cristina Kirchner's presidential candidacy. The Kirchner team almost certainly sought to extend its stay in the presidency beyond two terms. Yet as we have seen, an effort to modify the constitution to permit Néstor a third term would almost certainly have met widespread societal opposition. Cristina's presidential bid—which would allow

Néstor to run again in 2011—was legal, but it nevertheless smacked of institutional manipulation, especially since Ms. Kirchner enjoyed most of the privileges of incumbency during the campaign.

Persistent institutional weakness has had serious consequences for the quality of Argentine democracy. Compared to other middle-income democracies in the region (Brazil, Chile, Mexico, Uruguay), institutions of horizontal accountability remain weak in Argentina, permitting a higher degree of executive domination. Compared to these other democracies, Argentina's legislative and judicial branches are underdeveloped.

The Argentine Congress has few experienced leaders, virtually no professional staff, and little technical expertise, and its committee system and oversight bodies are poorly developed.[19] Legislative ineffectiveness is rooted in several factors, including the military's repeated closures of Congress between 1930 and 1976. And whereas the Brazilian, Chilean, and Mexican legislatures grew steadily stronger during the 1990s and 2000s, Argentina's did not. Since 1989, core legislative functions have repeatedly been delegated away via "emergency laws" that have granted budgetary and regulatory "superpowers" to the executive. Moreover, few politicians have invested seriously in legislative careers: The average legislative career in Argentina is 2.9 years, compared to 5.5 years in Brazil, 8 years in Chile, and 9 years in Uruguay.[20] "Amateur" legislators are less likely to invest in specialization, in serious committee work, or in building effective institutions of legislative oversight.[21] Indeed, the Argentine Congress is deficient in all these areas. On the Congressional Capability Index compiled by Ernesto Stein and his coauthors, which measures technical expertise, committee strength, and the professionalization of legislators, Argentina scores "low" (along with Guatemala, Honduras, and Peru), whereas Brazil, Chile, and Uruguay rank "high" and Mexico ranks "medium."[22]

A similar story can be told about the judiciary. On the World Economic Forum's 2004 index of judicial independence, Argentina ranked thirteenth out of eighteen Latin American countries—below Ecuador, Guatemala, Honduras, and Peru. By contrast, Uruguay ranked first, Chile second, Brazil third, and Mexico sixth.[23] A major source of executive dominance over the judiciary is the insecurity of judicial tenure. Although lifetime tenure for Supreme Court justices has been enshrined in the constitution since 1853, it has been violated repeatedly since the 1940s.[24] This did not change with democratization. Indeed, three of the four presidents popularly elected between 1983 and 2003 (Alfonsín, Menem, and Néstor Kirchner) pushed successfully for the removal of sitting justices. Due to repeated court packing, the average tenure of Argentine Supreme Court justices between 1960 and 1995 was barely four years, which is less than half the corresponding figure in Brazil and less than a third of that found in Chile.[25]

Crisis and institutional weakness tend to be mutually reinforcing. Institutional weakness increases the likelihood of political and economic crisis, which in turn triggers efforts to circumvent or change the rules. For example, the 2001–2002 crisis gave rise to widespread demands that the institutional slate be wiped clean (again): There were calls for immediate elections, a purge of the Supreme Court, a new constitution, and an overhaul of the electoral system. The crisis clearly facilitated Kirchner's encroachment on legislative and judicial authority. Although his actions did help to restore credibility to many public institutions, they nevertheless reinforced the dominant pattern since 1930: When crises hit, the players and the rules are changed. The Supreme Court provides a clear example of this dilemma. During the 2001–2002 crisis, many Argentines complained about the absence of judicial independence *and* demanded a purge of the Court. Kirchner's purge produced a better and more publicly legitimate Court, but it came at the cost of another blow to the institution of secure judicial tenure, thereby reinforcing existing patterns of judicial weakness.

Missed Opportunities, Unfinished Business

Despite his successes, Néstor Kirchner missed several opportunities to improve the quality of Argentine democracy. Consequently, his wife inherited unfinished business on several important fronts. On the economic front, inflation—a longstanding problem that has often had deleterious political consequences in Argentina—rose considerably after 2003. Price controls and measurement shenanigans notwithstanding, the Kirchner government was unwilling to undertake growth-inhibiting measures that most economists deemed necessary to combat price hikes. Although favorable currency conditions and commodity prices limited inflation's impact on Argentina's international competitiveness, the government's "official index," which lacks credibility, could not disguise domestic price increases. Argentina also faces a looming energy crisis, as increasing demand—caused by price controls and economic growth—runs up against limited supply due to lack of investment. Argentina will become a net energy importer in 2008, and despite increased public-sector investment and scheduled price increases, the country may soon face costly shortages.

The new Kirchner government also faces a problem of public security. In the aftermath of the 2001–2002 crisis, the level of violent crime increased markedly—and, crucially, so did the public perception that crime was a problem. Moreover, governments had failed repeatedly to reform police forces that were known to be corrupt and complicit in criminal activity. Néstor Kirchner launched an overhaul of the police force, but his alliances with progressives and human rights groups and his own ideological orientation left him reluctant to adopt classic "law-and-order" policies that might threaten civil liberties. Indeed, Kirchner publicly rejected calls for "strong-hand" policies. He refused to use force against street blockades and other forms of civil disobedience, and he appointed Supreme Court justices known for their commitment to defendants' rights.

This opened up space for law-and-order appeals on the right. The salience of the public-security issue was evidenced by the rise of Juan Carlos Blumberg, a businessman who led a series of massive demonstrations in Buenos Aires after his son Axel was kidnapped and killed in 2004. Although the crime issue did not translate into electoral support for the right in 2007—Blumberg ran for governor of Buenos Aires and fared poorly—the issue still looms large in public opinion. Balancing public demands for security with her commitment to civil and human rights will be a major challenge for Cristina Kirchner. As in other Latin American countries with left-of-center governments, failure on the public-security front could fuel the rise of law-and-order populism, which could place many hard-won civil liberties at risk.

In the area of social policy, Néstor Kirchner missed an opportunity to redistribute wealth and reduce income inequality. Though widely considered left-of-center, the Kirchner government neglected social policies aimed at combating poverty. Indeed, despite unprecedented fiscal health, the government did not invest heavily in either conditional cash transfers to the poor, or health and education programs for them, as did the left-of-center governments of Brazil and Chile. Indeed, social programs established to deal with the poverty emergency created by the 2001–2002 crisis, such as the Jefes y Jefas (Heads of Household) program, were scaled back. Rather than create new social programs, the Kirchner government invested heavily in public works. Consequently, although unemployment and poverty rates declined sharply under Kirchner, these declines were rooted almost entirely in economic growth. In fact, levels of poverty and inequality remained higher in 2007 than they were during the mid-1990s.

Thus after four years of a left-of-center Peronist government with vast resources at its disposal, levels of inequality and social marginality, which had increased markedly since the 1970s, remained high. Although high demand for labor improved salaries and conditions for the formal-sector workforce, the conditions facing informal-sector workers, and particularly the "structurally unemployed," remained bleak. Until recently, high levels of marginality and inequality were relatively unknown in Argentina. If these problems are not addressed, they could lead to the kind of social polarization and conflict that has all too frequently threatened the stability of Latin American democracies.

Finally, Néstor Kirchner's government did little to strengthen political institutions. Mr. Kirchner's extraordinary popularity created a rare opportunity to invest in institution-building. By doing so, Kirchner could have avoided the fate that befell nearly all of his predecessors: seeing initial successes wiped away by subsequent crises and policy overhauls. For the most part, however, Kirchner did not engage in institution-building. Argentina's political and economic institutions remain strikingly weak—far weaker than those of Brazil, Chile, Mexico, or Uruguay. As a result, the economy and polity that his wife inherits remain vulnerable. Argentina has been down this road before. Good times notwithstanding, the specter of yet another crisis remains.

NOTES

1. Sebastián Etchemendy and Ruth Berins Collier, "Down but Not Out: Union Resurgence and Segmented Neocorporatism in Argentina (2003–2007)," *Politics and Society* 35 (September 2007): 363–401.

2. See Ernesto Calvo and María Victoria Murillo, "How Many Clients Does It Take to Win an Election? Estimating the Size and Structure of Political Networks in Argentina and Chile," paper presented at the Elections and Distribution Workshop, Yale University, 26–27 October 2007.

3. On average, Argentine provinces depended on the federal government for 50 percent of their income in 2007. See Mara Laudonia, "Las provincias agotaron los beneficios fiscales de la devaluación," *iEco* (*Clarín* [Buenos Aires]), 6 December 2007. Available at *www.ieco.clarin.com/notas/2007/12/06/01558399.html*.

4. See Enrique Peruzzotti, "Towards a New Politics: Citizenship and Rights in Contemporary Argentina," *Citizenship Studies* 6 (March 2002): 77–93.

5. Enrique Peruzzotti, "The Nature of the New Argentine Democracy: The Delegative Democracy Argument Revisited," *Journal of Latin American Studies* 33 (February 2001): 142.

6. Catalina Smulovitz and Enrique Peruzzotti, "Societal Accountability in Latin America," *Journal of Democracy* 11 (October 2000): 147–58.

7. Mariano Grondona, "El Despertar de la Resistencia Republicana," *La Nación* (Buenos Aires), 27 August 2006.

8. Mark Jones et al., "Congress, Political Careers, and the Provincial Connection," in Pablo T. Spiller and Mariano Tommasi, eds., *The Institutional Foundations of Public Policy in Argentina: A Transactions Cost Approach* (New York: Cambridge University Press, 2007).

9. Indeed, the difficulty of achieving legislative discipline helps explain why Cristina Kirchner sought an extension of emergency executive-decree authority—despite the PJ's overwhelming legislative majority—immediately after taking office.

10. *Página/12* (Buenos Aires), 2 January 2006.

11. *Clarín,* 13 July 2007.

12. Omar Sanchez, "Argentina's Landmark 2003 Presidential Election: Renewal and Continuity," *Bulletin of Latin American Research* 24 (October 2005): 457.

13. Enrique Peruzzotti, "Demanding Accountable Government: Citizens, Politicians, and the Perils of Representative Democracy in Argentina," in Steven Levitsky and María Victoria Murillo, eds., *Argentine Democracy: The Politics of Institutional Weakness* (University Park: Penn State University Press, 2005), 229–49.

14. Ernesto Calvo and María Victoria Murillo, "Who Delivers? Partisan Clients in the Argentine Electoral Market," *American Journal of Political Science* 48 (October 2004): 742–57; and Calvo and Murillo, "The New Iron Law of Argentine Politics? Partisanship, Clientelism and Governability in Contemporary Argentina," in Levitsky and Murillo, eds., *Argentine Democracy,* 207–26.

15. Marcelo Escolar and Ernesto Calvo, "Ultimas imágenes antes del naufragio: Las elecciones del 2001 en Argentina," *Desarrollo Económico* 42 (January–March 2003): 25–44; Juan Carlos Torre, "Citizens versus Political Class: The Crisis of Partisan Representation," in Levitsky and Murillo, eds., *Argentine Democracy,* 165–80.

16. See Carlos Nino, *Un país al margen de la ley* (Buenos Aires: Emecé, 1992); Guillermo O'Donnell, "Delegative Democracy," *Journal of Democracy* 5 (January 1994): 55–69; and Levitsky and Murillo, eds., *Argentine Democracy.*

17. Steven Levitsky and María Victoria Murillo, "Conclusion," in Levitsky and Murillo, eds., *Argentine Democracy,* 270–75.

18. Gretchen Helmke, *Courts under Constraints: Judges, Generals, and Presidents in Argentina* (New York: Cambridge University Press, 2004).

19. Scott Morgenstern and Luigi Manzetti, "Legislative Oversight: Interests and Institutions in the United States and Argentina," in Scott Mainwaring and Christopher Welna, eds., *Democratic Accountability in Latin America* (New York: Oxford University Press, 2003).

20. Ernesto Stein et al., *The Politics of Policies: Economic and Social Progress in Latin America, 2006 Report* (Cambridge: Harvard University Press, 2006), 55.

21. Mark P. Jones et al., "Amateur Legislators—Professional Politicians: The Consequences of Party-Centered Electoral Rules in a Federal System," *American Journal of Political Science* 46 (July 2002): 656–69.

22. Stein et al., *Politics of Policies,* 55.

23. Stein et al., *Politics of Policies,* 88.

24. Helmke, *Courts under Constraints.*

25. Stein et al., *Politics of Policies,* 86.

9

POLITICS, MARKETS, AND SOCIETY IN BRAZIL

Lourdes Sola

Lourdes Sola, *professor of political science at the University of São Paulo, is president of the International Political Science Association. She is author or coauthor of many works, including* Statecrafting Monetary Authority: Democratization and Financial Order in Brazil *(with Laurence Whitehead, 2006).This essay originally appeared in the April 2008 issue of the* Journal of Democracy.

Latin America and especially Brazil—whose 190 million people make it by far the region's largest country—have been enjoying new economic and political prospects whose full measure theorists of democratization have yet to take. Theory, by and large, is still stuck in the 1980s and 1990s—decades when external shocks buffeted the region and a generally restrictive international environment limited democracy's horizons. It assumes that the responses to economic crises followed a similar pattern in the relevant countries, with economic stabilization and market-friendly reforms preceding social reform and often at odds with it. Lately, however, an unprecedented liquidity bonanza, sustained hikes in commodity prices, the rising global weight of newly industrializing powers such as India and China, and the entry of tens of millions of new consumers into the world economy have brought fresh growth and possibilities and changed the strategic incentives facing elected leaders across the region.

As structural economic changes widen politicians' scope for discretion, a shift in analytical focus is needed. What happens when the economy becomes an *enabling* rather than a disabling factor for politicians in democratizing countries? Will the processes associated with democratization become more rather than less predictable? Will their quality rise or fall? How much did the specific mix of market discipline and social reform that Brazil adopted during "hard times" affect that country's chances to profit from the current international environment? Will Brazil soon find itself in a virtuous circle that links growing prosperity to greater equity and more robust, broad-based, and effective democracy? Or does such a question betray too great an emphasis on material factors, perhaps even amounting to economic reductionism?

The weakness of such reductionism becomes clear from a glance at current developments in Latin America, where different countries are taking various paths amid the new possibilities. In Bolivia, Ecuador, and Venezuela, elected politicians are turning back to an amply funded state as their preferred engine of transformation, with large doses of economic nationalism and illiberal constitutionalism added to the mix. By contrast, Chile even under Socialist presidents Ricardo Lagos and Michelle Bachelet has stayed faithful to both markets and liberal constitutionalism—the very model, as it were, of a happy match between economic liberalization and political democratization.

Brazil has been following a more convoluted path, although it appears to be managing a similar confluence, satisfying both investors and the voters who put the left-of-center Workers' Party (PT) into office. In Brazil's case, the market disciplines adopted by President Luiz Inácio "Lula" da Silva upon his 2002 election were meant to address the crisis of confidence that had accompanied his win, as investors feared a break with the macroeconomic policies and the moderately market-friendly reforms of his predecessor, Fernando Henrique Cardoso of the Brazilian Social Democratic Party (PSDB), who served as president from 1995 to 2002.[1]

Keeping investors happy was a political as well as an economic necessity, and explains why Lula and the PT—long the standard-bearers of Brazil's leftist opposition—chose continuity with Cardoso's macroeconomic and social policies. On the social front, continuity was eased by certain unique features that had characterized Brazil's previous responses to the adverse international environment. For in contrast to the dominant theoretical consensus, Brazil's 1980s drive toward social reform had *preceded* the adoption of market disciplines. In the 1990s, Cardoso's administration then pressed market-friendly reforms and a renewed drive toward social reform at one and the same time.

The contrast between the restrictive economic conditions of 2002 and the more prosperous ones that prevailed four years later, when Lula won a second term, provides a window onto the ways in which his administration's strategic decisions have changed while he has been in office. Among other things, this window can help us to assess how the strengths and weaknesses of Brazil's democratic institutions figured in the calculations of the new governmental elites. With the economic strains that once backed market discipline now lessening, we can ask: How firmly embedded are these elites' twin commitments to representative democracy and to market-friendly policies? Could it be that an improving economy—usually taken to boost hopes for democracy—is actually helping to expose and even to reinforce the constitutional weaknesses that beset Brazil's political system?

To embed democracy and secure economic stability takes time, patience, planning, and good leadership. This is all the more so in an extremely unequal society such as Brazil's, where democratic institutions are still consolidating, experience with citizenship is limited, and rights are poorly secured.[2] Looking back over the last two decades allows us to survey the distinctive democratization path that Brazil has followed as it has simultaneously sought to reduce inequality, pursue social reform, and open itself to the demands and promises of markets. Brazil's experience belies the notion that the debt crisis of 1982 and its consequences (including economic liberalization and stabilization) produced an "assault on the state" and socially regressive results everywhere.

The Distributive Dimension

Even as Brazil's "developmentalist state" headed toward a crisis of legitimacy and solvency in the 1980s, the country was witnessing a shift, eventually enshrined in the 1988 Constitution, toward the fuller social and political incorporation of those—such as rural workers—who had long been left on the system's edges. Macroeconomic instability and hyperinflation eventually passed thanks to structural adjustment and other reforms, but the extension of rights via detailed laws and the intense efforts of successive presidents endured.[3] In short, the socioeconomically conservative tenor that modernization had long assumed in Brazil was giving way to something more liberal, more thoroughly republican in spirit, and more friendly to the cause of democratization.

Yet broad currents of statism and economic nationalism continued to run strong. For example, the inclusion of rural workers in the 1980s took place through corporatist structures that had been devised fifty years earlier with organized urban workers in mind. Such arrangements, moreover, enjoyed a constitutional status that made them formidable barriers to economic liberalization and slowed Brazil's ability to respond to external economic challenges.

The broad social reforms that began in the 1980s gathered momentum and moved toward a tipping point in 1993,[4] even as the embrace of market-friendly changes in economic policy was growing stronger. Cardoso's administration oversaw the expansion of universal public programs in health, education, and assistance to the elderly and disabled, as well as the implementation of such conditioned cash-income transfer programs as Bolsa Escola, Bolsa Alimentação, and Projeto Alvorada. The Comunidade Solidária program targeted the poorest municipalities with basic social programs to help provide more and better health care, primary schooling, and (later) job training for people living there. Other targeted land-reform and poverty-relief efforts sought to assist rural dwellers.

This transformation of the welfare system appears all the more remarkable considering the external economic shocks that Brazil was feeling from the Mexican peso crisis of 1994–95, the Asian currency crisis of 1997, the Russian bond default of 1998, and the crisis of confidence surrounding Lula's election. And yet the engineering of new and elaborate institutions to make real the social rights declared by the 1988 Constitution went forward in tandem with the deepening of trade liberalization; the end of constitutional restrictions on capital mobility; the privatization of certain public enterprises as well as bankrupt state and private banks; and a Fiscal Responsibility Law that disciplined the relationship between the federal and subfederal governments while heightening transparency and accountability.

Although branded "neoliberal" by its foes, Cardoso's administration saw social spending rise more than ninefold, from US$1.3 billion in 1995 to $12.3 billion in 2002. The social-policy gains, moreover, appear to be sustainable. Brazil's Gini coefficient (a standard gauge of income inequality) showed a trend toward equality by dropping from 0.63 in 1989 to 0.56 in 2004, while the number of Brazilians living in poverty declined by a quarter over the same period.

Even as Lula has stood by his commitment to macroeconomic stability, favorable structural changes in the economy from 2004 on have enabled the growth of the conditioned income-transfer programs that began under Cardoso, and which are known collectively as the Bolsa Familia (Family Stipend). In just three years beginning in 2004, the number of Brazilians benefiting from these programs more than doubled. By 2006, 11.5 million households would be included. For the decade beginning in 1996, the overall impact of *all* conditioned income transfers was a 21 percent reduction in the Gini coefficient.

Lula's commitment to macroeconomic stability and to meeting Brazil's international financial obligations surprised many. The months leading up to his landslide 61 percent victory in the 27 October 2002 presidential election saw investors become so worried that he would reject market discipline and repudiate Brazil's debts that the country's currency lost half its value, while its Gross Domestic Product (GDP) shrank 6 percent and its borrowing costs spiked.

To one degree or another, the business community, the middle class, and voters in the smallest and poorest municipalities *(grotões)* shared investors' anxieties. Yet most Brazilians remained even more upset over the mediocre 2.3 percent annual economic growth that their country had struggled to achieve on Cardoso's watch, and they rated job and income growth as their top economic concerns. By mid-2002, as Lula's lead over Cardoso's designated successor José Serra was coming to seem ever more solid, the PT's strategists reached out to centrist and center-right voters with a platform promising to abide by the terms of a $30-billion bailout agreement between Cardoso's government and the International Monetary Fund. The platform also vowed to devote 3.75 percent of GNP to pay the interest on Brazil's foreign debt, to hit inflation-reduction targets, and to honor existing contracts. Marketing guru Duda Mendonça devised a communications strategy designed to win over various resistant groups in the electorate. Investors remained largely unpersuaded, however, and market skepticism prevailed.

Throughout 2003, Lula's young administration strove to close the critical gap between soaring electoral performance and abysmal economic credibility. The PT's strategists accepted the market's demands in the areas of macroeconomic policy, relative (but nonstatutory) autonomy for the central bank, and vowed to take further steps toward the restructuring of the public-sector pension system. Yet they refused to embrace microeconomic reforms to strengthen independent regulatory agencies and corporate governance in the public sector.

This early atmosphere of crisis was long gone by the time Lula faced reelection in 2006. Strong foreign demand for commodities and Brazilian-made goods plus the effects of structural adjustment had turned the country from a debtor into a creditor. Starting in 2004, the inflow of direct investment ran strong. Changes in the global economy—along with moderate economic liberalization—enabled Brazil to reap the benefits of rising exports, particularly in the commodities sector. As of 2007, Brazil's government was seeking to accelerate growth even further through the expansion of investment opportunities and credit.

A Tale of Two Elections

At first glance, the presidential elections of 2002 and 2006 seem remarkably similar. In each case, Lula won a runoff with slightly more than 60 percent of the vote, while his PSDB rival was stuck in the high 30s. Yet the commonalities mask critical differences. Not only did economic conditions change sharply, but so did the ways in which different regions and classes voted. In 2002, Lula won first-round victories in all but a trio of Brazil's 27 states, two of which voted for "favorite-son" candidates. In the 2002 runoff, he won every state except Alagoas in the Northeast. In 2006, by contrast, Lula lost the first round in eleven states, while the PSDB's Geraldo Alckmin, a little-known governor, finished the runoff having won seven states, mostly in southern, southeastern, and west-central Brazil.

The socioeconomic composition of the PT vote changed as well. In 2002, Lula had fared best in the more developed areas of the South and Southeast, and among the wealthiest and best-educated urban voters. In 2006, the Bolsa Família helped him to win the poorest municipalities, most of which cluster in the North and Northeast, the traditional redoubt of conservative parties. But the size of the record tallies that he compiled in those regions shows that his appeal there went beyond the poor to reach the middle and upper classes as well. The Bolsa plus a 15 percent hike in the minimum wage had, it seems, exerted a multiplier effect on local economies. Retirees and nonunion workers in the cities also benefited from Lula's wage and pension reforms.

Even as Lula was winning about the same share of the total vote (while losing in more states) from 2002 to 2006, his party was reeling from scandals and watching its losses pile up. Since much of the immediate fallout rained down on the core architects of the winning 2002 strategy and the first-term policies, the PT's troubles left the president with more autonomy vis-à-vis his party than ever.

What do these recent shifts imply about the prospects facing democracy in Brazil? Do the changing socioeconomic and geographic contours of Lula's base provide further evidence for the popular "two Brazils" thesis and its portrayal of a society sharply split between rich and poor?[5] Are we witnessing the birth of *lulismo,* a new political phenomenon based on Lula's popularity and his skilful creation of a direct relationship—largely outside the channels of a weakened PT and Congress—with unorganized interests and the poorest? Can Congress shake off the effects of scandal and executive dominance long enough to pass overdue tax reform as well as political and electoral reforms?

The strategies that Lula's government has favored since 2002 shed light on these questions, and also on the structural weaknesses from which Brazil's political system suffers even as certain of its institutions show a heartening degree of resilience. At the outset of his time in office, Lula laid down a pattern of political communication that has endured beyond its initial use in helping him to "triangulate" the complex challenge of simultaneously satisfying skeptical investors, his own left-wing base, and the wider electorate. Improving the market's expectations and checking renewed inflationary pressures—the key economic demands of 2003—required him to stick with orthodox macroeconomic measures, tighten monetary policy, and reform the public-pension system. These were all steps of the sort that Lula and the PT had long denounced while in opposition.

In order to draw attention away from the policy continuity underlying these measures—which were overseen by a PT-led coalition government that contained centrist and center-right parties—Lula and his team sought to project the image of an epochal departure from the past. This political strategy has received far less attention than its results in the form of improved economic governance. The strategy required trade-offs between responding to investors and satisfying the hopes of domestic constituencies that had voted for change.

Three mechanisms figured prominently. The first was the intensive use of symbolic assets and other political resources available to the presidency in a country whose constitution makes the executive the dominant branch of government. Duda Mendonça's communications strategy relied heavily on Lula's effective daily radio broadcasts to the nation as well as on his television exposure. The second was the crafting of a coherent governing coalition out of a heterogeneous electoral coalition. The third was the carefully engineered compliance of the president's party with an unpalatably "neoliberal" change of gear in economic policy. With some modifications due to changing circumstances, the interplay of these three mechanisms has remained highly influential to this day.

The Uses of Legitimacy

Economic stability underwritten by fiscal and monetary discipline serves the interests of both international investors and Brazil's poorest citizens, who have the fewest defenses against runaway inflation. The electoral rewards that President Cardoso had reaped by embracing currency stabilization in the form of the Real Plan made this point clear to PT strategists. Their task was to brighten the markets' gloomy expectations about Lula while winning over an electorate that had begun to take stability for granted and that wanted more growth to go hand-in-hand with greater equity and welfare. The strategists' answer was to employ lessons learned during the 2002 campaign by stressing the symbolism attached to the election of a working-class president who had quit school after the fourth grade: "He is one of ours!" ran the slogan they devised. Lula, fortunately for his advisors, had the personal flair and political acumen to make this proactive approach work. And he not only had the help of saturation media coverage that reached even the farthest corners of his vast country, but could also call upon a thoroughly modern and well-funded marketing and opinion-polling machine.

Other proactive tactics included the use of rhetoric designed to obscure any links or likenesses between Lula's economic policies and those of his predecessors, and even to create the impression that the country was being comprehensively refounded. The crisis of investor confidence was blamed on the "accursed legacy" of the Cardoso administration. Meanwhile, not merely Cardoso's but all past governments were lumped together with "the elites," while Lula was pictured as a father figure. The slogan "Never before in this country!" sought to underscore his government's responsiveness to the underprivileged. These appeals proved credible and effective, notwithstanding well-publicized evidence that Lula's policies were allowing bankers and other private interests to make large profits of the sort that the president and his party had strongly decried while in opposition.

Another of the administration's arguments sought to persuade citizens to use an extended timeline when weighing the costs and benefits of economic policy. The president and his allies dwelt on the noble long-range aspirations of the iconic Zero Hunger Program to great effect both at home and abroad, despite this ambitious scheme's poor results. Moreover, effective appeals for voter patience rested on realistic estimates by administration economists, who predicted that growth would get seriously underway by 2004. Opinion polls showed that Brazilians were indeed ready to extend their horizons of judgment much as the president had asked. In early 2003, majorities were telling pollsters from CNN and the Instituto Sensus that they would give Lula six months to make good on his economic promises. By the final quarter of that year, this self-reported grace period had tripled to eighteen months. The role of such strategies in assisting a smooth exit from the crisis years of 2002 and 2003 should not be underestimated: Lula's indices of popularity remained high notwithstanding a 13 percent fall in real average income, a significant increase in unemployment, and GDP that grew by a barely detectable 0.1 percent.

Lula and his advisors faced a fresh test of their communications acumen in May and June 2005, when news broke of political scandals involving key government strategists and leading figures in the PT. Throughout the rest of that year, the new communications strategy became essential in averting the defeat of Lula's 2006 reelection bid. This time around, the administration used a panoply of devices that varied from audience to audience. Long televised interviews, aimed at the best-educated citizens, depicted political corruption as part of "the system," a banal practice used to fund elections. Ignored were the distinctive aspects of the Lula administration's scandals, including their centralized nature and the use of public resources to serve a national political party rather than to buy votes on a particular bill or to enrich an individual.[6]

Poorer neighborhoods benefiting from the Bolsa Familia and the higher minimum wage and served by federally controlled or influenced local media heard reassuring daily messages asserting that "never before has a government been so engaged in investigating corruption." The Lula administration's sophisticated marketing and communications efforts were like nothing ever before seen in Brazil. They allowed the president to decouple his own image from his party's, and to keep his distance from the PT's problems despite a Federal Police investigation that uncovered well-funded maneuvering by close Lula advisors against José Serra's (eventually successful) candidacy for the São Paulo state governorship. Lula's winning of a second term owes much to these novel (for Brazil) public-relations methods. They added to the aura of the Brazilian presidency and helped to magnify the effects of both the symbolic assets and the political skills that are essential to Lula's mode of leadership.

In a democracy, the crafting of even a modestly coherent policy consensus depends in no small part on the political and institutional framework within which an electoral alliance must go about turning itself into a governing coalition. Brazil's political system is host to a structural tension between the majoritarian presidency and the power-sharing requirements of the other political institutions that make up the country's "coalitional" form of presidentialism. Moreover, given the executive dominance that is embedded in both constitutional text and political fact, devising a consensus approach to economic policy also depends on more contingent conditions, such as leaders' capacity to work with existing institutions in resourceful new ways. In the recent past, a modicum of policy stability and effectiveness has proven attainable so long as the federal executive respects the different electoral weights of the various parties and bargains with representative state governors.

Coalition Building Since 2003

How has Lula met this challenge? What new power resources has his administration created from existing institutions, and to what ends? Since Lula took office, the executive branch has applied its considerable discretionary powers to the delicate task of cementing a ruling coalition of eleven parties around an economic agenda of solvency and market discipline that many of these parties find less than congenial, even if they once grudgingly recognized the temporary need for it during the crisis of confidence. The coalition included small parties of the right and center-right known for clientelism and corruption, as well as parties to the left of the PT. Lula's coalition, moreover, at first held only 45 percent of the seats in the Chamber of Deputies (a figure that increased to 65 percent after the large Party of the Brazilian Democratic Movement [PMDB] split and most of its members decamped to the government). Cardoso, by contrast, had needed to manage a coalition of just four parties that together controlled 75 percent of the Chamber seats.

Given the opposition's preexisting commitment to economic stability and market-friendly reform, did Lula have to govern by means of such a large, mixed, and often-undisciplined coalition? This question became all the more pointed in the wake of news that certain rightist and center-right legislators were each receiving unprecedented payments *(mensalãoes)* thought to be worth about $12,000 per month in return for backing the administration. Although these lawmakers' parties may have disagreed with the administration's economic policies (the small clientelistic parties of the right and center-right tend to favor the expansion of state-controlled jobs and opportunities), the legislators themselves might have been expected to vote with the government in exchange for control over public-enterprise or executive-branch posts. However, discontent may have arisen from both the relatively scarce number of posts to be filled, and the preference shown to PT members when filling them.

The question, while understandable, was also naïve in a way, for much more than the economic agenda was at stake. The PT was carrying out a long-term power-building strategy designed to make it Brazil's perennially dominant party. The assets to be used in this approach included the PT's control over the largest single bloc of seats in the Chamber, its organizational roots and discipline, and Lula's 82 percent popularity rating. The first asset was less valuable than it seemed, however, for the PT's own share of the Chamber was not even 18 percent, and in Brazil only one party has ever held more than 20 percent of the legislature. This 20 percent ceiling explains why, by 2003, Lula was reaching out so vigorously to the center—and particularly to lawmakers from the fractured PMDB—in a bid to gather to his side at least a nominal legislative majority.

The government used its discretionary powers to insulate economic policy from the pressures of competitive politics, a standard move in cases of macroeconomic structural adjustment. In Brazil, this meant shielding the authority of liberal economists in the Finance Ministry and the Central Bank against attacks by economists within PT ranks.

At the same time, in a clear and novel politicization of public administration, PT members (mostly labor unionists) were given government posts and executive jobs in state-run companies, federal banks, and regulatory agencies. The upper reaches of the federal executive branch were turned into a virtual nest of defeated PT election candidates. This wave of personnel moves and its implications for effective and honest governance would loom large after February 2004, when various political scandals began to come to light. Brazil's federal executive still decides who will fill about twenty-thousand jobs that are kept exempt from merit-based selection criteria—a fact that those who decry the "neoliberal assault on the state" seldom if ever note. By boosting the number of ministries from 27 to 35, and by staffing the state bureaucracy, public enterprises, and state-run banks with PT members, the administration was acting on a "winner-takes-all" basis that was at odds with the unspoken rules of coalitional presidentialism.

Among the leading devices for padding a majority has been the practice of drawing opposition politicians to the ruling coalition's smaller parties (never to the PT) by taking advantage of the executive's control over state patronage as well as an electoral law that allows floor crossing. The PT's tactics have significantly drained opposition parties and undermined the positive trend, dating from the late 1990s, toward the distillation of electoral competition into five or six parties. Even though the PT held only two governorships, Lula commanded the partial cooperation of most governors. This was not surprising. Their states depended on federal approval to gain foreign loans as well as to share in the welfare gains expected in upcoming years.

The political costs of that power-building strategy became clearer in mid-2005, when the monthly-payments scandal broke. Congressional hearings led to the resignations of José Dirceu, the president's chief-of-staff and top political strategist; PT leader José Genoíno; and Luiz Gushiken, Lula's communications director. The hearings uncovered the complex network that had been set up to pay for the PT's power-building strategy. Large sums from state-owned companies had been funneled to selected legislators and other key figures through a little-known public-relations executive named Marcos Valério. Investigation also revealed that Duda Mendonça, Lula's top ad man, had been paid through illegal overseas accounts. The evidence that Eduardo Azeredo, the president of the major opposition party (the PSDB), had received cash from a subsector of the Valério network to fund his 1998 run for the governorship of Minas Gerais state helps to explain why the opposition refrained from consistently harping on the ethical shortcomings of the dominant party.

In March 2006, another crucial resignation—that of PT member and finance minister Antonio Palocci—ripped the veil off the PT's longstanding practice of using padded municipal contracts to fund its election campaigns. This turned a spotlight on the prevailing values of PT leaders, who reckoned illegal practices and the abuse of public funds morally acceptable so long as the goal was to serve the party rather than individual interests. The underlying illiberal assumption—that the Workers' Party is above the law—stood in sharp contrast to the long-held impression among educated Brazilians that the PT is somehow "exceptional." Sensing the value of this image, Lula (who as of this writing has not been personally implicated in the scandals) had earlier sought to obscure the novel nature of the Valério network by telling a television interviewer that such behavior was somehow "inherent in the system."

Such developments bring to center stage the issue of horizontal accountability. How effective are the institutions constitutionally empowered to check the powerful executive branch? The courts and the Federal Police played prominent roles in investigating the *mensalão* affair. Media scrutiny was intense. Much-publicized congressional hearings played a pedagogic role, albeit at the cost of further damaging the already low public standing of the Chamber of Deputies. The investigations, the coverage, and the hearings were all encouraging signs that horizontal accountability is alive in Brazil. On the disheartening side was the evident tolerance with which PT leaders viewed their colleagues' malfeasance, as well as the cavalier attitude that the PSDB had shown by not requiring the resignation of its president after it came out that he had availed himself of the same illegal network as the PT in order to support a campaign of his own.

Lula's Second-Term Prospects

Tarnished by scandal and looking into the jaws of defeat in 2006, Lula's administration responded with: 1) an expansion of Bolsa Familia coverage from 8.5 to 11.5 million families; 2) a 13 percent real increase in minimum wages and retirement pensions; and 3) steps to make it easier for poorer Brazilians to get bank loans. These policies helped the administration to make inroads into the *grotões* and secure reelection, but could not stop the significant shift away from Lula's camp by better-educated citizens in the southern, southeastern, and west-central parts of the country.

The "two-Brazils" thesis, according to which the elections reflect a split between rich and poor, needs qualification.[7] First, the severe economic crises that hit the Center-West and South hurt *all* social sectors. Second, Lula's commanding 2006 performance in the North and Northeast, where he gained 65 percent and 85 percent of the vote, respectively, included the support of local elites. The Northeast's entire economy benefited from the Bolsa Familia, the minimum-wage hike, low inflation, and the decline in value of the U.S. dollar (which made imports cheaper). During 2006, consumer spending in the Northeast grew at a Chinese-style pace of 13 percent (almost double the rate at which it grew nationally).

Finally, the partial shift of the better informed and educated away from Lula's camp needs closer scrutiny. Discontent among the middle classes of the wealthier regions had many causes other than higher unemployment rates. The share of national income going to these Brazilians has been shrinking even as their tax burden has been growing. They enjoy wide exposure to multiple and competing sources of information regarding rights abuses and corruption, including the recent PT scandals. Compounding their sense of disillusionment over the PT's lack of its once-vaunted ethical "exceptionalism" has been that party's poor follow-through on its campaign promises regarding health and education. The failure to spend money in these areas has galled well-informed citizens who are aware of the government's broad taxing powers and the bonanza that has been going on in areas such as the spectacularly profitable financial sector.

In the *grotões*, by contrast, local authoritarians run the show while media competition barely exists. Local television and radio stations dominate the airwaves in these impoverished areas, and local-broadcasting licenses have long been treated as "pork-barrel" concessions from the central government. The national media can cover whatever they like, but the local media will always act as a filter determining how national coverage "plays" in the poorer localities. There, the administration's official line that it was doing "more than ever before in this country" to fight corruption was the dominant story.

As Lula's second term approaches its 2008 midpoint, the question of how favorable economic circumstances and Brazil's new role in world trade and investment markets will affect the administration's strategic thinking remains open. Judging by recent developments, one can speak of mixed results and see reasons for anxiety. Good economic-growth prospects and proactive policies such as the Bolsa Familia, the higher minimum wage, and easier credit access have reduced poverty and inequality and helped many once-poor Brazilians to become members of a rising new middle class. These promising socioeconomic trends are vital to the spread of political equality, but in and of themselves they still do not guarantee that the stubborn problem of limited citizenship is being adequately addressed.

A Renewed Rise of the State?

There is also reason to worry whether the idea of market-based, representative democracy is really taking hold—not among the populace at large, but among policy makers themselves. Even as a dynamic private sector, led by a modernized financial system and Brazilian firms that are going global, spreads optimism in markets and the pages of the foreign press, existing political elites are relying ever more heavily on the state not only to change society but to help them cement an allegedly more stable governmental coalition. The traditional politics of pork is swelling in scale because Brazil is richer, and because politicians and party leaders have decided to reshape "coalitional presidentialism" in a way more consistent with the power-sharing logic already inherent in that model. The incentives for opposition deputies to migrate to the smaller parties in the government's coalition have been mounting, though the Supreme Federal Tribunal's September 2007 ruling that congressional mandates belong to parties rather than individuals could arrest that trend. In the face of congressional reluctance to vote for political reforms that would promote party discipline, the courts are acting in ways that promise to bolster the stability of Brazil's rather fluid party system, but which also threaten to further the "judicialization" of politics.

On the politico-economic front, meanwhile, badly needed structural changes languish, with no chance of being enacted. New moves from the government point to renewed restrictions to competition within major areas. Thus, the duopolistic structure in petrochemicals is being strengthened as the state increases its participation as Petrobras's main shareholder; and competition in telecommunications may be significantly restricted by means of a state-funded merger of two private firms, with the resulting new entity to be controlled by the state. The deliberate politicization of regulatory agencies compounds the picture. Among the necessary changes being ignored are not only tax reforms but also measures intended to foster better corporate governance and to reduce the regulatory and juridical uncertainty that limits long-term investment and with it Brazil's ability to compete in the global economy. Short-term calculation has been crowding out sound, long-range strategic thinking, and few elected officials seem to have reflected that now—while the economic bonanza is in full swing—is the best time to adopt politically costly reforms. The politically insulated central bank is maintaining monetary discipline, but the government remains fiscally profligate, spending at a much faster pace than its income is increasing. The central bank may remain staffed by people who respect markets, but other organs of economic policy making are seeing a "changing of the guard," with advocates of greater state interventionism and state-funded employment gaining preponderance. In the major planning institute, for instance, economic liberals critical of fiscal profligacy have been purged as never before.

On the political-institutional front, the PT and government-aligned lawyers have been calling for a constituent assembly and laying emphasis on plebiscites. One aim appears to be a set of constitutional amendments facilitating a third term for Lula. Given Lula's strong personal popularity and the deep mistrust with which most voters view "politicians" (meaning especially members of Congress), this is hardly out of the question.

The president and members of his administration often give voice to a plebiscitary conception of democracy. For example, Luiz Dulci, the secretary-general of the presidency, claimed that the Supreme Federal Tribunal's acceptance of the prosecutor-general's accusations against the forty persons involved in the *mensalão* scheme "has nothing to do with the government. . . . The government was judged at the voting booth, democratically, and received the consecrating approval of the Brazilian people. . . . The sovereign people are the judges in a democracy [and they] reelected President Lula."[8] Finally, the launching of the cabinet-level Communications Ministry and the well-funded TV-Brasil network (with its presidentially appointed guiding council) give additional cause for concern.

Contrary to what a reader of the dominant theoretical work on democratization might expect, Brazil's experience of political democratization and economic liberalization under the adverse economic conditions of the 1980s and 1990s did not bring about a neoliberal "assault on the state." On the distributive, socioeconomic side of things, the story of how democratization processes and social reforms have taken hold in Brazil under the novel political-legitimacy criteria laid down by the 1988 Constitution shows us how a definite departure from the "modernizing conservatism" of the past has gone forward hand-in-hand with moderately market-friendly reforms.

By comparing how Lula's 2002 and 2006 election bids unfolded, we can study a test case that reveals how shifting economic conditions (which we might sum up as "demanding in 2002, permissive four years later") affected the strategic decisions that Lula's administration made. As we peer farther ahead into the opening decades of the twenty-first century, we note with worry how democratization seems to be breeding (among key elites, at least) an ever greater reliance on the state not only as an engine of social transformation, but as a trough of party-political resources. We also feel concern, finally, as we note how the Brazilian polity's plebiscitarian leanings—checked somewhat so far by the judicial system and the media—have begun to emerge not amid crisis, but even as the good times roll.

NOTES

1. Lourdes Sola, "Financial Credibility, Legitimacy and Political Discretion," in Lourdes Sola and Laurence Whitehead, eds., *Statecrafting Monetary Authority: Democracy and Financial Order in Brazil* (Oxford: Center for Brazilian Studies, 2005), 237–59.

2. Sola and Whitehead, *Statecrafting Monetary Authority*, 4.

3. Sônia Draibe, "Social Policies in the Nineties," in Renato Baumann, ed., *Brazil in the 1990s: An Economy in Transition* (Houndmills, England: Palgrave, 2002); and "Social Policy Reform," in Mauricio Font and Anthony Spanakos, eds., *Reforming Brazil* (Lanham, Md.: Lexington Books, 2004).

4. Francisco Ferreira, Philippe Leite, and Julie A. Litchfield, "The Rise and Fall of Brazilian Inequality, 1981–2004," World Bank Policy Research Working Paper Series, 2006. Available at *http://ideas.repec.org/p/wbk/wbrwps/3867.html*.

5. Wendy Hunter, and Timothy J. Power, "Rewarding Lula: Executive Power, Social Policy, and the Brazilian Elections of 2006," *Latin American Politics and Society* 49 (Spring 2007): 1–30.

6. Maria Celina D'Araújo, *Governo Lula: Contornos sociais e políticos da elite do poder* (Rio de Janeiro: CPDOC, 2007).

7. David Samuels, "Brazilian Democracy under Lula and the PT," in Jorge Domínguez and Michael Shifter, eds., *Constructing Democratic Govenance in Latin América,* 3rd ed. (Baltimore: John Hopkins University Press, 2008).

8. Dulci's comments appear at *www.agenciabrasil.gov.br/noticias/2007/08/29/materia.2007-08-29.1997689595/view*. Author's translation.

10

PROBLEMS OF SUCCESS IN CHILE

Arturo Valenzuela and Lucía Dammert

Arturo Valenzuela *is professor of government and director of the Center for Latin American Studies at Georgetown University. He is the author of several books and numerous articles on Chilean politics. During the Clinton administration, he served in the White House as special assistant to the president and senior director for Inter-American Affairs at the National Security Council.* **Lucía Dammert** *is director of the Security and Citizenship Program at FLACSO-Chile. This essay originally appeared in the October 2006 issue of the* Journal of Democracy.

On 15 January 2006, Michelle Bachelet of the Socialist Party won a runoff for Chile's presidency with 53.5 percent of the vote, becoming the first female head of state in the Americas to be elected without any connection to the political career of a male relative. Her election was the fourth win in a row for the Concertación, the center-left coalition built around the Socialists and Christian Democrats that has held office since General Augusto Pinochet's seventeen-year military dictatorship came to a peaceful end in 1990. Chilean voters have rewarded the Concertación because it set their 16.5-million-strong South American nation on an admirable course of socioeconomic progress and democratic stability that has eluded many neighboring countries afflicted by weak governing institutions, faltering economies, and high levels of poverty and social exclusion.

While assuring that continuity would be maintained, Bachelet also signaled that she was the best candidate to preside over Chile's first "posttransitional" government. Her immediate predecessor and fellow Socialist, Ricardo Lagos (2000–2006), followed the pattern set by the Concertación's two Christian Democratic presidents, Patricio Aylwin (1990–94) and Eduardo Frei (1994–2000). All three presidents governed with the support of experienced party leaders who had begun their careers before the 1973 coup, had been deeply involved in the arduous journey that had led to Pinochet's defeat in a 1988 plebiscite, and had then proved instrumental in rebuilding democratic institutions. Bachelet promised that her government would bring into public office a new generation of Chileans.

The Concertación had moved cautiously from the start, intent on precluding any crisis that could risk triggering an authoritarian reversal. At the same time, the coalition laid the groundwork for what would become Latin America's most successful economy. A combination of robust growth and effective public investments in infrastructure and social programs cut the poverty rate from 40 percent in 1990 to less than 18 percent in 2006. Democracy and the rule of law fared so well, meanwhile, that Freedom House now ranks Chile as one of Latin America's freest societies, with ratings comparable to those of Costa Rica and Uruguay. Transparency International's Corruption Perception Index also gives Chile good marks, slightly below those of the United States but above France and Italy.

After some initial difficulties, Lagos left office with a 70 percent approval rating, the best since polling began. His administration erased such legacies of military rule as constitutional provisions establishing appointed senators, barring the president from dismissing military commanders, and granting the armed forces oversight of elected leaders.[1] Significant renewal in the army and growing willingness in the judicial system to uncover and account for Pinochet-era human rights violations furthered the work of completing the transition from authoritarianism to democracy.

Nevertheless, after sixteen years of coalition rule, Chile's democracy faces significant challenges. In 2000, Lagos himself came close to losing the presidency to a populist candidate of the right who capitalized on growing citizen alienation from the dominant parties and their leaders, who rotated from one top post to another. In 2006, Bachelet successfully portrayed herself as the candidate of renewal and change, promising to forge a more inclusive and open "government of citizens"—as implicitly contrasted with one run by and for politicians. She promised 36 specific measures to address issues such as inequality, education, health care, and crime.

The daughter of an Air Force general who opposed the coup and died while in military custody, Bachelet was a relative newcomer to politics. She had played no prominent role in either the struggle against the dictatorship or the early years of civilian rule. A pediatrician trained in Eastern Europe, she received her first official post from Lagos, who made her health minister in 2000. Weekends spent giving free medical treatment to children in poor neighborhoods led citizens to see her as a caring and approachable public servant. Whether Lagos meant to or not, he further burnished her credentials by making her defense minister. She became a figure who could project not only compassion but authority, drawing on her family background as she worked with reformist officers to cement the Chilean armed forces' return to their proper role as apolitical defenders rather than masters of a democratic society.

Bachelet's election to a single four-year term (cut down from six years by a 2005 constitutional amendment) put to rest the myth, picked up by the international press, that she faced an especially uphill struggle in what was characterized as a land of intense social conservatism. In fact, her victory is a reminder that Chile has long been a highly secular society with some of the Western world's strongest Marxist parties, as well as a democracy whose rise has been tied to the success of anticlerical parties strong enough to have enacted the separation of church and state early in the twentieth century. Indeed, Bachelet as a single mother was not out of step in a country where more than 50 percent of all births occur out of wedlock.[2] The new president quickly named a cabinet heavy with newcomers, half of them women. (She extended the concept of gender parity to regional and local appointments as well.) Another early project was her well-publicized effort to implement each of her 36 campaign promises within a hundred days of taking office.

Just months into President Bachelet's term, some of the high expectations surrounding her have already met with disappointment. Her administration failed to anticipate that so many students would strike to demand better secondary schooling and lower fees. Then—worse still—she and her team seemed inept at managing the crisis. Her approval rating has dropped, and she has replaced cabinet ministers in order to stanch the criticism.[3] While the general inexperience that was on display during her mishandling of the student strikes may be the proximate cause of her problems, her administration's uncertain start also reflects a deeper problem with her approach to governing Chile. Although Chileans are tired of politics as usual, the answer is not the replacement of a government of parties with a government of citizens. Rather the challenge facing her and Chile's political elites is to make parties more inclusive while safeguarding their essential role as instruments of democratic governance.

Secrets of a Success Story

Many commentators on Latin America persistently but misguidedly assume that Chile has become a regional standout because the military regime forced a series of enlightened reforms that laid the basis for today's economic dynamism and political stability. While there is no question that the military junta, and in particular Pinochet's embrace of free-market economic policies, helped to steer the country on a path to economic recovery and modernization through export-led growth, a full account of how this happened must include circumstances unique to Chile that contributed to the new government's success in implementing its reform agenda.

Decades of constitutional rule and competitive politics before the military coup of 11 September 1973 had left Chile's armed forces, un-like those of neighboring countries, a highly professional and apolitical establishment unbeholden to private economic interests. Such interests welcomed the coup for ending Salvador Allende's socialism, but hardly expected the new authorities to favor market-opening reforms that would level the protectionist walls which had benefited Chilean businesses in the past. Reforms enacted under democratic rule in the 1960s—particularly the overhaul of the highly unequal land-tenure system that had given traditional elites so much of their power—had made private interests less able to oppose trade liberalization. This contrasts sharply with the cases of Argentina and Brazil, where military juntas failed to implement market-based reforms. It is highly instructive that Chile's military did not return lands to their traditional owners, but instead allowed property in the hands of peasant cooperatives to be sold so that new owners could embark on the revolution in agriculture that would form a major part of the Chilean economy's success story.

The lesson should be clear: Anyone tempted to wish for a Pinochet-like figure willing to slice through the Gordian knot of modernization with an authoritarian blade should think hard about how much Pinochet's reforms actually relied on a strong legacy of democratic governance. Not only military autonomy and viable, transparent state institutions conforming to the rule of law, but also reformist or even radical redistributionist measures are part of the Chilean success story. Indeed, the Chilean case could be considered an exemplar of the need to implement "third-genera-tion reforms," including steps to strengthen state institutions and the rule of law, in order to ensure that macroeconomic reforms and structural-adjustment policies bear fruit.

While Chile's preexisting institutions made possible the relatively rapid implementation of economic reforms after 1973, the country's success-ful return to democracy after 1988 stemmed directly from the military government's failure to carry out its cardinal objective of eliminating the old parties and leaders. These not merely survived, but united behind a common strategy first to defeat Pinochet in the October 1988 plebiscite that he hoped would legitimize and prolong his rule, and then to beat the military-aligned rightist candidate Hernán Büchi in the December 1989 election that brought Patricio Aylwin to the presidency.

Few observers would have predicted such an outcome. Fragmentation had been the theme of Chilean politics theretofore. It was the inability of the Socialist Allende, elected in 1970 with just 36 percent of the vote, to retain centrist (Christian Democrat) support in Congress as radical elements pushed the country further to the left, that had led to stalemate, rising tensions, and finally the 1973 coup.[4] Chile's military rulers blamed the country's democratic breakdown not only on the left but also on the weakness of democracy, which they said made easy prey for demagogues, populists, and international Marxism. Pinochet and his junta set out to change not only the statist economic policies of the past, but the Chilean polity itself. In addition to repressing established parties and leaders, the junta redesigned the constitution in 1980 to limit popular sovereignty, to make the armed forces overseers of all elected representatives including the president, and to ensure that Pinochet himself would remain army commander whatever the outcome of any plebiscite.[5]

The continuing presence of Pinochet and the powerful military establishment had two effects. First, it reassured the right and the business community that the post-Pinochet government could not easily return to pre-1973 economic policies. Second and more important, it gave the Concertación partners a strong incentive to stick together while moving (however cautiously) toward the full restoration of democratic practices. Caution, plus the realization that free-market policies were benefiting Chile through job creation and high growth, led the coalition to keep these policies. While the dictatorship's market-based reforms had been unpopular with the parties that beat Pinochet and Büchi at the polls, the Concertación leaders' decision to support such policies helped both to legitimize them and to give Chile's new government the political running room to extend such policies further. At the same time that it was opening Chile up to markets, however, the Concertación was quick to enact new social policies that lifted more Chileans out of poverty.

Overcoming Authoritarianism's Legacies

It is important to stress that Chile's transition was not "pacted." The democratic parties never agreed to specific terms with the authoritarian regime,[6] and indeed signaled from the start that their goal was to end such undemocratic features of the 1980 constitution as appointed senators, limits on the president's power to promote and cashier military commanders, the military-dominated security council, an electoral law that overrepresented the right, and an amnesty law that barred investigating (let alone prosecuting) human rights abuses. The catch for the Concertación was that several of these features (especially the appointed senators and the overrepresentation of rightists) made it hard to gain the legislative majorities needed to change the other rules. Not until fifteen years after Pinochet stepped down would the Concertación be able to abolish the authoritarian legacies of military rule and the judicial system be fully able to hold human rights violators to account.[7]

Of all the issues with which Chile's transitional governments had to wrestle, the question of civil-military relations was among the thorniest. Pinochet used the army as a bastion while resisting accountability for human rights abuses. With backing from rightist parties, the military fiercely sought to bar any reduction of its constitutional prerogatives and opposed the naming of the Truth and Reconciliation Commission in 1990. The courts, however, gradually began to assert their own jurisdiction behind the idea that the absence of a body (as in the case of someone who had been "disappeared" under the junta) required keeping an inquiry open regardless of any amnesty law. The courts also came to accept the argument that, while the amnesty law could bar prosecutions, any grant of amnesty presupposed the determination that a crime had been committed, thereby opening the door to legal review of abuses.

Pinochet's arrest (on a Spanish warrant) in London in 1997 did not mark the beginning of the prosecution of military personnel for human rights abuses—that had already begun in the mid-1990s. It did, however, mark the beginning of his fall from grace even among his erstwhile supporters, a process that gathered speed in 2004 when Chilean authorities charged him with concealing millions of dollars in foreign bank accounts. In harsh contrast to his carefully cultivated image as a selfless and austere military officer whom destiny had called to save Chile from communism, Pinochet came to seem in many eyes like merely another corrupt "tropical dictator." His difficulties accelerated change within the army, which publicly acknowledged past abuses and dropped the doctrine of the armed services as "guardians of the nation" in favor of one that defines them as public servants in defense of the nation.

The Concertación's most important achievements were first to build the most successful coalition government in Chilean history, and then to preserve it beyond the first few years after military rule ended. Chile's elected presidents had long struggled to govern despite an intensely contentious party system that typically denied the chief executive both a popular-vote majority and majority support in Congress. The Concertación broke that pattern. Although Pinochet's constitution gave the president extensive formal prerogatives, there was never any doubt after 1990 that constant negotiations among the president, cabinet officials, legislators, and party leaders would be the norm in both the making of policy and the filling of congressional and local nominations, cabinet and subcabinet posts, governorships, and ambassadorships. Commissions formed by executive, legislative, and political-party leaders helped to institutionalize the bargaining system.

As a result, Chile presents a happy contrast to other countries in the region where legislative opposition forces, in effect preferring politics to governance, have decided that undermining minority presidents is better than working with them at the risk of boosting the electoral prospects of such presidents and their parties.[8] By reaching out to opposition leaders, Chilean governments since 1990 have made it clear that their country's "democracy of accords" includes more than just the parties of the Concertación. Coalitional discipline helped the Concertación to enlist rightist support for a hike in the value-added tax that paid for expanding social programs in the early 1990s, as well as to pass anticorruption legislation during Lagos's term. In foreign and trade policy, the Concertación frequently reassured the business community that market-opening policies would be continued and even enhanced. Skillful economic-policy management and proven respect for the Central Bank's independence gradually won the private sector's trust and convinced it that the Concertación's standing abroad was good for business.

Too Much of a Good Thing?

Chile's democracy is consolidated, but faces challenges that we should not downplay. Ironically, some of those challenges stem from the very model of governance that has helped Chile to succeed. Tactics that aided institutional consolidation just after Pinochet may now be growing increasingly counterproductive. A major trouble sign has been falling voter turnout, especially among the young. High rates of abstention coincided with dipping support for the Concertación parties and increased inroads by the Unión Demócrata Independiente (UDI). This party, the formation on the right most closely identified with military rule and the more conservative elements of the Catholic Church, managed in a December 2001 opinion poll to draw the support of 15 percent of the population, while only 12 percent backed the Christian Democrats, whose decline has been particularly dramatic. At the beginning of the transition, they commanded the loyalty of close to 40 percent of the electorate—more than twice the support enjoyed by their leftist partners in the Concertación. By early 2006, UDI's star had faded while the Christian Democrats were stagnating and saw the combined support of the Socialists and the Party for Democracy exceed their own. Tellingly, no single party commands the loyalty of more than 15 percent of the electorate in Chile today, and more than a third of all voters profess no party attachment.[9]

The UDI's initial success resulted from the imagination and hard work of its youthful leaders. They focused on some of Chile's poorest communities, garnering support by serving ably in local offices while using populist rhetoric. This same appeal helped to project Joaquín Lavín, the UDI mayor of Santiago, into the national spotlight. Lavín would give Lagos a serious run for the presidency in the 2000 election, mounting the biggest challenge that the coalition had faced since democracy's return and forcing the contest into a second round. Concern over Chile having its first Socialist president since Allende hurt Lagos, but so did the UDI's ability to present a new face while capitalizing on the growing lack of interest in traditional politics.

Lagos's leadership skills, a rebounding economy, and the serendipitous emergence of two women candidates as his likeliest successors helped the Concertación to reverse its declining fortunes. The parties of the right did the Concertación a huge favor by not renewing their leadership and by letting themselves become entangled in bitter internecine disputes and political scandals of their own making. Yet the overall lesson from Lavín's near-upset of Lagos remained: The traditional parties as a group had lost touch with their roots and their followers, and were failing to reach younger voters, all of which helps to explain the increased disenchantment of the citizenry with politics and democracy.[10]

The Concertación's recipe for effective governance—disciplined parties with leaders capable of forging agreements while rotating through cabinet posts and congressional seats—had opened a widening breach between leaders and followers. Public office had come to appear as the preserve of a tiny band of the same faces. Scandals related to under-the-table bonuses for high-ranking but low-paid officials, lucrative consulting deals for their friends and relatives, or dubious financing of party coffers added to Chileans' impression that cronyism was out of control.

More problematic still was the lack of vigorous competition for elected office. This shortage stemmed in large part from the military regime's reworking of the electoral system. In order to give parties of the right more congressional seats than they would have received in a more directly proportional system, the military-engineered electoral law set up districts with two seats apiece while also holding that the list with the most votes can gain both seats only if its vote share doubles that of its nearest competing list.[11] This means that in any two-list contest, the top list must get at least 66 percent in order to take both seats, while the runner-up list can win a seat (thereby matching the top list) with only a bit more than a third of the vote. Although this arrangement did help the right, it failed to produce the larger change that the military's constitutional architects wanted—namely, the replacement of multipartism by a system in which two large parties vie to woo the median voter.

Chile's traditional parties proved too resilient to let this happen. Faced with such an unfriendly law, they adapted by negotiating common lists, thereby retaining and even strengthening the individual identities of each major party in what was and is essentially a five-party system.[12] Even though the electoral law failed to produce a two-party system, could it have played an essential role in encouraging stable coalition government? This question is much debated in Chile. Some argue that the law gave the Concertación a crucial incentive to maintain cohesion. Others hold that even had the older system of open-list proportional representation been kept, coalitional discipline would have endured. The second view seems more plausible, for the first overstates the law's importance relative to such other factors as the fear of an authoritarian reversal and the advantages that a disciplined coalition gave the Concertación in keeping power and moving its agenda forward.

The Downside of Doing Well

Whether the Pinochet-era electoral law or some other array of factors has done the most to reinforce the practice of "democracy by agreements," the downside of that practice should now be clear. Narrow party elites acting behind closed doors decide how many congressional candidacies each coalition partner will get, how they will be allocated territorially, and who will fill them. When the Christian Democrats held the presidency from 1990 to 2000, the parties of the left argued for parity in congressional representation even though the Christian Democrats were the largest single party in terms of vote share. When in 2000 the presidency went to the Socialists and the Christian Democrats began losing popular support, the latter in turn began insisting on an equal number of "safe seats" to compensate for their "loss" of the presidency and their decline in electoral and popular support. A number of notorious squabbles over safe seats ensued among parties in the Concertación.

At times, party negotiators would force a popular incumbent off a ticket in order to make room for a candidate from another party, or bar from certain jurisdictions candidates who by winning might upset the careful internal balance of power that the coalition was seeking to maintain. With no genuinely open primaries, party followers in districts throughout the country had no choice but to accept leaders imposed by Santiago, most of whom lived in the capital and had few or no links with the people whom they were nominally representing.

Far from encouraging unity and discipline, it appears that over time the electoral system has fed interparty bickering, made worse by a tendency toward heightened ideological polarization.[13] The Christian Democrats' flagging electoral fortunes may be compounding this, as they are driving some party leaders to argue that Christian Democracy must distinguish itself more clearly from its partners to the left as well as its opponents to the right. Christian Democracy emerged in Chile in the 1960s as a third choice in a society riven by sharp differences between a Marxist left and a right identified with the economic elite. With the Cold War over and most Chileans now embracing constitutional democracy and markets, and with the threat of an authoritarian comeback receding, the Christian Democrats have found it harder to stand out as a genuine middle option.

The electoral law has had the further effect of continuing the "extra-parliamentary" left's exclusion from Congress—thereby driving another wedge between the mainstream parties and society's disaffected—even though nearly a tenth of all voters support this orientation. Coalition unity comes at the expense of openness and transparency in Chile's system of representation. The most successful governing coalition that the country has ever known increasingly strikes the public as distant at best, and self-serving and exclusionary at worst. While citizens' confidence in political parties has dropped across Latin America in recent years, Chile's decline from 1997 to 2002 was an especially dramatic 66 percentage points—more than double the regional average.[14] And although Chile has been ranked with Uruguay and Costa Rica as among the strongest democracies in Latin America, Chileans appear to be notably less satisfied with the quality of their democracy than their counterparts in those two countries.[15]

Despite the bargaining that goes on, the presidency retains the formidable, even overwhelming powers which it received from Pinochet's 1980 constitution. So long as the Concertación leaves this legacy of military rule untouched, Congress's relative institutional weakness will threaten to intensify the democratic-accountability deficit that already afflicts a legislature filled with candidates chosen through backroom deals. Before 1973, Congress was a major arena for public debate and compromise despite a volatile and polarized national political climate. Today, the legislature plays second fiddle to the executive in structuring agreements and moving legislation forward. Although it would be unfortunate if Congress tried to assert its authority in the absence of a stable majority coalition based on party discipline, the legislature's secondary role in policy formation could very well come to haunt Chile if a president's foes come to see Congress as a tool for undermining executive-branch proposals rather than putting forth serious alternatives to them.

The tale of strong elite agreements that bolster governance but then lead to decay amid their own tendency to alienate and shut out is not new to Latin America. The Pact of Punto Fijo, a power-sharing agreement that Venezuela's two main parties reached in 1958 to head off an authoritarian reversal, eventually came to seem a cozy deal in which elites split spoils (mostly from petroleum) while fending off potential competitors. A sharp decline in oil revenues left the parties too strapped to keep the patronage flowing, and one of Latin America's strongest party systems collapsed while populist and would-be coupmaker Hugo Chávez waited in the wings. In Colombia, the Liberal and Conservative party elites built an elaborate National Accord (1958–74) to end armed partisan conflict—agreeing to share power by alternating control over the presidency and dividing all other posts, including congressional seats, on an equal basis. Although the Accord ended a civil war, it stanched genuine political competition and excluded significant sectors of society from access to power, fueling extrasystemic movements and armed insurgencies that have brought Colombia a new iteration of bloody internal strife.

A Government of Citizens?

Chile is hardly likely to experience political crises as profound as those that have gripped Venezuela and Colombia. Its democratic institutions are stronger, and the very election of Bachelet revealed the system's capacity to generate change while maintaining continuity. Bachelet won by promising a new and more participatory style of politics while offering to address challenges that include Latin America's highest inequality levels outside Brazil—a problem that remains despite recent successes in reducing the poverty rate and the incidence of absolute poverty.[16] She moved swiftly to constitute a more representative cabinet, insisting on complete gender parity and new and younger faces. To implement her campaign program, she convened a series of commissions of experts and citizens to propose reforms in areas such as education, pensions, and the electoral system itself.

Bachelet's early steps, while appealing to the public, met with skepticism if not resistance within the parties of the Concertación. Her team was criticized for not consulting more widely on critical appointments. Her choices left many prominent leaders who had backed her candidacy and even managed her campaign out in the cold. Nor was it clear how she proposed to organize the consultation and decision-making process of her presidential office, or how new initiatives, such as the work of the independent commissions, would be funneled through executive and eventually legislative channels. Although Bachelet had held two major cabinet posts, she had been outside the central decision-making process under Lagos, and seemed hesitant and disorganized in getting her own team off the ground. It is understandable that she needed to place the imprint of her own authority on her government and not risk being controlled or managed by officials and party leaders who viewed the Concertación as their bailiwick. Particularly difficult for her was the enormous popularity of former president Lagos, who had projected reassuring strength and decisiveness while adroitly navigating the complex shoals of a coalition government.

It was Bachelet's misfortune to have her honeymoon in office end abruptly before she had a chance fully to calibrate her administration. The detonator was a surprising protest movement led by secondary-school students complaining about low educational standards, high fees, and barriers to postsecondary education. Student demonstrations mushroomed as schools throughout the country, including private institutions, joined in solidarity. The movement's leaders cut across party lines and included Socialists and Christian Democrats as well as students aligned with parties from the extraparliamentary left. As the media focused on their cause the students added new demands, calling for the revamping of a public-school system administered by municipal governments whose resources varied greatly from one jurisdiction to another.

As Chile's educational system came to a standstill, the government was slow to react—first implying that the student cause had merit, but then moving unsuccessfully to control it with hard-line tactics. After about a month, the protests were finally brought under control with help from party leaders and official assurances that the government would respond to grievances. A commission of 73 members, including student leaders, was appointed to study proposed reforms.

The new administration had hardly recovered from the student protests when it faced a new challenge from widespread flooding in southern Chile. Once again the authorities were caught flatfooted. Bachelet herself was embarrassed when, on a trip to survey the damage, she heard many complaints that government aid had failed to materialize. Attempting to respond to a chorus of criticism, Bachelet fired three cabinet ministers including those in charge of education and the interior.

Finally and unusually, Bachelet came under fire on a foreign-policy matter. When rumors went around that Chile was considering a vote in favor of Chávez-ruled Venezuela's bid for a seat on the UN Security Council, new Christian Democratic Party head Soledad Alvear reacted with a strong statement calling for Chile to vote against Venezuela. Her statement revealed disagreements within the Concertación on foreign policy, something that was rare in previous Concertación governments.

Bachelet's problems go deeper than the shakedown-cruise difficulties that any new administration, particularly one run by relatively inexperienced officials, must learn to weather. In practice, the president's campaign promise to create a "citizens' democracy" has meant appointing many technocrats without much party background or backing. In this, she has deviated sharply from the practice of her predecessors, all of whom consulted carefully with party leaders when filling key vacancies. Even more significantly, a governing style that seeks to project greater openness and less reliance on cutting deals with party leaders has deprived the government of the stalwart support that it needs in order to respond quickly to multiple challenges.

A Need to Shift Gears

There is little doubt that Bachelet and her team are right in thinking that the voters expect their new president to implement change. But it is one thing to put fresh faces in high posts, and quite another to structure a government whose officials lack strong and constant backing from the parties that make up the ruling coalition. In seeking to satisfy the demand for more participatory democracy, Bachelet risks making the same mistake that President Vicente Fox made in Mexico. He assembled a group of able technocrats whom he believed would satisfy the conditions for a "plural" government of "transition," but who proved weak because they simply did not come close to representing any of the real political forces in the country.

Bachelet needs to shift gears quickly and seek the support of key leaders in the parties and Congress. While she appears weak, the reality is that strong leaders with long governmental experience now head the parties in her coalition. Rooting her administration more firmly in these well-established parties will dispel the aura of weakness, but she must be careful at the same time to remember and take seriously the depth and extent of Chileans' hunger for a new approach to politics. Insofar as the parties have lost touch with their bases as elite agreements have substituted for more open and participatory discussions and citizen involvement, Chile's leaders need to reinvigorate parties rather than try to shunt them aside with appeals to an ill-defined ideal of "government by citizens."

An essential item on the agenda must be the strengthening of mechanisms for internal party democracy and greater openness in selecting party leaders as well as nominees for public office. Internal party reform needs to dovetail with the adoption of a new electoral law that will permit greater citizen input in the electoral process through open primaries or a more directly proportional system of representation built around larger district magnitude, open lists and preferential voting. One of President Bachelet's commissions, chaired by former senator and minister of the presidency Edgardo Boeninger, has suggested election-law reforms whose enactment would be a strong step in the right direction. The new law includes gender quotas to bring women into political life, including party organizations.[17]All the parties in the Concertación have an interest in seeing Bachelet succeed. In order for this to happen, however, they must move beyond the logrolling culture of the "politics of agreements" and join in an effort to promote reforms that will make the system of representation in Chile more open and broadly competitive.

Just as Bachelet must recognize that the parties are central to governance, the parties must realize that the quality of democracy is at stake and that reforms which promote participation should be at the top of the policy agenda. Congress, still severely limited by Pinochet's constitution, is the branch closest to the people. No participatory reform can be complete until legislative powers and prerogatives have been restored. The appropriate place for policy debates on critical policy matters is not an array of ad hoc citizen commissions that report to a dominant executive, but the halls of the legislative body with its public hearings and robust debate. A strong legislature provides an arena for forging compromises and agreements that are more transparent and inclusive. Party leadership will continue to be important, but redressing the executive-legislative imbalance that military rule left behind will help to create a more responsive and accountable representative body. At the same time, the government needs to rethink how efforts at decentralization and devolution of authority to provincial and local levels have been working. The student protests were a sign that the municipalization of education which began under the military government has serious drawbacks.

Chile's success has owed much to the ability of disciplined parties with roots in society to agree for the sake of governance. The country still faces many challenges—reducing inequality, renewing the educational system, and strengthening economic competitiveness, to name a few. Chile's leaders can best address them by working with the population to overhaul democratic institutions to make them more open, participatory, and responsive. A new electoral law shorn of the former military regime's distortions will be an excellent place to start.

NOTES

1. Robert Funk, *El gobierno de Ricardo Lagos: La nueva vía chilena hacia el socialismo* (Santiago: Universidad Diego Portales, 2006). See also Felipe Agüero, "Democratización y militares: Breve balance de dicisiete años desde la transición," in Manuel Alcántara Saéz and Leticia Ruiz Rodríguez, eds., *Chile: Política y modernización democrática* (Barcelona: Edicions Bellaterra, 2006), 313–35. This collection is the best on Chilean politics since the reestablishment of democracy.

2. J. Samuel Valenzuela, Eugenio Tironi, and Timothy R. Scully, C.S.C., *El Eslabón perdido: Familia, modernización y bienestar en Chile* (Santiago: Editores Taurus, 2006), 19. Chile's reputation as a conservative country stemmed from a misreading of the reasons why it lagged behind other countries in legalizing divorce. First, the Concertación lacked needed Senate votes due to the overrepresentation of the right that the military left behind. Second, the Chilean Church's prominent role as a defender of human rights during the dictatorship made coalition leaders reluctant to confront the Church over "moral issues." Finally, although the Church had distanced itself from the social liberalism of the Christian Democrats, the latter remained wary of pressing issues with the Church in ways that might cost them votes.

3. Valuable survey material is available from the Centro de Estudios Públicos at *www. cepchile.cl.*

4. Arturo Valenzuela, *The Breakdown of Democratic Regimes: Chile* (Baltimore: Johns Hopkins University Press, 1978).

5. For an overview of the military government, see Pamela Constable and Arturo Valenzuela, *A Nation of Enemies: Chile under Pinochet* (New York: Norton, 1991).

6. J. Samuel Valenzuela makes this point forcefully in "Los derechos humanos y la redemocratización en Chile," in Alcántara and Ruiz, *Chile: Política y modernización democrática,* 269–312. For an argument that the Concertación did at least implicitly pact with the military, see Felipe Portales, *Chile: Una Democracia Tutelada* (Santiago: Editorial Sudamericana, 2000). Portales was writing during the Frei government before some of the key "authoritarian enclaves" were removed.

7. J. Samuel Valenzuela, "Los derechos humanos y la redemocratización en Chile." See also Robert Funk, *El gobierno de Ricardo Lagos.*

8. Arturo Valenzuela, "Latin American Presidencies Interrupted," pp. 3–17 of this volume. Since the democratic transitions of the early 1980s, fifteen Latin American presidents have had to leave office early. In each case, the lack of a congressional majority and the consequent elusiveness of a stable governing coalition loomed large. The comparison between Chile and Mexico is particularly illustrative. Mexico's PAN, a center-right party similar to the Chilean Christian Democrats, was never able to ally with the leftist PRD even though both were battling the entrenched single-party PRI regime. Mexico has thus had divided government with the usual policy paralysis, a syndrome unlikely to improve in the wake of the disputed 2006 election in which no presidential candidate garnered more than 36 percent.

9. For survey data, consult the periodic surveys conducted by the Centro de Estudios Públicos, by far the best and most reliable. Unlike other Chilean pollsters CEP makes its data available to researchers free of charge. See *www.cepchile.cl.*

10. Alan Angell, "Hechos o percepciones ciudadanas? Una paradoja en la evaluación de la democracia chilena," in Alcántara and Ruiz, *Chile: Política y modernización democrática.* See also Alan Angell, "Party Change in Chile in Comparative Perspective," at *www.lac. ox.ac.uk/parties-ips.pdf.*

11. For an early discussion of the electoral law and its potential ramifications, see Peter Siavelis and Arturo Valenzuela, "Electoral Engineering and Democratic Stability: The Legacy of Authoritarian Rule in Chile," in Arend Lijphart and Carlos H. Waisman, eds., *Institutional Design in New Democracies: Eastern Europe and Latin America* (Boulder, Colo.: Westview, 1996), 77–99.

12. The Concertación is formed by the Christian Democrats, the Socialists, and the Party for Democracy (PPD) as well as several minor parties. On the right of the political spectrum are the Unión Demócrata Independiente (UDI) and Renovación Nacional (RN). The Communist Party and its allies continue to poll at about 3 percent.

13. Leticia Ruiz, "El sistema de partidos chilenos: Hacía una desestructuración ideológica?" in Alcántara and Ruiz, *Chile: Política y modernización democrática,* 86.

14. Alan Angell, "Hechos o percepciones ciudadanas? Una paradoja en la evaluación de la democracia chilena," in Alcántara and Ruiz, *Chile: Política y modernización democrática,* 185.

15. J. Mark Payne et al., *Democracies in Development: Politics and Reform in Latin America* (Washington, D.C.: Inter-American Development Bank, 2002), 34.

16. Dagmar Raczinski, "Radiografía de la familia pobre," in J. Samuel Valenzuela et al., *El eslabón perdido,* 294. As Alan Angell notes, leaving aside the richest tenth of the population, Chile is one of the most egalitarian countries in the Americas. Inequality is less than what one find in the United States. See Alan Angell, "Hechos o percepciones ciudadanas?" 171.

17. For an analysis of Boeninger's proposals, see Andrés Tagle Dominguéz, "Cambio del sistema electoral: Análisis del proyecto de reforma constitucional y propuestas de la Comisión Boeninger," Documento de Trabajo No. 365, Centro de Estudios Públicos, Santiago, August 2006, *http://cepchile.cl.* Tagle misses the point in criticizing the proposed reforms when he argues that they would not improve proportionality. The issue is not proportionality as much as the capacity of the system to provide for more citizen choice. Peter Siavelis's arguments in favor of a return to proportional representation are far more compelling. See his "Electoral Reform Doesn't Matter—Or Does It? A Modest Proportional Representation System for Chile," *Revista Chilena de Ciencias Políticas* 26 (2006): 216–25.

11

AN UNLIKELY COMEBACK
IN PERU

Cynthia McClintock

Cynthia McClintock *is professor of political science at George Washington University. Her current research focuses on the implications of runoff versus plurality presidential-election rules for democracy in Latin America. This essay originally appeared in the October 2006 issue of* the Journal of Democracy.

On 4 June 2006, Alan García of the American Popular Revolutionary Alliance (APRA) was elected president of Peru for a five-year term. García had achieved an astonishing comeback. By all accounts—including his own—his 1985 to 1990 administration had been calamitous, and many Peruvians had said that they would never vote for him again. Only six weeks before the April 9 first round of the 2006 elections, opinion polls placed him a distant third. In that first round, however, García squeaked past free-market candidate Lourdes Flores of the National Unity (UN) coalition to finish second, and then in the June 4 runoff defeated fiery ultranationalist Ollanta Humala of the Union for Peru (UPP) coalition.

García appeared likely to join the ranks of what Jorge Castañeda has called the "right left" in South America (which includes Chile's Socialist Party, Uruguay's President Tabaré Vázquez, and Brazil's President Luiz Inácio "Lula" da Silva).[1] Humala's loss was in all probability a defeat for the "wrong left," and dashed Venezuelan president Hugo Chávez's hopes for a second ally in the Andean region. To simplify further what Castañeda himself acknowledges is an oversimplified classification, the "right left" retains the left's longstanding commitment to social justice, but is now internationalist, committed to democracy, and respectful of free-market principles. In contrast, the "wrong left" is committed to social justice but is nationalist, authoritarian, and still wedded to "unreconstructed" statist economic policies.

The holding of free and fair elections represents a step forward for Peru in its uneasy return to democracy since November 2000, when the increasingly authoritarian and corrupt government of Alberto Fujimori (1990–2000) and his spymaster Vladimiro Montesinos imploded. Peru's electoral authorities performed ably in 2006. Although the first-round runner-up was decided by less than 0.5 percent and the runoff by only 5 percent, these results were accepted by the losing parties. Despite considerable disgruntlement with their electoral choices, voters turned out in large numbers; citizens chose a candidate who respects democracy, rather than one whose proclivities appear authoritarian. García is also the leader of Peru's only strong political party, whereas Humala's coalition was improvised.

These favorable outcomes were far from predictable. Both Fujimori and Montesinos remained political players. At numerous junctures, Humala threatened to repudiate the elections. Despite Humala's lack of political experience, the credible charges against him of committing human rights violations in 1992, and his complicity in his brother's bloody 2005 attack against a police station, the retired military officer won the election's first round and came close to winning the second. The UPP coalition won a plurality of 45 seats in the congressional elections, also held on April 9. The support for Humala underscored that, despite Peru's recent robust economic growth, the peoples of the southern highlands—most of whom are impoverished and of indigenous descent—continue to feel resentful of their social, political, and economic exclusion.

Toledo's Record and Legacy

Under the government of Alejandro Toledo (2001–2006), for the first time in its history Peru simultaneously enjoyed economic growth, political peace, and one-person-one-vote democracy. Nonetheless, Toledo's approval ratings bordered on single digits, and Peruvians' support for democratic government declined.

Economic-growth rates during Toledo's government were at their strongest since the government of President Manuel Prado (1956–62). Between 2002 and mid-2006, real annual GDP growth averaged about 5 percent—a record that might have been the strongest in the region, surpassing even those of Chile and Costa Rica.[2] Inflation remained low, about 2 percent annually, and fiscal management was prudent. As copper, zinc, and gold mines initiated or expanded production, export earnings skyrocketed from about US$7 billion in 2001 to more than $17 billion in 2005. Economic forecasts are now upbeat, reflecting the advance of the giant Camisea natural-gas project, the development of a highway between Peru and Brazil, and likely continued preferential access to the U.S. market. (If the U.S. Congress does not approve the U.S.-Peru Trade Promotion Agreement—a bilateral free-trade agreement that the Peruvian Congress ratified overwhelmingly in June 2006—then the Andean Trade Promotion and Drug Eradication Act will probably be extended.)

Yet the benefits of growth were limited primarily to the top third of the income distribution and barely reached the poor, who make up 48 percent of the population. Unemployment remained stubbornly high. Real wages were stagnant, and job-security provisions continued to erode. Many poor Peruvians sought policy changes; they felt betrayed by Toledo, who was Peru's first president of indigenous descent since 1931 and as a candidate had highlighted his ethnicity and made a commitment to the poor. As prices for raw materials rose and many international companies' profits soared, large majorities of Peruvians believed that the taxes and royalties these companies paid should be increased.[3]

The Toledo government remained vigilant against the Shining Path (or Sendero Luminoso, the Maoist insurgency), and the guerrillas did not resurge. Sendero remnants were estimated to number less than five-hundred people, operating almost exclusively in coca-producing areas. The military and police remained active in these areas and made several important arrests. Former Senderista leader Abimael Guzmán had been caught in 1992 and continued to serve a life sentence. Whereas more than 35,000 deaths were attributed to the Shining Path during the 1980s and 1990s, the U.S. State Department attributed fewer than fifty to the organization from 2003 to 2005. Yet Toledo's government received little credit for this achievement, in part because violent crime was perceived to be increasing.

Democratization advanced under Toledo. To understand the political violence of the 1980s and 1990s, the government appointed the Commission for Truth and Reconciliation in 2001; in 2003, the commission produced a detailed and rigorous, albeit controversial, report. The media, most of which had been mouthpieces for the Fujimori regime during its final years, became unshackled. Although judicial, police, and military reforms advanced haltingly, decentralization was achieved; elections for regional governments were held in November 2002 and regional governments were duly installed. A new law on political parties sought to reduce their prodigious number, requiring parties to win 4 percent of the vote in order to obtain any congressional seats.

The Toledo government tried to hold accountable Fujimori-era officials who were corrupt or guilty of human-rights violations. Recent estimates reveal that $1.8 billion was stolen from state coffers during the Fujimori government.[4] Prosecutors sought the extradition of Fujimori first from Japan, where the ex-president had fled in November 2000, and then from Chile, where he flew surreptitiously in November 2005. Montesinos, captured in Venezuela in 2001, was convicted on several charges and imprisoned. Also among the convicted were two finance ministers, a president of Congress, and several generals. In all, approximately 1,500 individuals were investigated on corruption charges, including many media magnates and politicians who had taken bribes from Montesinos.[5]

The democratic transition under Toledo was "unpacted"—there was no agreement between the outgoing authoritarian regime of Fujimori and the incoming democratic government. The Toledo government's judicial investigations threatened a significant swath of elites. Some of these elites, dubbed "the Montesinos mafia," still had money and friends in important positions and retaliated by scheming to bring about Toledo's downfall, hoping that a new government would approve an amnesty. In part because of the mafia's influence, media coverage of the president was unrelentingly negative. During coverage of Toledo's 2005 state-of-the-nation address, for example, the country's most important television news program repeatedly showed legislators snoring and yawning through the speech. Songs and subtitles ridiculed the president; newscasters commented that apparent Toledo supporters had been paid by the government.

How, in fact, should Toledo's leadership be judged? On the one hand, Toledo set priorities and moved to execute them. Although his Perú Posible party won only 38 percent of the seats in the 2001 congressional elections, Toledo fashioned a legislative majority. During crises, Toledo focused intently and worked hard to resolve them.[6] At the top levels of government he appointed highly qualified and respected professionals. On the other hand, Toledo faced problems related to his personal life. He was given to a lifestyle that many regarded as frivolous and insensitive to the poor; Toledo drank the best scotch and vacationed at a beautiful beach resort on Peru's north coast. At the start of his term, he raised his salary to $216,000 a year (which was repeatedly but inaccurately said to be the highest in Latin America).[7] Due to popular protest, it was reduced to roughly $144,000 a year, though Peruvians still considered this excessive.

By global standards, Toledo's lifestyle and salary were not outrageous. There were no rumors of lavish property purchases or of secret Swiss bank accounts. But Peruvians were not measuring Toledo by global standards; in part, they were measuring him against Fujimori. On Montesinos's orders, for years the Peruvian media had portrayed Fujimori as an austere workaholic, inaugurating one public-works project after another in remote villages. Peruvians were also measuring Toledo by their assumptions of what was appropriate for people of indigenous descent. One pundit said that if Toledo had vacationed in the southern highlands, his approval rating would have gained 30 points.

Toledo suffered from other personal and political weaknesses. He lost a great deal of moral authority in his first year when he refused to acknowledge paternity of his out-of-wedlock daughter. The Perú Posible party was a hodgepodge of politicians who often wrangled over government jobs, and Peruvians believed that the lower bureaucratic levels were full of incompetent party hacks. Accordingly, although it was Fujimori's government that had stolen $1.8 billion from the state (a sum virtually never mentioned in the media), Peruvians perceived an increase in corruption under Toledo, and their dissatisfaction with the "political class" intensified. In poll after poll, overwhelming majorities characterized politicians (which implicitly included democratically elected politicians) as thieves who break their promises and abuse their power. In a 1996 Latinobarómetro survey, 62 percent of Peruvians said that they were not very satisfied with the way democracy works in Peru, whereas by 2005, the figure had jumped to 80 percent (versus a Latin American average of 61 percent). In a 1996 Latinobarómetro survey, 63 percent said that "democracy is preferable to any other kind of government," whereas in 2005, the figure was a mere 40 percent (versus a Latin American average of 53 percent). The decline in support for democratic values was the region's most precipitous outside Paraguay and Panama.

In short, by 2006 both the economic and political legacies of the Toledo government favored a political outsider who could credibly promise social justice and moral authority. This was hardly new in Peru, but the 2006 election was one of the few in which the incumbent party could not field a presidential candidate, and Toledo's party won less than 5 percent of the vote in the following congressional election. (On the brighter side for Toledo, his approval rating was in the 40 percent range upon his departure from office, the highest approval rating ever recorded for an outgoing president in Peru.)

The Race Narrows

The early rounds of the 2006 campaign were full of surprises. First, Fujimori landed in Chile in November 2005 after almost five years in Japan, and was promptly arrested and denied contact with the media. This ended any possibility of his presidential candidacy. Although Congress had banned Fujimori from public office from 2001 to 2011, and though he faced prosecution on 21 criminal charges upon a return to Peru, Fujimori maintained that somehow these obstacles could be surmounted and in October proclaimed his presidential candidacy. Although the vast majority of Peruvians believed that Fujimori should be prosecuted, he continued to have the support of some 20 percent of the population. He likely left Japan for Chile in the belief that advancing a political campaign would be easier from a neighboring country.

Meanwhile, the pro-Fujimori party Alliance for the Future (AF) was in place in Peru. Its presumed goal was to obtain a bloc of congressional seats in order to pursue favorable judicial treatment for Fujimori. Its presidential candidate was a longtime Fujimori stalwart, the tough-talking Martha Chávez; at the top of the party's congressional ticket was Fujimori's daughter Keiko. Keiko had been a gracious acting first lady for her separated father, and she claimed to have tried early on to persuade her father to break with Montesinos.

A second surprise was the contest's rapid narrowing from 23 candidates to three frontrunners: Flores, Humala, and García. Fujimori aside, this narrowing was largely due to opinion polls and media coverage. Polls affected media coverage, and vice versa. As early as October 2005, poll results dominated the headlines. This favored candidates with strong name recognition and solid party backing who were already campaigning—namely, Flores and García. But what the pollsters and the media downplayed was that, as late as mid-March, a whopping 40 percent of voters remained undecided.[8] Presumably, these voters were dissatisfied with the frontrunners, but they were not receiving much information on other candidates, and they were being told that votes for candidates other than the frontrunners would be "wasted." Accordingly, several qualified but relatively unknown candidates were hurt; one example was Susana Villarán, a former human rights leader and center-left minister in the cabinet of Valentín Paniagua (the interim president from the Fujimori government's November 2000 implosion until Toledo's July 2001 inauguration).

A third surprise was that Paniagua was not among the three frontrunners. In polls, Paniagua scored the highest of any candidate for honesty and commitment to democratic principles. In virtually everyone's view, Paniagua's interim government—perceived as center-left—had been successful. But Peruvians worried that Paniagua, who was 69 years old, lacked drive and energy. Also, his campaign lost months to negotiations with potential coalition partners; in the end, Paniagua's more-or-less centrist Popular Action (AP) party joined two small center-right parties to form the Center Front. This alliance did not help him. By late January 2006, Paniagua's poll numbers had fallen to 10 percent, and Lima's pundits gave him no chance to win.

The fourth surprise was Humala's meteoric rise. He jumped into third place in November's polls, and into second in December's. If Venezuela's Hugo Chávez, Bolivian president Evo Morales, and Mexican 2006 presidential candidate Andrés Manuel López Obrador are the "wrong left" in Castañeda's classification, then Humala is the "very wrong left." Humala's economic platform emphasized the nationalization of Peru's natural resources and the repudiation of the Peru Trade Promotion Act. Humala appeared authoritarian, having threatened to reject the elections and destabilize a Flores government. As a former army lieutenant-colonel, he enjoyed such strong support within Peru's military that one pundit said that he was not an "outsider" but "an insider" hailing from Peru's oldest political party—namely, the military. Humala was also a virulent nationalist who regularly denounced Chile; his family's ideology was "etnocacerismo," named after General Andrés Cáceres, a Peruvian hero of the War of the Pacific (1879–83) who had resisted the Chilean invaders. Beyond all this, Humala had no political credentials and no coherent political party.

What was behind Humala's surge? First, he convinced many Peruvians that he would combat the corruption of Peru's political class, even threat-

ening to impose the death penalty on public officials caught stealing. A
second factor, albeit largely unspoken, was Humala's mixed ethnicity. He
is neither indigenous nor white. Peru's population is 15 percent white, 45
percent Amerindian, and 37 percent mixed; Peruvians in recent years have
sought out nonwhite presidential candidates, whom they probably trust
more. In 2006, Humala was one of only two or three such candidates.

First-Round Cliffhanger

From December 2005 through March 2006, it appeared that Humala
and Flores would be the two candidates to emerge from the April 9 first
round. Yet Humala and Flores were both dealing with serious challenges.
Previously undecided voters began to opt disproportionately for García,
who was positioning himself as the candidate of "responsible change" (this
was his key motto, whereas he called Flores the candidate of continuity
and Humala the candidate of "irresponsible" change).

Humala's rise was checked by indications that he was an imposter.[9] He
proclaimed indigenous roots, but he had been born and raised in Lima and
had studied at expensive private schools. He touted his nationalism, but
he had traveled to Venezuela in January and was feted by Hugo Chávez.
He stood for law and order, but in February he had been identified as
"Captain Carlos" and accused of extrajudicial killings in 1992 in a hamlet
in the coca-producing Upper Huallaga Valley. Investigative journalists
pointed out that Humala's second vice-presidential candidate, Carlos Tor-
res Caro, had served as Montesinos's lawyer, and that many candidates
on Humala's congressional list had been charged with serious crimes.
Journalists also investigated Humala's purported October 2000 uprising
against the Fujimori government—the event that had initiated Humala's
political career—and argued that it had actually been a smokescreen for
Montesinos's escape from Peru.

A final disclosure concerned the New Year's Day 2005 attack against a
police station in the remote province of Andahuaylas by Humala's brother,
Antauro. Antauro charged that the Toledo government was corrupt and
demanded the president's resignation. Four policemen were killed, and
Antauro was arrested. Ollanta—who at the time was Peru's military at-
taché in South Korea—tried to keep his distance from his brother's failed
rebellion, but taped messages from Ollanta indicated his knowledge and
support of the attack. In March, Humala's parents' interjections further
damaged his campaign. His father proposed an amnesty for imprisoned
insurgency leaders Abimael Guzmán and Víctor Polay. His mother said
that homosexuals should be shot.

In contrast to Humala, Flores was an experienced politician, respected
among Peru's elites and internationally. While still in her twenties, she
was a rising star in Peru's pro–free market and socially conservative
Popular Christian Party (PPC). She was elected to Congress for the PPC

in 1990, 1993, and 1995. She was the standard-bearer for the center-right UN coalition in the 2001 elections, losing a spot in the runoff to García by only 1.5 percent; the UN (which included the PPC, the staunchly Roman Catholic Renovation party, and the National Solidarity Party of Lima mayor Luis Castañeda Lossio) became the third-largest bloc in Congress.

Flores was perceived as intelligent, responsible, and sensible; she sought to highlight these qualities in her campaign motto, "Peru in firm hands." Pledging continuity with the Toledo government's market policies but also austerity and good governance, she enjoyed overwhelming business and media support. She advanced several promising economic initiatives, such as renovating ports in order to make Peru an economic power in the Pacific Rim. Although some feared that she would be vulnerable to smear campaigns as a childless single woman, Flores's gender probably brought her as many votes among women as it cost her among men.

In February and March, however, Flores's candidacy was hammered by Humala and García. Their charge was that Flores was "the candidate of the rich," primarily because her first vice-presidential candidate, Arturo Woodman, is one of Peru's wealthiest businessmen. It did not help that Woodman had had dealings with Fujimori and Montesinos, nor that Flores's political circles were narrow and lily-white, and included other high-profile former Fujimori allies. Astoundingly, Flores did not rebut the charge that she was "the candidate of the rich." Nor did she retaliate with negative campaigning against García and Humala. Flores's entourage undercut her promise of good governance, and she faced more and more difficulty in channeling Peruvians' desires for change.

In late January, García stood at only about 15 percent in the polls and appeared to be a long shot. Although APRA is Peru's oldest and only institutionalized political party, with strong roots on Peru's north coast, it is perceived by many Peruvians on both the right and the left as a corrupt and opportunistic cult. Historically, APRA was also populist. It rejected Marxism but championed the "little man" against the oligarchy, and when in power sought to satisfy everyone through deficit spending. Elected to the presidency in 1985 on a center-left platform, García aspired to lead Latin America against debt payment, which outraged the international financial community. His expansionary fiscal policies led to quadruple-digit inflation, food shortages, and the worst economic crisis in Peru's history. At the same time, the economic debacle fanned the flames of the Shining Path insurgency, which expanded into Lima. While García's counterinsurgency policies were criticized for different reasons by both the right and the left, he should be credited with the establishment of the Special Intelligence Group, which ultimately captured Guzmán.

García made rash, hot-tempered decisions. The most notorious was his attempt to nationalize Peru's private banks in 1987. Also, in June 1986 his government ordered the military to quell riots staged by Shining Path inmates in Lima prisons, and more than two-hundred Shining Path inmates were killed in the process. Peru's left in particular has long charged that García himself was complicit in these killings; their concerns were not assuaged by the appointment of retired navy admiral Luis Giampietri as García's first vice-presidential candidate for the 2006 elections. Giampetri had directed one of the prison assaults and had collaborated closely with the Fujimori regime.

Fujimori ordered García's arrest during the 1992 *autogolpe* (self-coup), but García managed to escape to Paris, where he spent the better part of the next eight years. Returning to Peru in January 2001, García came from behind in the 2001 presidential election to edge past Flores into the runoff, though in the end he lost to Toledo by six points. Still, after the 2001 legislative elections, APRA became the second-largest party in Congress, and García was Peru's most important opposition leader. For several years, García led voter preferences for the 2006 presidential ballot, but his lead dissipated. In July 2004, he made a controversial decision to support a national strike by the country's largest labor union; worse yet, during the march he kicked an APRA supporter, reinforcing concerns about his temper. Moreover, APRA's overwhelming victories in the 2002 regional elections proved problematic, as many APRA regional presidents would face corruption charges.

Nonetheless, most Peruvians still deemed García a brilliant and charismatic politician. García was introducing innovative economic proposals. In particular, his proposal for *la sierra exportadora* (the exporting highlands) integrated the left's concern with the poor and the "reconstructed" view that the way out of poverty was through the global free market. García proposed to expand vastly Peru's roads and irrigation canals and to offer low-interest loans aimed at dramatically increasing the export of some 26 highland-grown agricultural products. García advanced a plethora of additional reforms. He stipulated that the working day should be eight hours, with additional pay for overtime. He proposed a reform of the pension system and the elimination of temporary employment contracts that limited workers' rights. While Flores sighed that nothing could be done about international companies' windfall profits and Humala advocated nationalization, García said that his government would negotiate new terms with company executives. While Flores applauded the U.S.-Peru Trade Promotion Agreement and Humala excoriated it, García favored it—though with conditions.

The results of the April 9 elections are reported in the Table on p. 164. In the congressional contest, the UPP won a plurality, securing slightly more than a third of the seats. This percentage was identical to that held by Toledo's Perú Posible party in 2001. As in the 2001 to 2006 Congress, APRA had the second-largest number of seats and the UN the third. Fujimori's party was fourth with 13 seats, an increase from 3 in the previous Congress. Paniagua's Center Front finished fifth. After weeks of uncertainty, both Perú Posible and the evangelist National Restoration party passed the 4 percent threshold and secured a pair of seats each. Women fared quite well, winning 29 percent of the seats, an increase over 2001. Peruvians may also cast "preferential votes" for individuals on congressional tickets; under this provision, Fujimori's daughter Keiko starred, winning three times as many votes as any other candidate. The affable Keiko had campaigned with her outgoing new American husband and had enjoyed extraordinarily favorable media coverage.

The Second Round

Many Peruvians were unhappy with their two second-round choices. Still, almost all political analysts ultimately decided that García was the "lesser of two evils," often saying that if García became president, elections would be held in 2011—but not necessarily so if Humala won. In a postelection University of Lima poll, the most frequent explanations for Humala's loss were, first, "because he is authoritarian"; second, "because of the intervention of Hugo Chávez"; and third, "because he is very radical."

García and Chávez clashed during the first month of the campaign leading up to the June 4 runoff, stimulating nationalistic resentment of Chávez and his support for Humala.[10] On April 12 in Washington, D.C., Toledo signed the U.S.-Peru Trade Promotion Agreement. In response, at a meeting of several Latin American presidents on April 19, Chávez announced that the Andean Community of Nations was dead and that Venezuela would withdraw from it. García then said that "Chávez was asking that Peruvians and Colombians not negotiate with the United States when 80 percent of Venezuela's exports go to the U.S., and Venezuela has the equivalent of a free trade agreement for its oil." Chávez lost his temper, unleashing a torrent of insults against García; the former president was "a swine, a gambler, and thief." Chávez reiterated his hope that his "compadre" and "compañero" Humala would win.

At this point, Toledo repeated his request that Chávez stay out of Peru's elections. Chávez in turn called García and Toledo "two alligators from the same swamp." At about the same time, Bolivia's Morales called Toledo a "traitor [to indigenous peoples]" and Venezuelan officials derided him as a "U.S. puppet" and "Bush's office boy." Both countries withdrew their respective ambassadors, and Chávez threatened to cut diplomatic relations with Peru if García won. Such insults among Latin American political leaders are rare, and most Peruvians were shocked. In an Apoyo poll, 61 percent reported a negative opinion of Chávez and only 17 percent a positive one. García repeated that Humala was advised and financed by Chávez and said that only he could prevent Peru from becoming a "colony of Venezuela." At García's campaign rallies, crowds chanted, "Chávez, get out of Peru!"

TABLE—RESULTS OF PERU'S 2006 ELECTIONS

POLITICAL PARTY—PRESIDENTIAL CANDIDATE	PRESIDENTIAL RACE		CONGRESSIONAL RACE
	FIRST ROUND 9 April 2006 (% valid vote)	SECOND ROUND 4 June 2006 (% valid vote)	9 April 2006 (# of seats of 120 total)
Union for Peru (UPP)—Ollanta Humala	30.6	47.4	45
American Popular Revolutionary Alliance (APRA)—Alan García	24.3	52.6	36
National Unity (UN)—Lourdes Flores	23.8	—	17
Alliance for the Future—Martha Chávez	7.4	—	13
Center Front—Valentín Paniagua	5.8	—	5
National Restoration—Humberto Lay	4.4	—	2
Perú Posible—No presidential candidate	—	—	2
Other—14 additional presidential candidates	3.7	—	0
Citizen Participation			
Blank votes (percent of all votes cast)	11.9	1.1	
Null votes (percent of all votes cast)	4.2	7.4	
Did not vote (percent of all eligible voters)	11.3	12.3	

Source: Peru's National Office of Electoral Processes (ONPE) at *www.onpe.gob.pe*. Figures may not add to 100% due to rounding.

Although Humala tried to bounce back by portraying himself as a victim of the U.S. government and García as Washington's candidate, these gambits failed; to its credit, the U.S. embassy stayed outside the fray. Apoyo polls taken before April 9 had forecast that García would lose to Humala (when most Flores voters were probably saying that they would nullify their ballots), yet García surged to an 8-point lead on April 24 and to a 14-point lead on May 5.

For various reasons, García's margin of victory in the second round was only 5 points. By June 4, the García-Chávez clash was less salient. Also, García had become the establishment candidate, who in Peru almost invariably fares worse in the election itself than in early opinion polls. Furthermore, as García moved to the right to attract Flores and Fujimori voters, he lost others who then considered him too far to the right or too opportunistic. García's platform became more business-friendly; he began supporting the U.S.-Peru Trade Promotion Agreement and adopted Flores's call for the renovation of Peru's ports. At the same time, García made some populist promises that could prove difficult to fulfill, such as providing potable water for half a million Lima residents in six months.

For his part, Humala became somewhat less intemperate. He retreated from his call for the nationalization of Peru's natural resources and from his endorsement of the leftist military government of Juan Velasco Alvarado (1968–75). Apparently, he urged reticence on his parents. He emphasized a new pledge to slash gas prices by 30 percent, which was credible given Chávez's likely support of a Humala-led government. But the UPP candidate also continued to signal that he was not afraid to break rules: The most spectacular example was his behavior at the start of the May 21 presidential debate (the only debate of the campaign). With millions of Peruvians glued to their television sets, Humala arrived more than fifteen minutes late, and then lied, saying that he had been tardy because the road had been blocked by García supporters, when in fact he had been videotaped at a convenience store. Humala also placed a Peruvian flag on his podium and would not remove it, even at the request of the moderator (who finally removed it himself).

Two days before the debate, for reasons that are not entirely clear, Montesinos jumped into the campaign.[11] In an audiotape smuggled from his cell, the former spymaster charged that Humala had collaborated in Fujimori's fraudulent election and that Humala had staged his October 2000 uprising in order to camouflage Montesinos's escape from Peru (as investigative journalists had suspected). The immediate question became which presidential candidate would benefit from Montesinos's charges. Although presumably it would be García, during the debate Humala implied that García had made a deal to pardon Montesinos when he became president. Although overall García appeared to win the debate, questions about a García pardon for Montesinos persisted.

Ultimately, García prevailed. There was a deep regional divide. García won handily in Peru's relatively prosperous coastal area, including Lima. In the interior, Humala won all but two departments, and in the southern highlands—Ayacucho, Huancavelica, Cusco, and Puno—he averaged 75 percent of the vote. Turnout, almost 90 percent in both presidential rounds, was the highest for any election since Peru's 1980 return to democracy, save for 1985. (Peru has a system of compulsory voting, though it is not strongly enforced.) Blank and invalid votes, which had increased sharply in 2001, returned to average historical levels.

Prospects for Democracy Under García

Peru's elections have implications for Latin America's recent leftward trend. The left was predominant, and what Castañeda calls the "wrong left" was strong—but not as strong as the "right left."

By historical standards, the right and center-right did not fare badly. In elections during the 1980s, Flores's PPC averaged 11 percent of the vote. In 1990, when the PPC and Popular Action were allied under Mario Vargas Llosa, this coalition won 33 percent in the first round. In 2006, Flores's UN, Fujimori's AF, Paniagua's Center Front, and National Restoration won a combined 41 percent of the vote. Probably more Peruvians than ever before favor free-market economics, and a slim majority appears to support the U.S.-Peru Trade Promotion Agreement. If Flores had fielded a more appealing entourage, she might have won.

Humala appeared to be a "very wrong left" leader. In contrast to López Obrador and Morales, Humala was a military man with no political experience. He was a disciple of Chávez and in important respects an impostor. Especially because of his shady political allies and his hostility toward Chile, he was a very risky choice. Yet if not for Peru's runoff rule, he would now be president. Humala might also have been elected had it not been for Chávez's heavyhanded intrusions into the campaign. While Chávez's support for Humala—financial or otherwise—probably helped the UPP candidate in the early months, the Venezuelan president's April vitriol provoked nationalistic reactions. Savvy Latin American politicians, in particular Mexico's Felipe Calderón, quickly noted the popular desire for an electoral process free of interference not just from the United States but also from another Latin American nation. Chávez is the first Latin American president with the resources and the ambition to support presidential candidates outside his own country, and in 2006 he hoped to add both Humala and López Obrador to his camp; now his only possible addition appears to be Nicaragua's Daniel Ortega.

The 2006 elections may herald a reinvigoration of democratic values in Peru. Turnout was excellent, and the election authorities were respected despite the close runoff race. In a June 2006 poll conducted by Catholic University's public-opinion institute, 67 percent of Peruvians said that "democracy is preferable to any other form of government"—a large jump from 2005 figures. Upon García's inauguration on July 28, a majority of Peruvians were guardedly optimistic. But has García in fact changed? Are Peruvians' hopes likely to be fulfilled?

García's ideology has evolved in numerous respects. He has shifted his economic positions and has appointed as finance minister a strictly orthodox economist. While García had always sought partnerships with other Latin American nations and is now strengthening Peru's relationships with Chile and Brazil, his internationalist outlook no longer excludes the United States. Although García has always respected the electoral process, during his first administration he was challenged by human rights dilemmas; if all goes well, political violence will remain minimal during this administration, and he will not have to confront human rights problems. García has acknowledged the stereotype of APRA as corrupt and has signaled his intent to combat any such proclivities.

García appears to have matured personally. He was only 36 years old when he was inaugurated in 1985, and he is now 57. Over the years he has developed a respected group of APRA colleagues; in particular, Jorge del Castillo, García's prime minister, seems to be a reliable sounding board. Yet as García's infamous 2004 kick showed, he can still be impetuous.

Peruvians continue to worry about his ego, his honesty, and his ability to focus.

García still faces formidable obstacles. He must contend with vigilant political opposition from Humala, who is now preparing for the November 2006 regional elections. The AF is an important congressional bloc and will press hard for favorable judicial treatment for Fujimori and his allies. Of crucial importance, García made a multitude of promises, and he will be walking a tightrope in trying to fulfill them without overstepping market constraints. In contrast to García's first term, APRA does not enjoy a congressional majority. This is a good thing in the view of many analysts, as García will have to negotiate. APRA itself remains disciplined, and García was able to appoint some non-Apristas to cabinet posts without an APRA backlash. For the moment, García appears likely to secure approval for his initiatives from all parties except Humala's UPP. Over the longer run, given the fragility of Peru's political parties, the outlook is uncertain; the UPP is already in disarray, and both the UN and Center Front coalitions have suffered defections.

García emerged victorious because he promised what most Peruvians wanted: democracy and social justice, but also a respect for the market. Keeping this promise will not be easy. In contrast to the time of García's first administration, however, Peru's economy is now growing robustly, the country is by and large at political peace, and García has a good deal more experience. Under the García government, Peru's deep socioeconomic divides may at least be bridged, and its democracy may move closer to consolidation.

NOTES

I would like to thank Jo-Marie Burt, Michael Shifter, and Coletta Youngers for their very helpful comments on a draft of this article. I would also like to thank the Universidad San Martín de Porres, which, through the offices of Richard Webb, hosted me in Peru from March to May 2006.

1. Jorge G. Castañeda, "Latin America's Left Turn," *Foreign Affairs* 85 (May–June 2006): 28–44. Beyond overgeneralization, other criticisms include that the authoritarianism and nationalism attributed to the "wrong left" could be considered "rightist" and that "right left" leaders campaigned to the left but are governing at the pragmatic center. See Michael Shifter, "Chávez Should Not Steer U.S. Policy," *Financial Times*, 7 April 2005; and Sidney Weintraub, "Latin America's Movement to the Left," *Issues in International Political Economy* 75 (March 2006): 1–2.

2. The data in this article on Peru's economy are drawn from CEPAL (Comisión Económica para América Latina y el Caribe) and from the *Economist*, "Country Report: Peru," from numerous issues.

3. See the National Engineering University survey reported in Ana Núñez, "El país pide a candidatos," *La República* (Lima), 24 March 2006, 2.

4. *Economist*, 30 July 2005, 34. Estimates by historian Alfonso W. Quiroz are even higher.

5. *El Comercio* (Lima), 25 June 2003.

6. See Gustavo Gorriti, "Sucedió en el Pardo's Chicken," *Caretas,* 20 July 2006, 30–31.

7. The salary of Mexico's Vicente Fox was higher; see George W. Grayson, "Mexican Officials Feather Their Nests While Decrying U.S. Immigration Policy," at *www.csis. org/articles/2006/back306.html.*

8. Inés Flores, "A la caza de 41% de indecisos," *La República,* 14 March 2006, 2.

9. For details and sources on the information in this paragraph, see Cynthia McClintock, "Ethnic Politics in Peru and the Presidential Candidacy of Ollanta Humala," paper presented at the Latin American Studies Association meeting, Puerto Rico, 15–18 March 2006.

10. Among the various reports, see "With Friends Like These," *Economist,* 13 May 2006, 44, and "Solito Se Jaranea," *Caretas,* 4 May 2006, 16.

11. For an insightful analysis of Montesinos's likely motives, see ConsultAndes S.A., "Peru Key Indicators 06-269," 14–21 May 2006, 4–5.

12

COLOMBIA HEWS TO THE PATH OF CHANGE

Eduardo Posada-Carbó

Eduardo Posada-Carbó *is research associate at the Latin American Centre in St. Antony's College, Oxford. He is the author of* La nación soñada: Violencia, liberalismo y democracia en Colombia *(Bogota, 2006), and his current research is on the history of democracy in Latin America. This essay originally appeared in the October 2006 issue of the* Journal of Democracy.

The day after the Colombian presidential election of 28 May 2006, the newspaper *El Nuevo Herald* of Miami noted "the disappearance of the bipartisan system that had governed the country with the alternation of Liberals and Conservatives for over a century." Established in 1849–50, both parties have long stood out as among the oldest in the Americas. The recent voting underlines that while neither party has disappeared, the old party system has long been eroding. Given the extent to which this erosion has proceeded, it becomes important to ask precisely what is replacing the old system, why the change is taking place, and what it portends for the future of democracy in Colombia.

At first glance, the election results reveal an unfamiliar landscape. The historically dominant Liberty Party (PL) was relegated to third place with a mere 12 percent of the vote while the Conservative Party (PC), the Liberals' traditional opponent, chose for the second presidential race in a row not to field a candidate of its own. Instead, it backed the successful reelection bid of President Alvaro Uribe—a dissident Liberal running under the banner of Colombia First (a coalition of recently established parties and the PC)—who won a second four-year term with a 62 percent landslide. The runner-up was Carlos Gaviria of the Alternative Democratic Pole (PDA), a new party made up of various left-wing movements, which garnered 22 percent of the vote.

That the Colombian party system is undergoing change would seem unquestionable, although the direction of the change remains uncertain.

There are signs that a multiparty system is emerging, with at least five central protagonists: the two historic parties, PL and PC, plus the PDA and two major new "Uribista" parties—the Social National Unity Party (PSUN) and Radical Change (CR). Critics portray some of the new parties as mere façades being used by various factions of Liberals and Conservatives as they attempt to rebuild and maintain their traditional dominance around the leadership of President Uribe. Others write off Uribe as a right-wing populist who wields personalized power to the detriment of political institutionalization.

The 2006 voting thus raises a set of questions: How can the changes in the party system be characterized, and why did they occur? How does Uribe's resounding reelection impinge on the party system, and what sort of political regime is taking shape under his administration? How has the country's continuing internal armed conflict influenced recent political developments? Does Uribe's reelection buck a regional trend that some say is shifting Latin American politics to the left?

Uribe's Landslide

On 7 August 2006, Uribe took the oath of office as Colombia's forty-sixth elected president since 1830. His inauguration, to some extent an ordinary event in a country where presidents have come and gone regularly according to an almost uninterrupted electoral calendar, nonetheless had extraordinary features. For the first time in the republic's history, an incumbent president had been reelected.[1] A 2004 constitutional reform had made this possible by allowing presidents to run for a second consecutive term. The sweeping scale of his victory was also remarkable: He was returned to office with the support of 7.3 million of the 12 million Colombians (out of a total population of about 43.5 million) who cast ballots.

It is important to stress the magnitude of Uribe's electoral success. He faced three experienced and serious opponents—a situation that would seem to make a modest plurality win more likely than a landslide—yet nonetheless managed to sway more than three-fifths of the voters. Horacio Serpa, the PL candidate, could boast a long career as an accomplished and popular politician, and was running his third race for Colombia's highest office. Carlos Gaviria of the PDA had been Uribe's teacher in law school and then gained national repute as president of the Constitutional Court before winning a Senate seat in 2002. He had the support of some of the country's most widely read newspaper columnists. Antanas Mockus, the former rector of the National University and twice the mayor of Bogota, was a maverick running on the ticket of the Indigenous Social Alliance (ASI) party. While he performed dismally on election day, he had the kind of resumé and electoral record that made his candidacy difficult to dismiss beforehand.

Uribe won in 31 of Colombia's 33 departments. The only exceptions were Guajira on the northern border with Venezuela and Nariño on the southern border with Ecuador, both of which went for Gaviria. In another five departments, the president won with less than 50 percent, but these were minor setbacks compared to the towering majorities that he piled up in the rest of the country. His most impressive margins, moreover, came in the most populous departments: In those of the core coffee-growing region and in the central departments of Cundinamarca and Huila, he won about 70 percent. In Bogota, which is currently governed by the left-wing opposition, he won almost 64 percent, while in Valle, another important opposition-governed department, he won nearly 60 percent.

Some have suggested that this triumph is less formidable than it seems because turnout was only 45 percent. Such an observation, however, needs qualification. For almost two centuries, Colombia has been going to the polls regularly and frequently, and unlike most Latin American countries it has never had compulsory voting. Thus it may not be surprising that Colombian turnout has typically lagged behind the rate of voter participation in Argentina or Costa Rica, and more closely resembles turnout in the United States. High emigration has seen more than three million Colombians move abroad, yet overseas ballots accounted for only 120,000 of the votes cast for president in 2006. There are also reasons to believe that the electoral census is inflated and thus that abstention rates are lower than reported. In any case, Uribe's remarkable mandate cannot be doubted. He even increased his electoral support: Two million more people voted for him in 2006 than in 2002.

How can we explain this massive win? Uribe followed an electoral strategy of "more government than campaign."[2] Opponents and commentators alike criticized his refusal to take part in televised debates with his rivals or give press interviews. It was alleged that the campaign was devoid of substantive controversy. Yet a closer look shows a different picture, in which almost every single item on the government's agenda was contested, and electors could make clear choices from a relatively wide menu.

Concerns about the advantages of incumbency received airings throughout the campaign. In May 2005, however, the Uribista coalition reached a congressional agreement with one of the opposition movements that later formed the PDA to pass a guarantee bill. This law imposed restrictions on the president's activities during the official campaign period, guaranteed mass-media access to all candidates, and offered state funding to parties. As a result, candidates from the two major opposition parties, the PL and the PDA, could each count on a larger sum in campaign subsidies than could Uribe.

The campaign involved significant degrees of open and visible political mobilization in a country often portrayed as being engaged in "civil war." Public rallies regained prominence in a contest that, according to the Fundación Seguridad y Democracia, had been the least violent in the last decade. The Revolutionary Armed Forces of Colombia (FARC)—the Marxist-Leninist guerrilla group that in the past has tried to disrupt elections with violence—announced that it would not interfere with the polling day and invited votes for any candidate opposing Uribe.

At his lowest point in the regular Gallup surveys—the polls that came closest to predicting the final results—Uribe received more than 58 percent support from those who said that they intended to vote. Early in the campaign, in December 2005, this number stood at almost 71 percent. That he came within ten points of this figure on election day five months later is a testament to his skill as a campaigner. But his ability to register so much support at the outset of the race demands an explanation that ventures beyond the campaign and takes into account his achievements in office.

Votes for a Policy?

There is no denying the severity of the challenges against which Colombia has had to struggle in recent decades. Faced with far less serious problems, between 1985 and 2004 a total of fourteen presidencies were interrupted in ten Latin American countries in a series of debacles that form what Arturo Valenzuela calls "a sad arc of failure."[3] Various Colombian presidents have weathered grave storms, but Uribe is unique in having maintained popularity rates near or above 70 percent throughout his first four years in office, as well as in having actually *gained* voter support as his first term drew to a close.

Any attempt at explaining this achievement should start by recognizing the somber mood of 2002. Both in Colombia and abroad, a sense of impending catastrophe prevailed. With very high homicide and kidnapping rates and what seemed an ever-escalating conflict after three years of frustrated peace talks with the FARC, perceptions of a disintegrating nation were common. Unwilling to see their country explode or collapse, a desperate electorate turned to Uribe, then a 49-year-old lawyer with important political experience as a senator and as governor of his native department of Antioquia. He was not seen as a single-issue campaigner, but as the candidate most able to deal with a large set of problems. Having been a Liberal throughout his political career, Uribe carefully avoided a formal break with the PL, but did run a dissident campaign under the banner of a "catch-all" movement.

Francisco Gutiérrez Sanín has shown that Uribe interpreted the "centrist" feelings of the electorate regarding the complex conflict that involves not only the guerrillas and the government but also rightist paramilitary groups. He projected not extremism but an air of determination and moderation that made him an appealing figure across lines of party and social class. Although Uribe appeared to be the most "hawkish" among the candidates in 2002, he received significant support from "doves."[4] He was perceived as the candidate best able to lead the country to peace.

Uribe's campaign manifesto listed a hundred points. His main plank was a program of "security"—a controversial concept in academic and intellectual circles, and puzzlingly a neglected area of discussion in Colombia despite the country's long security crisis.[5] At every opportunity during the 2002 campaign, and later as president, Uribe kept insisting that he was not seeking to install a police state, but "security for all" as a "founding value of democracy." In June 2003, his government published a comprehensive document containing what was the most detailed state formula in decades aimed at tackling violence. Achieving security was the first though "not the only preoccupation of the national government."[6]

"Democratic security" remains the president's most controversial policy, particularly among foreign observers. Yet there are clear indicators that substantial progress has been made in this area during the last four years, though the problems are still immense and far from solved. It is the progress in security—together with the desire to give the president a chance to follow through with his policies—that explains Uribe's extraordinary success at the polls in 2006.

No other indicator reveals more clearly the improvements in security than the homicide rate. Homicides have dropped sharply since 2002, when there were some 29,000 killings. In 2005 there were still more than 17,000 homicides, though this was a significant reduction in the death toll, and the lowest rate in twenty years. Such advances are striking, particularly when set against the tragic background of the country's extraordinarily high levels of homicide since the late 1970s. Kidnapping rates also show clear improvements. The number began declining in 2000, two years before Uribe took office, but between 2002 and 2005 kidnapping plummeted 73 percent. It continues to be a serious problem, together with the large number of people whom criminals continue to hold captive. The decline is nonetheless significant: Kidnapping is a major source of finance for the guerrillas, and a tool of wider social intimidation.

It is of course hard to say precisely how much of the decline in homicides and kidnappings is due to the government's policies against the major illegal armed groups, which include not only FARC but also the National Liberation Army (ELN), the second-largest Marxist guerrilla group, and the rightist paramilitary United Self-Defense Forces of Colombia (AUC). But the progress has been palpable, even if doubts about the final results remain. Whether FARC has really suffered a grave loss of capacity or has opted for a tactical retreat is debated, but government forces have at least regained the offensive, with an expanded presence and degree of control throughout the country. The most detailed statistical study of the conflict during the first two years of Uribe's administration shows "incomplete but nonetheless unmistakable evidence" that his policies have had "significant success in fighting the guerrillas while reducing civilian deaths."[7]

The government opened a demobilization process with the AUC at the end of 2002, when the paramilitaries announced a unilateral cease fire.

Since then, more than 27,000 of their members have demobilized and have surrendered sizeable amounts of arms. Concerns about the paramilitaries' intentions, their political influence, and their continued involvement in the drug trade and other criminal activities have all been publicly raised and widely discussed throughout this process. Discussions about justice for the paramilitaries' victims have also been intense. These preoccupations, while valid, tend to overshadow the gains that have been made. The AUC's demobilization does seem to have led to an important drop in killings. Statistical studies suggest that, on average, homicides have declined by 13 percent in areas where the demobilized paramilitaries operated.[8] While there are major variations across different parts of the country, the studies conclude that demobilization has improved human security. As state forces provide more security, paramilitaries are becoming more exposed publicly and more vulnerable to prosecution.

What should now be more fully recognized in the wake of Uribe's huge win is how much these improvements have meant to Colombians. In July 2005, 71.3 percent of respondents told Gallup pollsters that "the country is more secure than a year ago"; ten months later and a few weeks prior to the presidential election, those answering the same way still made up a strong 64.1 percent majority. In the May 2006 Gallup poll, Uribe was seen as the most able candidate by far when it came to handling security issues such as combating guerrillas, narcotraffickers, paramilitaries, and common delinquents. Most of those whom Gallup surveyed said that the major challenges of Uribe's second term will lie not in the area of security, but in the socioeconomic arena. Here also, however, the president's first administration made visible headway.

Colombia's recent economic performance may not be as strong as that of some other Latin American countries, but 2005's 5.1 percent GDP growth stood in sharp contrast to the deep recession of 1999. Though the economy was already on its way to recovery when Uribe took power in 2002, there remained signs of postrecession stagnation until 2003. Recent improvements are partly explained by a growth in investment rates, led by the private sector, and more widely by a "favorable external environment with adequate financing conditions for emerging economies and strong commodity prices."[9] Inflation is at a relatively low 4.1 percent. The fiscal deficit, while still high, appears to be under control. Unemployment fell from 19 percent in 1999 to 13 percent in 2005. Rising employment helped to reduce poverty levels during the last five years, though the extent of that improvement has been much questioned.[10] The government can also show progress in education and health, though income inequality continues to be high. In sum, the picture is one of moderate to good progress, which has encouraged what the Colombian economist Alejandro Gaviria calls "a trust boom" linked to the government. Though he warns that the "boom" may be temporary, the campaign-period Gallup polls do show that citizens saw Uribe as better positioned than any rival to deal with problems such as extreme poverty, housing for the poor, and the needs of people displaced by violence.

Uribe's style of governance—his personal austerity, commitment to long working hours, and strong leadership—may explain part of his popularity. But to understand fully his overwhelming electoral victory in 2006, it is important to acknowledge that his government has so far delivered more security for Colombians, who now see better prospects for their economy and society after a succession of severe crises. Javier Sanín notes that in 2006, as in no campaign since 1982, promises of change failed to prevail over the promise of continuity.[11] Yet the "continuity" that most voters chose was continuity with the substantial *changes* that Uribe's first administration had brought.

The major opposition candidates seem not to have made a proper assessment of Uribe's first-term accomplishments—an oversight that led them into a campaign of denials which could not finally prove persuasive. Carlos Gaviria of the PDA kept repeating that as a result of a "manipulated public opinion," Colombians were living in a "virtual country" under a "sort of collective anaesthetic" that prevented them from seeing a reality of insecurity and deteriorating human rights. Security is still not recognized by the PDA as a problem in itself, but is seen as derivative of other "structural" problems, a view shared by the PL's Horacio Serpa. The word "security" appeared in the PDA's platform only in relation to "integral social security" or "sovereignty"; the words "homicide" and "kidnapping" did not appear at all.

Mockus of the ASI did acknowledge some of the administration's achievements at the beginning of his campaign, when he announced that he was a "post-Uribe" rather than an anti-Uribe candidate. Following his party's defeat in the March 2006 congressional elections, Mockus changed tracks and hardened his discourse, becoming heavily critical of Uribe's policies toward the paramilitaries. Similarly, the statist vision of the economy held by the two major opposition candidates could not persuade the vast majority of voters that these candidates offered viable alternatives to government policies.

Taken together, the 2002 and 2006 presidential elections offer a relevant case study for the theory of "critical elections"—that is, votes which produce significant reorientations in government policies or a "sharp and durable electoral realignment between parties."[12] While it may be clear that voters have acted to change the direction of government since 2002, the precise contours of the party-system realignment following the "critical elections" of the last four years remain less clear.

The Two-Party System's Long Twilight

Until recently, some scholars continued to classify Colombia as having a "two-party system" of "uncommon" electoral stability.[13] Yet as we have seen, the evidence from the 2006 presidential election suggests a changed scene, with the Liberal candidate finishing a distant third, the Conservatives running no candidate of their own, a number of new parties forming to back Uribe's coalition, and the PDA standard-bearer emerging as the surprise runner-up. What then is left of the so-called bipartisan system?

To arrive at a proper answer to this question, we would first need to discern the true nature of the party system at the time that Uribe first came to power. The label of bipartism has survived to this day in spite of an almost continuous process of fragmentation since 1958 and the emergence of a large number of new parties. Giovanni Sartori questioned the validity of the label, calling Colombia a case of "façade two-partism," since the electoral units were not the parties as such but rather "patronage-based networks organized around individual politicians that present several different party lists." As Sartori observed, "If that is a two-partism, then I do not know what two-partism is."[14]

By 2002, there were 74 political parties and movements registered with the electoral authorities, and more than forty had seats in Congress. It is true that some of those had been established by former Liberals and Conservatives to optimize their electoral prospects in a proportional-representation (PR) system that had few entry restrictions and allowed for multiple party lists. It is also true, however, that even as lists pro-liferated, parties and movements were becoming independent electoral organizations; this reflected an ever-increasing personalization and a loss of party control over candidate selection and policy formulation. The 1986 adoption of direct popular elections to fill municipal offices such as mayoralties not only increased the number of locally based parties and movements, but also helped to undermine the local-level influence of the national Liberal and Conservative parties. Neither, for instance, has elected a mayor of Bogota since 1994.

It is hard to tell whether changes in the party system shaped subse-quent electoral reforms, or the other way around. The introduction of popular mayoral elections in 1986 was followed by the adoption of a comprehensive set of new electoral institutions contained within the 1991 constitution. These included elected governors (they previously had been appointed by the president), a single national district for the election of senators, two-round presidential elections, referendums, and congressio-nal representation for ethnic minorities. These were all components of a relentless effort of constitutional engineering directed in part against the two-party system. It all added up to what Rodrigo Losada calls "a whole battery of measures" to bombard "the strength of bipartism."[15]

A weakened bipartism meant neither the disappearance of the two traditional parties nor the immediate emergence of any third strong party, though the Democratic Alliance–April 19 Movement (AD-M19)—a coalition that incorporated the demobilized M19 guerrillas—managed to capture 25 percent of the seats in the 1991 Constituent Assembly elections. Despite its inability to consolidate itself as a party, some of its former members continued to play prominent roles in both national and local politics. The incentives for party fragmentation and new-party formation abounded, and they included access to state funding for electoral campaigns since the passage of a 1994 law. Scholars puzzled over the emerging party system, which defied simple classifications.[16]

Pressures for further reform persisted.[17] By the late 1990s, the long-term critical conditions that Pippa Norris has identified as major spurs to electoral reform were present: significant changes to the party system, a series of political scandals that sapped public confidence in the status quo, and the existence of a constitutional provision allowing referendums, with all their potential to break party interests.[18] The attempts of President Andrés Pastrana (1998–2002) to enact electoral-system reform met with defeat in Congress. Yet the results of the 2002 congressional races—in which the PC and the PL each saw its caucus shrink—together with Uribe's election set in motion a renewed drive for electoral-system reform.

In October 2003, Uribe called a referendum on a lengthy and complicated questionnaire which included, among many other matters, changes in the electoral system. The referendum failed, but at almost the same time, Congress began deliberations of its own that led to the passage of a substantial electoral-reform bill. The law adopted the D'Hondt seat-allocation formula, a method of distributing votes in a list-PR system that usually favors larger parties or coalitions. The law also forced parties to present single lists in elections and required a minimum threshold *(umbral)* in order to take any seats in Congress.[19] It was "one of the most fundamental reforms of an electoral system carried out anywhere in the last decade or so."[20]

Although Colombia's original two-party system was long gone before Uribe took office in 2002, this does not mean that he stepped into an institutional vacuum. The party system had not suddenly collapsed, but had been undergoing a long process of transformation. That the press was still asking in 2006 whether or not Uribe's reelection had "killed" bipartism reflects the extent to which the language of political analysts has been lagging behind the pace of political change in Colombia. The many recent changes have left behind a party system whose final shape remains uncertain, but the 2006 congressional and presidential election results suggest that a limited multiparty system—with four or five parties as major protagonists—may finally become established.

Parties: The Shape of Things to Come

President Uribe has played and will continue to play a significant role in reshaping the party system, but the realignment that is taking place also follows an institutional dynamic which is beyond his control. Congress's 2003 electoral reform passed independently of the president's will. It had a visible and immediate impact, drastically reducing the number of competing party lists and hence the number of parties that have seats in Congress. More significantly, the reform law encouraged the forging of alliances among previously separate groups, and thus the formation of new parties—the most important being the PSUN, the CR, and the PDA.

Uribe's coalition of the PSUN, CR, the Conservatives, and three small parties obtained a clear majority at the congressional elections on 12 March 2006, winning 61 of the 102 Senate seats, and 90 of the 166 seats in the Chamber of Representatives. The two main opposition parties, the PL and the PDA, won a total of 28 seats in the Senate (18 and 10 respectively), and 42 in the Chamber (35 and 7 respectively). Minor parties, such as those representing indigenous groups and various regionally based movements, took 13 seats in the Senate and 34 in the Chamber.

The government coalition's future is debatable. During the process of electing the leaders of Congress's two houses and their various committees, the coalition's unity proved fragile. In order to prevail, coalition leaders had to accept the partnership of two minor parties that had been excluded from Uribe's reelection campaign due to questionable funding sources or alleged ties to paramilitaries.[21] The nature of the new Uribista parties also remains debatable, but the point to stress here is the emergence of a multiparty governing coalition, including the PSUN, the PC, and the CR, under Uribe's leadership.

The demise of the two-party system in Colombia is often confused with the end of the two traditional parties. Yet neither of them has disappeared. Their power may have diminished, but they have also been experiencing significant changes in organization and in personnel, suggesting that the possibility of renewal cannot be ruled out. The PL, moreover, remains the single largest party in the lower house, followed by the PSUN and the PC.

The PL, Colombia's historically dominant party, has become a particular focus of discussion after its disastrous performance in the 2006 presidential election. There has been much talk about a possible reunification of the PL around the president, who as a dissident Liberal maintains an ambiguous stance toward the party—distant from the hierarchies but appealing to the rank and file. There have also been doubts about the permanency of the new Uribista parties (which at times have been portrayed as Liberals in disguise), particularly since the CR's leader has said that his party and the PSUN are "transitory phenomena." The PL's reunification, though not impossible, would be fraught with difficulties. Vested interests already exist in the CR and the PSUN, not all of whose leaders have come from the PL. Significant portions of the CR and PSUN electorates probably feel distant enough from the traditional parties that the old Liberal label might prove a liability. The PL's current leader, former president César Gaviria (no relation to Carlos Gaviria of the PDA), has explicitly reiterated that the party will remain in opposition. Specula- tions have also been floating that Uribe might be trying to reinvent the traditional two-party system. Yet even if the PL reunifies, and the PSUN and the CR prove to be temporary, there will still be a third protagonist to consider—the PDA.

Although the PDA is only the fifth-largest party in Congress as a whole, its representation in both houses is significant. Its morale received a huge boost from the second-place finish in the presidential race. The party also controls two important posts, the mayor's office in Bogota and the governor's in Valle, the department that contains Cali, Colombia's third- largest city. The consolidation of the PDA will have to overcome several obstacles, including the rivalries that have long troubled the Colombian left. Nonetheless, there are serious reasons to believe that, as the president of the Conservative Party acknowledged, the PDA "is here to stay as one of the parties that will define the political future of the country."

Colombia, then, has moved to a multiparty system not merely as regards the number of parties, but also as regards what Peter Mair calls "the breadth of ideological polarization."[22] It would be misleading to identify the PDA as belonging to the "extreme left"—its leader has re- peatedly opposed the armed struggle and the party cannot be considered to be "outside" the system. Indeed, in many ways the PDA possesses the features of a "cartel party" as described by Mair. Nevertheless, the PDA's presidential platform was clearly at the leftward end of the politi- cal spectrum, if by that we mean general hostility to the free market and backing for state-interventionist policies.

It would be similarly misleading to identify the Uribista parties as "extreme right." In both camps, there are internal tensions that may be pulling their respective component parties in different directions, but the "extremists" are probably in minority, while the PL would seem to be settled in the center-left. Only time can tell whether the emerging party system will be one of moderate or polarized pluralism, but for the moment it looks as if there has been a shift in the pattern of ideological distance among the most relevant parties.

Opponents of President Uribe accuse him of undermining representa- tive democracy by treating political parties with disdain. Before becom- ing president, however, he had always been a Liberal Party man.[23] He counted on the support of political parties in his two successful presi- dential campaigns. Rather than disappearing under his administration, political parties of all persuasions appear to have gained strength. In his victory speech on 28 May 2006, Uribe acknowledged the parties of his coalition as well as the institutional limits that now bind his dealings with Congress, including a new law that requires parties in Congress to work through groups *(bancadas)* rather than through individual legislators' relationships with the executive branch. He showed that he envisions a significant role for the parties of his coalition by quickly handing the crucial interior and defense ministries to the leaders of the PC and the PSUN, respectively.

Democracy's Time

Beyond its impact on parties and the party system, Uribe's reelection raises questions about the future shape of Colombia's democratic polity. His reelection in itself represents a fundamental change in the temporal dimension of Colombian democracy.[24] In a country where for almost two centuries (excepting the years from 1886 to 1902) presidential terms have generally been four years, or even as short as two years, having a president in power for eight continuous years is a substantial break with tradition that may yield unforeseen consequences. In order to overcome the most serious challenge that Colombia has been facing for the last several decades—its internal armed conflict—perhaps the country needed to extend the time horizon of its government as the best guarantee for the continuity of a policy that has had some successes.

The FARC and the ELN share the unlimited conception of time that characterizes authoritarianism, but now they face a determined government which will be in power for longer than the usual four-year cycle that they are used to outlasting. Perhaps this may finally force them to accept settlements. The ELN is already engaged in peace talks with the government. Complications becloud the prospects for separate talks with the FARC, but there are signs that both sides are exploring the terrain amid a climate of opinion that is again tending to favor negotiations. The demands for Uribe to deliver peace are indeed pressing. His government has to ensure the paramilitaries' demobilization, which entails dismantling their mafia structures and preventing them from turning back to crime. Inasmuch as the armed conflict is financed by the narcotics trade, the government must continue its fight against drugs.

Uribe's second term represents an extraordinary opportunity, but if things go wrong a weary electorate will find its patience being put to the test as never before. Expectations are high. The morning after his victory, the press was quick to note the challenges ahead: In addition to ending the armed conflict and eradicating illicit crops, his administration would be expected to sustain economic growth, reduce poverty, finalize the free-trade agreement with the United States, manage relations with Venezuela's populist leader Hugo Chávez, persuade Congress to adopt new tax and health reforms, and combat corruption—a full agenda that also has to leave room for unforeseen events. Second terms can be "the nemesis of presidential reputation,"[25] and Uribe's opponents are banking on that nemesis, with their eyes on 2010. Since his first term, pundits have seized upon every drop in his opinion polls to announce the end of Uribe's "honeymoon"—only to see his popularity rise again. Uribe may be able to prove that second terms are not always a curse, but can provide the additional time that democratic governments often need to tackle severe crises.

Presidential reelection does not mean that Uribe's mandate has ceased to be "government pro-tempore," to use Juan Linz's definition of democracy. Uribe's foes have cried that "autocracy" will fall upon Colombians, that under Uribe democracy will be "trimmed," that what he aims for now is to perpetuate his own power. These warnings sound more like expressions of frustration than sensible political analyses. With the recent significant advances of the PDA (in local and departmental offices, in Congress, and in the presidential elections), Colombia has today—under the provisions of the 1991 constitution—a more pluralist structure of power than before. In the first press interviews that he gave after his reelection, Uribe rejected out of hand any suggestion of a third term. Meanwhile, the country is preparing itself for another round of local elections in 2007, when possible candidates to succeed Uribe will be gathering their forces.

After Evo Morales's December 2005 election to the presidency of Bolivia, as Latin Americans looked ahead to a busy 2006 electoral calendar, the international press became obsessed with what seemed to be a new wave of left-wing or populist movements sweeping the continent. A lucid article by Uruguay's former president Julio María Sanguinetti surveyed the situation more accurately: There was no shift to the left in Chile after its January 2006 presidential election, and while the governments in Brazil and Uruguay are leftist, both have been moving toward the center. Recent elections in Peru, Costa Rica, Colombia, and Mexico confirm Sanguinetti's analysis: The emerging pattern is best described as complex, not as a simple drift to the left.[26] Chávez's populism looks a bit lonely. Some cannot avoid the temptation to compare him with Uribe as a fellow "populist"—a misguided exercise that confuses two different styles of government and two different institutional settings.

The time has come to examine national politics in Latin America beyond such easy stereotypes. There has been a tendency among students of the region to lump its politics into the simplistic categories of caudillismo (strongman rule) and populism, and this has once again become fashionable with the rise of Chávez. Leadership and individual agency do matter, but so do institutions, ideas, and history. In Colombia, democratic institutions have proven themselves resilient despite the odds. Resilience does not mean resistance to change. It is in the context of a changing political landscape, where parties continue to play a significant role, that President Uribe's achievements and limitations should be understood.

NOTES

1. The 1886 constitution allowed presidents to seek reelecion but only if they had not exercised power within eighteen months before election day. Thus when Rafael Núñez was

reelected in 1892, the incumbent was Acting-President and Vice-President Miguel Antonio Caro. See José María Samper, *Derecho público interno de Colombia,* 2 vols. (Bogota: Biblioteca Cultural de Cultura Colombiana, 1951), 2: 323–25.

2. See Eduardo Posada-Carbó, "Las elecciones presidenciales en Colombia," *Análisis del Real Instituto Elcano* 61, 24 May 2006, available at *www.realinstitutoelcano.org.*

3. Arturo Valenzuela, "Latin American Presidencies Interrupted," pp. 3–17 of this volume.

4. Francisco Gutiérrez Sanín, "La radicalización del voto en Colombia," and Gary Hoskin, Rodolfo Masías, and Miguel García, "La decisión del voto en las elecciones presidenciales de 2002," in Gary Hoskin et al., eds., *Colombia 2002: Elecciones, comportamiento electoral y democracia* (Bogota: Universidad de los Andes, 2003). See also Fernando Cepeda Ulloa and Eduardo Posada-Carbó, "The Congressional and Presidential Elections in Colombia, 2002," *Electoral Studies* 22 (December 2003): 785–92.

5. See Eduardo Pizarro Leongómez, "A New Approach: Alvaro Uribe's Democratic Security Project," Inter-American Dialogue Working Paper, July 2003; and Eduardo Posada-Carbó, "Colombia, la democracia a prueba," in Carlos Malamud, ed., *América Latina, 2002–03* (Madrid: Real Instituto Elcano, 2003), 218–33.

6. See Colombia (Presidencia de la República), *Política de defensa y seguridad democrática,* Bogota, 2003.

7. Jorge A. Restrepo and Michael Spagat, "Colombia's Tipping Point?" *Survival* 47 (Summer 2005): 132.

8. Michael Spagat, "Colombia's Paramilitary DDR: Quiet and Tentative Success," available at *www.cerac.org.co*; and A. González and J. Restrepo, "Desmovilización de las AUC: Mayor seguridad humana?" *UN Periódico* (Bogota), 21 May 2006.

9. Colombian Ministry of Finance, *Colombia Is on the Way to Sustainable 5% Growth: How Vulnerable Is the Recent Recovery?* (Bogota: Imprenta Nacional, 2006).

10. On the question of employment and poverty, see Alejandro Gaviria, "Evolución reciente del mercado laboral urbano y alternativas de política," unpubl. ms., May 2006.

11. See "El politólogo Javier Sanín analiza la contundente victoria del presidente Alvaro Uribe," *Revista Credencial* (Bogota), 6 June 2006.

12. V.O. Key, Jr., "A Theory of Critical Elections," *Journal of Politics* 17 (February 1955): 3–18. For an interesting reassessment, see Richard L. McCormick, *The Party Period and Public Policy: American Politics from the Age of Jackson to the Progressive Era* (Oxford: Oxford University Press, 1986), 64–88.

13. Erika Moreno, "Whither the Colombian Two-Party System? An Assessment of Political Reforms and Their Limits," *Electoral Studies* 24 (September 2005): 486.

14. Giovanni Sartori, *Comparative Constitutional Engineering: An Inquiry into Structures, Incentives and Outcomes* (London: Macmillan, 1994), 177, 180–81.

15. Rodrigo Losada, "Deterioro progresivo del voto partidista tradicional en Colombia, 1974–1998," *ALCEU: Revista de Comunicação, Cultura e Política* 6 (January–June 2003): 190.

16. See, for example, Francisco Gutiérrez Sanín, "Se ha abierto el sistema político colombiano? Una evaluación de los procesos de cambio (1970–1998)," *América Latina Hoy* 27 (April 2001): 213; and Lawrence Boudon, "Party System Deinstitutionalization: The

1997–98 Colombian Elections in Historical Perspective," *Journal of Inter American Studies and World Affairs* 42 (Autumn 2000): 33–57. On the degree of institutionalization of the Colombian party system, see Ronald Archer, "Party Strength and Weakness in Colombia's Besieged Democracy," in Scott Mainwaring and Timothy R. Scully, eds., *Building Democratic Institutions: Party Systems in Latin America* (Stanford: Stanford University Press, 1995).

17. For a detailed analysis of the long process of reform, see Arturo Sarabia Better, *Reformas políticas en Colombia: Del plebiscito de 1957 al referendo del 2003* (Bogota: Norma, 2003).

18. Pippa Norris, "Introduction: The Politics of Electoral Reform," *International Political Science Review* 16 (January 1995): 3–8.

19. The *umbral* for the Senate was 2 percent of the national vote, and for the Chamber half of the electoral quotient (the total of ballots cast divided by the number of seats to be allocated) in the respective departments.

20. Matthew Shugart, Erika Moreno, and Luis E. Fajardo, "Deepening Democracy by Renovating Political Practices: The Struggle for Electoral Reform in Colombia," in Christopher Welna and Gustavo Gallón, eds., *Peace, Democracy and Human Rights in Colombia* (Notre Dame: University of Notre Dame Press, 2007). Available at *www.icpcolombia. org/documentos/Deepening_democ_Col.pdf.*

21. See "Cuánto cuesta el apoyo de los purgados?" *www.semana.com,* 25 July 2006; and "La coalición del presidente creció este jueves en el Congreso," at *www.eltiempo.com,* 20 July 2006.

22. Peter Mair, *Party System Change: Approaches and Interpretations* (Oxford: Clarendon Press, 1998).

23. See John C. Dugas, "The Emergence of Neopopulism in Colombia? The Case of Alvaro Uribe," *Third World Quarterly* 24 (December 2003): 1117–36.

24. Andreas Schedler and Javier Santiso, "Democracy and Time: An Invitation," *International Political Science Review* 19 (January 1998): 19–38.

25. Jack Beatty, "The One-Term Tradition," *Atlantic Monthly,* September 2003, 38.

26. Julio María Sanguinetti, "Ola de izquierda?" *El Tiempo* (Bogota), 23 March 2006.

13

VENEZUELA: CHÁVEZ AND THE OPPOSITION

Javier Corrales and Michael Penfold

Javier Corrales *is associate professor of political science at Amherst College. He is author of* Presidents Without Parties: The Politics of Economic Reform in Argentina and Venezuela in the 1990s *(2002).* ***Michael Penfold,*** *associate professor at the Instituto de Estudios Superiores de Administración (IESA) in Caracas, is editor of* Costo Venezuela *(2002). This essay originally appeared in the April 2007 issue of the* Journal of Democracy.

For the past few years, Venezuela's President Hugo Chávez Frías has enjoyed a favorable political situation at home. Economic growth, fueled by rising oil prices, has been spectacular since 2003. Chávez and his allies have won four decisive electoral victories since 2004, the most recent being his sweeping 63 percent walk to a fresh six-year term in the December 2006 presidential race. And since 2005, the opposition has become increasingly tame, while street turmoil is on the decline and seldom results in violence. In addition, Chávez has achieved complete control of all check-and-balance institutions, including the unicameral National Assembly, which after the opposition boycott of the December 2005 elections now contains not a single opposition legislator. These political advantages would be the envy of any world leader. And yet, Chávez has been governing as if Venezuela faces some kind of emergency. He has been busily concentrating more authority, even receiving a grant from the National Assembly of "enabling powers" to rule by presidential decree for eighteen months starting in February 2007.

How did a movement that began in 1998 as a grassroots effort to bring democracy back to the masses turn into a drive to empower the executive branch at the expense of every other actor? The acceleration of authoritarianism in Venezuela cannot be explained by recourse to functional theories. These theories, which draw on Guillermo O'Donnell's famous explanation of the origins of bureaucratic authoritarianism in 1960s Latin

America, posit that authoritarianism grows out of chronic governability crises which prompt actors—whether in office or opposition—to seize and centralize power in order to cope with dire circumstances.[1] Prior to 2004, one could argue that Venezuela was suffering from a governability crisis—albeit one that was likely at least partly fabricated—and that this crisis might justify some of Chávez's increasing concentration of powers. Since 2004, however, Chávez has had almost no reason to feel politically threatened or encumbered yet has notoriously leaped in the direction of authoritarianism.

A necessary condition for this leap has been what Nancy Bermeo would call "elite intentions"—that is, the ideologies of elected politicians as well as their "misreadings" of the preferences of larger constituencies.[2] But motive alone is not sufficient; means and opportunity are needed as well. In Chávez's Venezuela, these have come in the form of economic resources at the state's disposal *together with* weakened institutions of representation. In addition, it is crucial to underscore the president's deliberate political strategies: his use of polarization, clientelism, offers of the opportunity to engage in corruption with impunity, and discrimination in favor of supporters when filling government-controlled jobs coupled with threats to see to it that foes are fired. A review of key moments in Venezuela's transition toward authoritarianism will make it easier to see how state resources both tangible and intangible can interact with rising authoritarianism.

Venezuela's New Political Regime

Chávez never tires of proclaiming a commitment to participatory rather than liberal democracy. He is right that Venezuela is moving away from liberal democracy, but he is not replacing it with more participation. Instead, Chávez is creating what many classical-liberal thinkers feared most: a quasi-tyranny of the majority. The Chávez regime has emerged as an example of how leaders can exploit both state resources and the public's widespread desire for change to crowd out the opposition, and, by extension, democracy.

Between 1999 and 2003, the rise of authoritarianism in Venezuela followed a consistent pattern: The government would target institutions almost one at a time, attempting to strip each of power in turn. The opposition would protest, and the government would answer by becoming more hard-line and exclusionary.[3] Starting in late 2003, this game took a turn as the government wheeled out a fresh tactic—heavy barrages of state spending aimed at rewarding loyalists and punishing dissidents. This new artillery, as we will show, left the opposition disarmed.

Chávez, a former army lieutenant-colonel who had spent time in jail for leading a 1992 coup attempt, began the process of regime change with the rewriting of the constitution shortly after he won his first presidential election in December 1998. He could have started by focusing on the flagging economy, but instead aimed to rewrite the rules governing relations among the branches of government in order to make the presidency stronger. In what is now becoming a trend in the region, Chávez began 1999 by appealing to voters' widespread antiparty feelings and convoking a National Constituent Assembly explicitly designed to kill the *partidocracia* (party dominance) that had characterized Venezuelan politics since the late 1960s. The weakening of the nonexecutive branches he sold as a means of "stabbing to death" the "moribund" traditional parties that were holding onto power within and through those branches.

Chávez's first conquest was to ensure himself overwhelming control of the Constituent Assembly. He did this by manipulating a self-serving system for selecting delegates (elections were by plurality and took place within districts of varying sizes at the state level) through a clever nomination strategy that rationed candidates from his coalition across districts and coordinated the vote from his supporters using ad-hoc lists (known as "kino cardboards") which helped to identify official candidates with the adequate numbers for each district.

The new president's camp drew only 53 percent of the vote but wound up with 93 percent of the seats and a free hand to rewrite the basic law. The predictable result was the most heavily presidentialist constitution in contemporary Latin America.[4] The presidential term went from five to six years, with the possibility of a single reelection. The president obtained complete discretion over military promotions with no need for legislative approval. The Senate was eliminated. The president gained the power to enact laws and to hold any kind of referendum without support from the legislature. Public financing for political parties was banned. The constitution did introduce the possibility of recalling mayors, governors, or the president, but only under highly stringent conditions.

By dramatically raising both the advantages of holding office and the costs of being in opposition, this constitution produced what scholars call a "high-stake power" political system.[5] In such a case, incumbents' incentives to share power shrink, as does the opposition's room to accept the status quo. The opposition, feeling shut out and stripped of other means to affect policy, soon begins staging street protests in hopes of guarding what few bastions it still holds.

Chávez replaced the old party-based system with a new focus on the presidency. The old system had begun with the 1958 interparty agreement known as the Pact of Punto Fijo. By the 1970s, the system was well known worldwide as a paradigmatic example of how such deals can lead to democracy even in unlikely places. By the 1990s, however, Venezuela had become famous as a case study of how pacting parties can ossify until voters reject them in disgust. Chávez exploited this disgust to weaken legislative powers, after which it became easier for him to pack the high court and tighten control over the attorney-general, the comptroller-general, and the military. The executive branch also acquired control over the National Electoral Council (CNE), the body that governs electoral affairs. For the first time in Venezuela's democratic history, doubts began to arise concerning the fairness of electoral rule.[6] With the executive rampant, the next step was to rearrange state-society relations.

The Politics of Polarize and Punish

In 2001, Chávez obtained from the legislature "enabling powers" to rule by decree in certain policy areas, mostly having to do with property rights in the hydrocarbon and agricultural sectors. When he threatened to seek the same sort of control over public education, broad sectors of society expressed shock at what seemed a gratuitous power grab. Then they responded with what amounted to a kind of allergic reaction in the body politic: Business and labor groups, civil society organizations, and political parties both old and new began to promote national protests, including a two-day civil stoppage in December 2001. By 2002, the country was gripped by the worst polarization that Latin America had seen since the heyday of the Sandinistas in 1980s Nicaragua.

For two years, the opposition seemed to have the upper hand. Between 2001 and 2003, the ruling coalition suffered defections in record numbers (from the cabinet, the legislature, and even the military). On 11 April 2002, in the midst of one of the most massive civil protests in Latin America's history, business leader Pedro Carmona and a military faction staged a coup that briefly removed Chávez from power. Carmona swiftly turned highly punitive against *chavistas,* dissolved the National Assembly, and dismissed the elected state governors. His support collapsed and Chávez returned in less than 48 hours from exile at an offshore navy base. Although many in the opposition had abandoned Carmona almost immediately, the episode damaged the anti-Chávez cause by tarring it with the *golpista* (coupmaker) label.

With international mediation efforts failing and Chávez refusing to negotiate, the opposition chose as its new tack a two-month strike by workers and managers from the state oil company, PDVSA. As oil production dried up, Chávez fired almost 60 percent of PDVSA's staff and ordered the military to take over the hydrocarbon industry. The hard times that ensued—GDP shrank by 17.6 percent in 2003—hurt the president less than it hurt the strikers, and they blinked first.

The opposition then went to Plan C: a recall referendum. This first truly electoral challenge to Chávez faced a high hurdle, however, for the 1999 Constitution demands that proponents of recalling a president must first collect valid signatures from a fifth of all registered voters and then must obtain not merely a majority but more votes for recall than the incumbent gained in the previous election. Although the Chávez camp bombarded the opposition with an array of legal and administrative obstacles to valid-signature collection, the CNE finally ruled in March 2004 that the opposition had gathered more than enough, and that there would be a referendum. This was the administration's weakest moment—the closest it came to succumbing. Polls showed the opposition far ahead. Again, however, the government did not respond by softening its exclusionary policies. Instead, it met this new threat from below with that familiar standby of Latin American politics, vintage populism.

Before the April 2002 coup, Chávez had been relatively inattentive to social spending, and in fact had dismantled most of the social programs left behind by the previous administration. Social spending declined in real terms during the early Chávez years, and the only social programs that survived were mainly delegated to the military. But in late 2003, reaping an oil windfall and facing the prospect of a real electoral challenge, Chávez launched what on his weekly television show he liked to call "missions to save the people." The deluge of money that he poured out in 2004 (close to 4 percent of GDP) enabled him to turn his low 2003 approval ratings of around 45 percent into a 59 percent victory in the August 2004 recall referendum. Dismayed oppositionists claimed fraud, but international observers from the Organization of American States, the Carter Center, and the UN Development Programme found no merit in these charges.

Dumbfounded by the stunning reversal of fortune that Chávez had engineered in just four months, the opposition went into a postreferendum coma and barely contested the October 2004 elections for regional office. Chávez's partisans took over 21 of the 23 state governments and more than 90 percent of the municipalities. In addition, the administration packed the Supreme Court with a dozen new judges, each one an avowed friend of the president's "Bolivarian revolution."

In short, Venezuela switched from a situation of heightened power competition in 2003 to one of political-energy asymmetry in 2005: The regime grew bolder, and the opposition grew more hopeless. Exhausted and discouraged, opposition leaders greeted revelations that the government could use the automated voting system to trace voter identity with a decision to sit out the December 2005 National Assembly elections.

By early 2006, the opposition had virtually capitulated. Every one of its strategies had failed. Massive mobilizations, labor strikes, the recall, appeals to the international community, and electoral participation had produced nothing but waning power and fewer concessions from the government. The opposition ran out of options and gas at least in part because in Venezuela, as in any oil-exporting country in which the state dominates the petrochemical sector, the government controls the fuel both literally and figuratively, and can give it to friends while keeping it away from foes.

Unlike the recall vote two years earlier, the December 2006 presidential election resulted in no claims of fraud. The CNE approved a manual audit of the votes that both local and international observers regarded as confirming the official results. Chávez won at least 50 percent in every state, including Zulia, the home of opposition standard-bearer Manuel Rosales. The election featured both the highest level of turnout (just under 75 percent) and the widest margin of victory in Venezuelan history, adding one more to the string of consecutive elections since 1998 in which Chávez has broadened his margin among the voters. Chávez garnered a larger share of the vote in rural states, in four of the five oil states, and in urban centers such as the Capital District of Caracas. The one glimmer of hope for the opposition was the concentration of its vote in just two parties, Un Nuevo Tiempo and Primero Justicia. This could be a sign that opposition voters are rethinking their post-1992 tendency to turn away from parties—a trend that has weakened society's capacity to hold authoritarianism in check.[7]

Social Spending and Rising Authoritarianism

Between 1989 and 1998, Venezuelan voters repeatedly turned against efforts by presidents to concentrate power.[8] How did Chávez manage to prevent this electoral sentiment, so strong in the 1990s, from unseating him in the following decade?

To understand Chávez's electoral fortunes since 2004, it helps to clarify the symbiotic relationship between clientelistic spending and declining check-and-balance institutions. When such institutions lose power amid a growing economy, the incumbent can raise spending while making it more discretionary. Opportunities for clientelism expand and with them the votes that the incumbent commands, while institutions of accountability suffer more erosion.

Clientelism is one approach to social spending. Other approaches include: 1) underfunding, 2) cronyism, and 3) spending that is meant to and actually does benefit the poor (what the World Bank calls "pro-poor spending").[9] Underfunding happens when governments fail to provide sufficient funds for social programs. Cronyism consists of social spending that in reality is mere camouflage for direct subsidies to elites, mostly "friends and family" of incumbents. Clientelism refers to spending that, unlike cronyism, is directed toward nonelites, but is nonetheless offered conditionally: The state expects some kind of political favor back from the grantee. Finally, pro-poor spending occurs when aid is offered on grounds of true need and without political conditions attached.

All democracies engage in all four types of spending, though proportions vary across countries, programs, and eras. The key question is which direction a newly elected administration takes when it changes the inherited proportions. We suggest that the answer depends on the degree of political competition and the strength of domestic check-and-balance institutions at the relevant time.

Table—Four Types of Social Spending

	Constrained by Institutions	Not Constrained by Institutions
High competition	Pro-poor spending	Clientelism
Low competition	Underfunding	Cronyism (friends and family)

Political competition refers to the difference in political force between the incumbent and the opposition. Competition is relatively low if the opposition musters few votes, has reduced access to state office, or has no immediate opportunity to challenge the government at the polls. Institutional accountability will be stronger when presidents face constraints from the legislative branch, whether structural (such as high levels of legislative authority over budgets) or circumstantial (such as when the opposition party or coalition controls a legislative chamber). An opposition that is competitive and in possession of robust accountability tools will be better able to oversee the administration, and contain the executive's temptation to use social policy self-servingly. All this favors "pro-poor" spending over "vote-buying" spending.

Varying degrees of these two democratic conditions—competiveness and accountability—will yield different results in terms of social spending (see Table). The worst situation for the poor is low political competition. Incumbents feel no pressure and thus have no incentive to seek more (or more reliable) votes through expanded spending. Social spending will remain sparse and, if institutions of accountability are weak, all too easily divertible toward cronyism. Heightened competition will drive incumbents toward the cultivation of wider voter support and thus promote spending, but with no guarantee that it will be aimed at helping the poor rather than at helping administration clients. The best safeguard against clientelism comes from the other key variable: checks on the arbitrariness of state officials.

In short, pro-poor spending is most likely to occur when both political competition and institutional constraints are strong. This proposition helps to explain social policy under Hugo Chávez. The first stage, from the approval of the new constitution in 1999 to the beginning of the recall campaign in 2004, represented the political shift from high to low accountability, leading to underfunding leavened by cronyism. The second stage saw rising political competition as the opposition began to focus on the recall referendum. Competition prompted the executive to spend, and declining accountability allowed it to spend opportunistically.

It is hard to estimate the totality of state spending under Chávez, but the best sign of its magnitude is that, despite the five-fold oil-price increase over the last three years, the accumulated fiscal deficit reached 2.3 percent of GDP in 2006.[10] The government has created special nontransparent funds, free of legislative oversight, that are believed to hold more than US$15 billion from the recent oil windfall. In 2005, the National Assembly approved a modification of the Central Bank law to create one such fund by transferring $6 billion from international reserves. Known as the Development Fund (FONDEN), it is controlled by the executive branch through the Ministry of Finance rather than the Central Bank (Venezuela's Central Bank, like most, was designed to be relatively insulated from direct executive-branch influence). There is no information on how or even whether this money has been used. In February 2006, the National Assembly approved another transfer of $4 billion from the Central Bank, and the president announced that PDVSA would transfer $100 million dollars a week into FONDEN throughout the year, adding another $5.2 billion.

Evidence shows that Chávez has distributed resources according to different political criteria for different programs, but clientelism figures heavily in most of them.[11] While a program such as Misión Ribas was influenced by considerations of poverty relief, it has also been used to "buy votes" at the municipal level. Clientelism and poverty thus interact closely. Cash transfers distribute oil income to the very poor—and also cement support for Chávez. Other programs such as Barrio Adentro and Mercal spend according to political criteria as well as demographic considerations, namely, the size of the population. In these two "mission" programs, poverty variables have no influence in explaining the distribution of resources at the state and municipal levels. What matters are the degrees of administration loyalty that governors and mayors display, plus the sheer numbers of potential voters who live in a given area.

The combination of opportunistic social spending and declining accountability has had decisive political effects. On the one hand, it leads to favoritism and thus polarization.[12] On the other hand, it creates a state that is virtually impossible to defeat through voting, since that state can always heavily overmatch whatever resources the opposition can bring to bear.

In short, state spending is born from democratic pressures (heightened political competition), but beyond a certain threshold of irregularity, it begins to undermine democratic institutions, creating a playing field that is far from level. Spending has given the Venezuelan government an advantage in competing for votes: The opposition campaigns with words; the state, with words plus money.

Ambivalent Groups and Intangible State Resources

Clientelistic spending has not been Chávez's only tool. *Chavismo* also relies on two less tangible but equally powerful instruments. It offers supporters de facto impunity to engage in corruption, and it practices job discrimination in their favor while using negative discrimination against those seen as government foes. These tools are reminiscent of the "inducements and constraints" typical of traditional Latin American corporatism.[13] Yet there is a difference. In classic corporatism, organized labor was typically the object of inducements and constraints; under Chávez and other neopopulists,[14] these tools are applied to groups that are not necessarily organized and that may even be amorphous. In Venezuela, these groups consist mainly of voters who are neither strongly for nor strongly against Chávez.

Locally, they are called the "ni-nis" (neither-nors). Since early on, pollsters have found substantial evidence of their salience. By July 2001, for instance, one reputable poll was beginning to classify some Venezuelan voters as "repented *chavistas*."[15] This category swelled from 14.7 percent in July 2001 to 32.8 percent in December. Some of these *chavistas* became mild opponents of the president, while others remained mild supporters. As late as 2006, as many as 30 percent of all those polled were professing themselves to be in either "slight agreement" or "slight disagreement" with government policies.[16] Thus, even in contexts of polarization, swing groups are nontrivial and likely to grow in size. Consequently, even radical leftist governments will still need to learn how to deal with the ambivalent middle. Impunity from prosecution and job discrimination have been Chávez's answers to the problem.

Impunity from prosecution differs from clientelism in that the benefits pass from one strong actor (in this case the state) to other strong actors (the military, perhaps, or business groups). Like clientelism, the offer of impunity is an appeal tailored to reach those who are not strongly aligned. Because strong actors can wield a veto, not merely over policy but even over the administration's very survival, a government in a polarized setting must deploy significant resources to assuage them.[17] Furthermore, in situations of radicalization it helps to have a mechanism for coopting military and perhaps also business elites, if only as a shield against coups. This might explain why in Venezuela there is no competitive bidding for most government contracts, and why few individuals close to the government have been jailed for corruption. Like clientelism, impunity has the effect of making beneficiaries intensely conservative—that is, it makes them dread the prospect of a change in government out of worry that such a change might end their privileges.

Job discrimination, both positive and negative, is Chávez's other strategy for winning or at least overawing ambivalent groups. His administration says repeatedly that government jobs, contracts, and subsidies will go exclusively to supporters. To make its implied threats of negative job discrimination more pointed, the administration does all it can to publicize the notion that it knows people's voting behavior. The two best-known examples of this tactic are the Súmate and Lista Tascón cases. Súmate is a nonprofit organization that Chávez said had broken the law by receiving a $31,150 grant for voter education from the U.S.-based National Endowment for Democracy.[18] This modest sum mattered less to the government than did Súmate's heavy involvement in collecting signatures to make the 2004 recall referendum possible. The Lista Tascón bears the name of its compiler, *chavista* legislator Luis Tascón, and includes voting data on citizens who signed the recall petition. The list was openly published on the Internet and was explicitly used to make citizens withdraw their signatures or else face being fired or denied access to public contracts and social benefits. The Chávez administration's intention is clearly to convey that loyalists can gain and dissenters lose a great deal, a dual signal meant to reach groups that are mostly untouched by ideology and polarization.

After eight years in power, the *chavista* coalition has changed enormously. In 1999, it offered a progressive ideology that promised to free Venezuela from the stranglehold of the old parties and repeated economic crises. This agenda favored change but not radicalism, and drew vast majorities. Since then, the agenda has turned radical, winning the loyalty of the extreme left but at the cost of polarization, with a large cluster of ambivalent groups in the middle, together with a substantial number of new and old elites. The lavish use of corruption, impunity, and job discrimination keeps these groups in Chávez's camp when it counts, and allows his government to increase its vote beyond what the extreme left can deliver by itself.

The Opposition's Dilemma

Dealing with an uneven playing field, however daunting, is not the worst challenge that the opposition faces in electoral contests where guarantees of fairness are flimsy at best. The opposition also needs to overcome its internal divisions and, more significantly, the tendency of its voters to abstain. In preparing for the 2006 presidential campaign, the opposition took significant steps to correct these problems, but still did not go far enough.

The first step was to seek internal unity. The race began with three reputable opposition candidates from varying ideological backgrounds. The first was Teodoro Petkoff, a 1960s guerrilla leader who had been planning minister under President Rafael Caldera in the 1990s and then became editor of the well-regarded daily newspaper *Tal Cual*. Petkoff was joined by Julio Borges of the new Primero Justicia party, which controlled a few municipal administrations, and Governor Manuel Rosales of Zulia, an oil-producing state in the west. For a while, it seemed that unity would prove impossible, and midyear arrived with no agreement as to how a unity candidate might be chosen. To everyone's surprise, the candidates amicably agreed to let opinion polling identify the strongest candidate. By early August, that was clearly Rosales. His rivals endorsed him—another surprise that gave the opposition a boost.

The strong current of abstentionism posed a harder problem. Six months before the December voting, many in the opposition (aware of Chávez's advantages) were still undecided about whether they would even bother to cast their ballots. The conditions needed for a fair and transparent contest remained in doubt. The opposition claimed constitutional and electoral-code violations including: 1) a lack of independence in the CNE; 2) an electronic voting system open to manipulation; 3) a suspicious swelling in the ranks of likely pro-Chávez voters after the unscrutinized issuance of a record number of voter registrations;[19] 4) a media tilt in favor of the president;[20] and 5) the administration's breaking of campaign-spending limits set by the CNE.

Over the course of 2006, the government addressed a few of these complaints. The CNE allowed the Center for Electoral Assistance and Promotion (CAPEL), a group affiliated with the Inter-American System of Human Rights, to audit the registration system. The CNE also allowed a group of Venezuelan universities to audit voter registration, but the three most prestigious schools[21] disagreed with the CNE's proposed statistical methodology and declined to take part. Neither CAPEL nor the universities' study found evidence that registration was rigged, although they confirmed that the system did not guard against the casting of ballots by unregistered voters as fully as it might have.

As with voter registration, reforms regarding the actual voting system were partial. During the runup to the 2005 legislative elections, analysts had learned that officials could use polling-place fingerprint-identification machines together with the electronic voting machines themselves to find out how individuals had voted. The alarmed opposition asked for manual voting, but the CNE dismissed this request, arguing that the law required automated voting. At the last minute, the opposition withdrew from the race, leaving every seat in the National Assembly to be filled by pro-Chávez candidates. In preparation for the 2006 presidential elections, the OAS gave the CNE technical assistance to reduce the possibility of tracing voting records through fingerprints, but the opposition pressed for more changes. The government then agreed to remove the fingerprint machines from a minority of polling stations, none of which lay in the most heavily peopled precincts. The opposition claimed that by keeping fingerprint machines in these key spots, the government was trying to scare opposition voters away from the polls.

The question of state funding—which was flowing solely to Chávez— lay foremost in the opposition's mind. In response, the CNE agreed to ban public officials from using official acts for electoral purposes and to limit the daily amount of televised advertising that each candidate could broadcast. When it came to enforcement, however, the CNE was a no-show. In November 2006, for example, PDVSA president Rafael Ramírez was caught on videotape telling employees to vote for Chávez because the state-owned company was "red, very red" *(roja, rojita)*, a reference to the colors of the ruling party. Far from firing or even reproving Ramírez, Chávez congratulated him and urged other ministers and officers to repeat the message. International observers in 2006 criticized the excessive state spending that was helping Chávez just as they had in 2005, but in neither case were these complaints of much avail.

The failure to restrain the unaccountable, politically minded spending machine that Chávez had set up in 2003 meant that the conditions for fair competition were worse in 2006 than they had been during the December 2005 National Assembly elections or the August 2004 recall balloting. Even media access, once an opposition strong point, had been reversed in the incumbent's favor by a wave of cash. The government invested more than $40 million in upgrading the state-owned television station and the government news agency, established three more television stations, acquired more than 145 local radio stations and 75 community newspapers, and created dozens of administration-friendly websites.

The prospect of a merely partial reform of the electoral system faced the opposition with a dilemma. Going along would mean that many opposition voters would remain dissatisfied, fearful, and inclined to abstain. Yet rejecting the reforms as insufficient would lay the opposition open to charges of recalcitrance and disloyalty and possibly damage its international reputation. The opposition leadership took a gamble in favor of going along. But this hurt them with the absentionist anti-Chávez forces even as it arguably helped to bolster the opposition's appeal in the eyes of the ambivalent. The wisdom of this gamble will likely remain a topic of debate within opposition ranks for years to come. Nor, in all likelihood, will this be the last time that the opposition must make a hard strategic choice with uncertain results.

"Nothing Can Stop the Revolution"

Chávez celebrated his 2006 victory by proclaiming that "Nothing can stop the revolution!" He may well be right. All that the opposition can do for now is watch him try to build what he calls "the socialism of the twenty-first century." His plan seems to have five parts. The first is full use of his 2007 enabling law to change more than sixty pieces of legislation without legislative approval. The second is the creation of a "presidential committee" that will put to referenda such proposals as allowing the unlimited reelection of incumbents and attaching even stricter conditions to recall votes. The third is a redrawing of the administrative and political map to curb the influence of governors and mayors. The fourth is a renewed effort to expand the role of the president's "Bolivarian" ideology in the hiring and training of public-school teachers. Finally, Chávez wants to found a yet-to-be-specified set of "communal assemblies" that will compete with existing local authorities. Chávez's new vice-president Jorge Rodríguez, who was the CNE's president during its least transparent period, calls this new phase of the regime—apparently without irony—a "dictatorship of true democracy."

At the same time, Chávez has announced plans to nationalize the telecommunications and electricity sectors as well as to boost the state's involvement in agro-industry and banking. The telecommunications policy will assert government control over CANTV, the firm that controls the transmission of data from the automated voting system. Once this happens, citizen confidence in ballot secrecy will plummet further and abstentionism by oppositionists will rise. Moreover, by denouncing the local private media company RCTV as *golpista* and refusing to renew its broadcast licenses, the Chávez government has made itself the first popularly elected administration in Latin America since the 1980s blatantly to curtail press freedom. The RCTV affair shows how open is the partisan political bias that now infects the government's handling of economic affairs.

Chávez's twenty-first–century socialism looks much like Latin America's mid-twentieth–century "hard corporatism" without the physical coercion.[22] In Venezuela today, the opposition has ever fewer means and even incentives to incur the cost of trying to stop authoritarian leaps. The problem goes beyond mere internal divisions within the opposition, crippling as those might be. The core problem is that the opposition finds itself on the short end of a sharp asymmetry in political resources vis-à-vis the state. Private donations are the opposition's only recourse, but the state's offers of impunity and threats or promises of contract discrimination threaten to close these off too as business elites become coopted by the new order.

One often hears that the *unlimited* spending of money on election campaigns hurts democracy. Yet *uneven* campaign financing may be still worse. In Venezuela, this unevenness has come about not simply because the state under Chávez has raked in more oil money, but also because institutional constraints have been wearing away under a deliberate assault. This erosion of constraints generated the 2002–2004 governability crisis, rather than the other way around. Chávez turned back this critical challenge to his rule with policies of polarization, selective impunity, and job discrimination, in the process building a dominant coalition of radicalized ideologues and plentiful economic winners. Clearly some of these winners are low-income Venezuelans. But others are members of old-fashioned elites and do not look all that different from such winners of the Punto Fijo era as military officers, government employees, and state contractors. As of now, this coalition is majoritarian, but it is hardly being mobilized for democratic gains. The story of Venezuela since Chávez's rise to power shows how, when democratic institutions are defective, social spending may all too readily be bent not toward correcting, but rather toward entrenching and even exacerbating these defects.

NOTES

1. Guillermo O'Donnell, *Modernization and Bureaucratic-Authoritarianism: Studies in South American Politics* (Berkeley: Institute of International Studies, University of California, 1973).

2. Nancy Bermeo, *Ordinary People in Extraordinary Times: The Citizenry and the Breakdown of Democracy* (Princeton: Princeton University Press, 2003).

3. Javier Corrales, "In Search of a Theory of Polarization: Lessons from Venezuela, 1999–2005," *European Review of Latin American and Caribbean Studies* 79 (October 2005): 105–18.

4. Michael Coppedge, "Venezuela: Popular Sovereignty versus Liberal Democracy," in Jorge Domínguez and Michael Shifter, eds., *Constructing Democratic Governance in Latin America,* 2ⁿᵈ ed. (Baltimore: Johns Hopkins University Press, 2003); and Javier Corrales, "Power Asymmetries and the Rise of Presidential Constitutions," paper delivered at the annual meeting of the American Political Science Association, Philadelphia, 31 August–3 September 2006.

5. Douglas C. North, William Summerhill, and Barry R. Weingast, "Order, Disorder, and Economic Change: Latin America versus North America," in Bruce Bueno de Mesquita and Hilton L. Root, eds., *Governing for Prosperity* (New Haven: Yale University Press, 2000); and Adam Przeworski, *Democracy and the Market: Political and Economic Reforms in Eastern Europe and Latin America* (New York: Cambridge University Press, 1991). For an application of these arguments to Venezuela, see Francisco Monaldi et al., *Political Institutions, Policymaking Process, and Policy Outcomes in Venezuela* (Washington, D.C.: Inter-American Development Bank, 2005).

6. Miriam Kornblith, "Elections versus Democracy," *Journal of Democracy* 16 (January 2005): 124–37.

7. Javier Corrales, "Strong Societies, Weak Parties: Regime Change in Cuba and Venezuela in the 1950s and Today," *Latin American Politics and Society* 43 (Summer 2001): 81–113.

8. Jennifer L. McCoy, "From Representative to Participatory Democracy? Regime Transformation in Venezuela," in Jennifer L. McCoy and David J. Myers, eds., *The Unraveling of Representative Democracy in Venezuela* (Baltimore: Johns Hopkins University Press, 2004), 263–96.

9. See *Making Services Work for Poor People* (Washington, D.C.: World Bank, 2004).

10. Francisco Rodríguez, "Why Chávez Wins," *www.foreignpolicy.com/story/cms. php?story_id=3685.*

11. Michael Penfold, "Clientelism and Social Funds: Evidence from Chávez's Misiones," *Latin American Politics and Society* 49 (Winter 2007): 63–84.

12. See Youssef Cohen, *Radicals, Reformers, and Reactionaries: The Prisoner's Dilemma and the Collapse of Democracy in Latin America* (Chicago: University of Chicago Press, 1994).

13. Ruth Berins Collier and David Collier, "Inducements Versus Constraints: Disaggregating 'Corporatism,'" *American Political Science Review* 73 (December 1979): 967–86.

14. Kurt Weyland, "Neopopulism and Neoliberalism in Latin America: How Much Affinity?" *Third World Quarterly* 24 (December 2003): 1095–1115.

15. José Antonio Gil Yepes, "Public Opinion, Political Socialization, and Regime Stabilization," in McCoy and Myers, eds., *The Unraveling of Representative Democracy in Venezuela,* 231–60.

16. These figures are from a survey taken in January and February 2006 by the independent Venezuelan polling firm Consultores 21, *www.consultores21.com.*

17. See Bruce Bueno de Mesquita et al., *The Logic of Political Survival* (Cambridge: MIT Press, 2003).

18. On similar trends elsewhere, see Thomas Carothers, "The Backlash Against Democracy Promotion," *Foreign Affairs* 85 (March–April 2006): 55–68.

19. The opposition wondered about the hard-to-explain 11.7 percent increase in registered voters that was noted during the brief time between April and October 2004.

20. By September 2006, Chávez was using three times the airtime allowed by CNE regulations, and this count leaves aside his famous *Aló Presidente* Sunday television show, which would add another several hours per week. See the report of Ciudadanía Activa, "Abuso Presidencial en los Medios de Comunicación del Estado," Caracas, 2006.

21. These were the Universidad Simón Bolívar, the Universidad Central de Venezuela, and the Universidad Católica Andrés Bello.

22. Alfred Stepan, "State Power and the Strength of Civil Society in the Southern Cone of Latin America," in Peter Evans, Dietrich Rueschemeyer, and Theda Skocpol, eds., *Bringing the State Back In* (New York: Cambridge University Press, 1985), 317–43.

14

ECUADOR: CORREA'S PLEBISCITARY PRESIDENCY

Catherine M. Conaghan

Catherine M. Conaghan *is professor of political studies at Queen's University in Kingston, Ontario. She was a visiting scholar at FLACSO-Quito in 2006–2007. Her most recent book is* Fujimori's Peru: Deception in the Public Sphere *(2005). This essay originally appeared in the April 2008 issue of the* Journal of Democracy.

In his first year as Ecuador's president, Rafael Correa scored two electoral victories that went far toward turning his promise of constitutional revolution into a reality. On 15 April 2007, Correa's proposal to call elections for a constituent assembly charged with writing an entirely new constitution won a massive 82 percent "yes" vote. At the end of September, the electorate handed Correa the second of the two prizes for which he had vigorously campaigned, awarding 80 seats in the 130-member constituent assembly to his Movement for a Proud and Sovereign Country (MPAIS).[1] In a land long plagued by fragmented parties and divided governments, the astounding majority that voters delivered to the 44-year-old U.S.-trained economist and former economy minister was unprecedented. Ecuador's new constitution will be written on terms set by the charismatic and hugely popular young president.

In the months preceding the September elections, Correa depicted the assembly race as the "mother of all battles," an "all-or-nothing" contest on which rested the future of his proposed "citizens' revolution." The language, while dramatic, did not exaggerate the administration's ambitions. Elected in a 26 November 2006 runoff, Correa debuted as a president fully identified with the most radical current in Latin America's widely discussed political "left turn."[2] At his inauguration, he embraced presidents Hugo Chávez of Venezuela and Evo Morales of Bolivia, and hoisted a replica of Simón Bolívar's sword (a gift from Chávez) while delivering his first address to the nation. Promising to end what he often referred to as the "long and sad night of neoliberalism," Correa pledged to put Ecuador on the road to achieving a "socialism of the twenty-first century."

Like Chávez and Morales, Correa came to office with the view that winning the presidency was, at best, a prelude to a more profound struggle for political power, one that would involve confronting rivals both within the state and in society at large. Each of the three presidents sees a new constitution in his country as the essential starting point for a leftist transformation there. Correa, like Chávez in his first presidential run in 1998, campaigned as the quintessential outsider, a maverick backed by his own antiestablishment organization. Blocking the road to Correa's proposed "deep and radical" constitutional revolution was an array of state institutions that remained largely in the hands of the traditional *partidocracia* (party dominance) that Correa so derided. Equally resistant to change, in Correa's view, was the business establishment. Reconfiguring the "correlation of forces" was how Correa described his mission as president. "Let's not be naïve," Correa advised supporters. "We won the elections, but not power. Power is controlled by economic interests, the banks, the *partidocracia,* and the media connected to the banks."[3]

In his quest to shake up Ecuador's power structure, Correa used his first year in office to fashion a presidency that can be called plebiscitary in a double sense. First, true to the literal meaning of the word, the president tied his administration, his very continuance in office, to winning two elections in a row: first to approve the idea of a new constituent assembly, and then to fill the seats in this body with supporters of his views. He framed both votes as referenda on his presidency, warning that a defeat would mean "I'll go home." More opportunities for the electorate to line up for or against Correa lay ahead, as 2008 promised to bring a referendum on the new constitution, followed in all likelihood by fresh national elections. Correa has insisted all along, moreover, that he is leading a "permanent campaign" and fully intends to run again.

Second, the Correa presidency also fits and extends the definition of a plebiscitary presidency as originally described by political scientist Theodore Lowi. Analyzing the evolution of the U.S. presidency, Lowi proposed the term as a shorthand expression for the way in which presidents can use direct, unmediated appeals to public opinion in order to govern "over the heads" of other institutions, especially legislatures.[4] Putting his own charisma and a savvy media team to work, Correa quickly mastered the art of mobilizing public opinion via polls, the media, and the streets in order to disorient, demoralize, and disorganize political opponents during his relentless pursuit of the constituent assembly. Never have Ecuadorians seen a president so obsessed with, and so skillful at, communications and public relations.

In this extreme version of the plebiscitary presidency, Correa did

more than just govern "over the head" of Ecuador's 100-member, unicameral National Congress. With the public's overwhelming approval,
he rendered Congress totally irrelevant. Campaigning to win hearts,
minds, and votes, Correa managed to upend what was left of Ecuador's
tattered institutions and craft a potent presidency. In doing so, Correa
appears to have closed the book on a decade of political instability.
Whether this powerful president and the constituent assembly will work
in concert to produce a new generation of genuine, sustainable democratic institutions—or whether the hyperplebiscitary presidency becomes entrenched in the new constitutional order—is the question that
hangs over Ecuadorian politics as Correa enters the second year of his
administration.

In Search of Presidential Power

Ecuador with its roughly 14 million people is the world's largest ex-
porter of bananas, and is also among Latin America's major oil exporters (with more than half its hydrocarbon exports going to the United
States). According to the World Bank, Ecuador's is a lower–middle-
income economy. Like its neighbors in the Andean region, the country
wrestles with poverty, severe income inequality, and tensions rooted in
regional, class, and ethnic cleavages. In the 1990s, Ecuador's politics
was marked by the ascent of one of Latin America's most active indigenous movements, led by the Confederation of Ecuadorian Indigenous
Nationalities (CONAIE). At the same time, Ecuador became synonymous with political upheaval and the syndrome that Arturo Valenzuela
has described as "presidencies interrupted."[5] Between 1997 and 2005,
three elected presidents—Abdalá Bucaram, Jamil Mahuad, and Lucio
Gutiérrez—were forced to leave office early when political crises and
street protests handed Congress and the military pretexts for unseating
them.

Analysts attributed this record of instability to multiple dysfunctions
associated with the party system and its leadership.[6] Since the transition away from military rule in 1979, Ecuador has been among Latin
America's leaders in party-system fragmentation and electoral volatility. Ideological and programmatic consistency have been rare commodities as party elites have acted according to unpredictable mixtures of
electoral calculations and personal animosities. In Congress, alliances
have been ersatz and transactional. Governmental accountability has
been nonexistent.

The legal system, widely seen as a corrupt extension of the party
system, has little credibility. Fielding one of the larger caucuses in Congress, the rightist Social Christian Party (PSC) was able to dominate the
process of selecting higher-court judges, feeding the sense that the judiciary is the thoroughly politicized tool of partisan forces. In the "any-

thing goes" atmosphere of Ecuadorian public life, cold-blooded career calculations and personal vendettas have routinely trumped principles. The party elites' short-term and instrumental approach turned the constitution and laws into malleable contraptions, easily manipulated in the face of this or that shifting exigency. Removing presidents from office became the most extreme manifestation of the instrumentalism that had come to permeate the political system.[7]

Average citizens saw little reason to believe in a game so awash in avarice, corruption, and incompetence. The economic crisis of 1999–2000, played out during the implementation of neoliberal reform, was a jarring and dislocating experience that led massive numbers of Ecuadorians to go abroad in search of work. The traumatizing freeze on bank deposits in 1999 and the subsequent dollarization of the economy in 2000 only deepened the public's resentment of politicians. Surveys reflected the acute crisis of legitimacy that afflicted Ecuador's institutions. Democracy audits, conducted in 2001, 2004, and 2006, respectively, showed Ecuadorians expressing extremely low levels of confidence in Congress, the parties, and the national government generally.[8]

Rafael Correa entered the 2006 presidential race keenly aware of the public's antipolitical mood and the precarious tenure of presidents. His own meteoric rise to prominence had come on the heels of the mass demonstrations in Quito that had forced President Lucio Gutiérrez to abandon the presidential palace in April 2005. Known as the rebellion of the *forajidos* (outlaws), the Quito protests exploded when Gutiérrez made a political deal that allowed for the return from exile of Abdalá Bucaram, the former president who had been ousted in 1997 and accused of corruption.[9] Correa, a young economics professor with a doctorate from the University of Illinois, joined the demonstrators demanding Gutiérrez's ouster. Vice-President Alfredo Palacio, the incoming president, tapped Correa to serve as minister of the economy. His tenure was brief but notable. He quickly established himself as an ardent nationalist and virulent public critic of neoliberal policies.

Drawing support from small, dispersed groups on the left and what remained of the *forajido* movement, Correa quickly assembled MPAIS as his electoral vehicle for the 2006 race. Establishing his antisystem credentials, Correa made two key decisions that shaped the course of the campaign and set the parameters for his first year in office. Embracing the *forajido* movement's demands for drastic political reform, Correa promised voters that he would do everything in his power to convene an assembly to write a new constitution. In Correa's view, a new constitution would not only redesign governmental institutions, but would lay the legal basis for reestablishing the state's central role in regulating and managing the economy. A new basic law would cleanse the body politic of its dysfunctional institutions and at the same time mark a definitive break with neoliberalism. To ensure that the assembly would be true to its transformative mission, Correa argued that this body would need to be invested with "full powers" to overrule or dissolve and replace all existing institutions. With such authority, the assembly could do anything from suspending the 1998 Constitution to disbanding the incumbent Congress and handing greater powers to the president.

Correa matched his "maximalist" position on the constitutional assembly with another critical decision. He announced that MPAIS would decline to run any candidates in the congressional elections that were to be staged concurrently with the first round of the presidential election in October 2006. With this one bold stroke, Correa both unequivocally identified his candidacy with the voters' deeply antipolitical mood and accepted the risk that, if elected, he would assume office with zero assurance of legislative support and far greater assurance that legislators might move to oust him at any time.

The possibility of another interrupted presidency loomed, especially when it became clear that parties led by Correa's bitterest rivals were poised to control the incoming Congress. While not enjoying an absolute majority, the Institutional Renewal National Action Party (PRIAN) and the Patriotic Society Party (PSP) emerged from the October race with the two largest congressional caucuses. PRIAN was the electoral vehicle of Alvaro Noboa, the bombastic banana billionaire who is Ecuador's richest citizen. Known for sometimes falling to his knees and praying at campaign appearances,[10] Noboa was making his third bid for the presidency. Former president and returned exile Lucio Gutiérrez headed the PSP, with unmasked antipathy toward Correa and his *forajido* followers. Joining the anti-Correa alliance was the PSC, a once-powerful party led by former president León Febres Cordero (1984–88) that would see its support greatly diminish in the 15 October 2006 voting for Congress.

Garnering 22.8 percent of the vote, Correa took second place in the October 15 first round. This result assured him a runoff against Noboa, who had come in first with 26.8 percent. Correa's challenge was not just to win the second round, but to win in a decisive way and lay claim to a mandate for what was shaping up as a likely showdown with Congress over the constituent-assembly issue.

Crisscrossing his small, mountainous country as the contrarian candidate of change, the energetic Correa turned in a campaign-trail performance that was as nearly flawless as that of his savvy media and public-relations team.[11] Young, handsome, and tireless, Correa was marketed as the hip, passionate, and tough leader who reveled in taking on Ecuador's establishment. By comparison, Noboa seemed mired in the past, reprising his evangelical style and the populist bravado of previous failed campaigns. Just hours after the polls closed on November 26,

Correa's victory was clear. In the final vote count, Correa bested Noboa by 56.7 to 43.3 percent.

By the time Correa took the presidential oath in early 2007, he was even more popular, boasting a 73 percent approval rating. Putting their substantial political capital to use, the president and his cabinet immediately embarked on an integrated, multifaceted strategy to change the "correlation of forces" and push forward their design of transforming Ecuador by means of a new constitution. To achieve these aims—and to guard his presidency against being "interrupted"—Correa needed to buttress executive power, keep his opponents on the defensive, and paint his administration as fulfilling its promises of change.

Inducing Institutional Implosion

Throughout his 2006 campaign, Correa had laid the groundwork for a confrontation with Congress. He pilloried the political veterans of the legislature as dinosaurs, a class doomed to extinction. While Correa acknowledged the legislature's legal status, he insisted that the body lacked underlying political legitimacy, pointing to the dismal ratings that it received in public-opinion polls.

With the 2007 Congress under the control of a majority that opposed the new president and his plan for a constituent assembly, the stage was set for a potentially explosive showdown. On his inauguration day, Correa signed an executive decree mandating a nationwide vote (*consulta popular*) to approve the convening of a constituent assembly. Opponents called the decree unconstitutional, citing articles in the extant constitution that gave Congress a primary role in vetting constitutional reforms. Correa offered a contrary reading, pointing to an article that allowed the president to bypass Congress and hold a national vote on any issue of "transcendental importance." Correa asserted that the national consultation on the assembly did not constitute a project of "constitutional reform" per se. Rather, it was a plan to scrap the current constitution altogether, and therefore unarguably of transcendental importance.

Admittedly, the 1998 Constitution's confusing language gave both Congress and Correa ample room to assert the legitimacy of their rival claims. Yet both sides understood that the conflict's outcome would hinge less legal arguments than on public opinion and the calculations of various legislators and authorities in other key institutions, especially the Supreme Electoral Tribunal (TSE) and the Constitutional Tribunal (TC).

With 73 percent of the public backing the idea of an assembly and 59 percent siding with the executive's plan to bypass Congress, Correa went on the offensive. Sending his executive decree to the TSE, Correa warned that should that body (then headed by a PRIAN appointee) refuse to execute his order, he was prepared to create an ad hoc electoral tribunal. The TSE thereupon punted the plan to Congress for approval and amendments. Correa called for public protests against the TSE and the legislature. With pressure building and its own ranks divided, Congress backed down and approved the plan for a national consultation to convoke constituent-assembly elections, but added language meant to curb the "full powers" of that assembly and prohibit any future dissolution of Congress. The TSE quickly announced that the elections would be held on April 15. But unexpectedly and with no explanation, the TSE voted to approve a revised decree submitted by the president which restored the "full powers" provision in the statute authorizing the assembly elections.

Correa's foes in Congress howled that the TSE must have surrendered to government bribes or threats. In a move that violated the standard procedures for removing TSE appointees, the congressional majority voted to sack TSE chief Jorge Acosta. The TSE replied in kind, voting to strip 57 legislators of their seats on the grounds that they were obstructing the electoral process by trying to remove the electoral tribunal's head. When the deposed legislators showed up for work, they were greeted by angry mobs and the National Police barring them from entering the building. Under orders from the Ministry of Government and Police, law officers ushered in 57 new legislators, the legally designated substitutes *(suplentes)* for the deposed incumbents. Leaving their previous partisan loyalties with PRIAN and PSP at the door, many of the new legislators declared themselves to be independents who would support the Correa administration.

The TSE's government-backed sacking of opposition legislators led to another institutional conflict. Arguing that their removal had violated the constitution, deposed legislators took their case to the TC. When that body ruled in their favor, an angry progovernment mob converged on TC headquarters, giving justices no choice but to evacuate the building under police escort. Correa immediately dismissed the TC's ruling, suggesting that the justices should be prosecuted.[12] The next day, the new pro-Correa majority in Congress voted to dismiss nine of the TC's justices, making the TC's ruling moot.

The net result of all the feuding was good for the administration. Without any need for Correa's direct intervention, the opposition and the other branches of government had been rendered powerless to stop the assembly process. While Correa led an aggressive public campaign to keep the pressure on Congress and the TSE, Minister of Government Gustavo Larrea worked effectively behind the scenes. He cajoled and enticed authorities to jump on the assembly bandwagon while making sure that the police were in place to control access to the disputed offices. Instead of smashing institutions and political opponents outright and risking the ire of the international community, Correa had engineered a process that had weakened and delegitimized the assembly's foes and the institutions that they had hoped to wield to stop it.

Permanent Campaign, Permanent Confrontation

From the start of his presidency, Correa clearly grasped the necessity of using the office as a bully pulpit for shaping public opinion and advancing his agenda for the constituent assembly. Correa has emerged as Ecuador's version of the "great communicator"—a leader who skillfully conveys popular, commonsense messages by means of a persona that appeals to a wide spectrum of the public. Guiding Correa's communications strategy as secretary of public administration is Vinicio Alvarado, the Guayaquil public-relations guru who designed Correa's innovative media strategy for the 2006 campaign.

The hallmark of a plebiscitary presidency is the drive to connect the president directly to voters, with minimal interference or "filtering" by parties, civil society groups, or the media. Continuing with the radio strategy developed during the campaign, Correa inaugurated his presidency with a two-hour weekly broadcast called "The President Dialogues with His Constituents." The Saturday-morning show, which airs on 154 stations around the country, provides Correa with a regular outlet for trumpeting his government's accomplishments and scolding his opponents. The program often airs in conjunction with the "traveling cabinets," during which the president and various ministers visit different locales to meet with local authorities, greet members of the general public, and appear at concerts or cultural events. The festive atmosphere surrounding Correa's visits provides fertile ground for politicking; the government made good use of the events to raise support before both the constituent-assembly referendum and the subsequent assembly elections.

Correa's media operation is coordinated by the Secretariat of Communication and run out of the presidential palace. The Secretariat has made deft use of paid advertising to publicize presidential initiatives and engage in what is referred to as a "values" campaign to promote national pride and patriotism. One frequently broadcast television commercial featured a montage of happy Ecuadorians singing the nostalgic grade-school song *Patria* (Homeland). Critics have offered a less sanguine interpretation of the government's goals, pointing to how the advertising messages seemingly collapse any distinction between the state and the Correa presidency. For example, Correa's party slogan has morphed into the official motto that appears on all government advertising, "La Patria Ya Es de Todos" (Now the Homeland Belongs to Everyone). Every government-sponsored television commercial ends with the same signature shot: Viewers see a vibrant man, photographed from a distance, who greets a spectacular Andean sunrise. His arms pump in a victory salute, an image that readily evokes the familiar sight of Correa on the campaign trail.

Matching this proactive communications strategy is Correa's own hyperactive approach to the presidency. He is a ubiquitous presence, the staple of every news cycle thanks to his tireless speechmaking and enthusiastic appearances at public events of every sort. Correa believes that among his roles as president should be that of unabashed cheer-leader-in-chief. He has even gone so far as to say that his principal duty is to be a "motivator" who can "raise people's self esteem and morale."[13]

Correa's uplifting rhetoric, especially his emphasis on restoring dignity to downtrodden citizens and engendering national pride, has been an important part of the president's strategy. Equally important is the pattern of permanent attacks on all perceived opponents. During the first months of conflict over the constituent-assembly issue, politicians opposed to the assembly were the primary targets of the president's harangues and heard themselves called everything from mafiosi to clowns, vipers, wolves, fakes, cadavers, sell-outs, and swindlers. When Guayaquil mayor Jaime Nebot and notables from that city's civic board questioned government policies, they too found themselves on the receiving end of a presidential tongue lashing, dismissed as *pelucones*—reactionary bigwigs.

Correa's list of purported enemies has expanded to include segments of the mainstream media. While Correa enjoyed generally favorable coverage as a presidential candidate in 2006, his relationship with the media soured when he stepped up criticism of individual journalists and media owners whom he accused of conspiring to destabilize the government. Correa has begun routinely trashing the media as the tool of Ecuador's "oligarchy" and has invited voters to tune out the privately owned media in favor of his own radio show.

Replaying the antiestablishment card that served him so well in the 2006 race, Correa continued bashing his critics in the lead-up to the September 2007 elections for constituent-assembly representatives. But "going negative" was not the only, or even the most important, arrow in the government's quiver. Delivering on the promises of the 2006 campaign would be crucial to maintaining Correa's popularity and making his personal appeal work for MPAIS candidates as the 2007 constituent-assembly election neared.

Credibility, Performance, and Policy

During his first year in office, Correa enjoyed strong and mostly steady job-approval ratings ranging between 60 and 70 percent. He ranked as one of the most popular presidents in the Americas, sharing the top slot with Argentina's Néstor Kirchner. Like Kirchner, Correa began his presidency with a hugely popular move, slashing his own salary by nearly half.

Correa and MPAIS strategists insist that their success to date is explained by a simple fact: They have kept the promises that they made during the 2006 campaign. According to Secretary of Public Administration Vinico Alvarado, Correa's greatest political resource is his credibility, which hinges on the public's perception that he is a straight-talking leader who is driving the government to produce meaningful improvements in the quality of life.[14]

Partly out of political necessity, Correa's approach to governance is based on speed. To keep his poll numbers high in anticipation of the April and September 2007 election battles, Correa delivered a flurry of executive decrees that pleased a variety of constituents. Windfall profits from Ecuador's booming oil economy paved the way for increased government spending. Among his first executive decrees was an order that doubled the regular welfare payments to poor households from US$15 to $30 a month, a move that benefited nearly a tenth of all Ecuadorians. Correa also doubled the amount available for individual housing loans to $3,600. The poor got another boost when Correa enacted subsidies that halved the price of electricity for low-usage consumers. A variety of other programs expanded credit to microbusinesses, youth, and women. Social spending has been greatly eased by the president's power to declare "emergencies" that start the money flowing with virtually no red tape. From January through July 2007, Correa dispersed $215 million by declaring emergencies in ten sectors, ranging from education and health to the prison system. Emergency road construction, assigned to the army's corps of engineers, has been a boon to the military, helping to strengthen the ties between Correa and the armed forces.

Increased social spending has been one front in the broader push to recast public administration in line with Correa's vision of activist government. The makeover of the public sector is both substantive and symbolic. Highlighting his concern for the plight of Ecuadorians abroad, Correa created a new National Secretariat of the Migrant. To emphasize a new focus on citizenship rights, Correa renamed the Welfare Ministry the Ministry of Economic and Social Inclusion.

These and other administrative changes are meant to reach constituencies that are important to building support for the president's project. Coordinating the presidency's programming directed at social movements and indigenous communities is the new Secretariat of Peoples, Social Movements, and Citizen Participation. As a counterweight to the powerful municipal administration led by political rival Mayor Jaime Nebot in Guayaquil (Ecuador's largest city, major port, and de facto economic capital), Correa created a new Ministry of the Littoral, a superagency that headquarters the operations of central-government ministries in Guayaquil. Not surprisingly, the ministry houses an office for the president, used during his frequent trips to the coast from the inland capital of Quito.

The activist approach is also apparent in economic policy. In keeping with Correa's promise to consign neoliberalism to the "trash bin of history," the administration has reasserted the state's strategic and regulatory role in the economy. For the first time in a quarter-century, the government in 2007 issued a comprehensive national-development plan. In a show of his more muscular approach to business regulation, Correa hiked taxes on foreign oil companies, raising the royalty tax on windfall profits from 50 percent to 99 percent. In keeping with his promise to increase regulation over the national banking system, Correa hounded bankers into lowering charges on banking transactions. Setting a frenetic pace along with a tone decidedly critical of the United States, Correa is forever at the forefront of new economic projects, seeking investment partners in Venezuela, Iran, and China, and reaching out to the Middle East by having Ecuador rejoin the Organization of Petroleum Exporting Counties (OPEC).

While critics dismiss many of Correa's policies as yet another example of the region's "petropopulism," public opinion has aligned firmly in favor of the president and his policies. In his high-energy approach to governance, Correa has successfully cast himself as the central protagonist of public life—the president who takes on multinational corporations, theorizes about "twenty-first–century socialism," delivers school uniforms and books, and regales listeners with his opinions on every facet of Ecuadorian life. As Lowi noted, the plebiscitary presidency is, by its very nature, a personal presidency: an office in which the public willingly invests great power with the expectation that the chief executive will act in extraordinary, perhaps heroic ways to solve problems. Correa has actively and systematically built such a presidency, methodically accruing ever-greater powers as he projects the image of an indefatigable, audacious leader.

The Assembly and Beyond

Both in personal appearances and on television, Correa campaigned fiercely in the weeks leading up to the September elections with his party's assembly candidates at his side. MPAIS reaped the benefits by sweeping the elections to a degree that few pundits had predicted. The president's movement took 80 seats in the 130-member assembly (73 for MPAIS itself and 7 for MPAIS in alliances with minor parties), leaving opposition parties trailing far behind. Gutiérrez's PSP, regarded as a big winner in the 2006 races, secured just 18 seats.

Even worse was the performance of Noboa's PRIAN and the once-dominant PSC, which ended up with just 8 and 5 seats, respectively. The magnitude of MPAIS's victory was evident in the number of voters who cast straight tickets. A whopping 41 percent of all voters cast straight-ticket ballots for MPAIS. By comparison, the PSP and PRIAN garnered a mere 4 and 3.9 percent of their respective votes from straight-ticket voters.

MPAIS should find willing allies in small leftist parties including the indigenous-backed Pachacutik Movement, which won 6 seats. Moreover, MPAIS's control over the assembly is assured by the assembly statute approved in the April referendum. This law stipulates that only a simple majority of 66 votes is required to approve articles in the new constitution. As Correa readily acknowledged, the Ecuadorian assembly was expressly designed by the executive to avoid the stalemate and chronic conflicts that dogged Bolivia's constituent assembly thanks to its two-thirds majority rule.

In the absence of any significant opposition bloc inside the constituent assembly, Ecuador's political future now lies squarely in the hands of Correa and MPAIS. To date, the group has functioned as an umbrella for Correa supporters from a wide variety of backgrounds; former *forajidos,* leftists, and populists jumped on the Correa bandwagon, envisioning the presidency as a vehicle for reforms and perhaps even revolution. But MPAIS was born as an electoral operation, not a political party. Correa and a small circle of confidants (including assembly president and former energy minister Alberto Acosta) have kept a tight rein on the organization, as evidenced in the process for choosing assembly candidates.

While Correa is sensitive to the demands emanating from local communities, the disconnect between MPAIS and organized civil society, including groups on the left, is striking. In keeping with his plebiscitary style, Correa prefers to forge direct ties with particular constituencies rather than act through intermediaries such as CONAIE or other organizations of the left. As for business organizations, Correa has been decidedly aloof and uninterested in meeting with them.

On 29 November 2007, the constituent assembly convened at its official headquarters in Montecristi, a town in the coastal province of Manabí. In its first act, the assembly asserted its "full powers" vis-à-vis all existing institutions, including the Supreme Court and the TC. Delivering Congress the final *coup de grâce,* the assembly assumed all lawmaking powers and declared the old legislature to be "in recess." In addition, the assembly sacked such congressionally appointed officials as the attorney-general, the controller-general, and the superintendents of banks and companies. With no institutional oversight and with the *carte blanche* provided by the assembly's majority, Correa is expected to enact swift, far-reaching changes in economic policy. These could include enhanced price controls in certain markets, more extensive state regulation of the mining sector, changes to ownership laws governing telecommunications, tax reform, and a greater role for state-run corporations.[15]

How much consensus or dissent might envelop the MPAIS caucus over the course of the assembly is an open question. Assembly president Alberto Acosta is regarded as an environmentalist who favors tight controls on future petroleum exploration while Correa has leaned toward maximizing oil revenues to support the government's development plans. Another potentially divisive issue is the debate over regional autonomy. The government's proposal creating new territorial divisions modeled after Chile's regions and making the cities of Guayaquil and Quito into separate districts is likely to galvanize local opposition and dismay assembly members who feel committed to the interests of the existing 24 provinces. Other hot-button issues will include debates on abortion and homosexual marriage. As a deeply religious Roman Catholic, Correa opposes both, putting him at odds with feminists and progressives in his own organization.

Undoubtedly, one of the biggest issues at stake in the assembly's deliberations is the powers of the presidency itself. Thus far, Correa and the MPAIS faithful have justified the nearly untrammelled use of executive power as crucial to breaking the logjam created by Ecuador's corrupt, discredited institutions and clearing the way for a new democratic institutionalization that will enhance transparency and citizen participation. But now that they have won the battle for a new constitution, is it reasonable to expect that Correa or his movement will have any real interest in placing effective restraints on executive powers and prerogatives, especially in light of the larger plan to restructure the economy and transform Ecuadorian society? And if there is little concern with the matter of restraining the executive, how can such a powerful, unchallenged presidency be reconciled with MPAIS's pledge to develop deliberative, empowering forms of grassroots democracy?

Correa derided the unlimited reelection recently championed by Chávez—and denied him by the voters of Venezuela—as "absurd." And yet the Ecuadorian president—who was elected under a constitution that barred the chief executive from reelection to consecutive terms—strongly backs the idea of allowing presidents to serve two consecutive terms.[16] Alberto Acosta opposes this and favors instead a six-year presidential term, with an incumbent permitted to run again only after having rotated out of office for at least one term. One should note, however, that if Correa's first election, which took place under the 1998 Constitution, is discounted, then Acosta's proposal could pave the way for Correa to remain in power until 2015. Should MPAIS opt for presidential reelection with consecutive terms of five or more years, Correa's stay in office could last until at least 2019.

No matter how the question of presidential reelection is resolved, if key features of the plebiscitary presidency are left intact then democratic institutionalization is likely to suffer. Before the 2006 assembly elections, opposition candidates complained frequently about the "uneven playing field" that they faced, with the TSE mostly standing by while Correa spent government money on advertising and used public events for electioneering. With fresh votes to fill the presidency and a new-model legislature likely to take place in 2008, the problem of unfair campaign practices is bound to recur as Correa seeks his own reelection and an MPAIS majority in the new congress. Should Correa secure such a majority, it could be a springboard for additional constitutional changes, more referenda, and even more powers for the executive branch. Keeping in mind Ecuador's long history of constitutional makeovers and legal improvisation, analysts would be wise to regard the new constitution as a working draft, not an immutable text.

However Correa's hyperplebiscitary presidency evolves over the long term, it has already succeeded in profoundly altering the landscape of Ecuadorian politics. Speaking to the public's deep-seated desires for a dramatic break with traditional actors and past political practices, Correa has championed a clean sweep of institutions. His goal of changing the "correlation of forces" has been realized through electoral victories that have humiliated parties such as the Christian Democratic Union, the Democratic Left, and the populist Roldosist Party. Once powerful, none of them has any significant national presence today. The poor performance by PRIAN, PSP, and PSC in the assembly elections has left them thoroughly sidelined as well. The traditional parties of the left, meanwhile, have found themselves completely eclipsed by MPAIS. Having swept away the past, MPAIS's leaders and followers must grapple with important questions about their movement's identity and future: Can it assume sufficient autonomy to become a democratic political party of the left or will it remain an electoral vehicle under Correa's personal control?

During his first year in office, Correa turned himself and his presidency into the political system's center of gravity. He is the leader and his is the office that define the country's agenda. Others can do little but follow or watch. The most telling measure of Correa's centrality to the political system is how much rides on his desires and his vision of the future. With no meaningful opposition from the parties or civil society, and with the president's own organization more an electoral movement than a governing party, Ecuador's political development seemingly hinges solely on Rafael Correa: his personality, his ambitions, and his decisions about what kind of "left turn" best suits the country. That one man's intentions weigh so heavily in determining the trajectory of change is a worrisome condition as Ecuadorians write their republic's twentieth constitution.

NOTES

1. Although Correa's organization is still designated as MPAIS (List 35) in the official electoral registry, the name has undergone slight modifications over the course of elections. Alianza País (*país* of course means "country" in Spanish) was the name used

to denote the electoral coalition that backed Correa's run for the presidency in 2006, while Acuerdo País was the moniker favored in the 2007 constituent-assembly elections. Blue-and-green banners bearing the name "Acuerdo País" appear on the homepage of its website at *www.acuerdopais.com*. Correa's own political website can be found at *www. rafaelcorrea.com*.

2. See the essays collected under the title "A Left Turn in Latin America?" in the October 2006 issue of the *Journal of Democracy*.

3. These remarks of 14 July 2007 can be found on the presidency's official website at *www.presidencia.gov.ec*.

4. Theodore Lowi, *The Personal Presidency: Power Invested, Promise Unfulfilled* (Ithaca, N.Y.: Cornell University Press, 1985). The plebiscitary nature of Latin American presidencies is also central to the notion of "delegative democracy" as originally described by Guillermo O'Donnell.

5. Arturo Valenzuela, "Latin American Presidencies Interrupted," pp. 3–17 of this volume.

6. On the evolution of the party system, see Simón Pachano, *La trama de Penélope: Procesos políticos e instituciones en el Ecuador* (Quito: FLACSO-Sede Ecuador, 2007), 133–72.

7. For a discussion of instrumentalism as a pervasive problem in Latin American politics, see Leonardo Avritzer, *Democracy and the Public Space in Latin America* (Princeton: Princeton University Press, 2002).

8. Mitchell Seligson, *Democracy Audit: Ecuador 2006* (Quito: CEDATOS Editions, 2006), 67–69.

9. The demonstrators adopted the "outlaws" tag as a badge of honor after Gutiérrez began calling them that. See Franklin Ramírez Gallegos, *La insurrección de abril no fue solo una fiesta* (Quito: Ediciones Abya-Yala, 2005).

10. Monte Reel, "In Ecuadoran Vote, Rhetoric Gives Way to Popular Pledges: Runoff Today Pits Banana Tycoon, Leftist," *Washington Post,* 26 November 2006. Available at *www.washingtonpost.com/wp-dyn/content/article/2006/11/25/AR2006112500774.html*.

11. On campaign strategy and tactics, see Catherine Conaghan and Carlos de la Torre, "The Permanent Campaign of Rafael Correa: Media and Politics in Ecuador," Paper prepared for the 27th International Congress of the Latin American Studies Association, Montreal, 5–8 September 2007.

12. "El Tribunal Constitucional restituye en sus cargos a 50 destituidos," *Hoy* (Quito), 24 April 2007.

13. Remarks by President Correa, 6 September 2007. Available at *www.presidencia. gov.ec*.

14. "Lo que mantiene la imagen del Presidente es su coherencia," *El Universo* (Guayaquil), 29 June 2007.

15. "Legal and Institutional Overhaul," *Weekly Analysis of Ecuadorian Issues* 43, 5 November 2007.

16. "Es absurda la reelección indefinida," *El Universo* (Guayaquil), 10 November 2007.

III

Case Studies: Mexico, Central America, the Caribbean

15

MEXICO'S CONTENTIOUS ELECTION

Luis Estrada and Alejandro Poiré

Luis Estrada is a lecturer on voting behavior and political methodology at the Instituto Tecnológico Autónomo de México (ITAM). **Alejandro Poiré** is Antonio Madero–Fundación México Visiting Scholar and a visiting professor of political science at Harvard University. He has published widely on Mexican political parties, elections, and public opinion. This essay originally appeared in the January 2007 issue of the Journal of Democracy.

Even before it culminated in an intense political drama that made headlines around the world, the Mexican presidential election of 2 July 2006 was arousing keen interest. The prospect of a left-wing government taking office as a result of the vote was a real one. Such a turn of events would have meant both a first in the country's twelve-year-old democratic history, and a major addition to an alleged leftward trend in the politics of Latin America. Instead, the election result turned out to be a razor-thin plurality victory for center-right candidate Felipe Calderón of the National Action Party (PAN), which had ousted the long-ruling Institutional Revolutionary Party (PRI) in the previous presidential election six years earlier.

Calderón's main rival, Mexico City mayor Andrés Manuel López Obrador of the Party of the Democratic Revolution (PRD) objected strenuously to the result, which was unanimously declared official on 5 September 2006 by the Electoral Tribunal of the Federal Judiciary (TEPJF), the country's highest institutional arbiter regarding all electoral matters. López Obrador had finished with a tally of 35.33 percent of the vote as compared to Calderon's 35.89 percent—a margin of 233,000 votes out of more than 41 million ballots cast in a nation of more than 100 million people. (The PRI's Roberto Madrazo had come in a weak third with 22.2 percent.)

The TEPJF's verdict, though unsatisfying to those who wanted a full recount of the vote, closely followed precedent set through ten years of jurisprudence, and further strengthened the basis for the settlement of electoral disputes peacefully through the rule of law, an achievement that is now a hallmark of Mexico's democracy.

Despite the massive challenge that the slim margin of victory implied, the 2006 presidential election was the best organized and cleanest in modern Mexican history. The minor mistakes made in the vote count and other irregularities were duly rectified through the established judicial process.[1] Moreover, approval of the process has been common among international election observers, the media, and most political actors, with the nontrivial exception of the presidential runner-up and his coalition, who claim that the vote was the most fraud-ridden since 1988. While winners have been sending the message of respect for the rule of law, losers have been refusing to acknowledge the results and denouncing Calderón as a spurious, illegitimate president. It is not unlikely that López Obrador will attempt a run for the presidency in the future, and that his campaign will draw on charges of an election allegedly stolen by "the forces of the right." What is less obvious is whether he will attempt to continue prompting mass mobilization and protest in a way that challenges the institutional setting more broadly. In order to offer some clues to deal with this question, we present an analysis of the campaign and its outcome, and then turn to examine the bases of the protest that ensued.

López Obrador's strong electoral showing helped the PRD and its two minor coalition partners, Convergencia and the Labor Party (PT), do well in the congressional races held concurrently to fill all seats in the 500-member Chamber of Deputies and 128-member Senate. The PRI (in a coalition with the Green Party, PVEM), did better in Congress than Madrazo did in his run for the presidency, but was nonetheless reduced to its lowest showing in history. The PAN emerged as the single strongest force in both houses, with a total of 41.2 percent of the seats in the Chamber and 40.6 percent in the Senate, as compared to the PRD's 25.4 and 20.3 percent respectively, and the PRI's corresponding 20.2 and 25.8 percent. The PT and Convergencia each have 3.9 percent of the Senate (5 seats), while the former has 3.2 percent of the Chamber seats and the latter 3.4 percent. It should be noted that since the election took place, the PRD, Convergencia, and PT coalition has renamed itself the Broad Progressive Front, which indicates the willingness of these three parties to coordinate with one another on a more lasting basis.

The Green Party will hold 4 percent of the seats in the Chamber of Deputies and 4.7 percent in the Senate, and two new parties gained congressional representation: New Alliance—a teachers' union–led PRI splinter—obtained 1.8 percent of the Chamber and a single Senate seat, while the Social-Democratic and Peasant Alternative won 0.8 percent of the Chamber but no seats in the Senate. In the new Congress, the PAN holds a strong legislative position, and should be able to pass ordinary (that is, nonconstitutional) legislation without great trouble, most likely with the support of New Alliance, the Green Party, and most of the PRI legislators. But it is now impossible for any two-party combination to pass constitutional reforms, which will strengthen the bargaining power of the smaller parties—and implicitly of their senior coalition partners. An additional challenge for Calderón is the extent to which PAN legislators will respond to his own priorities.

The close-run contest and its bitter aftermath revived Mexico's supposedly long-gone travails with contested elections and fraud charges, and prompted some of the largest and most intense protests in the country's history, with crowds in the capital at one point topping a third of a million people. Scholars concerned with the phenomenon of "losers' consent" and political protest suddenly have an unexpected case to study, one that highlights how, even in the presence of massive institutional investments and a fairly successful electoral experience stretching over more than a decade, leadership incentives and partisanship can still prompt massive (albeit nearly wholly peaceful) unrest and political protest.

Key Novelties in the Race for President

Open candidate-selection procedures have been a rarity in Mexican politics. Before 1999, when the PRI used a nationwide primary, that party would "unanimously" announce its nominee, who had always become the next president. The PAN, for its part, favored using party conventions for most of its history until 1999, when Vicente Fox, then the governor of the central-highlands state of Guanajuato, won an uncontested primary. The PRD, which came into being as a breakaway from the PRI during the years from 1987 to 1989, nominated the same uncontested candidate in both 1994 and 2000. In 2006, however, with each of the three major parties seemingly in a strong enough position to win the presidential election, nomination processes would matter as never before in setting up the contest.[2]

The PAN opted for a sequential, semiclosed primary in which slightly more than a million voters cast ballots in a series of three regional votes, each of which covered a different third of Mexico's 32 states. When it was all over, Calderón, a PAN founder's son who had served as the party's president, and briefly been President Fox's energy secretary, had bested rivals Santiago Creel (Fox's interior minister from 2000 to 2005) and Alberto Cárdenas (a former environment secretary and governor close to the PAN's more conservative and religious wing). Although Creel—originally the best known of the three and the one with the most support among independent voters—had been the early favorite, Calderón won a slight majority that allowed him to avoid a runoff and position himself as a strong new PAN standard-bearer. Paradoxically, the contender with the oldest ties to the party had ended up representing political renewal and a credible "inside" alternative to the Fox administration and its shortcomings.

The PRD featured a nominally open process in which only López Obrador participated. A onetime president of the local PRI branch in his southern home state of Tabasco, López Obrador was a founder of the PRD back in the late 1980s who had then run in Tabasco's 1994 gubernatorial election. When he lost—to Roberto Madrazo, as it happens—López Obrador and his followers cried fraud, blockaded roads and oil wells, and marched to Mexico City in order to stage sit-ins. After information surfaced which allegedly proved that PRI spending on that race had been about sixty times over the legal limit, the PRI administration of President Ernesto Zedillo tried and failed to unseat Madrazo.[3]

Later, López Obrador became the national leader of the PRD, and captured his party's candidacy to succeed Cuauhtémoc Cárdenas (the PRD's principal founder and first party president) as mayor of Mexico City in 2000. López Obrador's masterful use of the national visibility of his office (Mexico City television is broadcast nationally) soon made him a presidential frontrunner, as he even weathered storms that included financial scandals involving some of his closest associates. His calls for social justice and higher spending, combined with his knack for "getting things done"—sometimes without much regard for the rule of law—and huge doses of media coverage made him very popular in Mexico City and beyond.

A turning point in López Obrador's quest for Mexico's highest office came in April 2005, when the PRI and PAN in the Chamber of Deputies stripped him of the legal immunity *(fuero)* attached to his office, and thus exposed him to criminal charges for allegedly having disobeyed a court order in a land-use case. Massive, fiery public protests forced federal authorities to back down and drop the charges, which would have effectively barred him from running for president. From the *desafuero* dispute López Obrador drew two lessons that would become major themes in his campaign: 1) The Fox administration had been ready to use a legalistic sleight of hand to sideline him; and 2) "the people" had mobilized to stop this ploy in its tracks and save his political career. López Obrador's own pompous and oft-repeated public claims of "political invincibility" seemed to have been vindicated. Nothing could stop him now. Indeed, regardless of López Obrador's political interpretation of the episode, the ambivalence of the Fox administration—which originally filed the *desafuero* claim—regarding the proper enforcement of the rule of law underscores shortcomings in the process of democratic consolidation.

As it had in 2000, the PRI held an open presidential primary in 2006. Madrazo, who had lost the nomination to Francisco Labastida in 2000, had become party president in a nationwide primary in 2002, and had used his office to control access to federal candidacies and to steer party funds (Mexico has a generous public-financing law) to friendly state chapters. According to most polls, Madrazo personified the corrupt legacy of the authoritarian PRI, but his rivals within the party managed only to field an opponent (Arturo Montiel, governor of the populous central State of

Mexico) who had to withdraw almost immediately amid charges of illicit enrichment. Madrazo emerged from his easy primary triumph without the expected "nomination bounce" and failed to improve his poor personal standing with voters. He began his campaign facing billboards and hecklers repeating, "Do you believe Madrazo? Me neither!"

Mostly due to Madrazo's weakness, Mexico was set to experience its first presidential election since the founding of the PRI in 1929 in which that party's candidate never really seemed to have a chance of winning. According to *Reforma* (Mexico City's leading newspaper and most credible pollster), Madrazo peaked in February—almost five months before the vote—and even then only came within 9 percentage points of the lead. This made it easier for Calderón and López Obrador to campaign almost exclusively against each other, and polarization predictably intensified.

A second unusual feature of the race was the scale and personal nature of negative campaigning. The Federal Electoral Institute (IFE, the autonomous election-management body running the contest) and the TEPJF issued bans on 29 "denigratory" ads put out by one or another of the three main parties, but campaign strategists easily found ways around such obstacles by changing ads to avoid repeating the specifically prohibited material. In similar fashion, unions, NGOs, and particularly business groups found ways to pay for political ads despite a law that allows only parties the right to broadcast "messages oriented toward the attainment of the vote" during the campaign season. In this sense, the 2006 campaign inaugurated Mexico's struggle with the question of limits to free speech and "issue advocacy." To this was added the relatively novel regulatory challenge posed by the high media activism of President Fox and other elected officials from all parties, which contrasted with the personal discretion that then-President Zedillo had observed during the 2000 campaign.

Another major novelty of 2006 was the unabashedly left-wing nature of López Obrador's campaign proposals regarding economic policy. Although López Obrador sent emissaries abroad to reassure investors that he was a Mexican Lula, and fairly successfully portrayed his ideas as a fiscally responsible statesman's necessary innovations on a failed economic model, the main topic of his campaign during its final month was his promise to bring about a 20 percent immediate increase in the income of all those with annual earnings of less than 9,000 Mexican pesos (the equivalent of about US$850), a group comprising roughly 64 percent of the population. The "immediate increase" plan included reductions in energy prices, as well as direct cash transfers, to be financed through government austerity in other spending areas. The PAN campaign pounded away at the credibility of the plan, implicitly admitting what they feared might be its vote-getting power.

By December 2005, Calderón had lost most of the impetus of his primary win, and began the campaign on a down note with a widely seen interview in which the most salient topic was his personal conservatism. By February, however, he had righted himself, fired most of his newer advisors, and mounted a surge based on two key moves. The first was a relentless negative campaign against López Obrador's authoritarian personality and fiscal irresponsibility; López Obrador unwisely played into this by persisting in coarse rhetorical attacks on Fox in which López Obrador compared the president to a noisy species of native bird. Calderón's second tack was more positive and centered on his own portrayal of himself as a modern, honest, and well-educated policy expert who would provide the continuity needed to ensure macroeconomic stability, and who had a sensible proposal to deal with every public problem. Mostly due to Calderón's early travails, López Obrador peaked in March, when his lead stretched to 10 points despite a lackluster campaign.

The combination of Calderón's negative campaign and López Obrador's decision to skip the first presidential debate on April 25 spelled doom for the former mayor. Calderón used this debate to put Madrazo out of contention for good; by mid-May, the PAN candidate had cut away at López Obrador's lead and made the race extremely close. López Obrador eventually responded by talking less about his past accomplishments and more about the specific benefits that voters could expect from his presidency. He also used his appearance in the second debate on June 6 to begin a massive and effective negative campaign of his own against Calderón's "clean-hands" reputation. The central allegation was that Calderón's brother-in-law, Diego Zavala, had been involved in an illicit scheme to procure government contracts while Calderón had been energy secretary. No indictments came down and indeed no evidence of wrongdoing ever surfaced—Zavala did obtain government contracts, but not on his relative's watch. López Obrador's attacks, however, resonated with an electorate still vividly conscious of PRI corruption and wary of anything that smacked of nepotism and crony capitalism in the circles around Fox. With all the negative appeals from both major contenders, it is hardly surprising that election day found citizens polarized, and that a razor-thin margin in the context of such a young democracy was seen as contestable by the losers.

Perhaps the most important question stemming from the election is whether the protest led by López Obrador is based on a major loss of citizen trust in the country's democratic institutions, or whether it is more of a short-term, elite-driven strategy designed to rouse support for a restructuring of the Mexican left around López Obrador's leadership. In order to answer this question, we will look more closely at the respective support bases of Calderón and López Obrador as these emerged on election day, and then turn to an analysis of the reasons behind the postelectoral protest.

What Shaped the 2006 Presidential Vote?

The literature on Mexican voting behavior has evolved considerably in recent years.[4] Based on these studies, and using the nationwide exit poll sponsored by *Reforma,* we used a statistical model to estimate the effect on the probability of voting for each candidate of a number of different possible determinants. These included social and demographic correlates (such as gender, age, and income); retrospective evaluations of the Fox administration's performance; party identification; ideological orientation; whether the voter received aid from government social programs; and a summary measure of voters' opinions regarding the two frontrunners, Calderón and López Obrador.[5]

The election indeed featured a substantial north-south divide, with northwestern states (where the PAN organization has long been stronger, and where globalization's effects have been most palpable) clearly favorable to Calderón and unfavorable to López Obrador. The PRD contender's strong showing in the Federal District (Mexico City) is properly explained by left-wing ideology, PRD partisanship, and the degree to which López Obrador's mayoralty cemented his personal appeal—all of which were significant determinants of his vote nationwide, and major influences in Mexico City. After we controlled for Mexico City residency, we found that the elderly were less likely to vote for López Obrador and more likely to support the PRI, a finding consistent with previous research,[6] but counterintuitive if we consider that López Obrador campaigned heavily on the economic benefits that he promised to deliver to the elderly—he apparently was unable to make this case convincingly to those living outside his metropolitan bastion.

Being an independent increased the probability of voting for Calderón by 15 percent, and the probability of voting for López Obrador by 23 percent, while decreasing the likelihood of voting for Madrazo by 38 percent. Calderón balanced this relative disadvantage against López Obrador with significant support from PAN partisans and those on the ideological right, as well as those who approved of Fox's performance and who had positive retrospective evaluations of both their own personal economic situation and the country's economy as a whole—an effect unseen in Mexico's presidential elections since 1994. Interestingly, López Obrador did not seem to capture the support of those dissatisfied with Fox. Instead, the lion's share of what one might call the "fed up with Fox" vote went to Madrazo of the PRI.

Madrazo drew from the core support base that had sustained his party during its seven decades of rule. Rural, older, and less-educated voters, as well as women, were all more likely to support the PRI. Moreover, most of the factors that helped Calderón hurt Madrazo: Voters who were independents, from Mexico City, approved of Fox's administration, and positively evaluated the economy turned against Madrazo. Interestingly, neither recipients of the Seguro Popular—a health-benefits program for uninsured Mexicans inaugurated by Fox—nor recipients of Oportunidades—the internationally recognized conditional-cash-transfer poverty-alleviation program that began more than ten years ago and which now reaches one in every five families in Mexico—seemed decisively to support Calderón over the alternatives.

The north-south divide, however, must not be overstated. Neither income, nor education, nor religion, nor rural status made a difference in the vote between López Obrador and Calderón. This was not an election of rich against poor, Catholic against secular, or urban against rural—indeed the only significant variable among these has Madrazo benefiting from the rural vote. The "north-south" distinction is better understood as representing an increasingly prominent left-versus-right debate over economic policy *that cuts across all segments of the electorate.* There is indeed a higher level of support for the left in the southern part of the country, for reasons related both to the history of the various parties' organizational development and to differing levels of economic development.

In addition to the effects of ideology, retrospective evaluations, and partisanship, the model captures a strong candidate-centered effect on the vote. Both López Obrador and Calderón's campaigns successfully exploited voters' partisan predispositions, intensifying opinions about both the favored candidate and his opponent in each partisan base. Those who wanted to vote for López Obrador (or against the PAN or Calderón) were biased to pay attention to those messages that reinforced the issue or issues which distinguished their candidate from the competitor, and vice versa.[7] The negative nature of the campaign and the fact that it was a close race until the very end further strengthened this effect, and in a three-party election in which the PRI represented the centrist alternative to the incumbent, a more moderate campaign approach by either López Obrador or Calderón probably would not have made sense.[8]

The respective campaigns were successful in reinforcing each side's stance. The polarization of attitudes was evident not only with regard to voter preferences and the closely related opinions that people held of the various candidates, but also extended to views about how the campaign had unfolded, about what had happened on election day, and about the postelection conflict. The type of discourse that dominated the campaign raised the potential for protest to such a height that the credibility of various authorities and voters' favorable opinions concerning Mexican democracy proved to have only weak dissuasive power once López Obrador determined on a course of political mobilization.

The Importance of "Losers' Consent"

A recent addition to the growing literature on "losers' consent" argues that in newer democracies, individuals tend to lack sufficient political experience to help them handle defeat.[9] The idea is that election losers are more likely to engage in political protest, and that this effect is heightened owing to lack of experience with democratic events (such as elections). As the authors of this analysis put it, "Being in the political minority heightens citizens' political protest potential."[10]

The Mexican case, we argue, illustrates that not all political losers are created equal, and that the way in which election campaigns are conducted makes a difference as regards ensuing political protests, especially in the context of newer democracies. Some citizens may be more convinced than others of the country's democratic virtues, and therefore less easily swayed by calls for protest. Some may have certain social and demographic characteristics that make them more or less likely to be mobilized for protest. Especially in cases such as that of Mexico—where massive investments in boosting the credibility of elections have been a centerpiece of recent, landmark democratization efforts—one would expect electoral credibility to have some calming or appeasing effect, perhaps in conjunction with the large-scale and intense voter-education efforts that the IFE is legally mandated to implement. More believable elections, in other words, should be helping to reshape Mexican political culture in the direction of greater trust. Hence there should be less readiness to mobilize for protest in the event of an adverse election result.

In order to test such expectations, we proceed in two steps. First, we try to determine the extent to which Mexican voters were convinced that they lived in a democracy and would remain so convinced *independent of the election's outcome.* We show how partisanship determines even these stable opinions: There were more citizens convinced that they were participating in a democracy in Calderón's camp than in López Obrador's. Then we look at how these opinions of democracy might influence the potential for protest—in addition to the independent effect of having lost the election—and conclude that the protest itself has a strongly partisan character, and that misgivings about whether one is living in a democracy have little effect. These conclusions lead us to argue that the postelection protest is likely to be shorter-lived, and indeed less telling of deeper social dissatisfaction, than perhaps apparent.

We use the *Mexico 2006 Panel Study*[11] to identify four groups of individuals according to their respective perceptions of Mexico's democracy. First, we identify voters who, *convinced that Mexico is democratic,* were willing in each wave of the questionnaire (before the campaign season, during it, and after the vote) to affirm their belief that Mexico is a democracy. Second were the *convinced skeptics,* who said in response to all three waves of questioning that Mexico was not a democracy. The final two groups contained respondents who reported having changed their opinion. The third, or *disappointed,* group was home to those who had gone from thinking that Mexico was a democracy to thinking that it was not. The fourth and final group—we call them the *optimists*—was filled with those who, despite prior misgivings, eventually became convinced that Mexico was in fact a democratic country.

The Table shows how the members of these four groups are distributed across the range of their self-reported voting behavior. The data are somewhat encouraging, since more than half the voters interviewed systematically indicated their belief that Mexico was a democracy, while

TABLE—PERCEPTIONS OF DEMOCRACY BY REPORTED VOTE

	CALDERÓN	MADRAZO	LÓPEZ OBRADOR	OTHER	TOTAL
Mexico is a democracy (all waves)	54.2%	20.8%	21.8%	3.2%	100%
	n=154	n=59	n=62	n=9	n=284
Mexico is NOT a democracy	19.4%	18.1%	54.2%	8.3%	100%
	n=14	n=13	n=39	n=6	n=72
Disappointed (switched "yes" to "no")	27.3%	13.6%	54.5%	4.6%	100%
	n=24	n=12	n=48	n=4	n=88
Optimistic (switched "no" to "yes")	40.3%	29.2%	30.5%	0.0%	100%
	n=29	n=21	n=22	n=0	n=72
Total	42.8%	20.4%	33.1%	3.7%	100%
	n=221	n=105	n=171	n=19	n=516

Pearson chi^2(9)=67.94; Pr=0.00

The *Mexico 2006 Panel Study* consisted of three waves: the first one carried out October 7–10 and 15–18 (n=2,400); the second one carried out May 3–16 (n=1,770); and the third one carried out July 15–30 (n=1,594). Federal elections were held on 2 July 2006. A total of 1,378 respondents were interviewed in all three waves, which included an oversample for the Federal District and rural areas. The Table shows data from the national sample only. Further information on the *Mexico 2006 Panel Study* is available at *http://web.mit. edu/polisci/research/mexico06/index.htm.*

only 14 percent consistently rejected this assessment. The remaining 31 percent wavered in their opinion during the course of the campaign, with roughly half this group ending up disillusioned and the other half optimistic. Those convinced of Mexico's democratic character were more than twice as likely to support Calderón rather than López Obrador, while convinced skeptics were nearly three times more likely to support López Obrador over Calderón.

As expected, "disappointed" voters reported much higher levels of support for one of the losing candidates than did "optimistic" voters. According to the data, one's perception of Mexico as either democratic or nondemocratic was strongly associated with the victory or defeat of one's favored candidate, exactly as the authors of the "losers' consent" study would expect.[12] It would, however, be helpful to learn what lies behind the stable attitudes toward Mexican democracy, especially those independent of the specific election outcome. The structure of the study lends itself to such an inquiry, by allowing us first to identify groups with opinions that remained constant from before to after the election, and then to attempt to explain why these opinions have been held so steadily.[13]

The most important determinants of "democratic certainty" (whether it is the "positive" certainty that democracy is present or the "negative" certainty that it is absent) are contextual and political variables. Highly educated individuals' opinion of Mexico's democracy was slightly more volatile, but was not statistically distinguishable from opinion among less-educated groups. In particular, some of the same variables that were important in determining a voter's choice between López Obrador and Calderón also seemed to be at work in distinguishing between convinced democrats and convinced skeptics. These variables were: 1) retrospective evaluations of Fox and the economy, and 2) favorable evaluations of López Obrador and negative evaluations of Calderón, which in turn made it increasingly likely for an López Obrador defeat to bring about electoral protest.

Protest and Democratic Certainty

The above findings raise the possibility that not all electoral defeats have the same implications regarding the likelihood and nature of follow-on protests. What factors maximize the potential for protest? Can institutional arrangements be strong enough to induce attitudinal changes that will restrain outbreaks of protest after an election? After asking respondents during the course of the campaign whether they would take part in a postelection protest should their favored candidate denounce the outcome and urge them into the streets, we assessed a set of possible determinants, in particular including citizens' certainty regarding the democratic quality of Mexico.[14]

The results of our model are compelling: Those who felt sure that Mexico is a democracy, along with those whose opinions changed (for better or worse), and those who felt convinced that Mexico is *not* a democracy, were *all equally likely* to report themselves ready to protest the outcome of the election should their standard-bearer choose to contest it. Neither the credibility of the IFE as Mexico's electoral authority nor voters' confidence in the cleanliness of the election made any difference in the likelihood of a voter to protest.

The evidence shows that those with the highest likelihood to protest a disliked outcome were individuals with low education, and Mexico City residents with specific sociodemographic characteristics such as old age and low income—both groups being the target of social programs that López Obrador instituted early in his mayoralty. The same is true for voters who hewed to more extreme ideological views (whether of the right or the left),[15] partisans of all stripes,[16] and López Obrador sympathizers who felt completely certain that their candidate would win. In other words, we found that those who felt strong emotional or ideological ties to a political party were more likely to protest in the event of their candidate losing, no matter how clean they thought the election had been, whether or not they perceived Mexico as a democracy, or how much they trusted the election's official arbiter.

Similarly, while opinions about Mexico's democracy and its institutions made little difference in explaining the potential for protest, mobilized partisan bases, and in particular those of the PRD, were found to align closely with segments of the electorate that had a higher latent potential for protest—in particular in Mexico City, which was the scene of the largest demonstrations. Although strong partisans of all stripes were (not surprisingly) more likely to protest than were voters who failed to identify with any party, PRD partisans exhibited a much greater propensity to protest than did backers of the PAN or the PRI (the effect was about 50 percent stronger).

Moreover, potential for protest was strongly influenced by campaign dynamics: Those who said that they would definitely vote for López Obrador, and who were completely certain that he would win, were substantially more likely to say that they would engage in protest, implying that expectation of victory is one obvious reason behind the finding that close elections lead to protests. The survey results show that López Obrador's supporters were more likely to protest than were Calderón's. Frustration with electoral defeat, especially among partisans, prompts individuals to engage in protests. Yet some partisans might have greater reasons to be frustrated—perhaps because they have been out of power for a longer time, or because the history of their movement and the context of the campaign make it harder to accept defeat. In the case of the Mexican election, two reasons made this defeat tougher to swallow: For one, the PRD has never held the presidency and was actually born from a failed attempt to capture this post in 1988, in an election that produced substantial evidence of fraud.[17] Second, the *desafuero* affair strengthened misgivings among López Obrador and his followers as to the overall fairness of the country's political institutions.

Interestingly, the social bases of protest in Mexico show a pattern more consistent with "mobilized" rather than "spontaneous" participation: It was not those with higher resources, education, or status who professed the most willingness to take the streets, but rather such readily mobilizable groups as the elderly, the less educated, and the poor. Union membership played little role in the propensity to be mobilized for protest. A larger factor was perhaps membership in clientelistic networks, hence the greater likelihood of protest among those belonging to groups targeted for benefits by Mexico City social programs.[18]

In light of these findings, López Obrador's decision to contest the election and mobilize massive protests appears completely rational. His partisan base and campaign strategy allowed him to rouse the support of those individuals with the lowest income and levels of education, in particular those in Mexico City, who were easily cooptable through selective incentives. Moreover, his repeated claims that obstacles were relentlessly raised to his pursuit of the presidency by "the system"—which in his telling was represented by the Fox administration and the Calderón candidacy, and comprised powerful private interests alongside the leadership of the IFE and the TEPJF—take on a new meaning. As much support as López Obrador enjoyed among those convinced that Mexico was not a democracy, neither the IFE's credibility, nor perceptions of democracy, nor expectations of a clean election made a difference at the mass level. Nevertheless, López Obrador's ability to add a "stolen election" to the stock of injustices committed against him and his followers by those in favor of "neoliberal" economic policies should be understood as a long-term gamble to strengthen his movement's position in Mexico's ideological spectrum, which before democratization had included a prominent prodemocracy-versus-antidemocracy dimension that had seemed mostly resolved by the year 2000.[19]

But the 2006 election proved that a well-regarded candidate with a credible left-wing economic platform might not be enough for the PRD to win the presidency. By renewing Mexico's apparently dormant *political* (that is, democratic-versus-antidemocratic) dimension of conflict, and placing everyone except his own backers on the "authoritarian" end of the spectrum, López Obrador was attempting to generate a broader political base for his movement as well as greater long-run differentiation from both the PAN and the PRI. Interestingly, the future credibility of electoral processes might become a minor ingredient in this gamble—after all, most people do believe that Mexico is a democracy, contested election and all. In a sense, López Obrador's bet was a wager that Mexico's *other* political institutions—especially those in charge of governance and enforcing the law—would show themselves unable to improve in fairness, efficiency, and effectiveness.

Looking beyond the Mexican case, it is apparent that our study builds upon previous analyses of protest in the aftermath of close elections in young democracies. We show that such elections are not *necessarily* preludes to political protest, since losers are not always equally likely to be mobilized. But even relatively strong and credible electoral institutions might not be enough to quell political protest in the presence of a polarizing campaign, especially if leaders and parties can effectively mobilize losers' underlying attitudes and electoral frustration.

Although our survey evidence does not suggest that flawed institutions were the principal cause of the protest, institution-building remains an imperative for Mexico. Better, more realistic regulation that effectively tackles problems such as the abuse of governmental resources before and during election campaigns is essential to achieving cleaner elections. The same is true in terms of enhancing the damaged credibility, autonomy, and regulatory effectiveness of electoral authorities. But our research clearly shows that these measures cannot, by themselves, be expected greatly to reduce the potential for protest. Rather, these institutional improvements are geared to altering politicians' incentives to engage in antisystem strategies. In this respect, the decision by López Obrador's electoral coalition, now called the Broad Progressive Front, to take its seats in both the Chamber of Deputies and the Senate could be seen as a basic indicator of the electoral framework's success and a favorable sign for the future. But it may also announce a more complex strategy, in which this leftist Front straddles both sides of the institutional game, deferring when politically expedient, defying when not.

However that may be, our results also underscore that the patterns of protest seen after Mexico's stunningly close 2006 election may be less democratic and less productive than many believe. Clientelistic, partisan-led protests that mobilize society's most susceptible elements are far from the kind of autonomous, grassroots participation that forcefully expresses substantive popular demands.[20]

For the time being, Mexico's political leaders face an enormous challenge. They must break the incentives for gridlock that have pervaded the system over the last decade, and engage in the kind of policy making that will promote greater levels of welfare and social justice. Should such an effort succeed, it might make Mexico's citizens less vulnerable to political manipulation and clientelistic mobilization—by any political party, winner or loser, sore or not.

NOTES

The authors wish to thank Alejandro Moreno and the Mexico City newspaper *Reforma* for access to its 2006 exit poll; and Marco Fernández for his comments on an earlier version. Alejandro Poiré acknowledges financial support from the David Rockefeller Center for Latin American Studies at Harvard University.

1. We examined López Obrador's charges and found no evidence of systematic wrongdoing that could have benefited Calderón's vote total. See Alejandro Poiré and Luis M. Estrada, "Allegations of Fraud in Mexico's 2006 Presidential Election," paper delivered at the 102nd Annual Meeting of the American Political Science Association, Philadelphia, September 2006.

2. See Alejandro Poiré, "El Bueno, el Malo y la Incógnita: Ensayo Sobre las Primarias Partidarias del 2005," *Bien Común* 11 (December 2005): 7–10.

3. Ultimately, "[t]he Supreme Court . . . upheld Madrazo's contention that campaign spending was an internal state matter" and the case was filed. Susana Berruecos, "Electoral Justice in Mexico: The Role of the Electoral Tribunal under New Federalism," *Journal of Latin American Studies* 35 (November 2003): 810.

4. For a review, see Jorge I. Domínguez, "The Scholarly Study of Mexican Politics," *Mexican Studies/Estudios Mexicanos* 20 (Summer 2004): 377–410, esp. 405–10.

5. We assess the independent causal effect of each of the explanatory variables on the probability of voting for each of the three major candidates, using a multinomial logit model. For model coefficients and other detailed statistical information, see *www.journalofdemocracy.org/articles/gratis/PoireGraphics-18-1.pdf*.

6. See Beatriz Magaloni, "Is the PRI Fading? Economic Performance, Electoral Accountability, and Voting Behavior," in Jorge I. Domínguez and Alejandro Poiré, eds., *Toward Mexico's Democratization: Parties, Campaigns, Elections, and Public Opinion* (London: Routledge, 1999), 203–36.

7. The more intense the partisan allegiance, the more biased the analyses and interpretation of the political environment. See Donald Stokes, "Party Loyalty and the Likelihood of Deviating Elections," in Angus Campbell et al., eds., *Elections and the Political Order* (New York: Wiley, 1966).

8. Left-right ideology does not influence the Madrazo vote, underscoring his explicit appeals on the campaign trail to centrist voters.

9. See Christoper J. Anderson and Silvia M. Mendes, "Learning to Lose: Election Outcomes, Democratic Experience, and Political Protest Potential," *British Journal of Political Science* 36 (January 2006): 91–111.

10. Anderson and Mendes, "Learning to Lose," 91.

11. Participants in the *Mexico 2006 Panel Study* include Andy Baker, Kathleen Bruhn, Roderic Camp, Wayne Cornelius, Jorge Domínguez, Kenneth Greene, Joseph Klesner, Chappell Lawson (principal investigator), Beatriz Magaloni, James McCann, Alejandro Moreno, Alejandro Poiré, and David Shirk. Funding was provided by the National Science Foundation (SES-0517971) and *Reforma*; fieldwork was conducted by *Reforma* under the direction of Alejandro Moreno.

12. Anderson and Mendes, "Learning to Lose," 94.

13. The discussion in the next paragraph stems from a multinomial logit model of "democratic certainty," where the dependent variable had three categories: convinced Mexico is a democracy, convinced Mexico is not a democracy, and opinion switchers.

14. The discussion in this paragraph and the ones below uses results of a logit model where potential for protest, as measured in the second wave of the panel, was the dependent variable.

15. This result is consistent with Anderson and Mendes, "Learning to Lose," 103–4.

16. With the exception of PRI partisans in Mexico City, where this party has very weak support.

17. The evidence suggests that the fraud was not meant to stop a PRI defeat, but to guarantee a PRI majority in the Chamber of Deputies. See Arturo Sánchez Gutiérrez, ed., *Elecciones a Debate, 1988: Las Actas Electorales Perdida* (Mexico City: Diana, 1994).

18. For a critique of López Obrador's performance, including his clientelistic policy making, see Roger Bartra, "Fango Sobre la Democracia," *Letras Libres,* September 2006, 16–22.

19. See Juan Molinar Horcasitas, *El Tiempo de la Legitimidad: Elecciones, Autoritarismo y Democracia en México* (Mexico City: Cal y Arena, 1991), 171–200 for the original description of the two dimensions of the party system, and Beatriz Magaloni and Alejandro Poiré, "The Issues, the Vote, and the Mandate for Change," in Jorge I. Domínguez and Chappell Lawson, eds., *Mexico's Pivotal Democratic Election: Candidates, Voters, and the Presidential Campaign of 2000* (Stanford, Calif.: Stanford University Press and Center for U.S.-Mexican Studies, 2004), 293–319, for an assessment of issue voting in the 2000 elections.

20. Anderson and Mendes discuss the latter type of protest in "Learning to Lose," 98.

16

THE MOBILIZATION OF DISTRUST IN MEXICO

Andreas Schedler

Andreas Schedler *is professor of political science at CIDE in Mexico City. He is editor of* Electoral Authoritarianism: The Dynamics of Unfree Competition *(2006) and author of* Democratization by Elections: Mexico in Comparative Perspective *(forthcoming 2008 in Spanish). This essay originally appeared in the January 2007 issue of the* Journal of Democracy.

Right after the historic alternation of power in 2000 that put the final touch to Mexico's protracted transition away from decades of electoral authoritarianism, the country looked like a consolidated democracy. To be sure, its appearance was that of a normal Latin American democracy, beset by a weak rule of law, glaring social inequalities, dizzying levels of societal violence, a complacent political class, an ineffectual policy-making process, and deep popular disenchantment. Still, it appeared decidedly stable, untroubled by any antisystem actors of relevance. With parties and politicians glued to the electoral calendar, politics seemed to find its fulfillment in the cyclical suspense of the electoral "horse race" at all levels of the political system. Yet one thing seemed capable of provoking serious trouble (albeit at intervals of no less than six years): a close result in a presidential election.

In professional terms, election authorities in new democracies the world over fear narrow opposition defeats more than anything. There is nothing as troublesome for these authorities' credibility, and nothing as hard for the losing party to swallow. A close outcome tests the defeated candidate's democratic commitment and the democratic system's resiliency. In Mexico's 2006 presidential election, this worst-case scenario came to pass, and it turned out to be even worse than anyone had imagined. The losing candidate, Andrés Manuel López Obrador of the Party of the Democratic Revolution (PRD), finished second to Felipe Calderón of the National Action Party (PAN) by only 0.56 percent of the valid votes cast. López Obrador claimed fraud, urged his supporters into the streets, and launched something like a rhetorical revolution. Refusing to concede defeat, he adopted an incendiary antiestablishment discourse, declared that a "neofascist" gang of corrupt politicians and entrepreneurs had kidnapped democracy, announced his intention to rewrite the constitution, and had a cheering crowd proclaim him the "legitimate" president of Mexico. What had gone wrong to drag the country, within a few short weeks, from the tempered excitements of democratic routine into the epic drama of postelectoral conflict?

As the campaign began, the 2006 presidential race seemed to be a story foretold. For years, López Obrador had been leading opinion polls by wide and stable margins against all possible contenders. He seemed bound to win. Yet as tends to happen in a world where voter preferences are not written in stone, the campaign mattered. By the end of April, with barely two months to go before election day, Calderón had used an effective mixture of positive appeals and personal attacks to turn the race into a tight two-way affair.

In response, López Obrador began reverting to a note that he had struck before in his political career by charging his adversaries with foul play. Mexican law provides generous public financing to all parties, and overall the media have granted fair treatment to presidential candidates.[1] Notwithstanding this, López Obrador complained that he was facing a "state-controlled election" orchestrated by President Vicente Fox as well as a "dirty war" led by the PAN. Echoing themes of past democratizing struggles, López Obrador seemed to be preparing the ground for a challenge of the result in the event of his defeat.

The campaign came to a close in an atmosphere rife with tension. What had once promised to be a placid stroll to victory by an "indestructible" candidate ended with a troublesome two-headed uncertainty: Who would win, and would the loser accept the verdict? Election day went smoothly and calmly as the polarizing dynamic of the campaign gave way to established organizational routines and civic habits. National elections in Mexico, like those in any large, populous, and diverse country, require an enormous logistical effort. Almost 42 million voters, or roughly 58 percent of the electorate, went to the polls. More than half a million citizens acted as election officials at 130,231 *casillas* (precincts or polling stations) spread across 300 electoral districts. Well over a million party representatives, almost 25,000 national observers, and 693 international observers watched over the voting. Neither electoral authorities, nor political parties, nor the media reported any serious incidents. Observers were unanimous in hailing an exemplary exercise of civic participation. As anticipated, the trouble would begin later, after the polls had closed and results had started trickling in.

Official results in Mexican federal elections emerge from the review and computation of tally sheets at the district level three days after the election (Wednesday, July 5 in this case). In order to relieve the suspense, the Federal Electoral Institute (or IFE, Mexico's autonomous electoral-administration authority) displays preliminary results in real time, as they arrive. These preliminary figures lack any legal validity. They contain small margins of error whose precise magnitudes are unknown, and they are likely to be off at first since urban results come in quicker than rural ones (which is why the real-time results showed Calderón with a considerable early lead that aroused PRD suspicions).

To dispel uncertainty on election night, the IFE had also prepared a quick count. Quick counts (or "parallel vote tabulations" as they are more formally known) provide independent estimations of election outcomes by computing results drawn from a representative sample of polling stations. Election observers across the world have been using quick counts since the mid-1980s to check the conduct of election authorities. It was strange, however, to see an election commission itself employing this method. The IFE quick count, a professional exercise based on a large sample of 7,673 polling stations, was obviously not meant to be an instrument of administrative self-control. Ironically, though meant to dispel the uncertainty of election night, it touched off more than two months of tantalizing uncertainty over the identity of the winner.[2]

At 11 p.m. on election night, after the major television networks had reported that they were finding themselves unable to predict a winner based on their exit polls, IFE president Luis Carlos Ugalde stepped before the cameras to explain that the distance between the two leading candidates lay within statistical margins of error. The election was too close to call; everyone would have to be patient. He called for "prudence" and asked candidates to refrain from publicly declaring victory.

Ugalde was following a precise script agreed upon beforehand with the political parties. Yet unluckily, he missed an opportunity to create procedural certainty in the midst of substantive uncertainty. He neglected to explain that voters would be best advised to ignore the preliminary figures. He omitted to indicate that official results would be computed three days later, in a transparent process that would allow doubts about specific polling-station results to be addressed. And perhaps most damagingly, he had failed to talk to candidates in order to ensure they would heed his friendly advice to keep silent. No sooner had the IFE president finished than López Obrador and Calderón each went on national television to declare himself the happy victor. The stage was set for conflict.

The Rhetoric of Revolution

On election night, López Obrador declared that he had won by "at least" half a million votes, that his victory was "irreversible," and that he would not allow the election to be stolen. While asking his followers to await the recount of votes "polling station by polling station," he urged election authorities to "respect our results." These early declarations set up the unfolding postelectoral drama. Calling forth the specter of electoral fraud, they flung open a Pandora's box of suspicion. Over the days to come, López Obrador would add multifarious accusations of vote-rigging as talk of fraud spread like wildfire among his followers. Within less than a week, the country, admired and applauded worldwide for the integrity and professionalism of its electoral apparatus, saw itself pushed back into the epic confrontations and rhetoric of past democratizing struggles.

Shocked and depressed to find themselves at the center of political turmoil, the electoral authorities withdrew into bureaucratic routines and declarations rather than take up the struggle for public opinion. Soon ignoring or seeking to discredit anything that came from the IFE, López Obrador turned to the courts and the streets to advance his case. Before the Electoral Tribunal of the Federal Judiciary (TEPJF), since 1996 the final arbiter of all electoral disputes, the PRD pressed a sloppily prepared and internally inconsistent lawsuit. Its key demands were: 1) a recount of all votes; 2) the annulment of results from specific polling stations on grounds of numerical inconsistencies; and 3) the invalidation of the entire election on account of before-the-fact irregularities alleged to have rendered the campaign unfair.

To keep electoral magistrates on the right track of "integrity and patriotism," the PRD carried out a campaign of "civic resistance" against the "imposition" of the conservative candidate. The protests involved a series of mass demonstrations in Mexico City and, in faint imitation of Ukraine's 2004 Orange Revolution, the erection of huge camping tents on the capital's central plaza, the Zócalo, and its most splendorous avenue, La Reforma. One central demand animated these large and peaceful protest mobilizations: a full recount, "Voto por voto! Casilla por casilla!" Without a complete recount, López Obrador insisted, the credibility of the presidential election would be damaged beyond repair.

Over several weeks, as electoral magistrates deliberated and the capital sank even deeper into traffic chaos, López Obrador publicly asked Calderón to back a recount. Calderón responded elliptically that the case rested with the courts, not with politicians, and promised that he would support whatever the Tribunal ordered. A more enlightened conception of his own self-interest might arguably have led him to embrace the recount demand instead, and to open talks with the PRD about the formal rules that might govern recounts in the future and inform judicial-decision making in the present (without agreement on such rules any recount would be too likely to become simply another bone of contention). Unsurprisingly, the leading candidate's evasive legalism did nothing to allay the political conflict. Even if correct on paper, it could easily be read as simple rejection. López Obrador promptly declared it "the firmest proof of fraud."

In early September, after two months of tension and suspense, an intensely cross-pressured TEPJF validated Calderón's close victory. López

Obrador responded with heightened rhetorical escalation. Comfortably playing on traditional populist themes, he placed his charges of election fraud within a larger narrative of historic injustice. He described the election as symptomatic of an old split between the people and a "rapacious minority" of "white-collar criminals and corrupt politicians" who had set up a "regime of corruption and privilege" that had turned Mexico into "an ocean of inequality." With its "fascist propaganda" during the electoral campaign, this "very powerful group" of economic and political elites had carried out "one of the most savage attacks on democracy" in Mexican history. Afterwards, shielded by "the conspiratorial silence of mass media," they had "blatantly falsified" electoral results in order to "impose" their "willing puppet" Calderón. To restore democracy, social justice, and public happiness, the defeated candidate called for a comprehensive (albeit unspecified) institutional, economic, and cultural refoundation and "purification" of the country. Ten days after the final court ruling, he had a crowd of followers declare him the "legitimate president" of Mexico, in charge of forming a cabinet and elaborating a new constitution. Though orderly and nonviolent, and sometimes even festive in character, at the level of rhetoric and ritual at least, the postelectoral conflict had led to a quasi-revolutionary situation.[3]

Imperfect Elections

The modern history of elections is replete with tales of defeated parties and candidates protesting the unwelcome results. Turning elections into "the only game in town"—in which all parties acquiesce no matter what the outcome—has been one of democracy's greatest challenges everywhere. Building and consolidating a democracy can often take many election cycles. Mexico itself has only recently emerged from decades of fraudulent elections and electoral protests. In Latin American history, closely fought elections have often been a prelude to armed rebellion and civil war. In the contemporary world, a fair number of electoral autocracies have been tumbled by popular mobilizations against flawed elections. Today as in the past, losers almost inevitably claim that they have been robbed. Since close elections dramatically heighten the potential impact of fraud, they are particularly powerful motors of opposition protest. The "fact that ballot rigging could be decisive" provides a strong motive for claiming fraud in close contests.[4]

Establishing the veracity of opposition allegations is simple in easy cases, but quite a challenge in more ambiguous situations. The 2006 presidential election in Mexico undoubtedly falls well outside the "easy" category. The PRD's fraud charges came in shifting waves, some of which were frivolous and easy to discard. Yet the most serious allegations concerned discrepancies in tally-sheet data—an opaque and complex topic that even well-informed citizens find hard to grasp.

In the 1980s and early 1990s, as Mexico was emerging from the decades-old hegemony of the Institutional Revolutionary Party (PRI), acts of electoral fraud followed by opposition protests were frequent, especially at the state and municipal levels. In the 1988 presidential election, for instance, the PRI candidate won amid credible claims that fraud had been committed against Cuauhtémoc Cárdenas, a founder and three-time presidential candidate of the PRD. As the regime was then still able to threaten large-scale repression, the losing candidate opted to have his followers stand down rather than risk disruptions that might lead to violence.

Almost twenty years later, evocations of the stolen 1988 election remained powerful, and López Obrador exploited them skillfully. The profound democratizing reforms of the 1990s, however, had in the interim transformed beyond recognition Mexico's system for administering and overseeing elections. Many of the reforms answered demands that the PRD itself had made with a view to preventing any replay of 1988. Precluding the possibility of fraud was these reforms' central purpose. In order to institutionalize electoral integrity, reformers pursued four major strategies. They created a dense network of bureaucratic rules (regulation), transferred election management from the government to the independent IFE (delegation), subjected the organization of elections to tight party supervision (oversight), and moved dispute settlement from the legislature to a specialized tribunal, the TEPJF (judicialization).[5]

To prevent vote-rigging on election day, reformers entrusted the management of polling stations to randomly selected citizens, working under the watchful eyes of party representatives. The selection by lot of polling-station officials, the extreme diffusion of decision-making authority across more than 130,000 polling places, and the presence of close party supervision have combined to render the commission of election-day fraud almost impossible. In a polity as open as Mexico's, organizing large-scale vote fraud is simply beyond the administrative capability of any party or state agency. Any attempt to rig the vote would require active collusion among citizens as well as party representatives, and aspiring cheaters would in all likelihood be found out and denounced. In the climate of good faith that tends to reign in Mexican polling stations, citizens often consent to minor rule breaches such as permitting a frail old lady to vote even if her name is missing from the voter list. On election day 2006, the IFE received *no* reports of anyone attempting to rig the vote.[6]

The tally sheet used in each polling place on election day forms part of Mexico's comprehensive system of electoral controls. It requires polling-station officials to write down not only the results of the vote count, but also to record turnout and to account for all the ballot papers handled at the polling station. At the end of the day, the voter-turnout figure, the number of ballots found in the ballot box, and the total number of votes cast should match. In addition, adding any of these figures to the number of leftover ballots should in each case yield the number of ballots initially supplied. Verifying these simple arithmetical balances and reconciling eventual discrepancies constitutes a fraud-control method that many countries use in one form or another. Precise records of ballot and turnout figures allow election authorities "to demonstrate that all ballots used at each voting station are genuine and that ballots have not been fraudulently deposited in ballot boxes or removed from the voting station."[7]

Herein lies the institutional failure of election management that beset Mexico in 2006: Going well beyond the provisions of the election code, the IFE required polling-station officials to keep account of ballots and voters, without doing anything to ensure that their accounts would be accurate. It asked for turnout figures and multiple counts of ballots, without asking anyone to check whether the results were consistent with each other. Moreover, in previous elections, the Institute had collected similar data but had never paid much attention to them (nor had anyone else), thereby signaling that these figures did not need to be taken seriously. A ballot-accounting system without purpose and without procedures for verifying its results and reconciling discrepancies is a failure waiting to happen.

These systemic faults, together with the multifarious possibilities for human error, turned the prevailing practice of ballot accounting into a major source of suspicion. Mexican elections, the vigilant denunciations of the loser taught us, are a sloppier affair than we had previously imagined. The manual counting and recording of turnout and ballot data produce an impressive amount of "noise." About half the roughly 130,000 tally sheets contained inconsistent data. Most of these "arithmetical inconsistencies" were tiny, although some were startlingly large, showing dozens of surplus ballots or missing ballots that could not be accounted for. The errors' average magnitude stood at plus or minus 4.4 votes (or 1.3 percent of the 328 votes cast at the average polling station), slightly lower than the figure that was recorded in the 2000 presidential election (when nobody had found such problems worth noticing).[8]

There are numerous innocent explanations for these inconsistencies, the chief among them being honest human error. Preliminary statistical analyses, which show that errors were evenly distributed across polling stations won by the two leading candidates, support such good-faith explanations.[9] It is easy to see in such a close election, however, how discrepancies in ballot data could feed explanations that assume bad-faith maneuvering by citizen poll managers. As Calderón carried the election by only 233,831 votes, in theory—and distrust, like jealousy, is a big theory builder—he could have fabricated his victory by stealing just a single vote from López Obrador at each of the 130,231 polling stations. The PRD's fraud allegations rested on that party's straightforward reading of missing or excessive *ballots* as evidence of stolen or added *votes*. A hypothetical manipulation of ballot numbers alone, however, has no bearing on the vote count carried out by polling-station officials. To alter actual results, fraudsters would have to tamper physically with the contents of ballot boxes, either adding or removing ballots. We have zero evidence that this happened on election day. Still, the numerous discrepancies in ballot accounts provided justification for López Obrador's demand of a full recount as well as for the partial recounts that the IFE and the TEPJF decided to carry out.

Imperfect Remedies

The Mexican electoral process contains two stages that offer opportunities to clean up messes of the sort that polling-station ballot accounts predictably leave behind: the district-level tally and the Electoral Tribunal. Mexican election laws, in contrast to those in many other democratic countries, do not provide for full recounts in close elections.[10] The laws do, however, allow the possible reconciliation of tally-sheet discrepancies during the district-level vote tallying that takes place during the week following a national election. At this stage, election officials are obliged to perform recounts of the ballots from those polling stations whose tally sheets contain inconsistent, incomprehensible, or missing data. For anyone with doubts regarding the results, this would be the legally prescribed time to spot and correct problems through the recount process.

Unfortunately, the IFE's top authorities failed to seize the moment during the critical week of July 3. Instead of publicly stressing the Institute's full readiness to address any doubts or complaints that party representatives might raise, IFE officials contented themselves with merely restating the formal rules in an internal communiqué. Accordingly, district councils followed their custom from previous elections and paid little attention to discrepancies in ballot accounts, while everyone moved through the process in a hurry. In one dramatic day, officials unsealed and recounted the data from 2,864 polling stations. At those where Calderón had won, the recount reduced his margin of victory by an average of 2.9 votes. Where López Obrador had won, the recount decreased his lead by an average of 7.5 votes. Since two-thirds of the recounted votes belonged to polling stations carried by the PAN (as the PRD had refrained from demanding recounts in its own strongholds), the overall adjustment in the two candidates' respective vote totals was minimal.[11]

The second chance for remedial action comes from the TEPJF. In the case that the PRD and its coalition partners brought before that panel, they challenged the results from 21,786 polling stations (or 16.7 percent of the total), distributed across 240 of Mexico's 300 electoral districts. On August 5, after a month of diligence and deliberation, the TEPJF rejected the coalition's core demand for a full recount of all ballots. Following legal precedent, the tribunal reasoned that given the decentralized nature of Mexico's voting process, irregularities at one polling place may not be taken as evidence of irregularities at others. Moreover, it maintained that results unchallenged by anyone must hold firm, since recounting them could introduce more uncertainties than it eliminates.

Nevertheless, López Obrador's street mobilizations induced a fruitful departure from prior and more narrow jurisprudence. The tribunal ordered the recounting of results from 11,839 (or 54.3 percent) of the PRD-challenged polling stations in order to resolve "evident" inconsistencies in their tally sheets that district councils had failed to address. In the absence of formal rules for judicial recounts, the tribunal drew up a detailed manual of procedures to which the parties largely acquiesced. Closely watched by party representatives, judicial-branch personnel executed this partial recount during the second week of August. On August 28, the TEPJF published its conclusions regarding each of the 240 district-level recounts. After recounting about 3.5 million ballots, again mostly in precincts that the PAN had carried (since the PRD understandably declined to question its own victories), the tribunal subtracted about 2,700 votes from Calderón's vote total, while adding about 2,100 to López Obrador's. The resulting net swing of 4,800 in the latter's favor represented barely 0.01 percent of total valid votes.

In addition, the tribunal annulled the results from 744 polling stations (or 6.3 percent of those subject to recounting), citing discrepancies in their ballot accounts. For that purpose, it adopted two decision rules. First, it drew a sharp distinction between "fundamental" and "auxiliary" tally-sheet data. Only discrepancies involving the former could be sufficient to trigger the annulment of results, while inconsistencies concerning the latter could not. Dealing López Obrador a blow, electoral magistrates placed the numbers of received and remaining ballots, numbers that stood at the heart of his complaints, into the category of "auxiliary" data.

Second, following precedent (not common sense), the TEPJF resolved to annul results only in those cases where the discrepancy in "fundamental" tally-sheet data was larger than the number of votes separating the two leading candidates at the polling station under consideration. Given the small magnitude of most inconsistencies, this implied that the TEPJF would almost exclusively invalidate results in "battleground" precincts, where the margin of victory either way was small. Predictably, since the annulment of such polling stations changed the overall distribution of votes at the margins only, the judicial invalidation of results left the distance between the two presidential frontrunners intact. Although he had carried most of the annulled polling stations, their elimination cost Calderón only 5,246 votes more than it cost López Obrador, an average of just seven votes per precinct.[12]

The partial judicial recount confirmed that even if their ballot accounts were often less than perfect, Mexico's citizen poll managers had by and large counted votes well. Therefore, despite the closeness of the presidential election, even a full recount as demanded by the PRD would have been unlikely to reverse the outcome and make López Obrador president. In addition, the partial recount made clear that even in the event of a full recount, the TEPJF would still have had to decide how to handle persisting discrepancies in ballot accounts. The decision rules that its jurists applied in annulling polling stations provoked harsh criticism. Yet *any* rules that the Tribunal might conceivably have applied would have been controversial. In consequence, although a full recount must be regarded as an eminently reasonable demand in any close election, it would have been unlikely to settle the postelection controversy.

The TEPJF was also a major player in the final act of the election, since the Tribunal's duties include the evaluation and validation of the entire electoral process. In a unanimous, yet openly contradictory ruling that reflected profound differences of judgment among its seven magistrates, the Tribunal added to the feeling of betrayal and bitterness among López Obrador's followers. On the one hand, it sided with the PRD in vehemently condemning the PAN's negative campaign style as well as outgoing president Vicente Fox's "activism" on behalf of the PAN ticket (a presidential posture that upset many Mexicans who recalled their country's long history of executive dominance and saw Fox as backsliding toward it). The chief executive's "indirect or metaphorical" pronouncements in favor of continuity in governmental policies, said the TEPJF, had put "the validity of the elections at risk." On the other hand, the Tribunal declared itself incapable of determining whether these "important irregularities" had exerted a "decisive influence" on the election's outcome. Lacking firm evidence about their causal impact, it concluded that it had no grounds for invalidating the election.[13]

As many actors and observers were quick to note, in an election as close as the race between López Obrador and Calderón, *anything* could have been decisive—including a host of factors less ponderous than breaches of presidential neutrality. Evaluations of electoral irregularities almost invariably demand assessments of causal impact. Yet by moving from legal reasoning to the social-scientific estimation of causal effects, the TEPJF's magistrates had ventured upon ground where they seemed to be at a loss. The upshot was that the jurists had established an offense but then let it go unpunished, taking shelter behind uncertainty about the precise consequences that the offense had entailed. This inconsistency gave critics ammunition that they could use in efforts to discredit not only the TEPJF but the electoral process itself. López Obrador was quick to denounce it as part of an institutional conspiracy against the left. His final judgment was categorical: "To the devil with these institutions!"

The Sources of Distrust

The bureaucratic, judicial, and political imperfections that emerged during the electoral process did not render it undemocratic—but they did make it vulnerable to the strategic mobilization of popular distrust. While López Obrador's talk of fraud found a handy purchase thanks to flaws in the electoral process, he was also tapping a reservoir of distrust that had been accumulating long before election day. Acting within a general context of (well-founded) citizen distrust toward state institutions, the PRD standard-bearer tied his fraud allegations to the left's longstanding fear of exclusion, a fear that had deepened during the 2006 electoral process.

In its seventeen years of existence, the left-wing PRD had conquered elective offices at all levels except the presidency, which remains the most valued prize in Mexican politics despite the limits imposed by the realities of divided government. The party's foundational experience was the large-scale electoral fraud that it suffered in the 1988 election. Since then, every presidential contest has reawakened PRD supporters' latent fear that their adversaries will use underhanded means to block the path to presidential power. Such fears of foul play have been fed by the party's own delusions. As PRD leaders tend to convince themselves that they articulate the objective interests of the people, so also do they tend to convince themselves that most citizens will support them at the polls—*unless* manipulative media or fraudulent electoral practices distort voters' subjective preferences. As López Obrador likes to insist, "A right-wing victory is morally impossible."

More importantly, however, the actions of the PRD's foes have repeatedly fed its anxieties. In 2003, in an act of acute myopia, the PRI and PAN appointed the current top managers of the IFE without securing the concurrence of the PRD. Matching their partisan sponsors in foresight and responsibility, these officials accepted their appointment without demur, despite the exclusion of precisely the player that was most likely to cry foul in case of defeat. The lack of interparty consensus did not mean that IFE officials were ready to violate their duties of professionalism and impartiality, but it did mean that the PRD would have an easy time dismissing them as agents of its adversaries. In a context in which personal credibility is still a vital source of institutional trust, the controversial appointment process was bound to damage the Institute as a whole.

Later, in 2005, the government's failed attempt to prosecute López Obrador for a minor infraction in his handling of a lawsuit could effortlessly be read as a politicized use of the law. (Prosecution would have barred him from the presidential race.) In the months leading up to the election, the negative campaign that the PAN ran against López Obrador solidified fears of exclusion in a pathogenic game of mutually reinforcing negative perceptions. As we know from the history of democratic breakdowns in Europe and Latin America, right-wing parties, businesspeople, and the military tend to turn against democracy if they perceive their left-wing adversaries as posing a radical threat to their own vital interests. We also know that such threat perceptions are more likely to develop in highly unequal societies.[14] Mexico is an abysmally unequal society, and López Obrador strove to assert socioeconomic inequality as the country's central political cleavage. In this context, the negative advertising by the PAN that described the left-wing candidate as "a danger for Mexico" suggested that the right had come to see him as an existential threat. Its dramatic warnings against left-wing populism lent credibility to López Obrador's indictment that the rich and powerful found his "alternative project" to be "unacceptable" and would "do everything" to "destroy" him. Both sides embraced the self-reinforcing logic of polarization, of perceptions of threat feeding perceptions of threat.[15]

Since vote-rigging is an illicit activity whose perpetrators strive to hide it, assessments of electoral fraud are often based on belief rather than firm knowledge. In the absence of factual certainties, public opinion tends to divide into communities of believers. Given the tentative nature of evidence and inference, citizens will tend to embrace the story that they hear from the source which to them seems most credible. Thus, taking everything together—corrosive fears of exclusion, the evidence of irregularities, and the confusing din of discordant voices commenting on these irregularities—it is easy to see why PRD sympathizers (about a third of the electorate) would lend credence to their candidate's rhetoric of fraud. It is no harder to understand why their adversaries, in particular the PAN supporters who found their candidate on the winning side of the contest, were happy to give the election their seal of approval.

As numerous polls taken in the months since the election have shown, about two-thirds of Mexicans remain convinced that the election was clean, express trust in the IFE and the TEPJF at aggregate rates close to those recorded in previous years, and disapprove of López Obrador's disruptive strategies. Had an immediate rerun of the election been held, López Obrador would have lost by a wide margin.[16] Since the postelectoral dispute has polarized the citizenry more intensely than did the preceding campaign, public opinion has worked as the losing candidate's primary resource as well as his principal constraint. Making possible and lending weight to his massive protest mobilization, it also put decisive brakes on the escalation of conflict.

The preliminary balance sheet of Mexico's 2006 presidential election is fraught with ambiguities. The system of electoral governance and dispute settlement worked reasonably well. Yet at the same time, it created too much noise and too many needless invitations to distrust. The country underwent an intense postelectoral dispute, but its institutions held steady; for all the drama of conflict, democracy proved resilient. The failures observed were less those of institutions than of actors. The loser reacted deplorably, but in many ways neither election authorities, nor the victorious party, nor the media acted in a manner that was beyond reproach.

Now that the immediate postelectoral tension has subsided, what comes next? What may we expect from the Calderón presidency? What shall be the consequences of his close and contested victory? Certainly, the new president will face unrelenting opposition in the legislature as well as the constant threat of disruptive action in the streets. The final outcome of this ongoing power struggle is uncertain. The most benign scenario would see the president taking advantage of the stirrings of fear felt by the elite and middle classes in order to push through decisive reforms of the justice system, the fiscal system, and public education, while imposing new standards of austerity and integrity in the civil service.

A much more troublesome scenario would see Mexico going through the extraconstitutional removal of its chief executive through street pressure, much as we have seen happen in the numerous "interrupted presidencies" of contemporary Latin America.[17] Considering the volatility of public opinion, the relative weakness of the Mexican state, the ambivalence of many citizens toward democracy and the rule of law, the lack of public-spiritedness among professional politicians, the high moral stakes of the conflict, and the organizational strength of the new president's opponents, a premature termination of the Calderón presidency appears to be a real possibility (perhaps only to be avoided if taken seriously). This implies that Mexico has lost one of its most precious historical achievements: the clocklike certainty of its electoral calendar. In 2000, after Fox and the PAN ended the PRI's seven-decade lock on the presidency, everyone, including the loser, immediately started speculating about the 2006 election. Today, the horizon of politics has contracted to the immediate future.

Let us nevertheless indulge in the luxury of thinking ahead and ask what might be done to prevent a reenactment of the 2006 drama. Limiting myself to the electoral arena, I wish to suggest three areas of institutional reform. First, to halt the corrosive judicialization of election campaigns, liberalizing reforms should reaffirm the principle of free speech in the campaign period. If the current trend toward regulating and censoring the content of campaign messages persists, election campaigns will either turn into acrimonious second-order disputes over election campaigns; or they will develop into baroque exercises of self-praise by candidates cut off from their critical faculties. Second, the IFE needs to improve its system of ballot accounting. It must establish a system for verifying and reconciling ballot accounts at the level of polling stations in order to make sure that the counting and recording of ballots are done well. Third, although Mexico may not experience another close presidential election in a century, the parties in Congress should consider devising a recount law that establishes the precise conditions and procedures under which parties as well as civil society actors may demand a full recount. Still, "a hard-fought election whose results are accepted without demur by those who lost is a precious collective achievement."[18] No amount of institutional engineering can substitute for the requisite "public-spiritedness" and "collective sense of responsibility"[19] by all involved. Ultimately, it is actors, not institutions, who produce and conserve the public good of institutionalized elections.

NOTES

1. The Federal Electoral Institute (IFE) continually monitored the media presence of parties and candidates during the election campaign. For an overview, see Raúl Trejo Delarbre, "Datos duros: La actuación de los medios," *Nexos* 228 (September 2006): 2–23.

2. In fact, the quick count was perfectly accurate in its statistical predictions. The final vote shares of all candidates lay within the confidence intervals estimated by the quick-count team at 10:15 p.m. Mexico City time on election night. See IFE, "Informe del Comité del Conteo Rápido de la elección presidencial del 2 de julio de 2006" at *http://pac.ife.org. mx/download/08/pac_down_informe_Comite-Conteo Rapido.pdf.*

3. A comprehensive collection of López Obrador's speeches can be found at *www. lopezobrador.org.mx.*

4. Fabrice Lehoucq, "Electoral Fraud: Causes, Types, and Consequences," *Annual Review of Political Science* 6 (June 2003): 248.

5. For an overview of electoral reform in Mexico, see Andreas Schedler, "Mexico's Victory: The Democratic Revelation," *Journal of Democracy* 11 (October 2000): 5–19.

6. Most of the 1,314 "nonresolved incidents" (88.7 percent of all such incidents) that the IFE reported as having taken place on election day concerned voters who pretended to vote, or actually voted (by accident or agreement), either without appearing on the voter list or without having their voter ID in order. Unfortunately, on July 2, political parties were not able to cover all polling stations. The PAN was present in 79.9 percent and the PRD coalition in 79.4 percent of the 130,231 polling stations. The average figure conceals considerable regional variation, as the presence of parties varies with their electoral strength. In the PRD stronghold of Mexico City the PAN was able to cover only a bit more than a third of the polling stations; in the northern state of Nuevo León, the PRD coalition was present in only a third. Did anything dirty happen at places not watched by specific parties? Bivariate regression analysis suggests that the "effects" of variations in party presence on vote shares (at the state level) were similar for the PAN and the PRD coalition. Thus, even under the strong causal assumption that party observers acted as agents of fraud as well as deterrents of fraud, the net effect for the two leading candidates, it seems, was neutral. See Javier Aparicio, "Representantes de casilla y voto presidencial: un análisis preliminar" (Mexico City: CIDE, 2006). Available at *www.cide.edu/investigadores/aparicio/elecciones.*

7. ACE Encyclopedia, "Reconciling Ballot Accounts," at *www.aceproject.org/ace-en/ topics/vc/vce/vce01/vce01a.* For a comparative overview of ballot-accounting and vote-counting procedures, see ACE, "What procedures are used in the initial count?" at *www. aceproject.org/epic-en/vc/Epic_view/VC05.*

8. Javier Aparicio, "Errores artiméticos en actas: Análisis comparativo para 2000, 2003 y 2006" (Mexico City: CIDE, 2006). Figures are based on preliminary results as provided by the IFE at *www.ife.org.mx.*

9. See Javier Aparicio, "La evidencia de una elección confiable," *Nexos* 28 (October 2006): 49–53; and AC Nielsen, "Análisis sobre Errores Aritméticos" (Mexico City, 2006). Calculations by the PRD are available at *www.lopezobrador.org.mx/actas/analisis/php.*

10. For a comparative overview of recount provisions in contemporary democracies, see Louis Massicotte, André Blais, and Antoine Yoshinaka, *Establishing the Rules of the Game: Election Laws in Democracies* (Toronto: University of Toronto Press, 2004), 150–53.

11. See Aparicio, "La evidencia," 52.

12. See Marco A. Zavala, "Cuándo cuenta un voto," *Nexos* 28 (October 2006): 10–13. Electoral magistrates made no effort to present their rulings in a format accessible to analysis without a previous trip through the jungle of legal text. Their sentences are posted in chronological order at *www.trife.org.mx*.

13. Tribunal Electoral del Poder Judicial de la Federación, "Dictamen relativo al cómputo final de la elección de Presidente de los Estados Unidos Mexicanos, Declaración de validez de la elección y de presidente electo" (Mexico City: TEPJF), 5 September 2006, 158–203.

14. Among many others, see Gerard Alexander, *The Sources of Democratic Consolidation* (Ithaca: Cornell University Press, 2002); and Daron Acemoglu and James A. Robinson, *Economic Origins of Dictatorship and Democracy* (New York: Cambridge University Press, 2005).

15. As public-opinion data show with respect to legislative elections in established democracies, citizens "who feel [that] their vital interests are threatened by the elected government are likely to be highly sceptical about the virtues of the electoral process." André Blais, "How Do Losers Assess Electoral Democracy?" paper delivered at the annual meeting of the Midwest Political Science Association, Chicago, 3–6 April 2003, 1.

16. See, for instance, the data presented in 2006 in the newspaper *Reforma* (Mexico City), esp. July 15, 25, and 30; August 9 and 27; and September 6.

17. Arturo Valenzuela, "Latin American Presidencies Interrupted," see p. 3–17 in this volume.

18. Massicotte, Blais, and Yoshinaka, *Establishing the Rules,* 150.

19. Laurence Whitehead, "Close Fought Elections and the Institutionalization of Democracy," *Taiwan Journal of Democracy* 2 (July 2006): 11 and 6.

LOOKING TO MEXICO'S FUTURE

Jorge G. Castañeda and Marco A. Morales

Jorge G. Castañeda *served as Mexico's foreign minister between 2000 and 2003 and is currently Global Distinguished Professor of Politics and Latin American Studies at New York University.* **Marco A. Morales** *is a doctoral candidate in political science at New York University. This essay originally appeared in the January 2007 issue of the* Journal of Democracy.

Mexico's amazingly close 2006 presidential election has already become the object of much written analysis and even more speculation. Many have discussed what the 2006 election was "really" about and which policies are likely to be implemented over the course of President Felipe Calderón's upcoming administration. Yet others have argued that no matter what Calderón's National Action Party (PAN) administration does, it will remain illegitimate, spawned from fraud. A different and perhaps more useful approach is to address the topics that are most relevant to the future of Mexican democracy in the long run.

Electoral rules and political institutions are intertwined, and cannot be thought of as independent from one another. Institutions generate incentives that interact with electoral rules—as when a ban on reelection makes members of Congress more responsive to their respective parties than to voters. And electoral rules, in turn, generate incentives that affect the ways in which power is exercised—representation in the Senate takes a different meaning when seats are assigned by a 2:1 ratio between the first and second most successful parties, than when only the winning party receives a seat for every state. Thus causality runs in both directions, and must be accounted for when analyzing events that have taken place under a particular institutional and electoral arrangement.

For Mexico, the interaction of rules and institutions means that the path to a more stable democracy will need to be like a road defined by two banks. One will be formed by improved electoral rules, while the other will be composed of far-reaching institutional reforms. Learning to approach the problem with both in mind will be crucial because it is precisely the link between institutions and elections that the electoral reforms of the last twenty years have ignored.

Institutions and elections together constitute the cornerstone of democracy, mainly because they define what can be expected of a political system. That is, by determining the rules governing competition for office, by establishing the mechanisms to determine the winner of an election, and by defining checks and balances between branches and levels of government, the interaction of institutions and electoral rules generates incentives for politicians to behave in a particular way. This straightforward conclusion appears not to be self-evident in Mexico; it was not self-evident in 1996, when the basic rules of the current electoral system were first adopted, and it does not seem to have gained much ground since.

The aftermath of the 2006 presidential election is simply the natural consequence of an institutional reform that has not been deeply thought about—much less fully enacted—since 1996. The 2006 races for both the presidency and Congress took place under 1996 rules and pre-1996 institutions. Not only have Mexican politics changed in the last ten years, but the sole objective sought at that time—minimizing the probability of large-scale fraud—is no longer the most relevant item on the list of what Mexico needs in order to achieve a better-functioning democracy. Any discussion of democracy's future in the country must analyze not only how and why some aspects of the electoral process succeeded or failed in 2006, but also the nature and direction of the changes that are needed to reinforce the successes and correct the failures.

Given the rules set forth in the electoral code, election-day logistics worked nearly to perfection. That is, 99.9 percent of the more than 130,000 polling places were installed and votes were cast virtually without incident; 87 percent of the polling places had representatives from at least one political party; and votes were counted in the presence of interested citizens. Nothing less would be expected in any proper democratic election.

While the logistics left virtually no room for a massive orchestration of fraud, they unfortunately did leave quite a lot of space for human error. In the end, it is citizens and not trained officials who count the votes, and especially in a country where the average person has slightly more than seven years of schooling, mistakes are prone to happen.[1] Is there any way to reduce these errors? Yes, but not without a tradeoff. Votes could be cast and counted electronically, but at a much higher cost and not necessarily with higher reliability—consider the U.S. case—or thousands of election officials could be deployed on election day to count the ballots, again at a much higher cost, and with somewhat less apparent independence than under the current, citizens-based system.

But we need to keep in mind that the suspicion of fraud arose in 2006 *because of* human error. An autonomous elections-administering entity such as the Federal Electoral Institute (IFE) and the practice of vote-counting by citizens were justifiable and perhaps even indispensable back when elections held under the decades-old rule of the Institutional Revolutionary Party (PRI) were synonymous with fraud. But today, when democracy is established and the probability of widespread fraud is negligible, it might make more sense to transfer the task of professionally organizing and supervising elections to the equivalent of a European or Latin American ministry of the interior, as is the case in Germany, Spain, or Chile. Some might say that if the government is allowed to intervene directly in the electoral process, fraud could be easily orchestrated and the possibility of sustaining a "real" democracy would soon die because of the irresistible temptation of government-sponsored tampering. But if that is the case, then our problems—constituting a still-unfinished representative democracy—run much deeper. Addressing how the votes are counted or who organizes the electoral process would not solve the core issue. Mexicans need to ask which change and set of accompanying costs seem most preferable (all things considered) to the current status quo, and reform accordingly.

What Went Wrong?

While losing candidate Andrés Manuel López Obrador's claims of massive fraud are far from supported by the preponderance of evidence, his underlying argument appears valid: A case can be built for a lack of fairness in the race.[2] But defining and measuring "fairness" or "unfairness" with precision are daunting tasks. It would be hard to argue, for instance, that the televised "issue-advocacy" advertisements which business organizations paid for in the campaign's final stages had absolutely no impact on the election's outcome, but no serious scholar would venture to estimate the magnitude or direction of these effects.

Likewise, it would be hard to argue that federal social policy did not produce a positive evaluation of the incumbent party that might have created a bias in favor of ruling-party candidate Calderón. But any citizen in a democracy where parties regularly rotate in office knows that incumbents often hold advantages derived from performance while in office, although they may also incur serious disadvantages. Besides, López Obrador benefited from having been the mayor of vote-rich Mexico City, where he beat Calderón two to one. During his first five years as mayor, López Obrador's programs included a direct monthly subsidy worth nearly US$60 to every senior citizen living in poverty. It is no secret that most of the money wound up in zones where the mayor's Party of the Democratic Revolution (PRD) was strong. In sum, it is easier to reject the hypothesis of an equitable race than it is to prove how much inequity there was and what it finally meant. Yet both IFE and the Electoral Tribunal of the Federal Judiciary (TEPJF) issued rulings to limit the constitutionally guaranteed right to free speech during this electoral process.

The "original sin" (as the PRD colorfully put it) that foreshadowed the electoral result was the 2003 controversy over the makeup of the IFE's General Council (GC). The PAN and PRI caucuses in Congress chose the GC's membership by themselves after the PRD walked out of negotiations over the body's composition and refused to submit candidates.[3] The IFE, so the PRD's complaint goes, thenceforth began to act as an instrument of these two parties. The argument is correct in pointing out an agency problem: The PRD cannot expect the GC to be the agent of a party that refused to vote for any Council members. But the argument is wrong in assuming, as has been done since 1996, that individuals involved in administering elections have no partisan preferences or ties. They do, and it is highly unlikely that someone with the necessary qualifications and no partisan links could be nominated by any party, let alone be selected.

The deeper problem is that the current institutional design provides no incentives for the three main parties to reach a consensual decision regarding the composition of the GC. In a tripartisan setting such as exists in Mexico today, if two parties can achieve a minimum winning coalition by themselves, there is no reason for them *not* to act in tandem when the third party makes unreasonable demands. Moreover, if the members of the GC are chosen on partisan grounds, it follows that their actions will have a partisan flavor and will be seen as having been performed to benefit the members' principals.

Yet whatever the GC's internal political struggles and questionable attempts at modifying electoral policy, the system remained strong enough to produce an election that was at least logistically sound. Unfortunately, the performance of the rest of the institutional structure fails to merit such a positive assessment.

When recommending changes in the current system, two things should be kept in mind. First, changes in the electoral rules must be consistent with what institutional reform aims to achieve. That is, the effects of new electoral rules must be aligned with those of institutional reforms in order for the desired result to come about. Second, there is no such thing as a perfect institutional reform. Each alternative will not only generate unforeseen as well as intended results, but also costs as well as benefits. Each and every alternative is inherently imperfect, so we must be content with choosing the one that is closest to the desired outcome.

Therefore, the most important matter is defining precisely what we want the outcome of the institutional system to be. Once we have determined that, we can choose institutional reforms accordingly. In our view, the outcome that would do the most to improve the future of Mexican democracy would be a system that fosters long-term political stability. The new equilibrium that this system would embody would flow from the removal of barriers against the entry of new political participants, from steps to make competition more equitable, and from measures to minimize any more-than-proportional powers in the hands of particular political actors. In order to achieve such an equilibrium, three types of reforms will be necessary. The first type will be electoral, the second will mix electoral change with institutional modifications, and the third will focus purely on remodeling institutions. While space constraints rule out detailed discussions of mechanics, it is at least possible to sketch the rationale behind each category.

Electoral reforms. The rules under which elections are conducted will have implications for institutional design. The beginning of wisdom is to recognize that there is no need to address problems which have already been solved. Specifically, there is no need to rewrite the rules in order to impede massive electoral fraud (now a virtual impossibility) or to enhance trust and credibility in electoral institutions (a goal already achieved, despite their performance in 2006).[4]

Three changes to electoral-system rules would be particularly helpful. First, the nature and origin of funding for political parties need attention. Currently, political parties get most of their money (a grand total in 2006 of about US$400 million) from the federal government, with limited amounts coming from private sources. Public financing grows substantially from election to election, and is doled out in a lopsided way that rewards any party which increases its vote share from the previous balloting and imposes an unjustified handicap on any party whose vote-getting performance slips. Most importantly, a large portion of these funds are spent directly on television and radio campaign advertisements—typically bought at prices that the rising flood of public funds tends to drive upward. It would make sense to eliminate airtime purchases and to substitute state-mandated free broadcast time for a large portion of public funds, as is done in Brazil, Chile, and most European countries except Finland. It would also be a good idea to modify the distributional formula to avoid the inequitable "rich get richer, poor get poorer" effect of the current system.

A second needed change would adjust the functions of the electoral authorities. The IFE, and to a lesser extent the TEPJF, were created as a response to state-orchestrated electoral fraud and the need to foster confidence in election results. Since that aim has largely been achieved, it might make more sense to transfer responsibility for election logistics to some other government agency and allow the IFE to have the responsibility (now borne by the TEPJF) of officially declaring winners. Likewise, in order to avoid the current legal confusion between purely electoral matters and other constitutional matters, the increasingly independent Supreme Court rather than the TEPJF should be the sole entity with power to decide legal controversies, including any involving the Electoral Code.

The third and fourth changes in electoral rules should be lowering the bar to entry for new parties and allowing independent candidates to run. There is no reason why the traditional parties need to be the exclusive channels to public office. Under the current rules, it is virtually impossible to form a new party without resort to corrupt clientelistic practices, and independents are barred from running for office. This makes it too easy for the established parties to keep elected officials more responsive to their party than to their constituents. If single-issue political views could more easily find expression in the form of new parties, moreover, a healthier and more representative party system would be the result. Similarly, eliminating the prohibition against independent candidacies might just be the boost that elected officials need to grow more attentive to voters. There are legitimate concerns about how to regulate the flow of public campaign funds to independent candidates, but these concerns can be met in ways that need not obviate the gains to be realized from independent candidacies.

Electoral-cum-institutional reforms. Since electoral reforms must act in coordination with institutional arrangements, the resulting incentives should be aligned to promote the desired outcomes. Certain reforms would affect both the electoral and the institutional arenas. The first would be the introduction of a runoff for the presidency. Given the tripartisan system that Mexico has had since 1988, and the high degree of electoral volatility evident in the last two presidential contests, it is highly unlikely that anyone will soon win the presidency with more than 50 percent of the vote. Going to a runoff when no candidate exceeds a certain threshold seems like a plausible route to chief executives with surer mandates and hence a better chance of delivering on their campaign promises.

A runoff is likely to produce party atomization in Congress, especially when executive and legislative elections are concurrent, since small parties have an incentive to run in both in the first round in hopes of amassing votes that they can trade for their respective endorsements in the second round of the presidential election. A plausible method of decoupling these effects could come in the form of an instant-runoff (single transferable vote) system in which voters rank all the candidates from most to least preferred. By having this information available in the event that no candidate surpasses the prescribed threshold, electoral officials can instantly reassign votes according to the ranking of preferences that each voter has indicated in order to identify the winner without the added cost of an additional election. Such an arrangement also gives voters a strong incentive to cast sincere rather than strategic votes.

A second electoral-cum-institutional reform would be to eliminate the single-term limit that is currently attached to the presidency and seats in both houses of Congress. As the academic literature suggests, the prospect of standing for reelection at the end of one's term fosters accountability, professionalism, institutional memory, and policy continuity, to name just a few desirable consequences. Given these positive features and their notorious absence in the Mexican context, there seems to be no reason why elected officials in Congress and the executive branch should not have the option of seeking consecutive terms. Reelection could also, according to some, strengthen the parties' grip on politicians, but this effect will be moderated if other reforms such as open primaries, easier entry for independents, and funding changes are enacted.

Another reform with both electoral and institutional effects would be to readjust the use of proportional representation (PR) in Congress. Currently, 200 of the 500 seats in the Chamber of Deputies and 32 of the Senate's 128 seats are assigned according to a PR formula (a Hare quota with the largest remainder applied to 5 national lists of 40 seats for the Chamber of Deputies and a single national list of 32 seats for the Senate) which effectively ensures that most of these seats go to the three major parties. In other words, since usually none of the 300 plurality districts are won by minority parties, the three largest parties obtain both PR and majority seats ranging in the hundreds, minority parties rarely receive more than a dozen seats each, and their relative weight in the legislature is effectively diluted. A viable option to allow for more alternative voices to be heard would be to reduce the number of PR seats in the Chamber and assign them *only* to those parties that exceed a low percentage of the total nationwide vote, but fail to win any plurality seats. As for the Senate, since its basic principle is to represent all states equally, having PR seats in that body is plainly redundant.

Institutional reforms. Even when rules reorient the *individual* behavior of political actors, it is institutions that coordinate them to act *collectively* toward a given end. In Mexico, where petty political interests seem to be a dominant force, a different institutional setting might be what is needed to restrain individual interests in favor of long-lasting political stability.

No Mexican president is likely soon to enjoy an adequate legislative plurality, which makes coping with gridlock a major problem. What is needed is a system that generates sufficient majorities to govern while also reflecting the relative weights of the various parties in Congress. A variant of the semipresidential model seems like a natural candidate for the task: Such a system would feature a president chosen by universal suffrage, mainly equipped with veto power backed by sufficient support in Congress to make the threat credible. Coupled with this head of state would be a figure resembling a prime minister, appointed by the president but subject to congressional approval, and responsible for making everyday executive decisions. The rationale for this reform lies in the observation that when a political party lacks a sufficient plurality to enact an agenda by itself and all other political parties have more to gain by maintaining the status quo, a mechanism for overcoming gridlock must be available. With a popularly elected president and a legislatively approved prime minister, parties will both be able to enjoy some of the responsibility of governing and be forced to internalize the costs of inaction.

Here we should pause to point out a crucial lesson that must be learned. It is that there is no single, technically correct institutional reform. Institutions are means to ends. Choosing a particular arrangement, therefore, is not a technical decision, but a political one. We advocate the reforms sketched above because we think that they will enhance the political stability which Mexico badly needs.

Making Choices

Returning to the current situation, one cannot avoid wondering what happened to López Obrador and the PRD. His own close advisor, Porfirio Muñoz Ledo, was a major figure in the writing of the 1996 rules that governed the 2006 election, rules that the PRD supported. Why, then, did the PRD complain about the rules only after the 2006 race rather than in 2000 or 2003? Why cry for a new set of rules *precisely* when they produce an unfavorable result? Furthermore, why not propose possible reforms to fix the rules that do not work, instead of calling for their destruction?

The one thing that democracy cannot tolerate is a player who denounces the faults of the game *only* when the rules are not beneficial to him. If fairness and an equitable competition were his concerns, López Obrador should have pushed the cause of reform in Congress, the proper channel to correct these biases, between 1996 and 1999 when he was the PRD's president.

López Obrador may be correct in complaining about flaws in Mexico's political institutions. This essay certainly points to some of them. Although the cause might be fair, the means—indefinitely extended street demonstrations, a refusal to recognize Calderón as president, and disregard for the rulings of electoral authorities, all of which later resulted in López Obrador becoming the "alternative" president—that López Obrador has chosen to achieve his desired result certainly are not. And one cannot dissociate the man from the means, especially when less disruptive alternatives are available. Making a point, even a fair one, cannot constitute a legitimate justification for disrupting the lawful workings of a democratic system of government.

The PRD candidate's actions are also likely to affect his party. When one wing of the party takes over Mexico City's government while López Obrador carries on with his "alternative" presidency and government, it is likely that the party will split into radical and reformist factions which will struggle for control. The radicals seem to be the best positioned to dominate, at least early on, by virtue both of their higher visibility and the powerful posts that they hold within the party. If reformists begin to find themselves losing every intraparty contest, what will be their reason for staying rather than leaving to start their own party? The surprising thing, even at this early date, is that the PRD has been able to hold together despite the polarizing pressures that López Obrador is creating.

By now, our main conclusion should be clear: The most important and far-reaching imperative facing Mexico's democracy is the need to win congressional approval for an agenda of electoral and institutional reform. These reforms are essential for the country to be able to address what public opinion regards as the most pressing problems (unemployment, insecurity, and the like). This is so even if public opinion does not consider the enactment of electoral and institutional reform to be an urgent priority. When almost half the populace works in the informal sector of the economy and needs steadier jobs with higher pay, it may be hard to convince them to support an institutional and electoral reform program that will in the long run—but only in the long run—produce precisely the results that are so badly needed. It is a politically tough case to explain that job creation would be much easier if a president had a stronger mandate and a larger majority in Congress as a result of a well-designed runoff provision, or if members of Congress felt more keenly interested in serving their constituents thanks to a well-conceived reelection reform.

President Calderón has a choice to make. He can work to make the case for long-term reform's urgent importance to Mexico's future, even though people's most immediate concerns seemingly lie elsewhere. Or, like former president Fox, Calderón can postpone reform in order to focus on "what the people really want" and, like Fox, get nowhere. Recent polls have consistently shown that postelection Mexico, like Gaul, is divided into three parts: One third backs the new president, one third backs López Obrador, and the final third cares little about politics. This means that pressing the cause of reform will involve either trying to carry out a policy with two-thirds of the country in varying degrees of active or passive opposition, or building majority support by convincing the unengaged and peeling off as many supporters as possible from the López Obrador camp. This seems much harder than generating ad hoc coalitions to support each step of the reform process. But negotiating well will inevitably require a clear strategy to achieve a given goal, the use of creative tactics, and the willingness to play hardball to get a result as close as possible to the ideal reform.

What this ultimately means is that the future of the Mexican democracy rests not only on electoral rules and institutions that generate the "right" incentives, but on the ability to implement them as a means of addressing what public opinion considers the "most pressing problems" facing the country, thus making it possible to produce long-lasting solutions.

Any reader with some background in Mexican history will conclude—correctly—that the basic terms of the country's dilemma have not changed much in the last century: Mexico should redesign its political system to rely more on institutions and less on personalities. The ultimate aim should be to equip the Mexican polity with a baseline level of institutional performance that does not depend on having a particularly skilled leader at the helm. Given a "good draw" of political actors, democracy should perform well above this level. And even with a "bad draw," it should never perform below such a floor.

Just as no service to democracy will come from ignoring the need for reform, no service will flow from a disjointed reform. But it is also important to make a distinction: The issue at stake is not whether this or that administration meets this or that set of expectations, but whether Mexicans can devise and agree on means rationally calibrated to achieve crucial long-term ends. Passing the test that this issue poses will require decisions that cannot be postponed much longer.

NOTES

1. It should not be surprising, then, that some ballots cast for president were counted in the congressional elections and vice versa, or that some valid votes were counted as invalid by mere human error.

2. Alejandro Poiré, a former senior official of the IFE, has published a lucid account of the most important issues pertaining to electoral fairness in Mexico. See Alejandro Poiré, "Reflexiones sobre la equidad de la elección presidencial de 2006," *Este País: Tendencias y Opiniones,* July 2006, 16–23.

3. Since the PRD approved the rules under which the GC members were selected, the party's real objection cannot be to the selection process but rather must be to the candidates themselves. It is also worth noting that PRD spokespeople have called TEPJF justices "corrupt" for certifying Calderón's election, even when those justices owed their seats on that tribunal to PRD support.

4. For instance, an 8–11 September 2006 poll taken by the survey firm Parametría found 62 percent of Mexicans saying that they trusted the TEPJF, while 66 percent said that they trusted the IFE. These are slightly higher figures than those found in polls taken after the 2000 election. For Parametría's full analysis and data on historical trends, see "El Tribunal Electoral pasó la prueba y aumentó la confianza en el IFE," *Excelsior* (Mexico City), 18 September 2006.

18

FROM TURMOIL TO STABILITY IN CENTRAL AMERICA

Consuelo Cruz

Consuelo Cruz *is associate professor of political science at Tufts University. She is the author of* Political Culture and Institutional Development in Costa Rica and Nicaragua: World-Making in the Tropics *(2005). Her essay "The New Military Autonomy in Latin America" (coauthored with Rut Diamint) appeared in the October 1998 issue of the* Journal of Democracy.

By most standards of democratic consolidation, Central America has been making good progress since the 1980s. Armed political groups have joined the formal political system, politicians compete vigorously for votes, political parties keep tabs on one another, and civil society groups try to keep tabs on all things public. If political development was linear, the isthmian countries might be seen as having embarked on the path first forged by Costa Rica, the oldest and arguably the strongest democracy in Latin America.

Developmental linearity, of course, is no longer a plausible illusion, but it was once an enthralling notion for Latin America's regime builders. In the early years of independence, Central American political elites sought to conform to the European and U.S. paradigms—most notably by establishing wholesale democratic institutions and enshrining the principle of popular sovereignty. Costa Ricans, however, diverged from their neighbors even then. They were self-conscious pragmatists who eschewed doctrinal concerns and focused instead on socioeconomic challenges and institutional innovation.

Yet, it was in Costa Rica that democracy was eventually firmly institutionalized, even sacralized, while the other countries in the region perennially failed at the most fundamental of regime tasks: arbitrating conflicting demands and grievances so as to provide a generally acceptable and sustainable degree of order *and* justice. In recent decades, the arbitration failures of "third-wave" democracies and attendant pressures have revitalized an old repertoire of practices once associated with the weak or Potemkin democracies of yore. Used by governments and other powerholders to cope with or exploit intractable political contestation, these practices range from *autogolpes* (self-coups) and national dialogues to pacts and plebiscites. Costa Rica—even after its keenly contested 2007 referendum on the Central American Free Trade Agreement (CAFTA)—remains the brilliant exception.

After independence from Spain in 1821, and the collapse of Mexico's ephemeral empire in 1823, the new nations of Central America proved early adopters of political democracy. Just as quickly, however, their debates over the proper organization of democracy and partisan struggles over control of its institutions bloodied the land and narrowed the political horizon. By the mid-nineteenth century, the most progressive liberals and the most sober conservatives, in agreement since before independence about the desirability of free trade, converged as well on the "lesson" that notions such as individual rights are impractical and dangerous where the people are not yet fit to choose the right leaders.

Yet few dared challenge the principle of popular sovereignty. Conservatives and liberals alike proclaimed instead their determination to forge discerning citizens. To this end, democracy might be postponed, suspended, restricted, and perverted, but the legitimating power of its foundational principle—the people as sovereign—could never be openly repudiated. Partly for this reason, authoritarian regimes ritualized sham elections; and mostly for this reason, both traditionalists and revolutionaries sought to justify their visions of order and justice by claiming a special relationship with the people. Into the 1960s, traditionalists offered a political and social structure held together by paternalistic authority—rule by the sage, the mystic, the strongman—over "naïve" and "immature" citizenries. By then, too, leftist revolutionaries offered rule by a morally superior leader or cadre, endowed with vast discretionary powers, that is charged with the task of uplifting the masses.

Viewed in this regional context, Costa Rica was different from the start. In the first decades of the nineteenth century, its elites remained relatively disengaged from democracy in general and popular sovereignty in particular. Analytical scrutiny of the period reveals 1) a shared fear of "contamination" by "anarchic" neighbors; 2) early adoption of pragmatic experimentalism; and 3) the establishment of an unabashedly hybrid regime that would come to be known as the First Republic (1848–1948). Under this regime, successive governments assigned the highest priority to socioeconomic development and political stability, which they attained through a blend of intra-elite negotiation, electoral fraud, and measured repression.

The First Republic was brought down by revolutionaries who were loath to bury it and quick to praise it. Their principal leader, José Figueres, even averred that the builders of the *ancien régime* had laid the foundations for the Second Republic, which he and his followers were about to found. The new founders, moreover, pledged to defend their nation's "industrious and law-abiding character" from the dangers of "ideological extremisms," and to do so without resorting to organized violence. Finally, in a region where leaders periodically chased the chimera of "scientific" rule, the founders explained that "modern" and "exact" statecraft calls for policymakers to focus not on "theoretical" problems but on a country's "actual" challenges, and to devise "practical" solutions congruent with local reality.[1]

The governments of the Second Republic meshed a variety of ideas and techniques—some taken from abroad, some from their own national experience—to create a singular story of developmental success. One administration after another, albeit with varying degrees of enthusiasm, contributed to a political economy which, until the 1970s, was based on market-shaped microeconomics and state-led macroeconomics—the relationship between the two mediated by institutionalized consensus-building practices, stabilized by a substantial welfare system, and legitimated by increasingly transparent electoral processes. The upshot was a sort of social democracy in the very heart of Latin America, a region best known around the world for its banana republics and tinpot dictators.

Haunted by civil conflict and authoritarian repression, riddled with corruption, perennially open to intervention by external powers, and fractured along local, ethnic, racial, and socioeconomic lines, the other Central American nations clung to the outward formalities of republican government. The president, whether in khaki uniform or a white linen suit, remained the guardian of the people's interests. In the 1960s, and increasingly in the 1970s, Marxist and Maoist guerrilla armies also began to claim the role of popular champion. In Nicaragua, the Sandinista National Liberation Front (FSLN) came to power in 1979. Through most of the 1980s, the FSLN regime simultaneously sought to revolutionize the national political economy and fought the U.S.-backed Contra army. During that decade, Guatemala and El Salvador also witnessed civil wars between the left and the right, while neighboring Honduras suffered the reverberations of these conflicts, and Panama endured the destabilizing consequences of caudillismo (strongman rule) run amok.

Yet during this decade, the global political environment grew less hospitable to this sort of politics. Democratization in South America seemed to extend Iberia's earlier advances, and democratization in Eastern Europe seemed to herald a new epochal spirit. By the early 1990s, this trend appeared confirmed, as the Soviet Union collapsed and the United States' prestige soared. The major contending political forces in Guatemala, El Salvador, and Nicaragua, exhausted by the bloodletting and increasingly vulnerable to pressures for negotiation from abroad, converged on political democracy as a means of internal pacification.

They proposed not merely to secure peace or to build democracy, but to do both. The one seemed hardly imaginable without the other.

Guatemala: Democracy for Peace

A democratic peace, though hubristic in retrospect, seemed perfectly logical at the time. Since the left and the right, each in its own way, consistently relied on the legitimating power of popular sovereignty, the concept retained its traditional appeal. And while popular sovereignty need not entail democratic institutions, decades of sham elections had generated pent-up demand for the genuine article. This was the case even in Guatemala, where by the 1980s barbarism had become a normal part of politics.

Guatemala by then had accumulated a grim record of severe polarization between left and right, military coups (including the U.S.-sponsored overthrow of a reformist government in 1954), guerrilla warfare, and state-sponsored violence. The armed forces even had adopted a counterinsurgency strategy that relied on gross violations of human rights and that militarized a significant portion of the rural population (through the Civil Self-Defense Patrols, or PACs). In this context, the 1983 dissolution of Congress by President Efrain Ríos Montt appeared to be merely an extension of local normalcy. So too did the sudden overthrow in August 1983 of Ríos Montt by General Oscar Humberto Mejía Victores, who proceeded to call elections for a National Constitutional Assembly.

The resultant constitution, in contrast, signaled a possible turning point, as it opened the way for general elections at a moment when the country's main centrist party was up to the challenge. In 1985, the Christian Democrats (DCG) prevailed at the polls, after offering voters a reasonably credible alternative to right-wing domination and left-wing violent opposition. The electoral outcome was momentous. While Nicaragua and El Salvador remained mired in their own gruesome conflicts, a new Guatemalan government and a critical mass of citizens now seemed to share a common vision in which duly elected powerholders committed themselves to the lawful resolution of the keenest of political disputes. The political implications were daunting as well: The DCG administration of President Vinicio Cerezo (1986–90) would have to negotiate with the various guerrilla groups that in 1982 had formed the Guatemalan National Revolutionary Union (URNG).

Negotiation was no military imperative. The URNG was never able to mount a significant offensive. If anything, it met with defeat more often than victory, and failed to develop a broad support base. Negotiation was a matter of political exigency. Right-wing paramilitary organizations and death squads continued to wage a counterinsurgency campaign based on the repression of opposition forces and the murder of thousands of (mostly Mayan) peasants suspected of subversion. If the

DCG and the Cerezo administration were serious about integrating *both* extremes into the formal political system, they had no choice but to seek a negotiated settlement with the URNG.

At a minimum, the DCG administration understood that if the electoral process had shown anything at all, it was voters' preference for a sustainable peace, a goal which the administration believed could be attained only through the formal integration of the two extremes. But the very same democratic system into which they aimed to integrate those extremes quickly found itself beset by a growing web of distortions. Political parties and governmental bodies came to be generally regarded as corrupt or ineffective; the armed forces' subordination to civilian authority remained uneven at best; and extremist groups continued to exercise de facto rights to commit political violence. In a stunning instance of perverse arbitration, high-ranking military officers suppressed two coup attempts against Cerezo, but did so as part of a bargain whereby the executive funneled resources to the armed forces in exchange for protection.

In retrospect, a pattern emerges. As truncated, contradictory, or unevenly enforced arbitration generates multiple points of dissatisfaction, new political forces emerge, seemingly defunct players rise again, and unlikely—even unholy—alliances develop. In the late 1980s, Ríos Montt formed the Guatemalan Republican Front (FRG) and formally established it as a political party in 1990 to advance his presidential ambitions. But it was the brand-new Solidarity Action Movement (MAS) that carried the 1991 elections. The MAS campaign's winning message may be summed up as follows: We have never had the occasion to sully our hands, and since our candidate is a Protestant, his superior morals will keep them clean.

The MAS administration of Jorge Serrano Elías, in a continuation of the pattern just outlined, resumed peace negotiations with the URNG, while political parties, politicians, the Congress, and the Supreme Court of Justice engaged in corruption, abused their prerogatives, and challenged the executive. In addition, the rules of electoral competition—the defining feature of political democracy—became themselves the object of dispute. For example, a constitutional ban against politicians with a record of coup attempts had blocked Ríos Montt's presidential candidacy, but after the FRG won ten congressional seats, it began the battle to overturn the "unjust" ban on Ríos Montt.

In "normal" times, these would have been classic conditions for an *autogolpe* (self-coup). Typically, an *autogolpe* is justified as an executive decision to deal decisively, for the good of the people, with flawed democratic arbitration. A duly elected president closes down institutions—such as congress and the courts—that the president claims are corrupt or partial. In May 1993, President Serrano made precisely this move, closing down the discredited Congress and the Supreme Court. But Serrano failed to understand that the times were anything but normal. The Soviet Union had recently collapsed, and Eastern Europe and Latin America were making the dual transition to free politics and markets. To the extent that one could speak of an international political-cultural stage, its center still belonged to democracy triumphant. Serrano, initially backed by the armed forces, was left alone to face near-universal condemnation at home and abroad.

After Serrano's resignation, Congress appointed as transitional president Ramiro de León Carpio (1993–96), the well-respected former human rights commissioner. He continued peace negotiations despite a wave of political violence that recalcitrant members of the armed forces had launched in an effort to derail the process. His government's most visible accomplishment was the 1994 Global Accord on Human Rights, which called among other things for the dismantling of the Voluntary Committees for Civil Self-Defense (CVDCs), previously known as the PACs.

Other developments were less visible but equally important. The advance of peace negotiations increased the appeal of political competition to both the right and the left. The FRG set out to enhance its electoral strength, managing to capture 32 seats in the congressional elections of 1994. Similarly, the left prepared to participate in an electoral contest for the first time since 1954 through a coalition called the New Guatemala Democratic Front (FDNG). Peace negotiations and the more inclusive boundaries of political competition also raised the stakes of the electoral game to such a degree that right-wing paramilitary groups threatened violent repression of emerging political forces.

In this context, a centrist offer proved unbeatable yet again. Alvaro Arzú of the center-right Party of National Advance (PAN) defeated Alfonso Portillo (FRG) and garnered 43 of 80 congressional seats. This was the first time that a single party had gained control of the executive and the legislature simultaneously. Thus the Arzú administration (1996–99) was able to complete and formalize the long-sought negotiated settlement with the URNG in December 1996, agreeing to constitutional reforms, the dismantlement of the CVDCs, and UN-supervised demobilization of the army and the URNG. In 1998, the URNG registered as a political party.

An incipient democracy thus settled a long-standing conflict between left and right in a country with an even longer history of socioeconomic exploitation and political repression. But in the process, nearly all else was compromised. In 1999, the constitutional reforms proposed in the peace agreement were rejected in a referendum in which the abstention rate exceeded 81 percent of eligible voters (too apathetic or too fearful to show up). That same year, the FRG prevailed unequivocally in the presidential and congressional elections. Once again, the party's presidential candidate was Alfonso Portillo.

Portillo's political career had taken him on an extensive tour of the ideological and partisan spectrum. Portillo was a former left-wing, pro-indigenous activist. He was also a former member of the Social Democratic Party (PSD), and a former member of the DCG. In 1995, following an unresolved dispute within the DCG, Portillo left the party and became an independent member of Congress, where he joined the congressional leader at the time, Ríos Montt.

Portillo's tour was significant but not unique. De León Carpio, who as a human rights commissioner had denounced Ríos Montt's violations, ultimately joined him too, and served as an FRG congressional representative. A dictatorial, paternalistic caudillo, Ríos Montt developed a base of supporters in the interior of the country, loyalists who perceived him as a fair, committed leader. In a competitive system, this base made the caudillo an invaluable patron to political aspirants, especially given the alternatives. In 1999, both left and center parties were weakened by internal divisions. The PAN's top leaders recriminated against one another for undemocratic and unfair conduct, as did the member parties of the URNG's left-wing coalition. Not surprisingly, the FRG prevailed decisively over the PAN in the presidential and congressional elections, while the URNG came in a distant third.

The Portillo administration (2000–2004) was the first since the Cerezo government (1986–90) to be unencumbered by the pressing challenge of peace negotiations. It was able to identify its own urgent objectives. One was correcting the "injustice" of the peace agreements, which provided for reparations to the victims of the civil war and their families but made no such provisions for former PAC recruits. The other was correcting the "unfairness" of the Constitutional Court, which had blocked the constitutional amendment that would have allowed Ríos Montt's presidential candidacy in 2003.

Portillo pressed for legislation mandating payment of US$3,000 to each former PAC cadre. The proposed law provoked immediate opposition across the political field. Not only did the PACs stand accused of gross human rights violations, opponents pointed out, but the country's finances were in crisis. Reparations for the PACs, opponents further claimed, were neither just nor fiscally responsible. Amid legal battles and organized citizen protests, the FRG reactivated and mobilized the PACs. On the day known as Black Thursday (24 July 2003), thousands descended on the capital city where, aided and abetted by the administration, they went on a two-day rampage.

The violence served its purpose, as the Supreme Court ultimately revoked the ruling by the Constitutional Court against Ríos Montt's candidacy. At last, the caudillo was able to run. He finished third. The FRG, moreover, lost its congressional majority. But the mobilization of violent groups in order to shape decisions by a democratic regime had proved effective, and two high courts, each for different reasons but in related ways, had been openly politicized.

One clear consequence of the erosion of commonly accepted sources of authoritative decision making is that different institutional and political domains become vulnerable to internal fragmentation. This fragmentation, in turn, renders the prospect of stable rule even more remote. The PAN, for example, splintered as party notables failed to settle their own disputes, and the most promising leaders left to join new parties or to form their own. Arzú went over to the Unity Party (PU), and Oscar Berger created the Grand National Alliance (GANA) coalition.

The party system remained prone to fragmentation. A total of eleven parties competed for the presidency in the 2003 elections. The newly formed GANA went against the newly formed National Hope Unity party (UNE), led by the left-wing Alvaro Colom. Ironically, Ríos Montt's FRG—formed only in 1990—was the most established of the top three contenders. It was Berger (GANA), with 34.3 percent of the vote, who prevailed in the first round over Colom and Ríos Montt, who garnered 25.4 percent and 19.3 percent, respectively. The URNG's electoral performance was so poor that its very survival as a party became doubtful.

The hallmark of the Berger administration (2003–2007) was its attempt to heed the public clamor for justice, specifically by trying to prosecute the worst offenders of the deeply corrupt Portillo government. It managed mostly to make enemies in the FRG. The latter's congressional representatives, in fact, forged unholy alliances against Berger with representatives from UNE and at times even the PAN. Political animosities reached the point where Berger had to undertake a "national reconciliation" process.

Such a political system can hardly be expected to address simultaneously the country's need for order and justice. Yet this remains the dual challenge. Death squads continue to operate from within the state apparatus. Organized crime wields increasing political and economic influence. An ineffective and corrupt police force is no match for the everyday violence that positions the country as second only to El Salvador in criminal fatalities. The rights of indigenous people are neglected or violated, and most citizens live in poverty.

As the 2007 general elections approached, contenders promised solutions to these problems. But in an environment thick with mistrust, recrimination, and corruption, relatively well-established political parties appeared, at times, to be little more than fractious ensembles of convenience. This was true of the incumbent's GANA, which lagged in the polls early on, and even more so of the PAN, which remained embroiled in internal fights and mired in scandal. In contrast, newer parties led by experienced candidates gained momentum—most notably the leftist UNE and the center-right Patriotic Party (PP). UNE's Alvaro Colom emphasized justice and welfare, while the PP's Otto Pérez Molina accentuated order and security. Neither candidate obtained the majority required to avoid a November runoff, but they came in clearly ahead of the rest. The much more inexperienced Rigoberta Menchú, candidate of the Covergence for Guatemala, received a negligible percentage of the vote. She did manage, though, to gain ground among young Mayan voters, even as many indigenous candidates and activists were slain in one of the country's most violent electoral campaigns.

The country's political system has become much more competitive. The competition, however, can include electoral violence. In addition, while political parties do play a crucial role in the competitive process, internal fragmentation and corruption render the life of political parties nasty, brutish, and short. Finally, because electoral competition is seen as the legitimate path to public office and public institutions are seen as deeply compromised, politicians resort increasingly to the tactics of caudillismo. Guatemala is now an electoral democracy with its violent history seemingly behind it.

El Salvador: Peacefully at War

Fraudulent elections, death squads, human rights violations, assassinations, kidnappings, and guerrilla warfare became normal politics in El Salvador as well. But unlike Guatemala's revolutionary army—which hardly qualified as an exemplar of tactical, much less strategic acumen—El Salvador's Frente Farabundo Martí de Liberación Nacional (FMLN, a coalition of guerrilla armies formed in 1980) successfully battled its way to a virtual stalemate with the armed forces. By the late 1980s, the government and the FMLN were engaged in talks to reach a negotiated settlement.

Powerful external pressures in favor of negotiation were also at work, mostly from the United States and the United Nations. The negotiations culminated in the Chapultepec Accords of 1992, which the first administration (Alfredo Cristiani Burkard, 1989–94) of the conservative Republican Alliance (ARENA) embedded in a broader discourse of openness and dialogue. The ARENA administration and its successor (ARENA's Armando Calderón Sol, 1994–99) continued to restructure the economy in ways that adversely affected both the weakest sectors of the population and traditional capitalist groups, who resented the new advantages enjoyed by the ascendant financial sector.

Dissatisfaction at the top and poverty at the base, however, were overshadowed at the time by the attainment of the accords' key objectives, namely the taming of the resistant armed forces and security apparatus, and the integration of the FMLN into the formal political system. Less than a year after Chapultepec, the Supreme Electoral Tribunal registered the FMLN as a legal political party.

Since then, the conservative ARENA and the FMLN have been the country's predominant political parties. The FMLN performed extremely well in the congressional elections of 1994, 1997, 2000, 2003, and 2006, but poorly in the presidential elections of 1999 and 2004. Inter-

estingly enough, despite severe internal strife, the FMLN did best in its
first presidential contest (1994). In coalition with its long-standing political ally, Democratic Convergence, FMLN candidate Rubén Zamora
was able to force ARENA's Calderón into a runoff election. But the
1994 elections returned ARENA to power, giving it control of both the
executive and congress.

The third ARENA administration (that of President Francisco Flores,
1999–2004) excelled at crisis governance in the face of catastrophic
events. Not only did it respond effectively to destructive earthquakes,
but it ably publicized its efforts, earning good marks from citizens. The
administration, however, neglected the socioeconomic conditions that
engendered great numbers of migrant workers. Even as migrant workers came to be treated increasingly as a safety valve and as a source of
remittances, socioeconomic and security pressures continued to mount.
To this day, El Salvador leads the region in criminal fatalities (with
Guatemala closing in) and poverty remains widespread.

As in Guatemala, El Salvador's democratic regime has yet to produce
a viable combination of order and justice. The FMLN and ARENA conduct politics as if it were war, engaging in rhetorical confrontations and
political clashes that either polarize or alienate citizens. Indeed, the mistrust and incivility reached such a point in the early years of this decade
that more moderate observers called for a national dialogue. National
dialogues presumably bring together a country's key political forces—
las fuerzas vivas—to deliberate on intractable issues. Such dialogues
are semiformal, claim to be representative in composition and scope, are
difficult to engineer, and usually yield few if any sustainable results. El
Salvador is no exception. The very conditions that led to the clamor for
dialogue made it unlikely to succeed.

Even if ARENA had wanted the FMLN as an interlocutor, the latter
was not up to the task. Not only did its internal disputes diminish its national appeal, but the party suffered high-profile defections amidst very
public fights in which party members leveled ethical and political accusations at one another. Indeed, the FMLN entered the 1999 presidential
election as it had in 1994—torn from within. Moreover, it was unable
to renovate its top leadership, either in substance or style. For the 2004
presidential elections, the party again nominated a former comandante,
Schafik Handal. And once again, as in Guatemala, El Salvador's electorate rejected candidates who had participated directly in the war.

This last point leads to the party's image problem. While ARENA
carefully selected energetic and personally successful candidates unencumbered by the country's bloody past, the FMLN chose the aging
Handal, who came across as petulant and was characterized by survey
respondents as a "dislikeable, rude man."

Image in politics is no superficial concern. During the 2004 campaign, ARENA emphasized Handal's history of violence, and played

up the appealing personality of its own candidate, Antonio Saca, who smiled as effortlessly as Handal scowled. Saca soundly defeated Handal in the first round with 57 percent of the vote, amid a record turnout of 65 percent of eligible voters.

This is not to say that the FMLN will never gain control of the executive. The 2006 congressional elections showed the FMLN's continuing strong support at the local level—ARENA won only two more seats than did the FMLN. In addition, the FMLN's chances for a presidential victory may have improved with Handal's death from a heart attack in 2006. A broadening perception that ARENA's long incumbency confers "unfair" advantages could also work in the FMLN's favor. Polls suggest that most voters now prefer an alternative to ARENA. The 2009 elections may settle that issue, but probably little else.

Nicaragua: Pacts, Patrons, and Clients

Revolts, coups, and civil war have plagued Nicaragua since independence, but its history has also included long chapters of political stability. An oligarchic republic survived for three decades in the second half of the nineteenth century. The liberal authoritarian regime that replaced the republic lasted sixteen years. The longest-lived regime was that of the Somoza dynasty. The family ruled for more than forty years until it was dethroned in the revolution of 1979.

The revolution's armed vanguard, the Sandinista National Liberation Front (FSLN), seized power and proceeded to implement a leftist vision of a "just order." The attempt failed. It also triggered a civil war between the FSLN and the U.S.-backed National Resistance (better known as the Contras). In the late 1980s, Nicaragua began the transitions to peace and democracy, which (as in Guatemala and El Salvador) were closely entwined processes. Nicaragua too has made visible progress. International observers have characterized as generally fair the four major elections held in the last decade and a half—1990, 1996, 2001, and 2006. In addition, four different administrations (those of Violeta Chamorro, 1990–97; Arnoldo Alemán, 1997–2002; Enrique Bolaños, 2002–07; and Daniel Ortega, 2007–) have been duly installed. In brief, the country has established a solid record of electoral continuity and peaceful transfers of power.

Beyond these accomplishments, however, the political system is hardly a case of high-quality democratic consolidation. Electoral competition is controlled by caudillos who traffic in votes, engage in influence-peddling, and occasionally resort to extortion and other types of threats. Caudillos not only abuse official powers and state resources behind closed doors but also monopolize the public role of electoral protagonists. Prior to 2006, the FSLN's Ortega suffered three consecutive presidential-election defeats, yet each time he stood again as his party's presidential candidate. A constitutional ban on consecutive re-election prevented the center-right Liberal Constitutionalist Party's (PLC) Alemán from running for a second term in 2001, but he retained the de facto prerogative of selecting the party's presidential candidate, a role he assigned to his vice-president, Bolaños. Furthermore, had he not been tried and convicted on corruption charges during Bolaños's term, Alemán almost certainly would have run again in 2006. But despite the scandal surrounding him, he was once again able to select the PLC's candidate, this time anointing José Rizo.

Caudillo-led parties brook no internal dissent or independent ambitions. The PLC expelled Eduardo Montealegre and the FSLN expelled Herty Lewites in 2005. Montealegre went on to assemble and lead the Liberal-Conservative Nicaraguan Liberal Alliance (ALN). Lewites went on to run as the presidential candidate of the Sandinista Renovation Movement (MRS) and its smaller coalition partners (Alianza MRS). Both challengers did well in the 2006 elections. Lewites and Montealegre led comfortably in opinion polls, with combined support at times surpassing 70 percent. Moreover, Montealegre went on to outperform Rizo of the PLC at the ballot box. The MRS campaign suffered a fatal blow with Lewites's sudden death in 2006. By most accounts, Lewites could have outpolled Ortega.

Regardless of particular electoral outcomes, winners and losers alike are trapped in a corrupt and corrupting political-institutional structure of their own making. Political pacts, salient in the Nicaraguan repertoire of coping practices, are the single most pernicious feature of this structure. In general, pacts are typically restrictive if not exclusionary but can be instrumental in the pursuit of broad, even ambitious goals. Pacts have been used in different countries to establish the foundations of new regimes and to restructure or repair existing ones.

Members of a pact can be coequals, but more often (as in the Nicaraguan case) they play the roles of junior and senior partner. In Nicaragua, in fact, partnership status shifts with the correlation of forces, which in turn depends on the partners' capacity at any given moment to inflict damage on one another, or conversely, to provide mutual help. Damage or help can be delivered through a variety of means that usually require the abuse of institutional power but are acceptable to the partners and their clients.

Pacts can have unintended consequences. Indeed, a pact is usually implemented in order to resolve some political conflict that it ultimately aggravates.[2] However, recent Nicaraguan pacts have been successfully engineered to afford the partners a modicum of governmental effectiveness, and to do so in ways that pact members can use to enhance or consolidate their own power to the detriment of excluded players.

Since the beginning of the 1990s, the FSLN has been the one constant player in pact-making, engaging in serial partnering with the Chamorro,

Alemán, and Bolaños administrations. In each instance, excluded political actors have opposed the pact as unjust and treacherous. As insiders
become outsiders and former outsiders are brought in, the same charges
are raised by correspondingly different sets of politicians. The upshot is
a loss of credibility among established politicians.

More important, because pacts often require pressuring reluctant
partners, and because they can either boost or block political ambitions,
they help turn governmental institutions into battlefields. A months-long
stalemate between the executive and the legislature during the Chamorro administration brought the country to the edge of a constitutional
crisis in 1995. The first years of the Alemán administration were rocked
by clashes between the FSLN and the PLC in the Assembly, and related
rioting on the streets.

Confrontation between the two branches was keen during the Bolaños
administration as well. After serving as Alemán's vice-president for
five years, President Bolaños promptly set out to convict Alemán on
corruption charges, an objective that required the National Assembly to
strip Alemán of immunity. Uncooperative at first, the Assembly eventually yielded in the face of public mobilization stoked by the president
(working in league with FSLN activists). Alemán was ousted as head
of the National Assembly, tried, convicted, and sentenced to twenty
years in prison. (After a brief stint in jail, he was placed under house
arrest.)

Through all this, Alemán retained the allegiance of most PLC deputies, who colluded with FSLN deputies to take revenge against Bolaños.
This renewed FSLN-PLC alliance was cemented by Bolaños's adamant
opposition to a new set of proposed constitutional reforms, which aimed
to increase the prerogatives of the legislative branch at the expense of
the executive. The confrontation reached the point where FSLN and
PLC deputies began to debate a proposal to impeach Bolaños for alleged campaign-finance violations, and stripped several of the president's ministers of their immunity from prosecution. The result was a
paralyzing standoff between the administration and the congress. Under
severe pressure from the U.S. State Department and with the Organization of American States publicly describing Nicaragua's democracy as
"imperiled," Ortega and Bolaños finally reached an agreement. Ortega
pledged to dismantle the impeachment machinery being assembled in
congress against Bolaños; and the latter, in turn, accepted the new constitutional reforms on condition that they come into effect only *after* he
left office.

The 1999 pact between Alemán and Ortega—the country's preemi-
nent caudillos—has proved arguably the most comprehensive and durable. Crafted through secret and direct negotiations that systematically
addressed both men's individual and shared concerns, this agreement
provided for a set of self-serving "reform" laws. On the electoral front,

the reforms aimed, for example, to enable Ortega—on a losing streak since 1990—to attain a first-round presidential victory. He was finally able to reap the benefits in the 2006 elections.

The electoral reform, in addition, called for the elimination of existing smaller parties and the stiffening of requirements for the creation of new ones. Containing the extreme proliferation of political parties was the stated objective. But smaller political parties argued that by raising the representation threshold from 3 to 4 percent in general elections, the reform enabled the PLC and the FSLN to appoint partisan Supreme Electoral Council (SEC) magistrates who could be relied upon in the future to raise and maintain barriers to entry to the electoral market.

On the institutional front, the reforms increased the number of Supreme Court justices, SEC magistrates, and comptrollers. This move was intended to create new positions available to the PLC and FSLN for allocation among loyalists. Reserved congressional seats for the outgoing president and the presidential runner-up, in turn, gave Alemán and Ortega extended immunity, while a two-thirds requirement made it extraordinarily difficult to strip them of it. In this respect, the National Assembly functions as a sort of domain of impunity.

The pact's 2005 expansion and attendant constitutional reform created a property agency to resolve long-standing property disputes involving vast amounts of land and millions of dollars in compensation. The pact's expansion also called for the creation of a regulatory body for the utilities and communications sectors. The partners of the pact, through congressional deputies, appoint heads of these new arbitration institutions.

Finally, the pact leaves open the door to a constitutional assembly, and such an assembly is likely intended for reinstating consecutive re-elections. In 1995, this issue helped to trigger a near-constitutional crisis that was ultimately settled peacefully due to the army's noninterventionist stance, foreign donors' pressure on the disputants, and Cardinal Miguel Obando y Bravo's moral authority. But the cardinal's authority has since eroded, as he seeks to influence electoral outcomes, extracts favors from powerholders, and engages in opportunistic alliance-making. (He is currently closely tied to both Ortega and Alemán.) Once above the fray, the cardinal is now in the middle of it, and the arbitration regime may have lost its most effective informal moderator.

This loss may have serious ramifications. The PLC and the FSLN appear to have established a power duopoly, but one that is both renegotiable and contestable. In addition, while congress is often weak in the exercise of its oversight and control functions, it is energetic in the use of its institutional powers as political weapons. In the current congress seated in January 2007, the FSLN holds 38 seats, the PLC 25, the ALN 24, and the MRS 5. If the underlying pact becomes frayed or unworkable and cannot be renegotiated, it is not hard to imagine a reprise of legislative paralysis and war between the executive and the legislature. In that event, neither the cardinal nor the judiciary possesses the credibility to moderate or arbitrate between camps. The only remaining option is the military.

The armed forces, a praetorian guard under the Somoza dynasty and a partisan extension of the ruling party under the FSLN regime, now shun political imbroglios. Their institutional identity appears to be tied to a professional code of conduct and a neutral posture. Indeed, the question that now arises is whether the military has grown too independent, arrogating unto itself the right to decide when to leave or return to barracks.

The question is more than academic. The opposition on both the left and the right deeply mistrusts the Ortega government. They view his new popular advisory councils, for example, not as instruments of direct participation by the people but as means of social control. The councils, such as the Zero Hunger Program, will likely function as loyalty networks that bypass institutions and bolster the capacity of individual leaders to expand their client base. In addition, the possibilities of the reinstitution of consecutive reelection and of postponing the 2008 municipal elections until the general elections of 2011 loom darkly ahead for the government's opponents. Finally, add to all this the severe internal frictions developing once again within the FSLN, especially the resentment caused at the highest levels by the accumulation of power in the hands of Ortega's wife, and the system's "structured chaos" begins to look uncertain. How the military would respond to outright disarray is something that even the generals may not yet know.

Honduras: Town and Country

Almost from the start, Honduran politics have been closely entwined with regional conflicts. Throughout the nineteenth century, the country participated in the liberal-conservative wars that convulsed its neighbors, sending and receiving partisan armies across boundaries. In the twentieth century, such troop movements appeared to become a thing of the past. Socioeconomic instability and political restlessness, on the other hand, continued to build internally. Indeed, internal pressures led to the scapegoating of Salvadoran immigrant workers, in turn followed by the July 1969 Soccer War between Honduras and El Salvador. But aside from that conflict, contemporary Honduras managed to remain mostly at the margins of the region's turbulence.

This marginal existence, the one blessing of the country's status as a regional backwater, was interrupted in the 1980s, when the country became the northern staging ground for the Contra War in neighboring Nicaragua. Unlike Costa Rica, the southern staging ground, Honduras lacked the political institutions and culture to keep its domestic life relatively separate from its role in the war. Briefly put, no regime had been able to establish anything like a "just order" in Honduras at that time. The armed forces, which seized direct control in the 1960s, provided order but failed at almost everything else, and in a diversionary move, actually encouraged the anti-immigrant sentiment that ultimately led to the brief Soccer War. Civilian rule, on the other hand, newly restored in the early 1980s, would prove incapable even of controlling the military's antisubversion campaign in the countryside, much less effecting the deep changes needed for high-quality democratic consolidation.

On the socioeconomic front, land-reform initiatives have been aborted or frustrated, leading to further injustice, such as new losses of peasant lands. And although peasant, student, and labor organizations have traditionally been strong, activists have paid dearly at the hands of security and paramilitary forces. On the institutional front, the country's democratic system is now characterized by competitive political parties, stable electoral cycles, intense influence-peddling, and low reform capacity.

"Candidates of change" tend to run on modernization, antipoverty, and anticorruption platforms. But once elected, such candidates typically meet with limited success at best. Not surprisingly, macroeconomic growth, even when robust, barely makes a dent in rural poverty, which remains quite serious, particularly in the interior of the country. To the extent that Honduran democracy assumes the form of an increasingly well-established but narrowly competitive process controlled by urban political elites, the concept of consolidated democracy "as the only game in town" applies only too literally to the Honduran case.

Panama: The Bearable Lightness of Peripheral Being

In 1903, Panamanian nationalists, backed by the United States government, successfully fought for independence from Colombia. The U.S. Army Corps of Engineers promptly began construction of an interoceanic canal—a project that the Colombian legislature had rejected—in the newly independent republic. To this day, the Canal bisects the country, but its strategic importance, once crucial to the United States and international trade, has been eroded by a century of advances in maritime transport.

The ten-mile–wide Canal Zone proved vital for Panama as well. Indeed, the Canal and U.S. policies shaped all that matters to Panamanians, from their economic interests to their nationalist sentiments. Early on, the Canal trained Panamanians' full attention on U.S.-Panama relations. Broader isthmian affairs became peripheral by comparison. Through the decades, Panama and its neighbors hardly took notice of one another. Nicaraguans and Costa Ricans even let go of their own canal dreams.

Panamanian politics, however, still bore a striking family resemblance to the politics of its neighbors. The Liberal and Conservative parties and an increasingly restive military dominated the political scene. Notable families, the so-called Whitetails, governed the country as best they could, which is to say, with considerable difficulty. Arnulfo Arias, a nationalist notable, was elected and overthrown three times. The last was the coup of 1968. Led by General Omar Torrijos, the coup ushered in a populist-nationalist "revolution," with the general as its self-appointed "Maximum Leader."

Torrijos endured through a mixture of authoritarian control, populist socioeconomic reform, and nationalist determination. "Compassionate dictatorship" is how he described his rule. Also crucial to Torrijos's endurance were his popularity and skill, combined with his good fortune when Jimmy Carter became president of the United States. In 1977, Carter and Torrijos negotiated the transfer of the Canal's control to Panama. Although the transfer was scheduled to take place in 1999, the agreement represented at that very moment nothing less than a nationalist pinnacle.

As is the case with every pinnacle, all moves from that spot were steps down—something that Torrijos saw vividly. In keeping with his commitment to Carter, and seeking to exit on a high note, Torrijos began a gradual political opening, or more precisely, a caudillo-led liberalization process. This process, however, deteriorated into keen political jockeying and unstable rule after Torrijos's death in a 1981 airplane crash. Out of the political wreckage, a former intelligence officer and CIA asset named Colonel Manuel Noriega emerged as ruler. Corrupt and ruthless, Noriega outdid the worst stereotype of the banana-republic dictator. He practiced voodoo, trafficked in drugs, enjoyed torture, unleashed the so-called Dignity Batallions (paramilitary thugs) on the opposition, and defied the United States with the self-assurance of a world power. In 1989, the administration of President George H.W. Bush sent a military force to hunt him down like a common criminal and usher him to the Florida jail in which he remains.

Since then, Panama has created a renovated variant of its old days. A magnet for tourists and foreign retirees, with a thriving financial sector, Panama has an open economy that is forging ahead. Beneath the balmy easy living and the bustle of bankers and merchants, corruption still reigns. In politics, personalism and clientelism reign. The Revolutionary Democratic Party (PRD), founded by Torrijos and inherited by Noriega, won the first postinvasion elections (1994). Four years later, political ghosts competed in the 1998 elections. Mireya Moscoso, the widow of Arnulfo Arias, ran for the Partido Arnulfista. Her opponent, Martín Torrijos, son of General Omar Torrijos, ran for the PRD, the party founded by his father. The campaign, more than a programmatic debate, was a popularity contest between dead caudillos. The Panamanian electorate turned out in large numbers, and chose Arias's widow. In 2004, they turned to Torrijos's son.

Costa Rica: Small Country, Big Difference

Personalism and patronage have not been absent from politics in Costa Rica. Yet its citizens have generally regarded their system as the source of a uniquely robust public good—a combination of peace, security, prosperity, freedom, and justice. The political parties and governments of the Second Republic, like those of the First, have been closely associated with particular notables. The improper or illegal distribution of favors among allies and followers occasionally causes a scandal, which in turn brings about the disgrace or even punishment of culprits. But almost invariably, those same notables, parties, and governments have emphasized the importance of broad socioeconomic development as a goal, and consensus-based reform as the preferred means.

The 1948 revolutionaries who overthrew the First Republic and ushered in the Second "modernized" the political economy in ways that preserved the country's best traditions. Almost half a century later, as the 1990s drew to a close, the Second Republic faced its own internal critics. Increasingly, the country's political class and intelligentsia began to call for the "renovation" of the socioeconomic and political system. Established elites and aspirants alike pointed to rapidly changing times and urged an innovative response. And as on previous occasions, they demanded that innovation not breach the core mandates of their national identity. They stressed both the need to keep up with the world and to do so the "Costa Rican way."

The capacity to do both quite well has been the hallmark of the Revolution's political party, the National Liberation Party (PLN). By the start of this new century, however, the PLN itself was increasingly regarded as a particularly rusty piece of an outmoded two-party system. That system was openly challenged in 2002 by Ottón Solís, cofounder and presidential candidate of the Citizens' Action Party (PAC). In the presidential election of that year, Solís ran against Rolando Araya of the PLN and Abel Pacheco of the Social Christian Unity Party. Solís lost in the first round, while Araya was defeated by Pacheco in the country's first runoff vote.

Determined not to suffer a third consecutive defeat in the 2006 elections, the PLN turned to former president Oscar Arias (1986–90), a winner of the Nobel Peace Prize for his role in Central America's peace negotiations. Considered invincible by most, Arias accepted the PLN's nomination and launched a campaign that was perceived as uninspired at best. In the tradition of his political forebears, Arias appropriated the opposition's message in three quick steps: He accepted as valid the argument that the country's two-party system was problematic, then added his own twist by characterizing the system as an impediment to consensus-building, and from there proceeded to welcome the new multiparty system as a positive development.

Arias's anticipated landslide victory, however, did not materialize. Instead, the quintessential insider Arias prevailed over the upstart Solís by a margin of 1.2 percent of the valid votes. Standard explanations for this slimmest of margins hinge on Arias's arrogant demeanor and his staid understanding of politics at a time when calls for change seemed to build into a clamor. There is some validity to these points, especially the first. But a much more fundamental issue was at stake in the election, namely the renegotiation of the regime's foundational social and political pact in an increasingly globalized world.

The trigger issue was CAFTA. Signed by President Pacheco in 2005, CAFTA immediately sparked a heated public debate and prompted public demonstrations from supporters and opponents alike. CAFTA's best-known critic, Solís, highlighted the damage that the free-trade agreement would inflict on small and medium-sized farmers, industrial companies, and organized labor, particularly in the public sector—all groups consistently and closely associated with the social-democratic model championed and solidified by Arias's own party, the PLN. Yet the Arias candidacy was generally and correctly perceived as a proxy for CAFTA's approval. Arias argued that all Costa Ricans stood to benefit from the boost that the treaty would give to the country's export economy.

If a substantial win by Arias might have settled the CAFTA controversy, the perilously close outcome heightened it. CAFTA opponents even won a legal victory when the Supreme Electoral Tribunal said it would authorize a referendum if presented with a petition signed by at least 5 percent of the voters.

Plebiscites and referenda are often justified in Latin America by appealing to the principle of popular sovereignty, of course, but also by sudden and temporary recognition of the people as a wise, just, and fair arbiter. In the Costa Rican case, however, there is nothing sudden or temporary about such recognition. The hallmark of the country's political culture is the long-standing and consistent valorization of the Costa Rican people.

Direct consultation, if orderly and transparent, can settle an intractable issue by submitting specific proposals to a popular vote. Spontaneous or manipulated consultation, by contrast, is often no more than a variant of populist demagoguery, and tends to degenerate into unfettered caudillismo. Costa Rica's strong electoral institutions make the latter unlikely.

Taking these factors into account, Arias made a virtue out of necessity. Once again, he resorted to the traditional tactic of advancing the cause by "building consensus" and announced that he would ask the Legislative Assembly to authorize the referendum. This time, however, tradition was used boldly. By going along with the referendum, Arias got to bet on a "yes" vote while he corralled all parties to the dispute within the confines of a procedure that was unprecedented but democratic. This meant that he was committed to accepting the results either way, but so was most everyone else. At various points, both foes and friends of CAFTA extolled the referendum as an example of direct participation by the people in the making of a landmark decision that transcends CAFTA and affects the Second Republic's foundational arrangements.

Popular support for the treaty, though considerable, suffered during the weeks leading up to the October 7 referendum. Moreover, the referendum's procedural legality became a point of contention, requiring a ruling by the constitutional court on whether CAFTA itself was constitutional. Through all this, passions ran high, even as both sides pledged allegiance to their democracy, whose dictates, they insisted, are indisputably binding.

Costa Ricans approved CAFTA by a margin so slim that the opposition demanded a ballot by ballot recount, as provided by law. Both the recount and the Supreme Electoral Tribunal confirmed the victory of the "yes" camp. What now remains to be seen is whether the camps will prove true to their word, and honor the outcome. If they do, as I believe they will, Costa Ricans are about to make exceptional history yet again.

Progress and Scandal

Attempts at democracy-building are not new to Central America. Soon after independence, the countries of the region organized their governments along distinctly democratic lines. Every place except Costa Rica, those early efforts were accompanied by passionate engagement with the European and U.S. experiences, particularly their democratic theories and institutions. And everywhere except Costa Rica, those early efforts were overshadowed by the civil wars and dictators that followed and by subsequent attempts at democracy-building that either fell short or collapsed.

Through these cycles, the concept of popular sovereignty was never explicitly repudiated by either the left or the right; and authoritarian governments from both ends of the spectrum typically felt compelled to manipulate and pervert elections. Prior to the 1980s, authentically democratic governments were as weak as they were rare, and authoritarian governments were able to impose order but seldom attained a significant degree of legitimacy. Only Costa Rica was able to establish a regime of arbitration capable of settling conflicting socioeconomic and political claims while garnering general citizen approbation.

Examined against this backdrop, and putting Costa Rica aside, the region's third-wave democracies represent a substantial improvement over their predecessors. Political parties are much more competitive, the media and civil society are free to act as watchdogs, and citizens' equality of rights is undisputed. These key advances, however, must also be assessed in terms of their effect on system dynamics. Democratic accountability requires that independent journalists and nongovernmental activists expose official corruption and abuses of power. But if the net result is most often scandal, not redress, then the spread of apathy, disappointment, and cynicism should not come as a surprise. Further, democratic competitiveness hinges on political parties that function effectively as mobilizational and electoral machines. But if parties tend to splinter and collapse under the pressure of internal strife, operate as little more than patronage channels, or become personalistic domains, then it is predictable that the quality of democratic representation will suffer.

Finally, the formation of a democratic political culture entails the exaltation and affirmation of equal rights. But if their exercise is subordinated to the caprice and prejudice of powerholders, then not just the poor and the weak but also members of the economic, social, and political elites will at various points feel and act as aggrieved citizens, unfairly treated by those who control the state. Indeed, if history is any guide, when scandal overflows the public sphere and a sense of unfairness prevails even among the powerful, new guardians of popular sovereignty come forth to battle disorder and injustice, to save the people from its own excesses and flaws, and if necessary, to defend the people from democracy.

NOTES

1. See Consuelo Cruz, *Political Culture and Institutional Development in Costa Rica and Nicaragua: World-Making in the Tropics* (New York: Cambridge University Press, 2005).

2. Enrique Alvarado Martínez, "Los pactos en la cultura política de Nicaragua," *Revista de la Academia de Geografía e Historia de Nicaragua* 55 (2003): 179–203.

19

THE CARIBBEAN:
DEMOCRACY ADRIFT?

Daniel P. Erikson

Daniel P. Erikson *is senior associate for U.S. policy and director of Caribbean programs at the Inter-American Dialogue, the Washington-based policy forum on Western Hemisphere affairs. He is coeditor of* Transforming Socialist Economies: Lessons for Cuba and Beyond *(2005) and a contributor to several books including* Looking Forward: Comparative Perspectives on Cuba's Transition *(2007) and* Taking Sides: Clashing Views on Latin America *(2006). The original version of this essay, coauthored with Adam Minson, appeared in the October 2005 issue of the* Journal of Democracy.

Nowhere is hurricane season more dreaded than in the Caribbean, where a series of record-breaking storms have ripped across vulnerable island nations in recent years, leaving a trail of devastation in their wake. In 2005, the one-two punch of hurricanes Dennis and Emily killed several dozen people in Haiti, caused widespread flooding in Jamaica, and claimed sixteen lives in Cuba. As the storms continued on toward North American shores, the estimated cost of restoring damaged property in the Caribbean ranged into the billions of dollars. Two years later, in 2007, Jamaica found itself in the crosshairs of Hurricane Dean, a category-5 storm so powerful that it caused another US$3 billion in property damage across the Caribbean. Dean forced the country's parliamentary elections to be delayed, and Jamaica's voters were left in such a foul mood that, when elections were finally held, they delivered a stinging defeat to incumbent Prime Minister Portia Simpson Miller, a popular politician who had won wide acclaim for becoming the island's first female prime minister.

Due to the annual hurricane seasons' recent ferocity, the small, mainly English-speaking democracies that make up the majority of Caribbean countries have begun to take the precautions necessary to minimize the impact of natural disasters. While dealing with this arduous task, governments also face the challenge of ensuring their countries' economic well-being and political stability.

Many Caribbean nations have long taken pride in the strength of their political institutions and democratic traditions. Of the fifteen countries that make up the Caribbean Community and Common Market (Caricom), a regional organization for trade and cooperation founded by the Treaty of Chaguaramas in 1973, only three—Grenada, Haiti, and Suriname—have experienced unconstitutional changes in government or external military interventions. In fact, most member countries have experienced peaceful transfers of power from ruling party to opposition and back again. During the last three decades, as much of the rest of Latin America transitioned from military rule to democracy only to see democratic governments collapse under popular discontent, Caribbean democracies have remained comparatively stable and well-functioning. Yet in many of these countries, unease lurks below the surface.

In the Caricom nations, ranging from relatively large Trinidad and Tobago to tiny St. Vincent and the Grenadines, there is concern that these small, vulnerable states are facing new and unprecedented challenges. Some leaders blame the region's woes on globalization and the indifference of larger powers. In 2001, St. Lucia's Prime Minister Kenny Anthony stated, "Our democratic traditions are being challenged, not by internal policy failures but by the effects of external change on our socioeconomic and political traditions."[1]

These unwelcome shifts include the dismantling of longstanding international-trade preferences for the Caribbean, the corrosive presence of the South American drug trade through the island corridor, and the rise of powerful gangs, fueled in some instances by criminal deportees from the United States and Europe. Other leaders recognize that internal factors also play a role. In 2002, the assistant secretary-general of Caricom noted, "Quality-of-politics issues such as accountability, integrity, tolerance, respect for diversity, responsiveness of governments and public participation in decision-making, have emerged as powerful citizen concerns to which our governments will have to respond."[2] Furthermore, in 2006, then–secretary general of the United Nations Kofi Annan outlined another series of threats to stability in the region, saying, "Caribbean democracies suffer from an unemployment-fueled assault of violence, drugs, and HIV/AIDS."[3]

If they seek positive models in the region, the small democracies of the Caribbean can find scant comfort in their larger neighbors. In communist Cuba, Fidel Castro has fallen ill but democracy shows few signs of flourishing, while nearby Haiti has only recently begun to emerge from its political and economic morass. Even the Dominican Republic, which is once again experiencing an economic expansion, suffered a sudden economic collapse in 2003 and remains much poorer than most Caricom members.

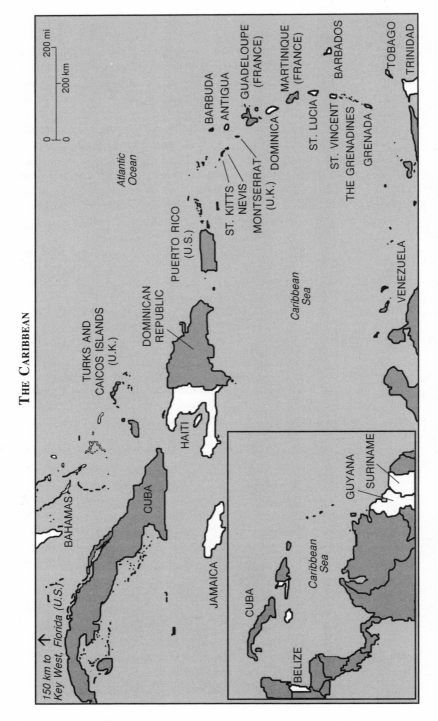

THE CARIBBEAN

Jamaica is a bellwether state in the Caribbean. With a population of 2.7 million, it is the region's most populous English-speaking country, and it became independent in 1962, earlier than most other Caricom member states. Jamaica's relatively high levels of public health and education, along with its vibrant cultural industry and reputation as a tourist destination, provoke the envy of many of its neighbors. Indeed, the country ranks as one of the most influential actors in the region.

Jamaica's recent political history has been characterized by an ongoing rivalry between the left-of-center People's National Party (PNP), long dominated by the late Michael Manley, and the more conservative Jamaican Labor Party, whose longtime leader was Edward Seaga. In the 1970s, the two parties developed sets of urban garrisons that by means fair and foul strived to bring their preferred candidates to power. The victor would share the spoils by channeling government funding into affiliated neighborhoods, while garrisons that supported the losing party went hungry. By 1980, clashes between the militant wings of the two parties had resulted in hundreds of fatalities.

Jamaica's political evolution has been marred by violence while producing few economic results beyond recurrent stagnation. Upon regaining power in 1989, the PNP, headed by Prime Minister Percival J. Patterson until his retirement in March 2006, managed to achieve a string of electoral triumphs despite sagging opinion polls, poor financial health, and high rates of unemployment (typically above 15 percent). Economic expansion has barely kept pace with population growth over the last decade, thus doing little to alleviate the deprivation facing the island's poor. The Jamaican economy remains heavily dependent on tourism, remittances from expatriates overseas, bauxite mining, and light manufacturing. At a time when competition from Asia has been sapping jobs from Central America and the Caribbean, entrenched bureaucracy and a 20 percent increase in the minimum wage in January 2005 have furthered Jamaica's reputation as a high-cost, low-productivity economy.

Even more worrisome than the country's political and economic problems is the steadily rising level of violence fueled by drug trafficking and youth-gang culture. An already high murder rate has risen to stratospheric levels in recent years. Jamaica's murder rate peaked at nearly 1,700 homicides in 2005, a grim statistic that was surpassed on a per-capita basis only by Colombia and South Africa.[4] It has since declined to about 1,400 annually, still a stunning rate for a country not at war. Many Jamaicans lay the blame for the violence at the feet of the drug trade, which has contributed to the widespread sense throughout Jamaican society that the country is beset by forces beyond its control. When a prominent Jamaican business leader described the island as a "failed state" in the spring of 2005, his comments prompted such a heated national discussion that the prime minister eventually jumped into the fray to refute the claim.

In 2007, Jamaican voters followed a regional trend of punishing the incumbent party at the polls by ousting the PNP from power for the first time in eighteen years. The 2006 retirement of Patterson had cleared the way for Portia Simpson Miller, also of the PNP, to win an internal party battle to become Jamaica's first female prime minister. Initially enthusiastic about Miller, voters soon cooled and voted her out in September 2007 in favor of Bruce Golding of the Jamaica Labor Party. In his inaugural speech, Golding focused on the challenges of economic debt, high levels of crime, corruption, and the country's sparse prospects for job creation. He also pledged to listen to "the persistent cry for justice from so many of our people to which we cannot continue to be deaf, to which we must respond." But the experience of Miller shows that Jamaica's voters are in no mood to grant a long honeymoon to its political leaders as they confront the island's deep-seated problems, and the new government will be under increasing pressure to show quick results.

Islands Under Stress

While not every nation shares Jamaica's woes, the ability to confront such challenges varies sharply among the Caribbean countries. Of Caricom's fifteen members, only the Bahamas has achieved the status of an upper-income country, with an annual per-capita GDP nearing $20,000. Most are middle-income countries, with GDP per capita hovering near $3,500 in Dominica, Jamaica, and St. Vincent and the Grenadines, and exceeding $12,000 in Antigua and Barbuda, Barbados, and Trinidad and Tobago (see Table.) While each of these nations is navigating a different set of political and economic circumstances, they also have many traits in common.

Trinidad and Tobago is celebrated as the home of calypso music and the birthplace of Nobel-prize–winning author V.S. Naipaul, who describes his native land as "a small island in the mouth of the great Orinoco river of Venezuela."[5] It is heavily dependent on oil-and-gas production, and high fuel prices have buoyed the country's living standards in recent years. The oil-and-gas industry now accounts for about 40 percent of the country's GDP and half of government revenues, which allowed the per-capita GDP to approach $14,000 in 2006.

Trinidad and Tobago remains captive to tense racial politics, characterized by frictions between the black and Indian populations, and reflected in the two main parties—the People's National Movement (PNM) and the opposition United National Congress (UNC) respectively. After several years of parliamentary deadlock, Prime Minister Patrick Manning of the PNM came to power in 2002 with the support of Trinidad's urban black population. He has since positioned himself as a regional leader, in part by offering grants to neighboring countries severely affected by high fuel prices. In 2007, Manning handily won re-election with 26 of 41 seats in Parliament.

TABLE—CARIBBEAN COMMUNITY MEMBER DATA

COUNTRY	POPULATION (2006)	AREA (KM²)	GDP PER CAPITA (2006 USD)	DATE OF INDEPENDENCE
Antigua and Barbuda	78,200	442	12,205	1981
Bahamas	327,000	13,939	18,961	1973
Barbados	270,000	430	12,523	1966
Belize	301,000	22,965	4,059	1981
Dominica	69,500	750	3,567	1978
Grenada	107,000	344	4,937	1974
Guyana	756,000	214,999	1,161	1966
Haiti	8,808,000	27,700	528	1804
Jamaica	2,667,000	10,991	3,877	1962
Montserrat	9,000	103	3,400	U.K.
St. Kitts and Nevis	39,000	261	11,954	1983
St. Lucia	171,000	616	5,602	1979
St. Vincent and the Grenadines	118,000	389	4,695	1979
Suriname	502,000	163,820	4,081	1975
Trinidad and Tobago	1,301,000	5,128	13,996	1962
Cuba*	11,294,000	110,860	—	1902
Dominican Republic*	9,021,000	48,671	3,653	1844
Puerto Rico*	3,927,000	9,104	14,460	U.S.

* Although not members of Caricom, Cuba, the Dominican Republic, and Puerto Rico are included for purposes of comparison. Due to Cuba's artificially high exchange rate, its estimated GDP per capita of $4,100 is not easily comparable to other countries and is thus excluded from the chart.
Sources: *Encyclopedia Britannica Book of the Year 2007* (Chicago: Encyclopedia Britannica Inc., 2007). Economist Intelligence Unit, *Country Reports 2007, www.eiu.com.*

Unfortunately, the improving economy has been accompanied by a dramatic upsurge in kidnappings. Gangs have especially targeted Trinidadians of Indian descent, who comprise 40 percent of the country's citizens and represent much of its upper class. Between 2001 and 2006, the number of kidnappings increased exponentially from 10 to more than 200 a year (out of a population of 1.3 million)—and Trinidad and Tobago now has the second highest rate of abductions in the world after Colombia.[6] The rate of kidnappings has begun to decline, but new threats of terrorism have emerged that may be linked to Jamaat al Muslimeen, a radical Islamic group that attempted to topple the government in 1990 and today has extensive criminal ties. In May 2007, four men from Trinidad and Guyana were arrested for conspiring to blow up a fuel line at New York's JFK airport. The sensational case shined a harsh spotlight on the Caribbean as a potential terrorist threat to the United States.

Many Indian-Trinidadians, who are disproportionately targets of abduction, blame the rise in violence and kidnappings on government corruption and police collusion, noting that insecurity worsened after Manning assumed power. By contrast, the police force has downplayed the threat to average Trinidadians, insisting that most murders and kidnappings are drug-related and that "very few innocent people are killed."[7] Meanwhile, the indictment on corruption charges of former UNC prime minister Basdeo Panday, who is of Indian descent, added to the ethnic and political tensions. Despite Trinidad and Tobago's economic dynamism, the country's democratic consensus faces increasing unease.

With a landmass three times larger than Trinidad and Tobago but only about one-third of the population, the Bahamas is one of several rays of light in the region's political panorama. As the Caribbean's only upper-income country, the Bahamas has established a model service economy, based on an impressive tourism sector—which accounts for 30 percent of national income—and offshore financial services. During more than thirty years of independence, the Bahamas has maintained a relatively clean record of stable democratic governance. The 2007 elections ousted the ruling PLP, sent its leader Perry Christie into opposition, and brought former prime minister Hubert Ingraham of the Free National Movement party back to power. Christie and Ingraham are close personal friends and business partners, which has left many Bahamians feeling that their country's politics are dominated by an exclusive clique. The economic and political policies of the Bahamas have remained remarkably consistent under both prime ministers.

Like the Bahamas, Barbados has a well-developed service sector, robust democratic traditions, and one of the highest standards of living in Latin America and the Caribbean. The country is one of the least corrupt in the world (it ranked twenty-third out of 179 countries in Transparency International's 2007 Global Corruption Index), and its levels of education and health care are among the highest in the region. The political scene features three parties that are moderate and have few major ideological differences—therefore, electoral competition centers on personalities and performance in office. Barbados enjoyed enviable prosperity during the fourteen-year rule of former prime minister Owen Arthur of the Barbados Labour Party, who was first elected in 1994 and successfully hammered out consensus with the opposition, the private sector, and labor unions on an array of issues. Still, in January 2008, Arthur's bid for a historic fourth term was rebuffed by the voters, who overwhelmingly elected opposition leader David Thompson of the Democratic Labor Party as the next prime minister. The sudden implosion of Owen Arthur's political fortunes underlined the volatility of Caribbean politics and highlighted the strong anti-incumbency sentiment that is sweeping the region.

Indeed, even well-governed countries such as the Bahamas and Barbados are struggling to meet the challenges posed by drug and arms smuggling and related security threats. In March 2005, Barbados suffered a prison riot that lasted for three days and led to a fire at the island's only penitentiary. The Barbadian government called on 120 security personnel from its Caribbean neighbors to help restore order and to evacuate the badly overcrowded, 150-year-old prison. Meanwhile, supported by the political parties, juries are getting tough on crime by sentencing violent criminals to death, and the government has appealed to the newly formed regional supreme court, the Caribbean Court of Justice, to allow the island's first execution in more than two decades.

Ongoing political turmoil in Haiti has profoundly affected the region as a whole, deepening political divisions among the Caribbean countries. Haiti officially joined Caricom in 2002, but was temporarily suspended when an armed uprising forced President Jean-Bertrand Aristide to flee the country in February 2004. Haitians elected a former president, René Préval, as their new leader in February 2006, following two years of inept interim government under Gérard Latortue. In 2007, Préval made some progress in improving Haiti's security situation and stabilizing the economy, but his relations with parliament became tense. Advances were made in purging corrupt police officers and vetting new recruits. Still, the 9,000-strong United Nations peacekeeping force is the main bulwark standing between Haiti and chaos, and Préval's pleas for continued international involvement were validated when the UN Security Council extended the mission's mandate until October 2008.

Another regional issue resulting from the Haitian chaos is the flow of refugees from that country. This has placed new pressures on the small surrounding countries, where managing the influx of Haitians draws on scarce public resources. The neighboring Dominican Republic has borne the brunt of this exodus, and its government has responded with forced repatriation of thousands of illegal Haitian immigrants. Similarly, the Bahamian government regularly repatriates thousands of Haitians who arrive there unlawfully. In May 2007, a harrowing incident unfolded on the high seas when a navy boat from the British territory of Turks and Caicos appeared to deliberately ram a sailboat crowded with Haitian migrants. The Haitian vessel capsized and sank, and more than sixty people drowned. Haiti's newfound political stability rests on the shaky foundation of severe economic deprivation, and the country is certain to continue posing a test for its democratic neighbors.

The Micro-States

In 1981, seven small-island Caricom members—Antigua and Barbuda, Dominica, Grenada, St. Kitts and Nevis, St. Lucia, St. Vincent and the Grenadines, and the British territory of Montserrat—created the subregional Organisation of Eastern Caribbean States (OECS), which promotes cooperation on defense issues, international diplomacy, and economic policies. The combined population of these countries is less than 600,000, and most have land areas only two or three times the size of Washington, D.C. The politics of this subregion has been shaped by its brief independence—most countries became independent in the 1970s and 1980s—and colonial legacies continue to reverberate.

Antigua and Barbuda saw a major political change in 2004, when the United Progressive Party's election triumph ended six decades of rule by the powerful Bird family. Since the 1940s, prime ministers V.C. Bird and his son Lester Bird had held on to power through massive patronage schemes, control of the economy and media, and eccentric authoritarian maneuvers. The Bird family still exercises some political influence through its family-owned radio station, which has recently been threatened with "antiharassment" legislation due to its vitriolic criticisms of figures in the current government.

Since independence in 1978, Dominica has been a relatively well-functioning democracy. The Labour Party, which has been in power since 2000, managed to retain its parliamentary majority in the May 2005 election—despite its controversial economic-austerity program and the deaths in office of two consecutive prime ministers. The 2005 victory, which hinged on a single vote in one electoral district, was disputed by the opposition United Workers' Party.

In September 2004, Grenada was all but ruined by Hurricane Ivan. The damage neared $900 million, more than twice the country's annual GDP. Agriculture and tourism were upended and unemployment jumped to 20 percent. But the devastation failed to inspire a detente between the government of Prime Minister Keith Mitchell and the opposition, which has sued to contest the government's one-seat majority in Parliament. The island's democracy has matured considerably since the United States invaded in 1983 to oust a Marxist-Leninist government that had taken power by force. In 2001, the government established a Truth and Reconciliation Commission to shed light on those events, yet subsequent delays and controversies suggest that the wounds from that period have yet to heal.

St. Kitts and Nevis, which has a population of 39,000, has enjoyed a long history of free and fair elections, although in 1993 election results were strongly disputed by the opposition. The ruling Labour Party is widely popular on the main island of St. Kitts, but authorities have been confronted with recurring efforts by·Nevis to secede from the federation. In 2007, St. Kitts and Nevis Prime Minister Denzil Douglas marked his twelfth year in power amid a slight economic rebound and growing fears about crime. Nevis held a special election to replace an opposition leader who had died of a sudden illness, but the balance of power in parliament remained unchanged.

Since independence in 1979, St. Lucia's democracy has been relatively stable. The United Workers' Party (UWP) was largely dominant until 1997. The country was then ruled by the Labour Party for nearly a decade, until Sir John Compton came out of retirement to lead the UWP to an unexpected victory in the December 2006 elections. Compton, who played a major role in securing St. Lucia's independence and served as it's first prime minister, soon fell ill and eventually died in September 2007 at the age of 82. He was succeeded by Stephenson King, a cabinet member who had served as acting prime minister for several months during Compton's illness.

In neighboring St. Vincent and the Grenadines, antigovernment protests in 2000 shut down the capital of Kingstown and prompted Caricom to intervene and broker early elections, which brought the opposition to power. In 2007, politics in St. Vincent and the Grenadines became increasingly contentious as Prime Minister Ralph Gonsalves of the Unity Labour Party (ULP) and the opposition New Democratic Party (NDP) sparred over issues including new taxes, regional integration, and foreign policy.

Trouble on the Mainland

Caricom includes three members on the mainland of Central and South America: Belize, Guyana, and Suriname. All of these countries—which have populations well below one million—face significant political challenges that threaten to hamper their development.

The tourist paradise of Belize saw a major democratic event in 2003, when the incumbent People's United Party became the first to win re-election since the country's independence in 1981. This victory was largely due to record economic growth during the party's first term in power, yet labor strikes and mass protests nearly toppled the government in April 2005. Revelations of mismanagement in the telecommunications sector led to a series of public-sector strikes and increasing calls for the prime minister's resignation. Protestors sabotaged power lines and severed fiber-optic cables, virtually cutting the country off from outside contact for days. When the armed forces were eventually deployed to stem the unrest, one fatality and hundreds of arrests resulted. Prime Minister Said Musa accused the leader of the opposition United Democratic Party of inciting the violence, although that party seemed to hold little sway among the protestors. The unrest dissipated by early May, but Musa has yet to regain the voters' trust, and his opponent Dean Barrow of the United Democratic Party is likely to win the next parliamentary elections due in the spring of 2008. Meanwhile, a long-running boundary dispute with Guatemala continues to simmer on Belize's western border.

Guyana is one of only two Caricom nations to be designated a Heavily Indebted Poor Country (HIPC) by the International Monetary Fund and the World Bank, which restructured more than half of Guyana's national debt in 2003. While Guyana reached "completion point" in 2007 and is no longer considered a HIPC, it remains a cruel twist of fate that one of Caricom's founding members—and the host of its secretariat—is among its poorest. With a per-capita GDP just over $1,000, Guyana consistently trails development indicators in the rest of the region. Most worrisome, however, are Guyana's bitter political and racial divisions, which are steadily undermining the country's stability. President Bharrat Jagdeo of the People's Progressive Party–Civic (PPP-C) draws most of his support from the Indian-Guyanese community, which comprises about half the population. Although the Afro-Guyanese constitute around 35 percent of the population, they have been largely excluded from political power.

The PPP-C has retained power under three prime ministers since 1992 by means of regular elections endorsed as free and fair by the international community. Yet the opposition People's National Congress–Reform or its militant supporters have challenged the legitimacy of every election, with tactics ranging from protests, rioting, and arson to a 14-month parliamentary boycott in 2002–2003. An effort at bipartisan dialogue ended unsuccessfully in 2004 amid allegations that the home-affairs minister was linked to extrajudicial police killings during a spate of ethnic violence; he was eventually acquitted but resigned his post under international pressure. In August 2006, following weeks of rising violence and political uncertainty, Jagdeo handily won another five-year term in office when his PPP-C received 54 percent of the vote and a 36-seat majority in the 65-member National Assembly. Still, against the backdrop of deep-seated political conflict and economic deprivation, hundreds of thousands of Guyanese have left the country to seek better lives abroad.

Socially and politically fragmented Suriname became the only Dutch-speaking member of Caricom in 1995. This nation contains seven distinct ethnic groups and nearly a dozen political parties that rotate between three main coalitions. Almost two decades of military rule came to an end with democratic elections in 1991, but former military dictator Desi Bouterse retained the leadership of one of the main political parties. Despite his 1999 conviction in absentia for drug trafficking by a Dutch court, he managed to reemerge as a competitive candidate against incumbent Ronald Venetiaan in the leadup to the July 2005 election of the president by the National Assembly. Facing possible defeat, Venetiaan tried but failed to widen his parliamentary coalition to include several opposition groups, including the former dictator's party. Eventually, however, the unpredictable Bouterse withdrew from the race at the last minute and Venetiaan was reelected. In 2007, Suriname's courts ordered the prosecution of ten suspects for the "December murders" of fifteen political opponents in 1982, and the indictment included Bouterse. Meanwhile, the ever-increasing drug trade continues to be a problem. Dutch authorities, in an effort to stop the relentless flow of drugs from this former colony, have instituted a "100 percent rule" mandating that every traveler originating in Suriname must be searched for narcotics.

Divided Loyalties

Most Caribbean democracies retain strong ties to the United States and Europe, which provide crucial sources of tourists, trade, and investment. Moreover, expatriates living overseas send billions of dollars each year to relatives in their home countries; the amount of such remittances now exceeds most other financial inflows to these nations. Yet many Caribbean governments have become increasingly frustrated with the perceived lack of attention and interest from Washington, Brussels, and other European capitals. The United States has periodically modified the trade-oriented Caribbean Basin Initiative, launched in the mid-1980s, but the measure's benefits have lagged behind the region's needs. Meanwhile, the European Union is phasing out trade privileges for exporters of bananas and sugar, causing heavy job losses in the agricultural sector throughout the Caribbean. The post-9/11 drop in tourism also hurt many island economies, although this industry has bounced back more quickly.

Faced with the need to prop up their flagging economies, many Caribbean countries have turned to China and Venezuela for economic cooperation. To a large extent, the Caricom countries also rely on Cuba to provide medical services and expertise throughout the region. While the diversification of economic and political partners is a wise—and indeed necessary—move for these countries and their fragile economies, it raises the question of whether the region's growing dependence on undemocratic partners will have negative political effects in the future.

Beijing has become an aggressive player in Latin America, driven by the need for commodities to feed China's remarkable economic growth. China is also determined to separate Taiwan from its remaining allies in the Western Hemisphere, with the objective of promoting universal acceptance of the "One China" policy. China's new strategy of engagement has already produced important dividends for a number of countries: Chinese trade with the Caribbean Community totaled $4 billion in 2006 and continues to expand. This increase reflects China's pursuit of raw materials such as Trinidadian oil and gas, Jamaican bauxite, and Cuban nickel. Beijing has also designated a number of Caribbean countries as "approved destinations" for the expected boom in Chinese tourism.

In early 2005, Grenada and Dominica became the latest Caribbean countries to revoke diplomatic relations with Taiwan in favor of Beijing. In return, Grenada received support for rebuilding its national stadium, 2,000 housing units, a $1-million scholarship fund, and $6 million in grants; Dominica received a total of $112 million pledged over six years. But the wind blows both ways in the Caribbean, and in May 2007, the newly elected government of St. Lucia awarded diplomatic recognition to Taiwan, thus ending a decade of full diplomatic ties with Beijing. In Haiti, China has used its participation in the UN mission to pressure that destitute country to scale back or even revoke its recognition of Taiwan. Haiti is currently one of only six Caribbean countries that continue to recognize Taiwan (the other five are Belize, the Dominican Republic, St. Kitts and Nevis, St. Lucia, and St. Vincent and the Grenadines).

Venezuelan president Hugo Chávez has stepped up his courtship of the Caribbean. In June 2005, Venezuela and a dozen Caribbean states established the joint oil venture PetroCaribe, which allows nations to repay Venezuela for oil purchases over 25 years with 1 percent interest as long as the price of crude is above $40 a barrel. Venezuela will invest in storage capacities in Antigua and Grenada, and seek to expand and modernize refineries in Jamaica and the Bahamas. A side agreement will allow signatories to pay for a portion of oil imports with sugar and bananas, traditional Caribbean exports that recently have lost their preferential access to EU markets. But the PetroCaribe proposal sparked strong opposition from Trinidad and Tobago, which feared that the country's position as a major oil and gas provider to the region would be undercut if Caribbean signatories received the promised discounts on Venezuelan oil. In December 2007, Chávez presided over a major PetroCaribe summit that coincided with the reopening of an oil refinery in Cienfuegos, Cuba, where he estimated that the Caribbean's collective debt for Venezuelan crude currently is near $1.2 billion and is expected to grow to $4.5 billion by 2010.[8]

PetroCaribe is a component of Chávez's Bolivarian Alternative for the Americas (ALBA)—a rejoinder to the U.S.-backed Free Trade Agreement of the Americas. The ALBA is part of a broader Chávez campaign to chip away at U.S. influence in the Caribbean, and some see it as an effort to shield his controversial domestic policies from condemnation by Hemispheric institutions. Although the Caricom countries have a combined population of only 6 million, together with Haiti they represent a 14-country voting block at the 34-member Organization of American States. (Cuba, which would represent the thirty-fifth member, is excluded.)

Chávez appears to have taken a page from the playbook of his friend and ally, Cuban dictator Fidel Castro. In contrast to China and Venezuela, Cuba's links to the Caribbean represent longstanding collaboration rather than a new political phenomenon. Cuba has been an active presence in the Caribbean for decades, mainly by virtue of sending doctors and educators to underserved parts of the region. Castro's communist government distributes generic drugs and HIV/AIDS resources, sponsors new hospitals and clinics, and regularly dispatches emergency and health personnel to help neighboring countries in the wake of hurricanes and other natural disasters. More than 2,600 students from Caricom countries study in Cuba, and tens of thousands of Caribbean patients have traveled to Cuba for eye surgery under a special program known as Misión Milagro (Miracle Mission). Though Castro's government scaled back its involvement abroad after the collapse of the Soviet Union, Cuba remains influential in the neighborhood.

Thus far, Caribbean governments have decided that the tangible benefits of engagement with China and Venezuela outweigh these countries' democratic deficits. Jamaica hosted the first-ever trade summit between China and the Caribbean in February 2005, and then–Prime Minister Patterson, voicing an opinion shared by many Caribbean leaders, declared that "the time has come to explore and exploit new avenues for economic and trade cooperation between China and our region."[9] Indeed, the Caricom countries are following in the footsteps of Europe and the United States by focusing on trade and investment with China—although Caribbean policymakers are acutely aware of the power imbalance and thus avoid broaching human rights issues. For its part, Chávez's government appears intent on using Venezuela's oil wealth to cement the support of Caribbean countries and to expand its influence in the Organization of American States and other Hemispheric bodies. Chávez's aid-based diplomacy is likely to deter Caribbean countries from challenging or even criticizing his undemocratic practices.

Staying the Course

The Caribbean Community represents one of the longest-standing integration efforts in the developing world. It has evolved from a cluster of small Anglophone nations to a multilingual group of countries that are extremely diverse in terms of political development, population, and living standards. The organization more than doubled its combined population and halved its average income with the admission of poverty-stricken Haiti in 2002, and current discussions regarding the possible membership of the Dominican Republic have the potential to yield another such major change.

Collaboration on regional initiatives—such as the Caribbean Court of Justice and the Caricom Single Market Economy—has significant future potential. In 2009, Trinidad and Tobago will host the Fifth Summit of the Americas, providing an opportunity to showcase the region's successful integration efforts and to further bolster the region's profile. But even Caricom's top officials predict that the road ahead will not be easy. As Caricom's assistant secretary-general stated in 2002: "Our constant vigilance is all the more necessary in the face of accelerating societal change, growing political and economic challenges, and the multidimensional nature of security threats which, if not confronted, could affect adversely the preservation and consolidation of democracy in our states."[10]

Caribbean democracies have recognized the need to band together to confront common security concerns and to create a mutually supportive environment for economic development and political stability. As Trinidad's Prime Minister Patrick Manning has warned: "In the Caribbean, no one country is able to stand alone. All countries are interdependent, and united we will stand and divided we will fall."[11] In their efforts to face the future, Caribbean leaders are betting that regional unity will provide a needed anchor during turbulent times.

NOTES

1. "St Lucia: Anthony Says Globalization a Threat to Caribbean Democracy," Cana News Agency, 22 April 2001. See *www.cananews.com.*

2. Colin T. Granderson, "Anniversary of the Democratic Charter: A Caribbean Perspective," address at the ceremony commemorating the first anniversary of the signing of the Inter-American Democratic Charter, Washington, D.C., 16 September 2002.

3. Address by United Nations Secretary-General Kofi Annan to the Fourth European Union–Latin America and Caribbean Heads of State Summit, Federal News Service, 12 May 2006.

4. Joe Mozingo, "Jamaicans Live in Fear as Homicide Rate Skyrockets," *Miami Herald,* 7 July 2005.

5. V.S. Naipaul, Nobel lecture, Stockholm, 7 December 2001.

6. Carol J. Williams, "Kidnappings in Trinidad Blamed on Gang, Copycats," *Los Angeles Times,* 10 January 2005; and Juhel Browne, "77 Kidnappings for year so far, says Joseph," *Trinidad and Tobago Express,* 19 June 2007.

7. Quote by Supt. Adam Joseph, head of the National Police Service's antikidnapping squad. "Kidnappings Send a Chill Through Sunny Trinidad," *Los Angeles Times,* 2 January 2002.

8. Anita Snow, "Chávez Presides Over Oil Summit in Cuba," Associated Press, 21 December 2007.

9. "Address by Prime Minister of Jamaica P.J. Patterson at Opening Ceremony China-Caribbean Economic and Trade Forum," Jamaica Information Service, 4 February 2005. See *www.jis.gov.jm.*

10. Colin T. Granderson, "Anniversary of the Democratic Charter."

11. Peter Richards, "Trade: Venezuela Oil Deal Rattles Caribbean Unity a Bit," Inter-Press Service, 13 July 2005.

INDEX